The Knopf Collectors' Guides to American Antiques

Robert Bishop & William C. Ketchum, Jr.
Series Consultants

A Chanticleer Press Edition

Silver
&
Pewter

Donald L. Fennimore

With photographs by Rosmarie Hausherr

Alfred A. Knopf, New York

This is a Borzoi Book
Published by Alfred A. Knopf, Inc.

Prepared and produced by
Chanticleer Press, Inc., New York.

Color reproductions by Colourscan Co. Pte. Ltd., Singapore.
Type set in Century Expanded by Dix Type Inc., Syracuse,
New York. Printed and bound by Dai Nippon Printing Co., Ltd.,
Tokyo, Japan.

First Printing

Library of Congress Catalog Number: 84-47638
ISBN: 0-394-71527-6

Contents

Introduction

Silver and Silver Plate
Pewter

Collecting Tools

Acknowledgments

Few projects of lasting value are the work of one individual alone. So it is with this book. It has been an immensely rewarding effort for the author, but can hardly be claimed solely as his. This volume could only have come about through the dedicated work and generous cooperation of many, all of whom deserve credit.

My thanks are sincerely offered to John D. Barr, Tom Benson, Scott Braznell, Mr. & Mrs. Charles H. Carpenter, Jr., Stuart P. Feld, Mrs. John Gorton, James H. Halpin, Tom Josten, Mrs. Harry Lunger, Ian M. G. Quimby, James P. Roosevelt, and Mrs. Seymour Schwartz.

I am especially grateful to H. Parrott Bacot, Director and Curator of the Anglo-American Art Museum; Kevin Stayton, Associate Curator of American Decorative Arts at The Brooklyn Museum; Roland Woodward, Director of the Chester County Historical Society; David R. McFadden, Curator of Decorative Arts at the Cooper-Hewitt Museum; Edmund P. Hogan, Curator of the International Silver Company Collections; Miss Margaret Stearns, Curator, and William Butler, Curatorial Assistant, at the Museum of the City of New York; Frank Horton, Director of the Museum of Early Southern Decorative Arts; Patricia E. Kane, Curator, and David L. Barquist, Assistant Curator, at the Yale University Art Gallery; and Karol Schmiegel, Associate Registrar, and Clarence Buffington, at the Henry Francis du Pont Winterthur Museum. All of these people have taken time from their full schedules to help with the task of including objects under their care in this volume.

To Rosmarie Hausherr I offer a special thanks for so skillfully manipulating her camera to show the objects included here to their best advantage. Her genuine interest and considerable talent contribute greatly to this book's appeal.

My thanks to Paul Steiner and the staff of Chanticleer Press: Gudrun Buettner and Susan Costello developed the idea for the series; Carol Nehring supervised the art and layouts; and Helga Lose directed the production of the book. A lion's share of credit is also due to Marian Appellof, Mary Beth Brewer, Michael Goldman, and Ann Whitman for so skillfully and cheerfully undertaking the formidable task of making the text of the book flow intelligibly. Finally, my thanks to Charles Elliott, senior editor at Alfred A. Knopf, for his encouragement and support.

It must be acknowledged with gratitude that Barbara and Gerry Ward were both instrumental in supplying insightful comment and thoughtful criticism for the manuscript. Their willingness to share their considerable expertise has added much depth and scope to this effort. Credit is also due to John Carl Thomas and Kevin Tierney, who kindly took time from their full schedules to share their considerable knowledge in assembling the Price Guide, and to William C. Ketchum, Jr., who reviewed the manuscript and made many helpful suggestions. Very special thanks go to Robert Bishop for sharing his enthusiasm and expertise.

For interest, support, encouragement, and other important intangibles I must thank my mother, Martha S. Fennimore, my uncle, Charles V. Swain, and my wife, Jean. I also owe a special thanks to Jackie Fiore for so selflessly giving of her time to type the manuscript, and I thank my boss, Nancy Richards, for her confidence that my daily responsibilities would not suffer with the undertaking of this book.

About the Author, Photographer, and Consultants

Donald L. Fennimore
Associate Curator and in Charge of Metals at the Henry Francis du Pont Winterthur Museum, author Donald Fennimore is an expert in the field of American metal objects, particularly early 19th-century silver. He has lectured widely on the subject and written articles for *Antiques*, *The American Art Journal*, *Art & Antiques*, and numerous other publications. Mr. Fennimore is also a member of the Pewter Collectors' Club of America, the Victorian Society, and the Decorative Arts Society.

Rosmarie Hausherr
The recipient of several awards, including grants from the Swiss National Council of the Arts, Rosmarie Hausherr was trained in industrial photography and worked as a photographer for an international press agency in Zurich. Her work, covering a wide range of subjects, has appeared in newspapers, magazines, and books both here and abroad.

Gerald W. R. Ward
Consultant Gerald Ward is Assistant Curator of the Garvan and Related Collections of American Art at the Yale University Art Gallery. He is the author of numerous articles and reviews as well as co-editor of or contributor to several books and exhibition catalogues, including *Silver in American Life: Selections from the Mabel Brady Garvan and Other Collections at Yale University.*

Barbara McLean Ward
As Exhibition Coordinator in American Decorative Arts at the Yale University Art Gallery, consultant Barbara Ward has participated in many exhibitions and served as co-curator, with Gerald Ward, of "Silver in American Life." Also a Teaching Associate at the Winterthur Museum, Dr. Ward has taught courses in American history and the decorative arts and has lectured on the construction techniques of early American silver. She is the author of articles that have appeared in *Antiques* and related publications and a contributor to several exhibition catalogues.

Robert Bishop
Director of the Museum of American Folk Art in New York City, series consultant Robert Bishop is author of more than 30 books, among them *Folk Art* and *Quilts* in *The Knopf Collectors' Guides to American Antiques*. He established this country's first master's degree program in folk art studies at New York University. Dr. Bishop is on the editorial boards of *Horizon Magazine* and *Antique Monthly*.

William C. Ketchum, Jr.
A member of the faculty of The New School for Social Research, series consultant William C. Ketchum, Jr., is also a guest curator at the Museum of American Folk Art in New York City and a consultant to several major auction houses. Dr. Ketchum has written 18 books, including *Pottery and Porcelain* and *Furniture 2* in *The Knopf Collectors' Guides to American Antiques*. He is an associate editor at *Antique Monthly*.

Preface

Silver has held a timeless fascination for mankind, both because of its innate value as a precious ore and because it has been fashioned into elegant and beautiful objects. When settlers first arrived in America, they no doubt carried with them silver and pewter from England and the Continent; until metalworking industries took hold in the new land, well-to-do individuals continued to import wares from abroad.

Large items made from silver have never been within everyone's means, yet there are scores of small, affordable, personal silver objects that are representative of American silversmithing. In addition, the introduction of electroplating in the 19th century brought objects coated in silver—and looking like their more expensive counterparts—within everyone's means. Today's collectors are drawn to silver plate because the diversity of silver-plated objects often reflects the changing fashions of the day.

Unlike silver, pewter was used for practical, down-to-earth objects—things as simple as spittoons and commodes, spoons and tankards. Because of its homely associations it was not until the 20th century that collectors began to appreciate pewter in its own right. When they reevaluated it, they saw the artistry and individualism of the craft in America. Today many pewter objects command prices as high as, or even higher than, their silver counterparts. Others, however, remain affordable investments.

Some collections are limited to pewter household items, while others are made up of eccentric Victorian creations; still others may contain classic Federal pieces made of sterling. No matter what your preference, this book will show you the full range of these crafts in America. Every major type of American silver, silver plate, and pewter is covered, from early handwrought pieces to those that were mass-produced in this century. The objects illustrated include such common forms as pewter and silver mugs and bowls as well as curiosities such as silver toys for children and pewter baby bottles.

To acquaint collectors with the fashions that helped shape American taste, we have also included a few representative English examples. Similarly, we feature some of the finest pieces of silver and pewter ever made in America; these objects illustrate the level of artistry achieved in this country and provide models against which other pieces can be evaluated.

To help collectors identify the objects they encounter, we have separated the silver and silver plate from the pewter, and then organized the illustrations by shape and function, rather than by chronology or decorative style. Each illustrated entry includes a thorough description of the object, then goes on to describe any makers' marks, as well as to tell where and when it was made. Further, it provides historical background along with practical hints on what to look for and what to avoid.

To help you determine what you can expect to pay in today's marketplace, we have included an up-to-date Price Guide, which lists current price ranges for the pieces illustrated, as well as prices for simliar objects. You will find that some items are no more costly than their modern-day equivalents, and you will see how collecting silver, silver plate, and pewter need not be a pastime only for the wealthy, but an enjoyable hobby for all.

A Simple Way to Identify Silver, Silver Plate, and Pewter

Since early Colonial times, the products of American metalsmiths have served a decorative and useful function in our society. From the simplest pewter spoons to the most elaborate tea services, objects made of silver, silver plate, and pewter have played a large part in the cultural heritage of the nation.

This guide presents the full range of American silver, silver plate, and pewter. Included here are common, inexpensive objects, made in large numbers and readily available, as well as some very fine, rare objects that represent important levels of achievement in metalworking. We have chosen more than 450 objects for full coverage with text and pictures; the selections are representative ones that will help you to identify, date, and assess the value of the pieces you encounter. The color plates and accompanying text have been divided into 2 major groups. The first includes silver and silver plate, and the second, pewter. Within these subdivisions, the pieces are arranged according to shape and function so that beginners with no previous experience in the field can find objects quickly. More knowledgeable collectors who wish to refer to the work of a particular craftsman may turn to the Index.

The introductions to the 2 major divisions will give you an understanding of the history of American silversmithing and pewtering. In addition, there are introductory essays that tell how silver, silver plate, and pewter are made, and how to care for your collection. For collectors who are especially interested in flatware, there is an appendix that illustrates some of the most popular and attractive flatware patterns, both antique and modern. As a quick reference, we have provided a table of makers and marks, listing the American craftsmen whose work appears in the book with illustrations of their principal marks, as well as information about the place and time period in which they worked. The Glossary defines special terms with which some collectors may not be familiar. Finally, the up-to-date Price Guide lists current price ranges for the objects featured in the book.

This guide is designed to make collecting silver, silver plate, and pewter more rewarding. The tools provided—the photographs, descriptions, essays, tables, and illustrated appendices—will help the collector, whether beginner or expert, find greater enjoyment and pleasure in this pursuit.

How Silver, Silver Plate, and Pewter Are Made

Although objects made of silver, silver plate, and pewter are superficially similar in appearance, the processes used to make them differ and give them distinguishing characteristics. An understanding of these differences will help collectors to recognize and evaluate the objects they encounter.

Silver

Silver occurs in both a relatively pure state as a native metal and as an ore mixed with other materials, typically gold, copper, lead, arsenic, sulfur, and other impurities. Before the silver can be worked by a silversmith, all of the impurities must be removed. By heating the ore to about 1500° centigrade (the melting point for silver), all the unwanted materials are burned off or liquefied. Pure silver is so soft that it will not stand up under continued use. To make it more durable, it is usually mixed with an alloy. Traditionally copper has been favored because it mixes readily with silver, and because these metals are similar in all physical properties except color.

Working Silver by Hand

Once the metal has been purified and an alloy added, it is ready to be worked. Historically, the preferred technique was to hammer it into shape. The silversmith held a block, disk, or sheet of the metal on an anvil and hit it with a variety of hammers. Each hammer had a different size, weight, and shape, and their selection—for forging, hollowing, raising, sinking, planishing, and other tasks—was governed by the shape of the object being manufactured.

Silver's very plastic nature allowed the silversmith great freedom as he shaped it; however, like all metals, it hardens as it is worked, becoming more resistant to shaping. To restore plasticity, it was periodically annealed—heated to cherry red and then plunged briefly in an acid bath to cool.

After an object was shaped, it was rubbed with a series of increasingly fine abrasives, creating a mirrorlike finish.

Techniques other than hammering have been used as well, largely for making ornament or for such things as handles, finials, and legs. For this kind of work, the silversmith often cast molten metal in sand molds. In another technique, drawing, he pulled a strip of silver through a shaped hole in a hardened steel die, forcing the soft metal to conform to the shape of the hole. Finished strips were used as moldings, both to decorate objects and to strengthen them.

Mass Production

In the past century and a half, new processes were developed to speed production, eventually becoming the mainstay of the large-scale factory system. The most basic of these was flatting, which increased production and obviated lengthy training of workers. In flatting, a silver ingot passed between a pair of steel rollers in a gear train. The rollers compressed the silver into thin sheets that could be easily cut and soldered to fashion many types of vessels.

Early in the 19th century, mechanized die stamping was also applied to silver production. Die stamping was done with a press. The press had a stationary lower steel die into which a movable upper steel die fit. The upper die was raised, a piece of sheet silver placed on the face of the lower die, and then the upper die was allowed to drop, stamping out objects quickly, efficiently, and with great uniformity.

Spinning came into use in the mid-19th century. In this process, a thin silver disk was placed on a lathe. As it rotated, the lathe operator forced it over a shaped chuck. In this manner, a limited variety of simple shapes could be made quickly and easily.

Decoration

Since the 17th century, American silversmiths have used casting, drawing, engraving, and chasing to decorate silver. Engraving was the most universally popular technique. In engraving, a silversmith cut grooves in the metal with a series of pointed steel tools known as gravers. Gravers varied in size and shape; some cut a single V-shaped groove, others multiple grooves, and still others zigzag lines.

In chasing, a silversmith indented a design into a vessel's surface using small punches and a hammer. Each punch had a face of a different size, shape, and texture. After filling the vessel with pitch to keep it from collapsing, the craftsman hammered the desired design into the surface.

Unlike chasing, in which the design is indented, repoussé decoration is raised. To accomplish this, a special hammer known as a snarling iron was placed inside the object and used to raise lumps on the object's surface. After the lumps were raised, chasing tools provided detail.

Repoussé work was fairly uncommon in American silver, but piercing was rarer still. The extensive labor required to pierce an object made the technique very costly. In piercing, shaped holes were cut into an object using a thin-bladed jeweler's saw. This technique was usually reserved for objects that needed holes to function, such as braziers or casters. Occasionally, however, piercing was solely decorative.

During the early 19th century, these decorative techniques were supplemented with innovations geared toward quantity production. In one process, die rolling, a strip of silver was cranked between a pair of steel rollers, one of which had decoration cut into its surface, pressing the ornamental pattern into the silver. The strips were cut to length, bent to shape, and then applied.

Just as die stamping had been used to produce simple objects, it was also employed to make ornamentation. Die rolling and die stamping, together with flattened sheet silver and spinning, revolutionized silvermaking, allowing it to progress from a craft to an industry.

Silver Plating

Sterling silver has never been within everyone's means, and silver-plated base metals provided an affordable substitute. Techniques to coat iron, copper, and brass with a thin layer of silver had been developed at least as early as the 9th century.

Close Plating and French Plating

Until the 18th century, iron was often used as the base metal for plated objects. The only way to coat iron with silver was through a technique known as close plating. In close plating, the craftsman first coated an object with tin; next he laid thin sheets of silver over it. By carefully manipulating a heated iron over the foil, the craftsman melted the tin underneath; on cooling, it formed a permanent solder joint between the iron and the silver. Copper and brass were used in a technique known as French plating. Sheets of silver foil were placed directly onto an object and the foil was rubbed with a heated and polished steel burnisher; this process bonded the silver foil to the copper or brass base.

Fused Plating
The introduction of fused plating in the 1730s made both close
plating and French plating outmoded. Its invention is credited to
an Englishman, Thomas Boulsover. Whereas close- and French-
plated objects were plated after they were made, fused plating
took place before an object was fashioned. A sheet of copper
faced on one or both sides with a thin sheet of silver was passed
between 2 steel rollers; heat and pressure bonded the metals.
The sheets could be shaped into any kind of object. The
craftsman then soldered silver wire to the raw copper edges.
Wares produced this way appeared to be made entirely of silver.
The speed and savings realized by fused plating allowed it to
quickly eclipse the other 2 plating methods. It dominated English
production for most of the 18th and the first half of the 19th
century. So far as is known, Americans were not capable of
making fused plate in the 18th century, and all that was used
here was imported from England.

Electroplating
As the invention of fused plating revolutionized the industry in
the 18th century, a second upheaval took place in the 19th—the
development of electroplating, which quickly supplanted all other
types of plating. In electroplating, an object was immersed in an
electrolytic bath along with a pure silver ingot. A direct current
of electricity passed through a tank of distilled water in which
potassium cyanide had been dissolved. As the electricity passed
through the bath, atoms were removed from the ingot (the
anode) and deposited on the object (the cathode). The first large-
scale commercial application of this process was undertaken by
the Birmingham, England, firm of Elkington & Company. With
their success, the technique quickly spread in popularity. It
became the first major plating process to be practiced in the
United States, and during the late 19th century, the industry
assumed major proportions in this country. Electroplating was
much less expensive than other plating methods. An added
benefit was that many metals could be plated in this process—
copper, brass, britannia metal (an alloy of pewter), and German
silver (an alloy of copper, zinc, and nickel). Britannia metal and
German silver were used extensively because their white color
was so similar to that of silver that when the thin silver coating
wore through, the underlying base metal was inconspicuous.

Pewter
Pewter is an alloy composed principally of tin. Although the ratio
and number of its constituent metals can vary substantially,
pewter usually contains about 95 percent tin with approximately
1 percent copper, 2 percent lead, and either 2 percent antimony
or 2 percent antimony and bismuth.

Casting Pewter
Most often pewter was cast in expensive molds made of brass or
bronze. Those who could not afford them, mostly country
pewterers, used less expensive materials, such as soapstone, for
their molds. Pewter has the fairly low melting point of about 250°
centigrade, making it relatively easy to cast. Each object a
pewterer made required one or more molds. Simple objects like
plates or spoons were made in 2-part molds. Larger and more
complicated objects required more complex molds, some of which
had 7 or 8 pieces. Tankards, for instance, had to be cast in a
multipart mold: one for the barrel, another for the lid, and yet
another for the handle. Once each of these parts was cast and

removed from its respective mold, it had to be finished and then the various elements soldered together. Most objects or parts of objects were cast solid. However, to save weight and material, some parts, like handles, were usually hollow. These hollow parts were made in a process known as slush casting. In slush casting, the pewterer filled the mold with molten pewter, allowing it to partially solidify against the walls of the mold, then quickly poured the remaining molten metal out.

While the various parts of most multipart objects were soldered together, there were occasional exceptions. The most notable of these were porringer handles and the tops of some teapot bodies, which were cast and attached in a single step known as burning on. In this technique, a special mold was used that, upon being placed against the body, allowed the molten metal of the handle to come into contact with it. This partially liquefied it and, upon cooling, formed a permanent bond between the 2 parts.

Finishing and Decoration

After an object was removed from its mold, it had to undergo several finishing steps. A circular object was placed on a lathe and skimmed, that is, scraped smooth. Next, it was polished with a mild abrasive to give it a smooth brilliant shine. Irregularly shaped objects, such as spoons or oval boxes, were burnished and then polished.

Most pewter was undecorated except for simple moldings and fillets. However, ornament was occasionally added. Engraving, the most common method of decorating pewter, was usually done to record an owner's name or initials. Less frequently, pewterers used sparing amounts of cast ornament. Porringer handles are probably the most common example of cast decoration.

Technical Changes

In the late 18th century, facing competition from other materials, pewterers improved their product by adding more antimony, which made the metal more silvery in appearance. It also made the alloy slightly harder, so that serviceable objects could be made with thinner walls and lighter weight. This innovation was first developed by English pewterers, who gave it the patriotic name britannia metal. American pewterers were quick to use the new alloy. At about the same time, and in part because of this improvement in the alloy, pewterers began to make objects by spinning sheets of the metal on a lathe. Although this technique sped production of pewter, it never completely supplanted casting.

Pewter began to decline in popularity by the late 18th century. Once ubiquitous for household objects, it was soon surpassed in appeal by attractive and inexpensive silver plate, which had become the more fashionable medium for such forms.

Parts of Representative Objects

Candlestick

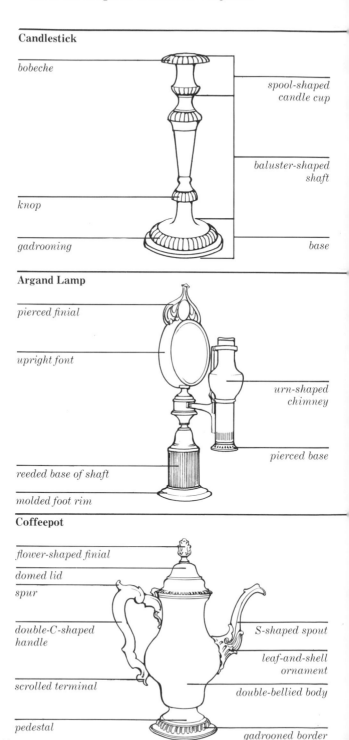

bobeche

spool-shaped candle cup

baluster-shaped shaft

knop

gadrooning

base

Argand Lamp

pierced finial

upright font

urn-shaped chimney

reeded base of shaft

pierced base

molded foot rim

Coffeepot

flower-shaped finial

domed lid

spur

double-C-shaped handle

S-shaped spout

leaf-and-shell ornament

scrolled terminal

double-bellied body

pedestal

gadrooned border

Sauceboat

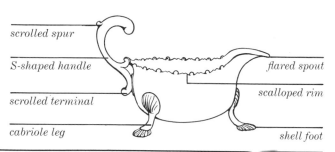

scrolled spur

S-shaped handle

scrolled terminal

cabriole leg

flared spout

scalloped rim

shell foot

Tankard

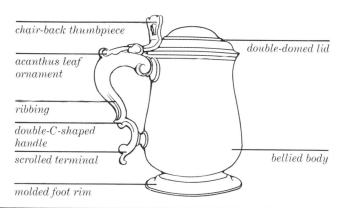

chair-back thumbpiece

acanthus leaf
ornament

ribbing

double-C-shaped
handle

scrolled terminal

molded foot rim

double-domed lid

bellied body

Sugar Bowl with Lid

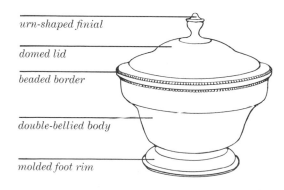

urn-shaped finial

domed lid

beaded border

double-bellied body

molded foot rim

Good, Better, and Best: Silver and Silver Plate

Good

It is easy to look at an object and say instinctively "I like it," but knowing why requires study and analysis. To explain its appeal fully, one needs to understand the era in which it was made and all the social, functional, economic, and technological factors that caused it to look the way it does. Specific aspects to address are how well the object is made, how widely respected the maker is among collectors, and how successfully the maker captured the spirit of the style in which he worked. This pitcher is technologically sound, having a separate liner built in to help keep its contents cold. It is decorated with a variety of motifs executed in several techniques. The ornament and the pitcher's spout, body, lid, and handle are pleasing individually, but together lack integration. Several features, such as the engraved leaves around the medallion and the handle terminals, lack strong and convincing definition. These drawbacks leave the viewer with a sense that the design of this pitcher is not fully successful.

Better

This pleasingly shaped pitcher is elaborately decorated with a variety of motifs. It is well proportioned and does not sit heavily, which cannot be said of the Meriden Britannia ice-water pitcher above. This example was made at a time when mechanization was becoming increasingly important in the production of silver. This fact does not necessarily take away from the value of an object; however, quantity production is inherent in the factory process. So, because this pitcher is one of many, one can compare it with numerous others. In its shape, this pitcher is typical of its time; however, it is quite light in weight; other pitchers of comparable size have a more substantial heft. The ornament encircling the body is ambitious, including an unusual and competently executed landscape scene; however, the ornament generally lacks the full vigor expected on objects of its era. This is particularly noticeable in the series of weak scrolls at the lip; moreover, the landscape does not fill the space on the body, and the borders on the pedestal are too narrow.

Best

This ewer, although less than a foot high, is visually monumental. Its great physical presence is principally owing to its well-thought-out shape and proportions. Some parts, like the lid profile, are complex, while others, like the shape of the body, are simple; yet all work together harmoniously, providing the viewer with a unified and satisfying design. And while this ewer fulfills its intended purpose very well, its maker went beyond creating a merely functional vessel. The engraved coat of arms on one side, the cast handle, and the thumbpiece capture the essence of the style in which he was working. All 3 elements are infused with a dynamic energy that urges the viewer's eyes from one point to the next in constant movement, imparting a gratifying assimilation of subtle nuances. In accordance with the dictates of the rococo style, these elements have been made truly asymmetrical—a surprising rarity in American rococo silver. For these reasons, this ewer serves as a standard against which other objects can be measured.

Electroplated water pitcher by Meriden Britannia, c. 1867

Silver ewer by Gale & Hayden, c. 1849

Silver ewer by Myer Myers, c. 1765

Good, Better, and Best: Pewter

Good

The measure of what makes an object merely good or the best of its type is often subjective and, in part, reflective of current fashion among collectors. However, a number of objective criteria can be applied in determining how an object compares to others of its type. Among the more important of these are proportion, clarity of outline, vigor of ornament, and the success with which the ornament is integrated into the form of the object. This mug is a very nice example, having features that are present in most American or English objects of this type. Its slightly tapered cylindrical body, simple flared and molded foot rim, encircling fillet, and hollow S-shaped handle are well designed and typical of pewter mugs made from the 17th through the 19th centuries. The fish-tail terminal on the handle is the single unusual feature; most mugs have a simple ball terminal. The handle terminal is the only feature worthy of particular note on this pleasing but otherwise average mug.

Better

While all the salient features on this mug are basically the same as those on the Frederick Bassett mug above, the manner in which they have been arranged and fabricated makes it considerably more interesting. Its proportions have been subtly but significantly altered, making the vessel taller and more visibly tapered and giving the mug more visual impact. The narrow fillet is located high on the barrel, a rather uncommon placement that successfully adds to the mug's pleasing and unusual proportions. The foot rim has a more elaborate profile than that on the Bassett mug, providing a stronger point of visual interest. The handle is quite unusual: While most are hollow and soldered onto the body, this handle is solid and cast in place. The slender curvilinear profile of the handle pleasingly complements the mug's tall slender form. Also important is the maker's mark, which is cast on the handle terminal; stamped marks are more common.

Best

Most American pewter mugs are straight-sided; only rare examples belly out in the pear shape so popular in silver mugs of the mid- to late 18th century. So shape alone recommends this cann to the serious collector. Added to that rarity is its visually successful composition: The lip flares just the right amount, and the bellied section is neither too gross nor wanting. Its maker has added a fillet at the outermost diameter to provide a visual accent. The diameter and height of the boldly flared and molded base are correctly proportioned to provide both actual and visual stability. The handle's complex taper, outline, and ornament complement but do not overpower the curved shape of the cann. The ruffled acanthus leaf on the handle and the sharply detailed and graduated volutes at top and bottom terminate the curves successfully without visual confusion. This cann's maker, William Will, was a prolific and innovative pewterer who has been extensively written about in this century; his popularity adds to the desirability of this exceptional example.

Pewter mug by Frederick Bassett, 1761–1800

Pewter mug by Nathaniel Austin, 1763–1807

Pewter cann by William Will, 1764–98

How to Use This Guide

Successfully identifying and evaluating American silver, silver plate, and pewter requires skill and knowledge in a variety of areas. It is important to know how objects are made and the different techniques and materials used. An appreciation of decorative styles and an understanding of makers' marks is also vital. The simple steps outlined below will make it easier to identify and evaluate the objects you encounter.

Preparation

1. Turn to the Visual Key to familiarize yourself with the organization of the book. The objects fall into 2 main divisions, one for silver and silver plate, the other for pewter. Within the first group, objects that are silver-plated are so designated in their titles; all other objects in the group are silver. Within the 2 large groups, objects are further classified according to their shape and function. The silver and silver plate section contains 10 such groups, the pewter section 6.

2. Read the essays preceding the main divisions, which give information about the history of the crafts in America. The brief essays preceding the smaller groups provide helpful information about the types of objects included in each one.

Using the Color Plates to Identify an Object

1. Compare the object you have found with the drawings in the Visual Key. Find the drawing that most closely resembles your object and turn to the entries listed above the drawing.

2. Compare the photographs in the entries with your object and select the photograph most like your object in function, style, and decoration. Remember that the article you are considering may be somewhat different from that shown in the photograph.

3. Read the entry, comparing your object to the one in the book.

4. Turn to the Price Guide for the current market value of the object illustrated in the photograph. Remember that prices depend on quality, condition, rarity, style, skill of execution, presence of a maker's mark, and many other factors.

Developing Expertise

1. To gain a thorough understanding of fabrication techniques, consult the introductory essay, How Silver, Silver Plate, and Pewter Are Made.

2. Become familiar with the Good, Better, and Best sections, which illustrate some of the considerations that affect the desirability of an object.

3. In the Illustrated Guide to American Makers and Marks you will find a list of makers whose work is included in the guide, along with illustrations of some of their marks. The Index will also refer you to works of a particular maker.

4. Consult the introduction to the Price Guide to understand some of the factors that affect price.

5. If you are considering a flatware object, the Flatware Patterns guide in the back may provide you with some information about the object you wish to purchase.

6. The essay on Caring for Your Collection provides information on the best way to clean, display, and repair silver, silver plate, and pewter objects.

7. For further reference, consult the Bibliography.

Information-at-a-Glance

Each color plate in the guide is accompanied by a full description of the object, pointing out the significant features that help identify the work. The plate number is repeated in the Price Guide. Technical terms are defined in the Glossary.

Title
The title of each object indicates the time in which the object was produced. The time periods are as follows:
Early Colonial: 1650–1710
Colonial: 1700–1740
Late Colonial: 1710–1775
Federal: 1776–1837
Late Federal: 1825–1837
Victorian: 1837–1901
Modern: 1901–present
These designations are simply for convenience; they are not stylistic terms. English objects are classified according to the monarch ruling at the time when the objects were made. In the section that includes silver and silver plate, the titles indicate which objects are plated; other pieces in the section are silver.

Description
Each description covers the general shape of the object, its decoration, and important features and appendages, such as handles, spouts, lids, and the like. Inscriptions are also noted. As a rule, the descriptions move from top to bottom, with the most important or conspicuous features described first.

Marks and Dimensions
Here the maker's mark or marks, when present, are described. Dimensions are in inches, with the largest measurement usually given first.

Maker, Locality, and Date
This section gives the name of the maker, his life dates (when known), the place where he worked, and the date or approximate date when the object was made. For partnerships and companies, the dates of the firm's operation are given if they are known.

Comment
Here we provide information about the history of the object, general observations about the form, and notes on the maker. Also included are descriptions of related examples, and information on how a specific object was made.

Hints for Collectors
These tips point out what to look for and what to avoid when collecting; how rare or common certain forms are; facts about an object's condition that may affect its value; tips on how to detect fakes and reproductions; what kinds of repair work will detract from the value of a piece; and information about the best way to care for your collection.

Visual Key

The objects included in this guide have been divided into 16
groups, 10 groups containing objects made of silver or silver
plate, and 6 with pewter pieces. For each group, a symbol
appears on the left along with a brief explanation of the types of
objects included. Drawings of representative pieces in the group
are shown on the right; the numbers above each drawing are
plate numbers. A few objects are similar to pieces included in
other groups; the plate numbers of these objects are followed by

Plates, Trays, and Related Objects *(Plates 1–13)*
The objects included in this group range from large oval trays to
small shell-shaped dishes. Silver plates are usually circular, while
trays may be circular or oval. Some trays are supported by 3 or 4
short feet and they may have a handle at each end. Also included
here are a tazza and a compote, forms that resemble plates but
rest on a central pedestal.

Spoons, Knives, Forks, and Related Flatware *(Plates 14–36)*
In addition to the familiar spoon, knife, fork, and ladle, this
group features such specialized pieces as oyster forks and berry
spoons. Some of these objects were made as parts of matching
sets, while others, such as the nut spoon, bear decoration that
symbolizes their function.

Table and Bar Accessories *(Plates 37–78)*
This group encompasses highly diverse objects, ranging from
grape shears to tea balls, caster sets, and corkscrews. All were
intended for use at the table or at the bar. Some, like the skewer
and the egg poacher, were elaborate versions of mundane pieces
used in the kitchen. Others, like the combination napkin ring and
vase, provided fancy embellishment for a well-furnished dining-
room table.

Tureens, Vegetable Dishes, Sugar Bowls, and Related Objects
(Plates 79–94)
Almost all of the pieces included here were made with a
matching lid. Primarily used for serving food, they include such
objects as soup and sauce tureens, butter dishes, and sugar
bowls. Many are elaborately decorated with plant, animal, and
human motifs.

an asterisk (*). The symbols and drawings for objects made of silver or silver plate are printed in one color and those for pewter in another.

silver and silver plate   *pewter*

1–4   *5–9*   *10–11*   *12–13*

14–17   *18–21*   *22–29, 3**   *30–36, 13**

37–40   *41–43*   *44–46, 48*   *47, 57–58*

49–56, 3*   *59–62, 69*   *63–70*   *71–78*

79–84   *85–88*   *89–92, 139*,*   *93–94*
                             146*

Porringers, Bowls, Cake Baskets, and Related Objects
(*Plates 95–117*)
These objects range from plain circular bowls to elaborate punch bowls and fruit baskets. Some, like the porringer, have one or 2 handles; others, like the compotes, rest on a pedestal or have a shaped base.

Teapots, Coffeepots, Pitchers, and Related Objects
(*Plates 118–150*)
All of these pieces have a pouring lip, a pouring spout, or a spigot, and most have a handle. In pitchers, creamers, and sauceboats, the spout forms part of the rim. Teapots and coffeepots have a tubular spout that is often attached near the base of the object. Also included here are hot-water urns, which have spigots, a cup with a long tubular spout, and 2 pitchers that tilt from attached stands.

Mugs, Cups, Chalices, and Beakers (*Plates 151–179*)
The objects in this group are drinking vessels, all similar in function but widely varied in shape. Cups, mugs, canns, and tankards have a handle; in addition, tankards have a lid. Also featured here are several 2-handled cups, plus beakers, goblets, and a chalice.

Candlesticks, Lamps, and Related Objects (*Plates 180–193*)
Most candlesticks are tall and accommodate a single candle. Others, known as chamber sticks, are low and have a handle, and still others are multibranched. Most have a disk-shaped rim, or bobeche, that catches melting wax. The lamps in this section were mostly designed to burn oil; the fuel is stored in a font that rests on a simple or shaped cylindrical base. Some lamps are equipped with mirrors or chimneys to enhance the light they project, while others have a shade.

95, 97–104, 110–111, 3*, 138*–139*

96, 3*

105–109

112–117, 138*

118–121

122–128, 138–139, 146

129, 131–132, 144–145, 148

130, 133–135, 139–140, 146–147

136, 138–144

137

149–150

151–153

154–156, 167–168, 3*

157, 159

158, 160–164

165–167

169–172

173

174–179

180–185

186–188

189–191

192–193

Boxes and Other Containers (*Plates 194–209*)
Both functional and ornamental, these small containers vary
greatly in size, shape, and decoration. Some were designed for a
particular use, such as holding calling cards, reading glasses, or
tobacco, while others probably served as all-purpose storage
vessels.

Sewing and Desk Accessories and Other Personal Objects
(*Plates 210–239*)
These enormously diverse objects include such pieces as
pincushions, whistles, brushes, ashtrays, and card receivers.
Some, like the buckle and the buttons, were fashioned for
personal adornment. Others, like the brush and the cigarette
lighter, are handsome interpretations of everyday objects.

Plates, Porringers, and Related Objects (*Plates 240–259*)
This section features plates, basins, serving trays, bowls,
and porringers. The plates and basins are mostly round, and the
trays oval. A few of the bowls come equipped with matching lids,
while others rest on a central pedestal. Porringers are bowl-
shaped vessels with one or 2 flat handles attached at the side.

Spoons and Ladles (*Plates 260–265*)
Pewter spoons typically have an oval bowl and a fairly simple
handle; a few examples included have a round bowl or a handle
that is somewhat ornate. Ladles included here have a circular
bowl; their handles are made either of wood or pewter.

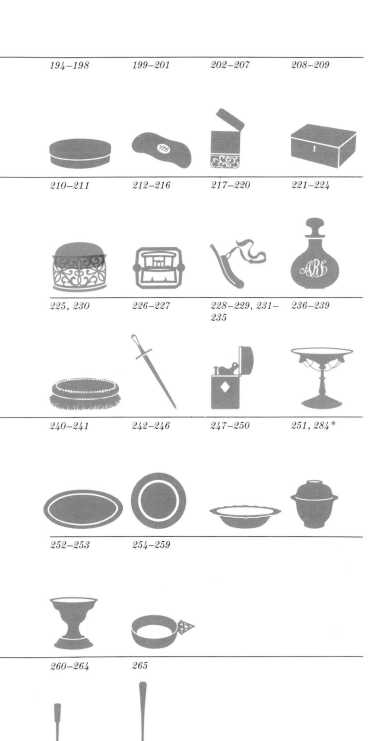

194–198   199–201   202–207   208–209

210–211   212–216   217–220   221–224

225, 230   226–227   228–229, 231–235   236–239

240–241   242–246   247–250   251, 284*

252–253   254–259

260–264   265

Teapots, Coffeepots, Pitchers, and Related Objects
(*Plates 266–292*)
Like their silver counterparts, these pewter objects typically have a pouring spout, shaped rim, or spigot; only a few flagons lack any spout. Most of the objects featured here rest on a foot rim or pedestal; a few have 3 legs.

Mugs, Chalices, Beakers, and Related Objects
(*Plates 293–308*)
Pewter drinking vessels are similar in form and function to silver ones, but they generally lack elaborate ornament. Mugs and tankards both have handles; tankards, in addition, have a lid. Beakers are tall vessels with gently sloping slides; usually they lack handles. Chalices rest on a tall pedestal-like base; they rarely have lids or handles.

Candlesticks, Lamps, and Related Objects (*Plates 309–322*)
Pewter candlesticks are usually tall and cylindrical. Some have simple incised decoration, while others are elaborately shaped. Like candlesticks, many lamps are tall and thin. They incorporate a small vessel known as a font in which the fuel is stored. Fluid lamps typically have one or 2 wicks; a few have mirrors, lenses, or arms—all devices intended to increase the amount of light cast.

Household Objects (*Plates 323–338*)
The articles featured in this section range from a humble bedpan and baby bottle to a fairly complex standish, a desk-top container fitted with compartments for nibs, quills, and other writing necessities. Other objects included here are a flask, a funnel, casters, a commode, and even a sundial.

| 266–267 | 268–270 | 271–276, 284 | 277, 279, 282–283 |

| 278 | 280–281, 284 | 285–292 | |

| 293, 295 | 294, 300–302 | 296–299 | 303–304 |

| 305 | 306 | 307 | 308 |

| 309, 311–314 | 310 | 315, 317–322 | 316 |

| 323–326 | 327–330 | 331–332 | 333–338 |

Silver and Silver Plate

Since time immemorial, silver has been held in the highest esteem—indeed, historians have traced its use to the fourth millennium B.C. Silver's ductility and malleability have enabled craftsmen to fashion it into an amazing variety of objects both functional and beautiful. The silversmith's craft is an art form, and silver has an enduring place in society.

Early Silversmithing in America

The tradition of apprenticeship, long practiced in England and elsewhere, was continued in the American Colonies. In order to become a silversmith, a boy apprenticed himself to a practicing artisan, or master, for 6 or 7 years. During that time, the apprentice lived with his master, serving him in any way necessary. In return, the master was obliged to teach the boy the art and mystery of the craft. Upon completion of his training, the new metalworker became a freeman; until he had his own shop, he worked as a journeyman for day wages or on a piecework basis. Many of these artisans did not work solely with silver, but also plied gold, and most referred to themselves as goldsmiths.

The earliest silversmiths in the Colonies were craftsmen from Europe, primarily England and Holland, who brought their skills with them to the new land. Although several goldsmiths are known to have settled in Tidewater Virginia, they produced very little silver; Captain John Smith recorded that this was "for the very best of reasons that there was none to find." The Tidewater region early turned its efforts to raising tobacco, but in New England, where the climate was harsher and crops poor, silversmiths found much work to do. Their raw material was primarily coin, melted down and fashioned into objects. In this way, the early Colonists provided themselves with a kind of savings security—for it was much more difficult for a thief to dispose of a recognizable object than it was to sell coins.

Detail of a goblet.

The earliest Colonial craftsmen known to us through work that survives today are John Hull and Robert Sanderson. These men worked in partnership in Boston for a short time, and were empowered by the British crown to mint money for the Colony of Massachusetts. Another figure of note in early American silversmithing is Paul Revere, Jr. He is better known today for his famous midnight ride, but this patriot, whose father was also a silversmith, had a lively trade in Boston at the time of the Revolution.

Regulation of the Silver Industry

Silver is a soft metal, and must be alloyed with copper in order to be worked. But since silver is also inherently valuable, and sold by weight, it was important to devise a means to guard against fraud. In Europe, different countries had their own standards of fineness—that is, the acceptable level of base metal that could be mixed with silver. In this Americans took their cue from England, where the sterling standard had been in effect since the 13th century.

This standard called for a minimum of 925 parts of silver per 1000 and was enforced by a governing board known as the Worshipful Company of Goldsmiths in the City of London. In Colonial America, there was no such overseeing body, and objects made here at the time tend to contain slightly less silver.

Although sterling has always been the standard for both English and American silver, the word "sterling" has never been used on English wares. American silversmiths are not known to have used the word on their silver before about 1870, except for a few craftsmen in Philadelphia and Baltimore between about 1810 and 1830. It was not until 1907 that the use of the mark in this country was mandated by law.

In order to document that an object was of the correct and accepted purity, England and other European countries required

Detail of a vase.

a system of marking. In England, 4 separate hallmarks (so called because they were stamped at the Goldsmith's Hall in London) were typically used. American silversmiths usually stamped only their name or initials on objects they made. However, by the 19th century, with the onset of large-scale manufacturing and national marketing, this began to change. Silversmiths often continued to mark their work, but their marks were frequently overstruck or had the name of the retailer, with whom the maker had a marketing arrangement, placed next to them. Sometimes 19th-century American silversmiths used multiple marks in imitation of British hallmarks, but these were not mandated by law and, as far as is known, do not have the same meaning as those used in England. The single and very important exception is Baltimore, where from 1814 to about 1860, a regulatory body organized to oversee the quality of the work of the city's silversmiths instituted a hallmarking system similar to that used in England. This body, however, proved unpopular and was eventually disbanded.

Silver Plate

It was not until the advent of electroplating in the 19th century that America produced plated wares in any quantity; most earlier such goods were fused-plated items that had been imported from England. Like silversmiths, the makers of silver-plated objects were considered craftsmen, but their work seems not to have been as rigidly controlled. The absence of an organized governing body in England is made evident by the rarity of marks on antique silver-plated objects.

By the middle of the 19th century, this situation had begun to change, and many American and English producers of electroplate placed their names on their products. In addition, they used numerous acronyms and symbols to tell the purchaser what he was buying. The most common of these is EP, which

Detail of a tobacco box.

stands for electroplate; EPNS stands for electroplated nickel silver, and EPBM for electroplated britannia metal. Other codes were also used, especially on flatware.

The Industrial Age
Following the American Civil War, the production of both silver and silver plate began to undergo tremendous changes. Mechanization brought with it new possibilities. Silver and silver-plate production became the realm of a few large manufacturers. Some of these firms, such as Gorham and Kirk, had existed for years as small shops or family partnerships. Others, such as the International Silver Company, were conglomerates.

These companies employed talented craftsmen to design and fabricate their products, but it was the company, rather than the individual artisan, that was responsible for the statement made by these products. In some cases, such as the manufacture of the Martelé line by Gorham, the styles were so distinctive and well made that the creation was limited to a few, or a few thousand, pieces. But in other cases, mass production was the rule; while its benefits were many, it incurred the inevitable loss of the individual silversmith's imprint.

Silver and Style
Style can generally be defined as the way in which an object is shaped or decorated. Although most forms have some basic structure—such as teapots, which always have spouts, lids, and handles—they can be worked in a limitless variety of ways. It is convenient to organize silver and silver plate according to the stylistic terms used in other decorative arts. However, too great an emphasis should not be given to these groupings because styles often overlap. One style does not cease abruptly to be replaced by another; the transition is often slow.

Detail of a tumbler.

Stylistic changes can be best understood as a reaction to what went before. In that respect, the movements of taste can be likened to a clock pendulum moving from one extreme to another, from simple to complex, chaste to flamboyant, naturalistic to stylized. The earliest stylistic category for American silver might be called baroque. The most fashionable objects made in this style date from the last half of the 17th and first few years of the 18th century. Baroque objects have bold curves with florid, 3-dimensional detailing, usually of leafy forms but sometimes with human motifs; the decoration at this time was very stylized.

The baroque evolved into a style commonly called Queen Anne, for the monarch on the English throne at the time. Objects made in the Queen Anne style were generally very curvilinear; the S-shaped or ogee curve, referred to as the line of beauty, generally predominated. These objects tended to be visually lighter than their baroque counterparts, with broad expanses of highly polished, undecorated areas. Proponents of the style were concerned with the integration of design; an object was conceived of as a visual whole rather than an assemblage of parts.

By about 1750 these design features had run their course, giving way to what is now known as the rococo. The principal feature of this style in silver was naturalism, and the most vibrant American examples have complex outlines. Their surfaces are heavily laden with ornament consisting largely of C-scrolls, S-scrolls, leaves, flowers, and vines.

Toward the end of the Revolution, Americans began to look to ancient Rome for stylistic inspiration in their silver. This ushered in the Federal style, which extended from about 1790 to approximately 1830. Objects made during this time were often urn-shaped and raised on pedestals. Those dating from the first half of this period are tall and slender, while those from the

Detail of a plate.

second half are shorter and broader. The early Federal objects are modestly decorated with beaded or narrow engraved borders and delicate engraved floral swags and pendants; all of these motifs are fairly abstract. Later examples are ornamented with increasingly realistic and sculptural features. The most ambitious flaunt botanically correct acanthus plants and accurate eagles, human heads, lion's feet, and serpents.

By the 1830s this style began to become more naturalistic. The forms and motifs used on much of the silver made between about 1830 and the 1870s recall those on rococo silver of about a century earlier; this style is therefore often called rococo revival. While much of the ornament on rococo revival objects is like that of the earlier rococo, it often has neoclassical overtones.

The era that fostered the rococo revival is generally referred to as the Victorian. At this time, silver experienced a tremendous growth in popularity, coupled with an extraordinary increase in availability because of mining in the Far West. The wares produced reflect an era of exuberance and plenty through their lush and extensive ornament.

The enthusiasm for large amounts of ornament eventually spawned a reaction toward simplicity, the Arts and Crafts Movement. Becoming manifest in American silver in the early 20th century, this style emphasized hand craftsmanship and minimal ornamentation. The slightly later Art Deco style was based largely on sharp, geometric angles and shapes.

No single style can be said to have dominated all others during this century. For example, the ever-popular, elaborate, mass-produced Kirk repoussé made in Baltimore coexists nicely with the much smaller amount of hand-hammered, sparsely decorated silver produced by The Kalo Shop in Chicago. The 20th century remains a time of diversity and experimentation in American silver design.

Detail of a cigarette lighter.

Plates, Trays, and Related Objects

Most plates, trays, and related forms made in America before the mid-19th century required an extensive amount of handwork in their fabrication. All were very difficult to make and, as a consequence, expensive. But in the mid-19th century, large-scale mechanized silver production provided householders with inexpensive and attractive pieces. By the beginning of the 20th century, many of these objects were made almost completely by machine. These articles, while often having much ornament, tend to be somewhat less flamboyant in character, their decorations rather stylized and restrained in comparison to earlier handworked examples.

Plates, Dishes, and Trays

Although silver plates were made by American silversmiths as early as the 17th century, they have never been common, and most were intended as communion or church collection plates. However, during the late 19th or very early 20th century, a few wealthy individuals had sets of up to 24 silver service plates made for their dining tables.

Trays, which are considerably more common than plates, range in size from 6″ to 3′. Those made before the American Revolution were typically round with 3 or 4 short feet at the edge; most made after the Revolution were oval. Larger trays, frequently used to carry a tea-and-coffee set, often had handles at the ends. Similar small examples made between about 1780 and 1810 often measured no more than 6″ across; today we refer to them as trays, but they were in fact teapot stands.

Tazzas and Compotes

A tazza, or footed salver, is a flat circular plate supported by a central pedestal. Limited quantities of tazzas were made by 17th-century American silversmiths, but the form fell from popularity in the early 18th century because tazzas tip over more easily than trays with feet. In the early to mid-19th century, compotes came into fashion; these dishes are similar to tazzas but have a bowl at the center. By the late 19th century, compotes were quite popular as table and sideboard ornaments; they were made in both silver and silver plate, and often came in pairs.

Decorative Motifs

Because large trays are expensive and valuable, an owner almost always stipulated that his name, initials, or coat of arms be prominently engraved on them. Most trays had no ornament in the center area except for this engraving. The edges, however, frequently had elaborate ornament. The most common design of the early 18th century was composed of alternating scrolls and stylized shells, sometimes with leafy flourishes. By the 19th century, this type of decoration had become much more vivid and elaborate, and extended over a larger area.

While most trays from the 19th century had foliate ornament, some were embellished with human and animal motifs. The most fanciful had ornament relating to the use of the tray.

The extensive use of machine processes in the 19th century spawned a reaction in a small but vociferous group of craftsmen who cultivated and practiced hand fabrication. Among the most famous of these makers were William Christmas Codman and his craftsmen at the Gorham Company, who made a type of silver known as Martelé. While some machines were used in its manufacture, the craftsmen reduced the evidence of this and emphasized, or even accentuated, the appearance of hand workmanship. Today, Martelé is a favorite of collectors.

Federal plate

Description
Circular plate with gadrooned edge. Shallow well engraved in center with coat of arms, crest, and motto "VIRTUS LIBERTAS ET PATRIA" (Virtue, Liberty, and Country) of Wetmore family of New York.

Marks and Dimensions
"F.&G." and "PHILADᴬ" each in rectangle stamped on reverse of brim. Diameter: 10″. Height: 1″.

Maker, Locality, and Date
Thomas Fletcher & Sidney Gardiner (1808–27), Philadelphia. 1812–25.

Comment
American silver plates from any period are rare. In England and on the Continent, sets were more common, sometimes consisting of as many as 24 plates. Because silver is soft and does not withstand abrasion from utensils, such plates were intended only for service. Smaller plates or bowls of porcelain or glass were placed on them, and these held the food. The plate shown here, however, one of a pair but without doubt from a larger set, has been eaten from directly, judging from the knife marks on its surface.

Hints for Collectors
Many showy or fancy European silver objects have no counterparts in America, where simpler, more practical forms from abroad were commonly adopted. Plates, which are usually both simple and practical, were seldom produced in this country. Although they may lack the visual impact of an elaborate tea set, silver plates deserve special attention, not only because of their rarity but also because they represent an interesting facet of earlier American life.

2 Victorian plate

Description
Circular plate with narrow molded edge. Rim cast with border of naked children playing in grape arbor. Well has molded edge; engraved with intertwined "LK" in foliate script. Engraved on back in script "From H.C.H. May 27ᵗʰ 1885."

Marks and Dimensions
"TIFFANY & C⁰/7344 M 8824/STERLING-SILVER" stamped incuse on back. Diameter: 8⅝". Height: ⅞".

Maker, Locality, and Date
Tiffany & Company (1853–present), New York City. c. 1885.

Comment
Silver plates were made by American silversmiths as early as the 17th century, yet they seem never to have been in great demand, probably because they were both costly and difficult to make. Plates tended to warp during fabrication, and it required a great deal of time and skill to make one that would lie perfectly flat. They are infrequently listed in silversmiths' order books and American household inventories. During the late 19th century, however, specialized plates, including ice-cream plates and soup plates, were made for table use. This plate might have served in any of these capacities.

Hints for Collectors
Rarity, often an important factor in evaluating silver objects, makes a plate like the one pictured here desirable. But rarity should not be the sole factor in selecting an object. A vigorous and visually pleasing design as well as substantial weight and fine workmanship should figure equally in any potential purchase.

Victorian child's eating set

Description

9 pieces decorated with cavorting children against mat ground. Straight-sided bowl with gilt interior and matching plate. Cylindrical mug with C-shaped handle and gilt interior. Narrow cylindrical napkin ring. Fork, knife, and spoon, each with tapered rounded handle; gilt fork tines, knife blade, and spoon bowl. Straight-sided porringer has flat, triangular, pierced handle with child's head amid scrolls; matching circular plate with decorated rim. "From Grandpa/Christmas 1893" engraved in script on underside of each piece but napkin ring.

Marks and Dimensions

"TIFFANY & C⁰ 5470 T 4166/STERLING"; globe superimposed over "T" and encircled with border containing "TIFFANY & CO"; all or some elements of this mark stamped incuse on underside of each piece. Bowl diameter: 5"; height: 3". Bowl plate diameter: 7⅜"; height: ⅝". Porringer diameter: 5⅜"; height: 2½"; width: 6½". Porringer plate diameter: 8"; height: ½". Cup height: 3⅜"; width: 4⅛". Napkin ring diameter: 1⅞"; height: 1¾". Knife length: 7⅜". Fork length: 6⅛". Spoon length: 6½".

Maker, Locality, and Date

Tiffany & Company (1853–present), New York City. c. 1893.

Comment

For centuries silver has been a requisite part of the life of well-born children. During the late 19th century especially, large silver manufacturers created an extensive array of silver objects —among them christening cups, baby spoons, rattles, and teething rings—that relatives and friends traditionally lavished

on the newborn. While any one of those might be given to a child, none was more appropriate than a porringer, mug, and utensils. Children's eating sets like the one shown here were both practical and ornamental, being often displayed as part of the family silver. Such displays were quite popular among affluent Americans during the late 19th and early 20th centuries, and sideboards heavily laden with silver, china, and glass were an important status symbol in the home.

Hints for Collectors

Children's silver utensils are readily available, but condition is all-important, since such objects were frequently battered and abused by their small owners. While an eating set with scratched gilt interiors, a chewed spoon, or a disfigured mug might retain its sentimental value, its monetary worth for collectors is substantially diminished. Usually children's utensils are found singly; it is rather uncommon to find an entire set in good condition. When you encounter a set that has especially attractive features, such as a documentable history of ownership or extensive amounts of tasteful ornament, it is a good idea to consider acquiring it, if it is fairly priced. Similarly, responsible collectors will refrain from breaking up such a set, even though selling the objects individually might bring higher profit than would selling the set as a unit.

4 Late Colonial/Federal tray

Description
Circular tray with scalloped, molded, and gadrooned edge.
Center engraved with coat of arms and crest (of Schuyler family
of New York) within foliate mantling. 3 short cabriole legs with
claw-and-ball feet.

Marks and Dimensions
"J•HEATH" in rectangle stamped on underside. Diameter: 15″.
Height: 1⅝″.

Maker, Locality, and Date
John Heath (dates unknown), New York City. 1760–80.

Comment
This silver tray is one of the largest 18th-century American
examples known. Except for some Boston-made examples that
were octagonal in shape, American trays, or salvers, of this
period were circular and had edges ranging from absolutely plain
to elaborately scalloped. Salvers of this period almost always had
3 short C-shaped legs, often ornamented with scrolls or shells.
This tray has claw-and-ball feet, which, although carved with
great frequency on late 18th-century furniture, were unusual
on silver.

Hints for Collectors
Trays of this type, regardless of size, were wrought from a single
piece of silver, and the raised edge was shaped with an iron
swage. To the edge the silversmith added a framing molding,
often with shell or scroll ornament; this molding was cast in
separate segments that were placed end to end to form a circle of
the desired diameter. Close examination of a tray's edge should
reveal evidence of this construction.

5 Federal tray

Description
Large, flat, oval tray with raised reeded rim. Center engraved
with oval containing script initials "ITCR" within leafy scrolled
mantling. 4 low feet decorated with shells and scrolls.

Marks and Dimensions
"S•C" in rectangle stamped on underside. Length: 16¼". Width:
12¹³⁄₁₆". Height: 1⅝".

Maker, Locality, and Date
Samuel Coleman (dates unknown), Trenton or Burlington, New
Jersey. 1790–1820.

Comment
Large silver trays were quite difficult to make, and most of those
known today were made in Boston, New York, or Philadelphia
by silversmiths who were adept at producing a large variety of
sophisticated forms. 18th-century examples were circular or
occasionally square, while 19th-century trays were almost always
oval, or occasionally rectangular with canted corners.

Hints for Collectors
For every large oval silver tray, dozens of plated examples exist,
many made in England of German silver. Plated trays can
be easily confused with silver ones. To avoid costly mistakes,
collectors should learn to distinguish the subtle difference in
color between silver and its base-metal counterpart. Also, the
base metal may show through at points of heavy wear, such as
the bottom of feet or the center of the top. Plated trays are
usually heavier than silver examples.

6 Federal teapot stand

Description
Flat oval form with cove-molded, reeded edge and 2 narrow engraved borders. Center engraved with "HT" in script in foliate circle. 4 flat and slender scroll feet.

Marks and Dimensions
"I•V" in oval stamped on underside. Length: 5¾". Width: 4¹¹⁄₁₆". Height: 1¼".

Maker, Locality, and Date
John Vernon (1768–1815), New York City. 1791–99.

Comment
During the late 18th century, silver teapots were sometimes made with accompanying small, traylike stands. By the second decade of the 19th century, teapots were designed with their own pedestals, which often had feet, obviating the need for separate stands. Teapots that used stands were of a basically simple shape—circular, oval, octagonal, or sometimes fluted. The trays on which they rested were of a conforming outline and fitted precisely to their teapots.

Hints for Collectors
Late 18th-century teapots have almost always been separated from their stands by later generations of owners. By themselves, the stands look exactly like miniature trays, for which many collectors mistake them. While teapot stands such as the one shown here are collected today in their own right, they are more desirable and valuable if they are still paired with their original teapot.

Modern bread tray

Description
Oval base with curved sides, higher at ends. Flared lip with rolled edge and narrow guilloche border; wider border below of alternating foliate panels and clusters. Elaborate foliate reserve engraved inside each end.

Marks and Dimensions
"LOUIS XIV/PATENTED/DEC. 23, 1919/STERLING/5887" and rampant lion within script "T"; all stamped incuse on underside. Length: 12¼". Width: 6¾". Height: 2".

Maker, Locality, and Date
Towle Silversmiths (1873–present), Newburyport, Massachusetts. 1919–50.

Comment
Table wares of machine-made sheet silver were quite popular and produced in considerable quantity during the early 20th century. Many different forms were made, each to fulfill a specific purpose. Breadbaskets, found on all stylish tables, were sometimes circular, but more often oval, to fit the shape of a loaf of bread. This example is ornamented with simple, stylized flowers and leaves, which were quickly and inexpensively replicated by means of heavy die-stamping machinery. Using downfall presses, diesinkers and machinists could reproduce attractive adaptations of the kinds of designs done by hand in earlier centuries.

Hints for Collectors
Silver of this type was made in great quantity, and today is readily available and inexpensive. However, it will eventually become scarce through attrition, especially since such pieces continue to be melted down for their bullion value.

8 Victorian platter

Description
Oval platter has molded and scalloped rim with 4 major lobes depicting a rabbit with radishes, an otter with a fish, a squirrel with acorns, and an opossum with a grasshopper. Shaped shallow oval well. "P" engraved in script on underside.

Marks and Dimensions
Anchor in shield under spread eagle flanked by lion and Gothic "G" each in clipped-corner square; "950-1000 FINE" and "8930" in rectangle; "16 IN" and sickle; all stamped incuse on underside. Length: 17¼". Width: 12⁷⁄₁₆". Height: 1³⁄₁₆".

Maker, Locality, and Date
Gorham Company (1831–present), Providence. 1899.

Comment
In its heyday during the late 19th and early 20th centuries, the Gorham Company was the largest silver manufacturer in the world, producing a vast array of utilitarian wares in myriad patterns. In the 1890s the company embarked on an ambitious project to make and market a limited line of silver that came to be known as Martelé, which is French for hammered. While Martelé pieces were always functional, they were considered art objects because of their aesthetic merit.

Hints for Collectors
Gorham made Martelé for only about 15 years, manufacturing fewer than 5000 pieces between 1895 and 1910. For this reason, Martelé objects are fairly rare and are becoming more and more expensive. Collectors should look for objects of the same high quality as this whimsically decorated platter. Martelé objects like this, already scarce, will disappear from the market in short order as demand increases.

9 Victorian tray

Description
Oval tray with raised molded edge having large border of beading. Arched loop handle at each end with beading and acanthus leaves. Well engraved with several plain, narrow, mat borders and 2 wide borders of scrolled acanthus leaves. Engraved coat of arms and crest (of Meade family of Philadelphia) in center.

Marks and Dimensions
"BAILEY & C⁰ CHESTNUT ST. PHILA" stamped incuse in oval enclosing "136" stamped twice; 3 pseudohallmarks (lion in clipped-corner rectangle stamped 6 times; "s" in oval stamped twice; and American shield stamped twice), all on back. Length: 30¾". Width: 12". Height: 2½".

Maker, Locality, and Date
Bailey & Company (1846–78), Philadelphia. 1846–78.

Comment
Large silver trays were difficult to make, required a large amount of silver, and were expensive. Although American trays are rare, the form was made in increasing quantity as the 19th century progressed.

Hints for Collectors
Trays as large and ornate as this one are almost always very heavy, weighing between 50 and 200 Troy ounces. Because of their cost, almost all had the owner's initials or coat of arms engraved in the center. A tray with a plain center has probably had its original engraving erased. A slight depression, a bright but smeared surface, and blurring of the surrounding ornament in that area are all signs that engraving has been removed. Since this lowers value, a collector should make a careful visual and tactile examination of an object before buying.

10 Modern compote

Description
Shallow circular bowl with wide border of pierced and applied foliate scrolls. Narrow rim with border of leaf tips. 2 tapered, pierced loop handles. Low, circular, flared pedestal with leaf-tip border at base. "R E B" engraved in script in center of well.

Marks and Dimensions
"STERLING/11 IN, 2995, MADE FOR TIFFANY" stamped incuse on underside. Diameter: 11″. Height: 4¾″. Width: 15¼″.

Maker, Locality, and Date
Unknown. Retailed by Tiffany & Company (1853–present), New York City. 1900–30.

Comment
Compotes, made singly or in pairs, were intended for the dining table or sideboard and frequently held fresh fruit. Most compotes do not have handles, but nearly all have applied ornament around the perimeter, typically in the form of a lush composition of leaves, flowers, and scrolls. This example is somewhat unusual in that its border is pierced.

Hints for Collectors
Compotes make attractive acquisitions and are readily available, especially those dating from the mid-19th to the 20th century. Collectors should seek those that have unusual features, such as the finely detailed, well-executed pierced border and tapered handles of the compote shown here. Avoid purchasing thin, lightweight examples, because these can be easily bent and damaged.

Early Colonial tazza

Description
Flat circular top with convex molded rim of gadrooning.
Trumpet-shaped flared central pedestal with gadrooned border
at base. Top engraved in script "Myndert Schuyler/b. 1672
d. 1755"; block letters "M + S" on underside.

Marks and Dimensions
"S/I•V" in trefoil stamped on bottom edge of pedestal. Diameter:
8¼". Height: 3".

Maker, Locality, and Date
Jacobus Vander Spiegel (1668–1708), New York City. 1680–
1708.

Comment
Tazzas, or footed salvers, are an early and uncommon form of
American silver. Most known examples date from the 17th and
early 18th centuries. Although unusual in appearance because of
the central pedestal, these salvers were used like a tray to
support or carry glasses, bottles, and other vessels containing
food and drink. This example was owned by Myndert Schuyler, a
prominent resident of Albany, New York, during the early 18th
century.

Hints for Collectors
The good condition, large gadrooned borders, and identified
original owner of this rare object make it exceptionally desirable.
The owner's name and birth and death dates engraved on the top
detract from its appeal, however, since they were added
considerably later. Judging from the kind of script letters and
their lack of wear, the engraving was probably executed in the
late 19th or early 20th century.

Description
Moderately deep bowl with scrolled lip; lobed side gently flared.
Beaded ring surrounds reserve in center of well.

Marks and Dimensions
"TIFFANY & C⁰ MAKERS STERLING 22954L" stamped incuse on
underside of lip. Diameter: 5¼". Height: 1⅛".

Maker, Locality, and Date
Tiffany & Company (1853–present), New York City.
c. 1941.

Comment
Botanical forms have influenced silver design for centuries,
providing an infinite variety of shapes ranging from the simple to
the complex and inspiring both naturalistic and highly abstract
interpretations. Frequently used in the handwrought silver of
the 17th and 18th centuries, foliate and floral motifs have
remained popular in today's predominantly machine-produced
objects. While in previous centuries these popular designs had
strong symbolic meaning, today they are enjoyed mainly for
their visual appeal.

Hints for Collectors
This dish is of a type produced in considerable quantity in this
century and is modest in both character and value. The vital
design should be of interest to beginning collectors seeking
visually pleasing objects at little expense. When buying an object
of this type, which was produced in large numbers, it is
especially important to acquire an example that is in very good
condition with clear maker's marks.

13 Victorian/Modern sweetmeat dishes and spoons

Description
Shallow bowl shaped like ribbed scallop shell, with incurved 3-part leaf handle. 3 small barnacle-shaped feet. Matching spoon with 3-part leaf handle, tapered shaft, and shallow oval bowl.

Marks and Dimensions
Dishes: Lion and "G" each in clipped-corner square, flanking anchor in shield; "65C J. E. CALDWELL & CO. STERLING"; all stamped incuse on underside. Length: 4¾". Width: 5⅜". Height: 2¼". Spoons: Lion; anchor; "G"; and "J. E. CALDWELL & CO." stamped incuse on back of handle. Length: 6⅛". Width: 1¼".

Maker, Locality, and Date
Gorham Company (1831–present), Providence. Retailed by J. E. Caldwell & Company (1848–present), Philadelphia. 1870–1920.

Comment
The scallop, or pecten, shell has been a favored motif among silversmiths for centuries, its form often inspiring the shape of an object or serving as applied decoration. It was particularly popular in England and America during the third quarter of the 18th century, and experienced great favor again in the late 19th century.

Hints for Collectors
Though modest in character and relatively inexpensive, these dishes are desirable for stylistic reasons. For instance, the feet are cleverly applied in a manner that imitates the way barnacles attach themselves to surfaces.

Spoons, Knives, Forks, and Related Flatware

It often surprises modern collectors to learn that before the mid-19th century the only flatware generally used at the dining table was the spoon. Knives were generally regarded as all-purpose utensils and not exclusively for an individual's use at the table. The fork was introduced to the table in 16th-century Italy, but failed to gain immediate acceptance. At least one early observer considered it "coarse and ungraceful to throw food into the mouth as you would toss hay into a barn with a pitchfork."

Early Table Settings
There are a very few large sets of spoons that date from the 18th century, but whole matching place settings did not become commonplace until about the time of the Civil War, when American tables began to be set with numerous and varied forms. Lettuce forks, sardine forks, cold-meat forks, cake forks, salad forks, and oyster forks were a few of the items generated by 19th-century taste. Also necessary for the well-appointed Victorian dining table were the salt spoon, bouillon spoon, orange spoon, sugar spoon, mustard spoon, preserve spoon, and ice-cream spoon, as well as the pie knife, butter knife, cake knife, and bread knife—not to mention asparagus tongs, crumbers, and food pushers.

Diners from eras earlier than the Victorian also used specialized utensils, but to a much lesser extent. One of the most interesting was the mote spoon; this had a pierced bowl to strain leaves from a teacup and a slender pointed handle that removed leaves from the base of the spout of a teapot. Another very early specialized utensil was the sucket fork. This unusual object, with a spoon at one end and a fork at the other, was used to eat fruits that had been preserved in a thick, sugary syrup known as sucket. Sucket was so popular in early America that it prompted one observer to state that "the women are pityfully toothshaken . . . by the sweetmeats." Although Americans have never lost their sweet tooth, sucket passed from popularity during the early 18th century.

Electroplated Flatware and Souvenir Spoons
With the invention of inexpensive electroplated tableware in the mid-19th century, elegant tables became much more affordable. Electroplated spoons, knives, and forks, costing a fraction of their silver counterparts but looking virtually identical, quickly became a part of many Americans' dining rooms.

The collecting of souvenir spoons was also a 19th-century phenomenon, and one that had nothing to do with eating. The popularity of these spoons can be deduced by an observation made in 1891 that "from Maine to California, from Minnesota to Florida, the cry is for souvenir spoons." To satisfy this demand, dozens of different companies made thousands of patterns. These spoons were usually fashioned to commemorate a special event, honor a hero, or document a notable place. They were often unusual and sometimes bizarre in design: One example commemorating the annual meeting of the Grand Army of the Republic has a handle shaped like a Civil War rifle.

Silver and silver-plated flatware continues to be produced by nearly all American silver companies. In spite of the advent of stainless steel, thousands of place settings in hundreds of patterns are sold every year to householders. A few contemporary craftsmen have also turned their attention to flatware design. Their dynamic and original interpretations of a very commonplace form give new importance to objects that we all occasionally take for granted.

14 Federal Onslow-pattern and octagonal-pattern ladles

Description
Left: Long, curved, tapered handle with flared, reeded, and scrolled end. Deep bowl with scalloped edge and tapered flutes radiating from juncture with handle. Right: Long, curved, tapered handle with faceted square end and letter "C" engraved on front. Deep bowl with raised triangle within rectangle on back.

Marks and Dimensions
Left: "WF" in rectangle stamped on back of handle. Length: 13¾". Diameter: 3¹⁵⁄₁₆". Right: "W. WOOD•Sterling" in rectangle stamped twice on back of handle. Length: 13".

Maker, Locality, and Date
Left: William Faris (1728–1804), Annapolis, Maryland. 1760–80. Right: W. Wood (dates unknown), probably Philadelphia area. 1790–1810.

Comment
Large ladles were popular for serving punch. While most, like the one at right, had plain hemispherical bowls, a few had bowls in the shape of a scallop shell. The uncommon handle tip seen on the ladle at left is derived from the so-called Onslow type, which was popular in England during the third quarter of the 18th century. Little is known about the maker of the ladle at right, except that he probably worked in the Philadelphia area.

Hints for Collectors
Although punch ladles are very common and old examples can still be obtained with ease, an unusual example such as the one at left will be hard to find and costly to acquire. The scarcity of its Annapolis maker's work adds to its interest and value.

15 Victorian fused-plated ladle

Description
Slender shaft with long, flared, French-plated brass socket riveted to flattened wooden handle and fused-plated bowl. Shallow circular bowl with rolled molded lip and curved spout at 90° to handle.

Marks and Dimensions
"C. ROUYER" in rectangle stamped on back of handle. Length: 11¾".

Maker, Locality, and Date
Pierre Casimir Rouyer (b. 1813), New Orleans. 1850–67.

Comment
Born in France, Rouyer settled in New Orleans in 1849, where he advertised himself as a goldsmith, silversmith, gilder, and plater. Most of his time seems to have been devoted to making flatware for the city's hotels and restaurants. In spite of the apparently large number of clients, Rouyer's business went into receivership in 1867, and relatively little of his work is known to exist today.

Hints for Collectors
Although this ladle is simple and lacking in elaborate ornament, it is of interest for collectors because it was made by a southern silversmith; works from south of Pennsylvania are less common than those from New England, New York, and Philadelphia. Additionally, the ladle is a very rare example of early American-made fused plate; prior to the Civil War, most plated wares were imported from England. Yet despite its historical appeal, this ladle would be fairly inexpensive, because of its simple form and because areas of its silver plate are worn away.

Federal and Colonial ladles

Description
Left: Slender baluster-shaped wooden handle attached to curved V-shaped bracket. Bracket attached to fluted oval bowl with 2 curved, flared pouring spouts. Right: Slender handle of twisted horn with small conical silver cap; fitted into tapered socket of flat narrow silver shaft. Shallow bowl with flared lip and spout.

Marks and Dimensions
Left: "S•E" in rounded rectangle stamped inside bowl. Length: 13⅛". Right: "J:WARNER" in rectangle stamped on back of handle. Length: 13¾".

Maker, Locality, and Date
Left: Samuel Edwards (1705–62), Boston. 1740–62. Right: Joseph Warner (1742–1800), Wilmington, Delaware. 1780–1800.

Comment
Although English ladles with horn handles are very common, there are few known American examples. Because the thin metal and attenuated form of these ladles make them fragile, they have often been strengthened by molding or a beaded border applied to the rim. In the example at right, the rim, although thick, was not applied; it bears traces of the letter-edged coin from which the bowl was made. The wooden handle and double spouts of the Edwards example at left are typical of 18th-century ladles.

Hints for Collectors
Before the Revolution, American silver objects were frequently made from European coins; after the United States Mint was established in 1794, American coins were used as well. Evidence like that discernible on the rim of the Warner ladle certainly adds to the interest of an object and perhaps to its value.

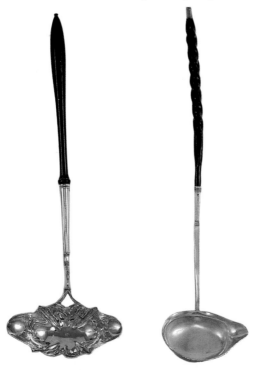

Federal repoussé ladle

Description
Long tapered handle with rounded downturned end and twisted shaft; elaborate grape-leaf cluster at juncture with bowl. Deep-bellied oval bowl with repoussé scrolled lip and 2 spouts; ornamented with grapevine and cluster border and acanthus leaves at base. "TP" engraved in script on front of handle end.

Marks and Dimensions
"CHAUDRON'S & RASCH" and "STER•AMERI•MAN•" each in S-shaped outline, all stamped on back of handle. Length: 15⅛".

Maker, Locality, and Date
Simon Chaudron & Anthony Rasch (1809–12), Philadelphia. 1809–12.

Comment
This ladle is unusual in several respects. The handle, with its twisted shaft, is lap-jointed and riveted to a separate ornamental bracket, which is cast rather than wrought. In addition, the bowl is elaborately decorated with realistic rather than abstract motifs. The acronym "STER•AMERI•MAN•" (Sterling American Manufacture) is unexpected, because the use of the word sterling on American silver was not common prior to the Civil War.

Hints for Collectors
The numerous atypical features of this ladle are intriguing and at the same time disturbing. When a piece diverges significantly from the norm, it may be either inauthentic or not of American manufacture, or simply an exception to the rule. Since Chaudron and Rasch made a number of unusual objects, this ladle is less questionable than it would be had it been made by a less innovative maker.

18 Victorian medallion-pattern pie server and fish knife

Description
Handles with circular end enclosing bust of bearded man wearing Roman helmet; below bust, reserve of imbricated scales and row of beading surmounted by crowned oval device. Left: Pie server has spade-shaped blade with convex notched sides and engraved panels of stylized foliate motifs. Right: Fish knife has wide, asymmetrical blade, pierced and engraved with panels of stylized and realistic leaves and flowers.

Marks and Dimensions
"W & H" stamped on back of handles. Left, length: 9⅝". Right, length: 11".

Maker, Locality, and Date
Henry Wood & Dixon G. Hughes (1845–99), New York City. 1871–99.

Comment
Of the many styles of late 19th-century flatware and hollowware, the so-called medallion pattern is one of the most easily recognized. Its principal motif is a male or female profile bust in a circle. Classical Greek or Roman garb was the preferred dress on these figures, although contemporary clothing was sometimes depicted. These figures were usually modeled in crisp relief and, in the most exuberant examples, looked almost like sculpture.

Hints for Collectors
Medallion-pattern silver is more popular with collectors than many other styles of late Victorian silver. Objects depicting identifiable mythical, historical, or contemporary figures are generally more highly esteemed and valuable.

Description
Flared handles with pointed notched tip and molded midsection; 2 applied fish on front; "B" engraved on back. Knife has asymmetrical, elaborately scrolled blade decorated with foliate scrolls. Fork has broad tines with foliate engraving.

Marks and Dimensions
"COIN" stamped incuse on back of each handle. Knife length: 11½". Fork length: 9⅞".

Maker, Locality, and Date
Unknown. Northeastern United States. 1860–1900.

Comment
In fashionable, well-to-do 19th-century households, fish was often served as one of several courses during the main meal. Many sets of matched knives and forks were specially made to serve the fish. Over the years, most of these paired utensils have become separated. When this happens, the fork usually loses its specialized identity, because it is so similar to other types of serving forks. But the knife, or slice, is always recognizable because of its uniquely shaped blade, which more frequently than not has a fish engraved on its upper surface.

Hints for Collectors
Although this set was not marked by its maker, it is of special interest because the 2 utensils have survived together; they retain their original silk-lined box (not shown); and the large fish on each is bolted to the front of the handle, a very unusual way to attach ornament to flatware. The heavy weight and excellent design of this set indicate that it was probably made by one of the major silversmithing firms in the Northeast during the late 19th century.

Federal fish knife

Description
Flat blade with curved edge and low ridge along one side; decorated with engraved scaly fish with leafy fins and pierced outline. Slender curved shaft with leafy shell at juncture with blade. Flat carved mother-of-pearl handle. Engraved "THS/to/ MMS" on underside of blade.

Marks and Dimensions
"L.QUANDALE" in rectangle; 2 eagles, each in rounded square; all stamped on back of blade. Length: 14½".

Maker, Locality, and Date
Lewis Quandale (dates unknown), Philadelphia. 1813–25.

Comment
Fish knives were very popular at the dining table from the late 18th century through the 19th century. These specialized utensils almost invariably had a fish depicted on the blade, denoting their intended purpose. Such iconography is not found on other flatware forms of the period. Made in both England and the United States, fish knives generally have fairly simple silver or ivory handles. This example has an elaborately carved mother-of-pearl handle and a large blade with spirited fish ornament; these features combine to make this knife one of the finest examples of the form.

Hints for Collectors
Because Lewis Quandale is a little-known maker, the exceptional silver knife shown here is likely to be less expensive than one by a better-known craftsman, making it an excellent buy.

Victorian crumber

Description
Flat rectangular blade with rounded ends; oblique lip with
scrolled edge on 3 sides; handle in King's pattern on top and
bottom. Blade engraved with landscape scene surrounded by
foliate circle on engine-turned ground with leafy edge.

Marks and Dimensions
5-pointed star; "J.CONNING" and "MOBILE" each in rectangle; all
stamped on handle back. Length: 12″.

Maker, Locality, and Date
James Conning (c. 1813–72), Mobile, Alabama. 1842–72.

Comment
The 19th century witnessed a growing emphasis on table
manners, most evident in the widespread publication of etiquette
books and a sudden profusion of tablewares. One of the new
utensils in genteel households was the crumber, which was used
to remove crumbs and other small bits of food from the tablecloth
between courses.

Hints for Collectors
This crumber is of particular merit for several reasons. The so-
called King's pattern of the handle is a fairly uncommon and
elaborate style. The landscape scene ornamenting the blade is
more interesting than the flowers and initials usually found on
such objects. And its southern origin lends this object special
appeal. James Conning's mark, in conjunction with the other
features, makes this crumber considerably more desirable than
typical examples from the Northeast.

Modern Chantilly-pattern flatware

Description
Left to right: Sugar spoon, teaspoon, tablespoon; oyster fork, pickle fork, lettuce fork, dinner fork, and meat fork; carving knife, dinner knife, and butter knife. Meat fork, carving knife, and dinner knife with hollow, pitch-filled, tapered, rounded handles, ornamented with loops and overlapping scrolls. Meat fork and carving knife have rectangular ferrule with incut corners and stainless-steel tines or blade; dinner knife blade also stainless steel.

Marks and Dimensions
"STERLING HANDLE" stamped incuse on back of handles and "STAINLESS" stamped on upper section of meat fork, carving knife, and dinner knife. "PAT. 1895 STERLING"; anchor, lion, and "G" or "GORHAM STERLING" in raised letters on back of handles of other pieces. Length (left to right): 6″, 5¾″, 6⅝″, 5½″, 5¾″, 6⅝″, 7½″, 8½″, 10⅛″, 9¾″, 6⅝″.

Maker, Locality, and Date
Gorham Company (1831–present), Providence. 1940–50.

Comment
The Chantilly pattern, seen in this dinner service, was created by William Christmas Codman, one of the chief designers for the Gorham Company. From 1895, when it was patented, until recently, Chantilly remained the most popular flatware pattern ever offered in the United States. In spite of the design patent, its extraordinary commercial success spawned many similar patterns by Gorham's competitors. It is interesting that the design employs no specific plant or animal motifs, but only highly abstract elements. Its simple, sinuous composition continues to appeal to Americans to this day.

The desire for elegant dining-table accoutrements persists from the last quarter of the 19th century, when many ornate flatware patterns still available today were first created. Though Codman designed over 50 flatware patterns for Gorham, none was favored for as long as this one. The enduring demand for a pattern like Chantilly can be partially credited to the fact that many current owners have inherited flatware in this style from earlier generations, and continue to fill out such sets when individual pieces are missing.

Hints for Collectors
A flatware service in the Chantilly pattern is easy to assemble. Knives, forks, and spoons are the most readily available early forms. If early serving pieces cannot be found, new ones can be bought from the factory. However, modern examples, though identical in every other respect to early production, are lighter in weight.

Late Victorian flatware

Description
Left to right: Sauce ladle, berry spoon, tablespoon, dessert spoon, teaspoon, meat fork, dinner fork, luncheon fork. All have tapered handles with rounded upturned end and border of leafy scrolls on edge of front and back. Bowls and tines in various shapes and sizes. Front of handles engraved with initials of various owners.

Marks and Dimensions
Fleur-de-lis in shield and "STERLING PAT. 91" stamped incuse on back of handle of each piece. Length (left to right): 5⅜", 9", 8¼", 7", 6", 9½", 7½", 7".

Maker, Locality, and Date
Junius H. Davis & Charles E. Galt (dates unknown), Philadelphia. 1891–1910.

Comment
During the late 19th century, a profusion of flatware patterns were created, and flatware became a vehicle for style in its own right, as hollowware had been all along. Makers' marks on late Victorian flatware of this period are often interesting. This group, for example, was made by the firm of Davis & Galt of Philadelphia, but the individual objects also bear various retailers' marks, including those of J. E. Caldwell of Philadelphia; Hennigan, Bates & Company of Baltimore; and Galt & Brother of Washington, D.C. Such marks provide insight into the way these wares were marketed.

Hints for Collectors

Collectors can assemble sets of late 19th-century flatware in a huge variety of patterns and forms. Many pieces are of substantial weight, well designed, and moderately priced. A great number of the objects that a collector will encounter bear the monograms of their original owners. Although an assembled set will have various monograms, these initials should be retained, since they are attractive and historically interesting. When attempting to assemble a set of flatware, or to find pieces missing from an existing set, collectors should pay close attention to minute details, since successful and popular designs by one firm were often closely imitated by another, regardless of restrictions imposed by patents. Check also for a maker's mark and, if possible, a patent date or pattern number to ensure that individual pieces you find on the market match others already in your collection. Note retailers' marks as well, since some tradesmen had sales agreements with specific makers; comparing such marks increases your chances of finding pieces that match correctly.

24 Modern Richmond-pattern electroplated flatware

Description
Left to right: Teaspoon, dessert spoon, tablespoon, luncheon or salad fork, dinner fork, luncheon knife, dinner knife. All have handles decorated on front and back with symmetrical scroll-and-leaf design; "EAR" engraved in script at top. Simple spoon bowls, fork tines, and knife blades.

Marks and Dimensions
"GORHAM ELECTROPLATE PATENTED 1897" and anchor, all in raised letters on back of handle. Length (left to right): 9½", 8¼", 7¾", 7", 8½", 7", 5¾".

Maker, Locality, and Date
Gorham Company (1831–present), Providence. 1897–1920.

Comment
This flatware pattern, like many produced since the 1870s, was made in both sterling and electroplate. Such pieces often bear a mark indicating the year in which their design was patented. In addition, a great variety of marks were used on plated wares to indicate the type and quality of the plating. The simplest was "ELECTROPLATE" (meaning silver electrolytically deposited on a nonprecious metal). Others were "A1" (2 ounces of silver deposited on a gross of teaspoons), "XX" (4 ounces of silver on a gross of teaspoons), and "EPNS" (electroplated nickel silver). The most familiar Gorham mark is an anchor flanked by a lion and a "G" in Gothic script. Holloware was often marked with a symbol designating the year a piece was made.

Hints for Collectors

Sets of late 19th- and early 20th-century plated flatware can be assembled easily and at modest cost. Often in highly elaborate patterns, these pieces are decorative in table settings. They are sometimes found with their silver badly eroded and their raised patterns heavily worn. Examples in poor condition should be avoided, since well-preserved pieces can be readily obtained. Replating electroplated wares is an affordable and legitimate option, but most collectors prefer the original plating.

Special care should be taken with flatware that is used for eating. Eggs and other foods with a high sulfur content will tarnish silver rapidly, and salt will cause corrosion. To stave off serious damage, clean flatware thoroughly after each use. When polishing, use only mild, relatively nonabrasive compounds that contain a tarnish-inhibiting agent, and always be certain to rinse off any traces of polish afterward, especially from recessed areas.

Late Colonial, Federal, and Victorian forks

Description
Forks with variously shaped handles and tines. Each engraved; 2 at right have embossed decoration.

Marks and Dimensions
Left: "MH" in rectangle, stamped on handle back. Length: 6¹¹⁄₁₆″. Center left: "WISHART" in rectangle, stamped on handle back. Length: 6⅞″. Center right: "W. B. JOHNSTON" in serrated rectangle stamped on handle back. Length: 6¹³⁄₁₆″. Right: "HARLAND" in rectangle, stamped on handle back. Length: 8⅜″.

Maker, Locality, and Date
Left: Marguerite Hastier (dates unknown), New York City. 1771–1800. Center left: Hugh Wishart (dates unknown), New York City. c. 1784 to 1825. Center right: William Blackstone Johnston (dates unknown), Macon, Georgia. 1832–50. Right: Unknown. Probably New York City. c. 1830–41.

Comment
Marguerite Hastier, whose mark appears on the fork at left, was the wife of the New York silversmith John Hastier. Upon his death in 1771, she continued to carry on his business. Her initials on this fork signify that she owned the shop, not that she made this fork herself.

Hints for Collectors
In the 19th century, the type of ornament seen on the Johnston fork was stamped onto handles using steel dies. This example is also desirable because of its southern origin and because forks were rarer than spoons until after the mid-19th century.

Description
Left: Rectangular paneled handle; long curved silver blade; crest and motto on handle. Center left: Rectangular onyx handle with chamfered edges and silver ferrule; short silver blade with "MGD". Center right: 6-sided, fiddle-shaped, hollow handle with molded ferrule; short silver blade; "E F Smith" on handle. Right: Oval reeded handle with foliate borders; rounded steel blade with embossed foliate scrolls and steamboat with inscription.

Marks and Dimensions
Left: "I.W.F." in rectangle and 4 pseudohallmarks (anchor; star; male head; and "C"), each in oval, all stamped on blade. Length: 8½". Center left: "JONES, BALL & POOR" in rectangle stamped on blade. Length: 6⅝". Center right: "J.MOOD" in serrated rectangle stamped on blade. Length: 5¾". Right: "13" in rectangle stamped on side of handle. Length: 7³⁄₁₆".

Maker, Locality, and Date
Left: John W. Forbes (1781–1864), New York City. 1820–38. Center left: George B. Jones, True M. Ball & Nathaniel C. Poor (dates unknown), Boston. 1852–65. Center right: John Mood (1792–1864), Charleston, South Carolina. 1830–50. Right: Unknown. United States. 1830–50.

Comment
Before the mid-19th century, most Americans used imported English table knives, so American examples from that time are uncommon. American knives usually have steel blades.

Hints for Collectors
Blades were attached to handles with pitch, which becomes brittle over time and will melt if exposed to extreme heat.

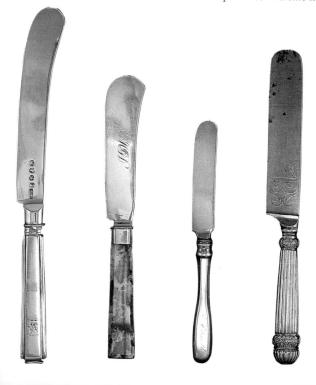

Child's Victorian Luxembourg-pattern spoon, fork, and knife

Description
Knife, fork, and spoon all have upturned handle with flared rounded end; ornamented with foliate C-scrolls on front and back. Knife has straight blade with rounded end. Spoon has oval bowl. Fork has 4 tines. All engraved "JKR" in foliate script on front of handle.

Marks and Dimensions
Lion; anchor; "G"; and "STERLING" in raised letters on back of spoon and fork handles and knife blade. Spoon length: 6". Fork length: 5¾". Knife length: 7¼".

Maker, Locality, and Date
Gorham Company (1831–present), Providence. 1893–1900.

Comment
Many handle patterns for silver flatware were created during the late 19th century, with large manufacturers producing a vast array of them each year. Some patterns were short-lived, while others attained a popularity that lasted from generation to generation. This pattern was introduced in 1893; known as Luxembourg, it was meant to evoke the exotic aura and rich history of this European country.

Hints for Collectors
Children's eating utensils were popular gifts during the 19th century; many survive today and are readily available to collectors. Most desirable are those in sets, which have added appeal if they retain their original box. Unusual patterns that enjoyed short-lived popularity are of special interest and often of greater value because of their relative rarity.

Modern traveling knife, fork, and spoon

Description
Knife with flat, petal-shaped, curved blade; curved, flared handle, rectangular in section, with 2 narrow pockets to hold spoon and fork. Spoon with slender, curved, flared handle and shallow oval bowl. Fork with slender, curved, flared handle; shallow oval bowl with 3 short curved tines.

Marks and Dimensions
"STERLING" and "GRAHAM" stamped incuse on end of handle of each implement. Knife length: 8¼". Fork length: 7½". Spoon length: 7¼".

Maker, Locality, and Date
Anne Krohn Graham (b. 1942), Newark, Delaware. 1978.

Comment
Although the knife and spoon had become essential to eating long before the 16th century, the fork, introduced at about that time in Italy, was slow to be accepted. All 3 came to be fairly common by the late 18th century. Although these implements are simple in function, each has provided a challenging design problem over the centuries; this unusual and graceful traveling set is an outstanding response to that challenge.

Hints for Collectors
These 3 modern utensils function exactly like their centuries-old prototypes. Yet their maker has fashioned a visually stimulating and aesthetically pleasing group while retaining their conventional serviceability. Collectors should seek out innovative designs, such as the set shown here, that are fresh solutions to age-old questions. In many cases, contemporary examples are made in very limited quantities, so that an eager collector may wish to contact a particular maker to commission an object.

29 Victorian dessert spoon and early Colonial spoons

Description
Spoons with shallow bowls. Left: Wavy fiddle handle with upturned tip; vestigial midrib on front; "AMD" in script. Center: Straight handle with leaves and scrolls; upturned 3-lobed tip; "C/IL" on underside of bowl. Right: Straight, tapered, squared handle; "P/MB" on tip.

Marks and Dimensions
Left: "S.C. JETT" in clipped-corner rectangle on handle back. Length: 7⅜". Center: "IB" in shield-shaped outline stamped on back of bowl. Length: 6½". Right: "IH", probably under rose, in hourglass outline in bowl; "RS", probably with sunburst above, in shield-shaped outline stamped on back of handle. Length: 6½".

Maker, Locality, and Date
Left: Steven C. Jett (dates unknown), St. Louis. 1848–60. Center: Jacob Boelen (c. 1654–1729), New York City. 1678–1729. Right: John Hull & Robert Sanderson (c. 1650–83), Boston. 1652–83.

Comment
The fiddle-pattern handle seen in the spoon at left was the most popular type of handle on American flatware produced between the War of 1812 and the Civil War. The spoon at center was often called a ceremonial spoon because of its cast ornamental handle; the style seems to have been peculiar to the New York area. The Hull and Sanderson spoon at right is among the earliest pieces of documented American silver.

Hints for Collectors
Early American silver spoons are common and usually inexpensive. Avoid examples with heavily worn bowls or broken handles, or that have had the initials of the original owner erased.

Victorian and modern souvenir spoons

Description
Left: Handle with eagle, portrait, and "WILLIAM H. SEWARD/ FATHER OF ALASKA"; below, another portrait, "THE ORIGINAL SEATTLE", totem pole, and gold mines. Parcel-gilt bowl with building and "MANUFACTURERS BLDG./A.Y.P./EXPO." Landscape and "ALASKA YUKON PACIFIC EXPOSITION" on back. Right: Handle in form of rifle marked "28th NATIONAL./1894/ENGAGEMENT./GAR" (Grand Army of the Republic). Gilt bowl shows bayonet, shield, castle, and "PITTSBURG".

Marks and Dimensions
Left: "STERLING" stamped incuse on back of handle; "PAT. NO./-38695-" with "M" and "B" flanking crossed pick and shovel, all in cast raised letters on back of bowl. Length: 5¾". Right: Stag's head, "RW&S" in gothic lettering, and "STERLING"; all stamped incuse on back of bowl. Length: 5⅞".

Maker, Locality, and Date
Left: Joseph Mayer & Brothers (1898–c.1945), Seattle. 1907. Right: Robert Wallace & Sons (1871–1956), Wallingford, Connecticut. 1894.

Comment
Commemorative spoons were most popular in the late 19th and early 20th centuries. The die cutting involved in elaborate examples, such as the spoon at left, is of the highest order.

Hints for Collectors
It is not difficult to collect an informative and diverse group of souvenir spoons. These spoons were commonly marked only with the name of the retailer; be willing to do some research to find out the maker of your acquisition.

Modern Art Nouveau berry spoon

Description
Handle with naturalistically modeled flowers, leaves, and raspberries on front and back. Large asymmetrical bowl with ribbing. "EAR" engraved in script on front of handle.

Marks and Dimensions
"TIFFANY & CO/MAKERS/STERLING/C" in raised letters on back of handle. Length: 9⅜".

Maker, Locality, and Date
Tiffany & Company (1853–present), New York City. c. 1905.

Comment
The stylish late 19th- and early 20th-century dining table was often elaborately set with a great quantity of silver flatware. Each part of the dining ritual had its own utensils; this berry spoon, appropriately decorated with raspberries, is an example of these specialized pieces. For the diner unschooled in the use of these objects, numerous books provided instruction in table etiquette.

Hints for Collectors
Variety was an important feature of turn-of-the-century silver flatware, and hundreds of patterns were designed and patented. Of these, many were illogical compositions of disparate motifs and are of limited interest to collectors. At the same time, many gifted designers directed their talents to table silver and produced practical objects of considerable aesthetic merit. Discriminating collectors should carefully study this vast array of designs not only to decide which they like, but also to learn to distinguish well-designed objects from their mediocre counterparts.

32 Victorian parcel-gilt nut spoon

Description
Cylindrical handle with seated squirrel eating a nut atop beaded disk at end; beaded collar near bowl. Deep, pointed gilt bowl with shaped shoulder and foliate piercing.

Marks and Dimensions
"BALL, BLACK & CO/NEW YORK/925" stamped incuse on back of handle. Length: 11⅛".

Maker, Locality, and Date
Ball, Black & Company (1851–76), New York City. 1851–76.

Comment
In earlier centuries, symbolism was very important in American architecture and the fine and decorative arts. Symbolic features ranged from the esoteric inclusion of periwinkles in a painting—to symbolize the pleasure of memory—to the more recognizable presence of Nike, representing Victory, on a national monument. This fondness for symbols even found pedestrian expression in everyday objects—like the use of a squirrel on this nut spoon. Although symbolism is still present in the American arts, it is neither as pervasive nor as well understood today as it was in previous generations.

Hints for Collectors
This nut spoon still retains its original fitted box (not shown). Many specialized table objects of the late 19th century were sold with such boxes, but most have lost their containers over the years. If a silver object is found with its original box, the latter should never be discarded, even if it is in poor condition. A vintage box enhances the interest and value of the silver it contains, especially if it is attractively decorated and bears the name of the manufacturer or retailer on the lid.

Victorian/modern oyster forks

Description
Left: Shallow, pointed, pierced bowl with stylized foliate ornament. 3-pronged fork at opposite end. Long cylindrical handle with oval pod having rope-and-foliate decoration. "D.E." engraved on underside of spoon bowl. Right: Shallow, oval, ribbed and pierced bowl. 3-pronged trident-shaped fork at opposite end. Flared tapered handle with central medallion enclosing man's head in helmet. "MCS" engraved in script on back of medallion.

Marks and Dimensions
Left: Lion; anchor; "G"; and "STERLING 78" all stamped incuse on back of handle. Length: 10¼". Right: Lion; anchor; "G"; and "PAT. 1864 STERLING" all stamped incuse on back of handle.

Maker, Locality, and Date
Both: Gorham Company (1831–present), Providence. 1870–1910 (left); 1864–1910 (right).

Comment
By the late 19th century, specialized equipment had evolved for eating oysters. Double-ended silver utensils such as these have a pierced bowl to strain the liquid and grit from the oyster, and a fork to spear it.

Hints for Collectors
Oyster forks from the 19th and 20th centuries are not rare and can be found singly or in sets. Collectors should seek out interesting examples by respected makers. These 2 forks are of greater interest than more standard examples, one because of the Roman medallion, the other because of the elliptical knop on the handle.

Early Colonial sucket fork

Description
Handle with flat, rectangular, slightly curved shaft; front and back engraved with foliate scrolled motifs. Fork end flared and with 3 tapered tines; spoon end has shallow oval bowl with low triangular ridge on back. Block initials "VR" conjoined over "S E" on back of bowl.

Marks and Dimensions
"I•K" in rectangle stamped on back of handle. Length: 5⅞".

Maker, Locality, and Date
Jessie Kip (1660–1722), New York City. 1682–1722.

Comment
This double-ended implement was designed to be used for eating plums or grapes preserved in heavy sweet syrup; the fork end speared the fruit, and the spoon held the syrup. Sucket forks were popular in England during the 16th and 17th centuries. There are approximately one dozen American examples known today; these date prior to the 1730s, by which time the popularity of these sweetened fruits had waned. All were made in Boston, New York City, or Philadelphia; most have 2 tined forks and were made singly or in pairs.

Hints for Collectors
Because sucket forks, with their peculiar double-ended design, are so rare, even the most curious collector might fail to recognize an example that comes to light. They are of great interest and value because of their age and because they provide insight into the eating habits of the period.

Early Colonial mote spoon

Description
Long, slender, round handle tapered to point; molded baluster near juncture with bowl. Small, shallow, oval bowl pierced with sunbursts and scrolls. "RT" scratched on back of bowl.

Mark and Dimensions
"IK" in rectangle on back of handle. Length: 6¹⁄₁₆".

Maker, Locality, and Date
Jesse Kip (1660–1722), New York City. 1700–10.

Comment
Mote, or strainer, spoons came into being with the rise in popularity of tea, which was first imported to Europe from the Orient in the early 17th century. The pierced bowl skimmed floating tea leaves from a cup of tea, and the needlelike handle removed clogged leaves from the strainer at the base of the teapot spout. All known American examples date from the 18th century.

Hints for Collectors
American mote spoons are very rare, although they do turn up on occasion. Because their small size and narrow surfaces made them difficult to mark, few bear a fully legible maker's mark. Be cautious in ascribing such imperfectly marked spoons to American silversmiths, since 17th- and 18th-century English silversmiths produced many more examples, and the English works are often similar to those made in America. As is true of most silver forms, American mote spoons are much more valuable than comparable English examples.

36 Colonial/Federal marrow scoop and Federal tea-caddy spoon

Description
Left: Short flat handle with 9 slightly concave sides, outlined with double narrow border. Fluted shell-shaped bowl. Right: Long slender utensil with shallow rounded scoop at one end and shorter broader scoop at other end; 2 ends separated by thin tapered segment with crest (unidentified) over "K".

Marks and Dimensions
Left: "J. Lownes" in script in conforming outline stamped on back of handle. Length: 3″. Right: "SS" in rectangle stamped on back. Length: 8¹⁵⁄₁₆″.

Maker, Locality, and Date
Left: Joseph Lownes (1758–1820), Philadelphia. 1785–1805.
Right: Unknown. England or America. 1750–1820.

Comment
Spoons were undoubtedly the most common form of American silver. While some examples are quite simple, others, like these, were highly specialized. The tea-caddy spoon was used to transfer tea leaves from a tea caddy to a teapot, and the marrow scoop was used to extract marrow from beef bones.

Hints for Collectors
A collector can assemble a large and fine group of American silver spoons with relative ease. Teaspoons are the most readily available; other forms, like the marrow scoop and tea-caddy spoon, are much harder to find and more expensive. The relative simplicity of these objects, when compared to hollowware, should not lull the collector into believing that spoons do not require study. They have been extensively faked, and the careful collector should pay close attention to detail.

Table and Bar Accessories

 During the past 3 centuries, silver and silver plate have been fashioned into an impressive variety of table articles. While the teaspoon has remained basically unchanged during its long history, the same cannot be said for most other forms.

Changing Fashions and Technologies

Many types of tablewares represent the popular fashions of their era and thus passed from use as quickly as they came into vogue. Grape shears are a good illustration. Used to remove a cluster of grapes from a bunch, these shears were very popular, judging by those that survive, during the late 19th century. Like the stiff white collar, they were part of a very formal life-style in which a large number of objects were developed for highly specialized activities. Along with this general way of life, grape shears have passed out of favor, and today's informality allows grapes to be merely plucked by hand.

Other objects represent the state of technology of their time. Table braziers, for instance, were used to cook food or simply keep it warm in the dining room. They were usually elaborately pierced, the holes serving both as decoration and as conduits for air that passed over the hot coals within. Although braziers were not regularly used in the kitchen, they were an outgrowth of an era, before the introduction of the enclosed cookstove in the mid-19th century, when cooking took place over an open fire.

Also popular once but now outmoded are the wine siphon and bottle label. The former, considered absolutely essential to the well-appointed wine cellar, was used to transfer wine from a bottle to a decanter without disturbing the sediment. However, most people today pour their wine directly from the bottle to the glass, so that the wine siphon has become unnecessary. Similarly, the metal label that was hung from the neck of a decanter to identify its contents has been replaced by paper labels attached to the bottle.

Other wine accoutrements, however, still remain in use. Since no stopper has ever been found to provide a better seal for wine bottles than the cork, the corkscrew has remained basically unchanged over the centuries, and continues to be a necessity for wine drinkers.

Updated Forms

Some silver and silver-plated objects have continued to be used over a long period of time, but only after being adapted for changing life-styles. In earlier centuries, for example, salt was very expensive and difficult to obtain, so containers for it were generally quite small and, befitting salt's valued place on the table, often made of elaborately decorated silver. Because salt is extremely corrosive, alternate materials, such as glass or even rock crystal, had to be used to line early salt containers. The easiest solution to this problem, however, was to use open containers that could be emptied easily after each use.

Casters were used for condiments other than salt—like dry mustard and pepper—since at least as early as the 18th century. Such objects, along with others like silver toast racks and elaborate condiment sets, tell us much about the lives of our predecessors, affording valuable insight into the appetites and customs of earlier times.

37 Federal spring-type sugar tongs and late Colonial/Federal sugar tongs

Description
Top: Flat tapered arms at right angle to bow; small convex oval tips; ornamented with stylized leaves, flowers, and narrow wriggle-work borders. "TEH" engraved in script on bow; "TR" in script on arms. Bottom: Scissors-type device with 2 irregular finger grips on short scrolled shafts attached to flat circular hinge and extending out on other side as 2 elaborately scrolled and molded arms ending in shell-shaped tips. "ATJ^{ur}" engraved in script against striated ground on hinge, with engraved flower on back.

Marks and Dimensions
Top: "I•OWEN" in rectangle stamped on each arm. Length: 6⅝".
Width: 2⅝". Bottom: "COB" in conforming outline, stamped on both finger grips. Length: 5". Width: 1¹¹⁄₁₆".

Maker, Locality, and Date
Top: John Owen (dates unknown), Philadelphia. 1804–10.
Bottom: Charles Oliver Bruff (1735–85), New York City. 1763–83.

Comment
The pair of sugar tongs on the bottom, typical of those made in the American Colonies during the mid-18th century, is one of the finest examples known. The elaborate and clearly delineated outline and surface ornament are well conceived and executed. The owner's engraved script initials, with their contrasting shaded ground, are exceptionally fine.

Hints for Collectors
The slender elements of scissors-type tongs are easily broken; in addition, they provide inadequate space for stamping a mark. So examine a potential purchase carefully, both for evidence of breakage and for any visible maker's mark.

38 Victorian grape shears

Description
Long loop-shaped handles with foliate diapered surface and pierced floral brackets in finger holes. Thick pointed blades; wide blade has steel edge.

Marks and Dimensions
"TIFFANY & C⁰/102 M 2306/STERLING" stamped incuse on one blade. Length: 6½". Width: 2¾".

Maker, Locality, and Date
Tiffany & Company (1853–present), New York City. 1869–91.

Comment
Grapes became an important decorative motif in the 19th century, ornamenting many forms in American silver—cake and fruit baskets, urns, and other objects, some of which had nothing to do with the fruit. Because grapes were also a popular food, 19th-century grape shears are frequently encountered. They were used at the table to remove a small cluster of grapes from a bunch.

Hints for Collectors
Silver grape shears are fairly easy to come by, but most are unmarked or have English marks. Acquiring a pair with an American mark is considerably more difficult. Look for the mark on the handle, which is most often the only part of these devices made of silver. In many instances, only the word "STERLING" will be found. Since English and Continental silversmiths of the late 19th century rarely used the word sterling, its presence on otherwise unmarked shears is a good indication that the object is of American origin.

Description
Cylindrical fluted shaft with morning glory and leaves at end.
Curved pointed pick at opposite end. Gilt overall.

Marks and Dimensions
Lion; anchor; "G"; and "STERLING"; all stamped incuse on top.
Length: 4⅝". Diameter: ⅞".

Maker, Locality, and Date
Gorham Company (1831–present), Providence. 1870–1920.

Comment
Walnuts, pecans, and other nuts are notoriously difficult to open
and equally frustrating to remove from the shells because of
their irregular interlocking shape. To make it easier and more
graceful to eat nuts, numerous mechanical devices have been
invented; some of these are simple, like nut picks, and others
complex.

Hints for Collectors
Silver nut picks from after the mid-19th century are quite
common, so collectors can exercise great discrimination in
selecting suitable examples to own. The nut picks shown here are
most desirable for several reasons. They are fully marked by a
well-known and respected maker. Their attractive design
incorporates a realistic morning glory at the top. Finally, these
picks are in good condition, and they are completely gilt, which is
fairly uncommon. Yet even with so many appealing features, the
set of one dozen from which these picks come would be fairly
modestly priced.

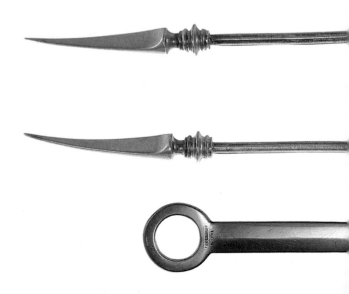

Description
Long flat blade with circular ring at wide end and straight sides tapering to point. Midrib on each side.

Marks and Dimensions
"J. CONNING" and "MOBILE"; each in rectangle, stamped on side. Length: 10 1/16″. Width: 1 1/8″.

Maker, Locality, and Date
James Conning (c. 1813–72), Mobile, Alabama. 1840–72.

Comment
In the 18th century, skewers made of iron or sometimes of wood were used to fasten meat to a spit or to help it retain its shape while roasting, and perhaps to ensure that the roast would cook evenly. Silver examples, too expensive to be used in such a mundane way, were substituted for the ordinary skewers before the food was brought to the table. Such luxuries were uncommon in early America and are thus infrequently encountered by collectors today.

Hints for Collectors
Because antique English silver skewers are quite common, collectors seeking American examples should examine potential acquisitions closely. Be sure that English marks have not been erased and, equally important, satisfy yourself that the American mark conforms in every detail to accepted strikes. This assurance is especially important for works by rarely encountered but widely respected makers; these objects command a premium.

Victorian and modern tea strainers

Description
Left: Tapered cylindrical wooden handle with tapered silver socket. Deep, pierced bell-shaped bowl; loop at rim opposite handle. Right: Tapered hourglass-shaped handle with leafy decoration on front and back. Pierced bowl in shape of poppy.

Marks and Dimensions
Left: "TIFFANY & CO 17997 MAKERS 21879 STERLING M"; stamped incuse on handle socket. Length: 9". Width: 2⅝". Right: "R" in shield flanked by eagle and lion; "STERLING/POPPY/PAT. SEP. 8, 1906"; all stamped incuse on exterior of bowl. "R" in shield flanked by eagle and lion; "STERLING"; all raised on back of handle. Length: 7". Width: 2¾".

Maker, Locality, and Date
Left: Tiffany & Company (1853–present), New York City. 1869–91. Right: Reed & Barton (1840–present), Taunton, Massachusetts. 1906–20.

Comment
There are numerous devices to separate tea leaves from tea. Strainers like the ones shown here were placed directly over the cup, and the tea was poured through them.

Hints for Collectors
Strainers of this general type were made as early as the 18th century, but most date from the 19th century. Heavy examples with inventive piercing are likely to have greater appeal.

42 Late Colonial punch strainer

Description
Deep circular bowl with flared sides extensively pierced with small holes forming stylized 6-pointed flower surrounded by "JABEZ BOWEN PROVIDENCE JANUARY 1765". 2 flat triangular handles at rim, pierced with symmetrical scrolled design.

Marks and Dimensions
"CLARK" in shaped rectangle, stamped on back of each handle. Length: 11⅞". Diameter: 4¹¹⁄₁₆".

Maker, Locality, and Date
Jonathan Clarke (1706–66), Newport or Providence, Rhode Island. c. 1765.

Comment
Strainers were a desirable amenity for punch drinkers. They were used to remove fruit pulp and, more importantly, strong spices like cloves and pieces of cinnamon that enhanced the flavor of punch but were not potable. Although most punch strainers had 2 handles, some had a single handle. The example shown here, with its original owner's name and the date punched into the bowl, is quite unusual, since most were punched with simple stylized foliate designs.

Hints for Collectors
The handles of strainers like the one shown here are easily broken off, and have frequently been reattached or even replaced. Sloppy soldering may be a sign that such damage has occurred. Also, carefully examine the bowl for exceptionally thin or smeared areas, which may indicate that English hallmarks have been erased and replaced with spurious American marks to increase the value.

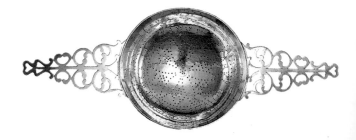

Victorian tea ball

Description
Sphere pierced with small holes and decorated with smiling man's face. Hinged lid. Chain attached to top of lid has loop at end.

Marks and Dimensions
Lion, anchor, and "G"; "STERLING/50"; and cross in square; all stamped incuse on rim of lid. Diameter: 1½". Length: 6".

Maker, Locality, and Date
Gorham Company (1831–present), Providence. 1886.

Comment
Elaborate Victorian social etiquette led to increasingly specialized forms of small silver table objects. Changes in the genteel ceremony of taking tea, for instance, generated a proliferation of new devices with the specific function of keeping unattractive and unpalatable tea leaves from being consumed with this popular beverage. Traditional forms such as strainers and mote spoons continued to serve this purpose for tea poured from a pot. Tea balls and spoons with hinged pierced lids were filled with tea leaves and immersed in a pot or cup to make tea, the perforations allowing hot water to pass through, but not the leaves.

Hints for Collectors
Collectors specializing in silver tea paraphernalia should be on the lookout for tea balls. Made in great variety, these small objects are usually modestly priced. The most desirable are as imaginatively ornamented as this sphere, which cleverly incorporates a human face in its design. Select examples that are in good condition and avoid those with dents, broken hinges, or sloppy solder repairs.

Federal bottle label

Description
Convex oval disk with engraved wriggle-work border
surrounding "LEMON". Chain attached to 2 loops at upper edge.

Marks and Dimensions
"N.VERNON & C?" in rectangle, stamped on back. Length: 1½".
Height: ⅞". Chain length: 5".

Maker, Locality, and Date
Nathaniel Vernon & Company (1802–08), Charleston, South
Carolina. 1802–08.

Comment
Before the advent of printed paper labels, liquor and wine bottles
often had a small silver plaque hung around the neck to identify
the contents. Labels used in America were generally made in
England of silver or silver plate. A few early American silver
examples are known, including this one marked "lemon,"
meaning the aromatic lemon bitters used as an aperitif or to
flavor a drink. Vernon was one of many Charleston silversmiths
who supplied his sophisticated clientele with objects he produced
as well as imported English wares.

Hints for Collectors
Southern silver is rare and therefore quite desirable among
collectors. Of the major southern silversmithing centers,
Charleston was perhaps the most important during the 18th
century. The silver made there was usually of fine quality and,
because of the city's strong trade ties with England, had a close
affinity to the best objects from London.

Victorian silver-over-ivory corkscrews

Description
Curved tapered animal tusk with silver cover pierced with interlocking foliate scrolls and leaves; engraved lines and foliage. Fitted with plated iron corkscrew on long molded shaft.

Marks and Dimensions
"BLACK, STARR & FROST STERLING" stamped incuse around base of corkscrew. Length: 8½". Height: 6½".

Maker, Locality, and Date
Unknown. Retailed by Black, Starr & Frost (dates unknown), New York City. 1876–1929.

Comment
Corkscrews have been designed in a great array of patterns, but all work on the same principle. The unusual design, large size, and exotic ivory of the examples shown here make them quite flamboyant, meant for uncorking a bottle in front of guests, rather than in the butler's pantry or kitchen. Silver is much too soft to withstand the torsion involved in removing a cork, so iron was used for the working portion of the corkscrew, which was then close-plated with silver for cosmetic purposes and to prevent rust.

Hints for Collectors
Examine silver-overlay objects to ensure that the silver, which is usually fairly thin, is not broken or missing in places; it is often difficult to spot losses on such pierced designs. Also check that the ivory is not chipped, cracked, or discolored. The loss of the close-plated silver on the screw portion is inevitable, but any remnants should be preserved.

Late Federal wine siphon

Description
U-shaped hollow tube with long flared arms. Curved segment faceted and flanked by narrow moldings. Shorter arm with several small holes near tip. Longer arm fitted with tubular pump having ivory-handled plunger; petcock valve at end of tube with tabular scalloped thumbscrew.

Marks and Dimensions
"F.M." in rectangle, stamped on petcock thumbscrew. Length: 21¾". Width: 5½".

Maker, Locality, and Date
Frederick Marquand (1799–1882), New York City. 1826–39.

Comment
Siphons like this were used to transfer wine from dark, squat, undecorated bottles to clear, stylish decanters for table use. By using a siphon instead of pouring directly from one bottle to another, spillage and the transference of sediment were made less likely. While most siphons have a simple mouth-operated suction tube attached to the longer arm to start the liquid flowing, this unusual example has a sophisticated suction pump. Marquand spent most of his productive life in New York City, but worked briefly in Savannah, which had a close mercantile relationship with New York via intercoastal trade during the early 19th century.

Hints for Collectors
Siphons are quite rare today because they were created for wine connoisseurs, who constituted a small segment of the population. Owing to their limited appeal, they have often been melted down into more useful or fashionable objects. Although siphons are no longer necessary for the enjoyment of wine, they are likely to appeal to aficionados of both silver and wine.

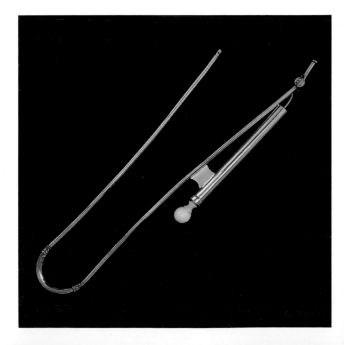

Late Colonial cream pail

Description
Small tapered circular vessel with 5 clusters of horizontal reeding encircling body. Hinged twisted loop handle joined to 2 molded loops at rim. "I:Tudor" engraved on underside.

Marks and Dimensions
"T:DANE" in rounded-end rectangle, stamped on underside. Height: 2⅞". Diameter: 2".

Maker, Locality, and Date
Thomas Dane (1726–c.1795), Boston. 1750–75.

Comment
Small pails of this type with either a hinged or fixed loop handle were used for clotted cream, a thick cooked concentrate of cream used as a topping for berries. Judging from the small size of these pails, clotted cream must have been used sparingly, perhaps because it was so rich. Only a few such pails are known today, all of which originated in the Boston area. The engraving on the underside of this pail—"I" commonly used to represent "J"—probably refers to John Tudor (1709–95), his son John (b. 1732), or his daughter Jane (1736–91).

Hints for Collectors
Because of their small size, cream pails can easily be mistaken for miniatures or toys, but they were actually full-size household objects. Most hollowware of this date was fabricated of a single piece of seamless silver. This type of cream pot is an exception, the sides being formed of one piece of vertically seamed silver, and the bottom made as a separate inset.

Victorian bottle coaster

Description
Circular bowl-like vessel. Flared lip with flower-and-leaf pattern.
Bellied circular side with ribbing. Inside bottom ornamented
with spiral swirl design. Base has narrow foliate molding. Foliate
script initials "CCS" engraved on side.

Marks and Dimensions
"TIFFANY & C⁰/5723 M 2792/STERLING-SILVER" stamped incuse on
underside. Diameter: 6½". Height: 2⅛".

Maker, Locality, and Date
Tiffany & Company (1853–present), New York City. 1869–91.

Comment
Bottle coasters, which apparently developed during the 18th
century, were used to hold liquor and wine bottles at the table.
Most were made of silver plate with wooden bottoms, or of
decoratively painted papier-mâché; both types seem to have been
made commonly in England. Very wealthy persons, however,
commissioned local silversmiths to fashion coasters of silver,
although at present few American silver examples are known.
Bottle coasters may have pierced or solid sides.

Hints for Collectors
Bottle coasters usually were made in pairs and are more
desirable as such, rather than individually. It is often difficult to
determine a price for antique American silver examples; since
the form so rarely appears in the marketplace, there is little
basis for comparison. However, one can be certain that a pair of
antique American silver bottle coasters offered at a public sale
would be expensive. For this reason, the collector should
thoroughly research the objects before buying.

Modern coasters

Description
Flat circular form with low flared rim and silver coin set into center. Left: 1874 Bolivian Boliviano coin; "Jessie Xmas 1941" engraved on back. Right: 1881 United States dollar; "Jessie Xmas 1946" engraved on back.

Marks and Dimensions
"STERLING" stamped incuse on underside. Diameter: 4¼". Height: ¼".

Maker, Locality, and Date
Unknown. United States. Left: c. 1941. Right: c. 1946.

Comment
Silver has traditionally been used for currency as well as for a wide variety of objects, from large and imposing forms to small, personal articles. Its universal appeal has also caused it to be made into unusual, idiosyncratic objects. Built around silver coins, these small coasters for drinking glasses were Christmas gifts, as their inscriptions attest.

Hints for Collectors
Collectors of American silver readily respond to typical and easily recognized forms like tankards and candlesticks. However, unusual objects can provide depth, variety, and richness to a traditional collection. Collectors should seek out the unusual as well as the typical; by acquiring both they will gain a better understanding and appreciation of the medium and the culture that used it. Common 20th-century silver objects such as these coasters are widely available at antiques shops as well as local auctions and flea markets; they can usually be purchased for moderate or modest prices.

Description
Rectangular plate with slightly convex sides and narrow molded edge. Rim decorated with hammered facets. Circular well with "Viola./1884." engraved in script.

Marks and Dimensions
"WM. WILSON & SON/STERLING/5" stamped incuse on back.
Width: 2¹⁵/₁₆".

Maker, Locality, and Date
William Wilson & Son (c. 1858–84), Philadelphia. c. 1884.

Comment
During the mid- to late 19th century, it was the fashion to serve each course of a meal on its own plate, and to include at each table setting a separate plate for bread and another for butter. This elaborate custom persisted into the 20th century, eventually giving way to more casual dining habits after the Second World War. Silver plates are not very common. The textured rim of the plate shown here follows the tenets of the Arts and Crafts movement, which held that objects should reflect the manner in which they were made, rather than be so highly finished that all evidence of workmanship is lost.

Hints for Collectors
Many people think that all silver objects are very expensive. However, interesting and enjoyable silver can often be acquired by the discriminating collector for relatively modest sums. This butter plate is a good example: Its small size, late 19th-century date, and little-known maker would probably make it fairly inexpensive. It is of special interest because it provides an insight into late 19th-century table etiquette.

51 Victorian knife rest

Description
Slender tubular rod, supported at each end by a magnolia-like seedpod and leaf cluster with flat back.

Marks and Dimensions
"STERLING"; "766"; and a fasces; all stamped incuse on underside of rod. Length: 3⅞". Height: 1⅜". Width: 1½".

Maker, Locality, and Date
William B. Kerr & Company (1855–1906), Newark, New Jersey. 1855–1906.

Comment
Small amenities for the table proliferated during the late 19th century. A knife rest, on which the carving knife was placed so it would not stain the tablecloth, was considered necessary for the well-appointed table. Most surviving examples are silver plated or ceramic. Silver examples are uncommon, although they were made by both large factories and smaller shops. They vary greatly in ornateness: Some have simple X-shaped ends, while others have elaborately sculpted animal supports.

Hints for Collectors
Because of their small size and generally outmoded purpose, knife rests might be easily overlooked by silver collectors other than those who specifically seek Victorian table objects and often use them as they were originally intended. Most informed collectors seek out marked examples that incorporate large quantities of well-defined ornament, such as birds, humans, or quadrupeds, into a pleasingly designed composition.

Description
Rectangular V-shaped trough supported at each end on 2 slender curved legs that cross and conjoin to form a loop above; seedpod hangs from top of each loop.

Marks and Dimensions
"DEMATTEO/STERLING/9" stamped incuse and "HANDMADE" in rectangle, all on one side. Length: 6⅛". Height: 1¾". Width: 1¾".

Maker, Locality, and Date
William G. Dematteo (1895–1981), Bergenfield, New Jersey. 1935–70.

Comment
After the Second World War, stainless steel, aluminum, and plastic usurped the place of silver as materials for most types of table objects, so that many of these small modern silver items are uncommon and thus appealing today. Since some of these pieces were highly specialized and are no longer used at the table, it is occasionally difficult to identify their original functions. Such is the case with this small trough-shaped object, which might have been a holder for sugar cubes—themselves a rarity today—or possibly a knife rest.

Hints for Collectors
Although the original purpose of this object is uncertain, it is an interesting, well-designed piece incorporating attractive plantlike motifs that relate to the kind of work done by the well-known Danish silversmith, Georg Jensen. Its maker, William Dematteo, was an accomplished silversmith whose work, like that of other talented 20th-century craftsmen, should be sought by collectors, since it cannot but appreciate in value.

Description
Slender baluster-shaped handle with small spherical finial.
Circular inverted cup with flared lip; upper half ornamented with
leaves, scrolls, and flowers. Long teardrop-shaped clapper.

Marks and Dimensions
"HOWARD & CO STERLING"; spread eagle; and "221D"; stamped
incuse into rim. Height: 3⅞". Diameter: 2¼".

Maker, Locality, and Date
Hiram Howard & Company (1878–1901), Providence. 1878–79.

Comment
Small, hand-held bells were used at dinner and tea tables to
summon servants. These bells—silver for the wealthy, silver
plate for the less affluent—were made as early as the 18th
century, but were most popular in the late 19th century during
the heyday of self-conscious gentility. While most of these bells
were held in the hand, some took a more fanciful form, such as
those affixed to a marble stand and supported by an elaborate
frame; such examples were rung by tapping a plunger with the
forefinger.

Hints for Collectors
Small objects like this bell usually have few places where a mark
can be discreetly stamped. In addition, the marks are frequently
small, making it easy to overlook them. Collectors should use a
magnifying glass to thoroughly examine such pieces, including
the edges, the underside of the rim, and any recesses, for
evidence of identifying marks.

Description
Baluster-shaped device with cylindrical socket at one end and mushroom-shaped handle at the other; tabular thumbscrew attached to side near socket end. "LS" engraved in script on end of handle.

Marks and Dimensions
"H. E. BALDWIN & CO." in arc; "NEW.ORLEANS" in rectangle; both stamped on thumbscrew. Height: 6¹³⁄₁₆″. Width: 1⅞″.

Maker, Locality, and Date
Attributed to Horace E. Baldwin & Company (1842–53), New Orleans. 1842–53.

Comment
This unusual object, unlike most Victorian silver, is not ornately decorated. Nonetheless, it illustrates clearly the niceties of the Victorian dining table. By attaching this handle to the bone of a ham or beef roast, a fastidious host could carve without soiling his hands. Although this object is marked "NEW ORLEANS," it was most likely made in Newark and retailed in the South, like many other 19th-century objects of northern manufacture. English silver and silver-plated bone holders were much more common than American ones and were imported here during the late 19th century. Horace Baldwin, whose New Orleans sales office retailed this object, was a partner in the Newark, New Jersey, silversmithing firm of Baldwin & Company. New Orleans proved to be a lucrative market for this company's products, as evidenced by the establishment of the sales office in the 1840s.

Hints for Collectors
Silver objects such as this generally hold more interest than value for collectors. Nonetheless, it is always a good idea to purchase objects in good condition and by well-known makers.

55 Victorian electroplated napkin ring with vase

Description
Oval ring with 2 narrow borders of flowers. Tall thistle-shaped vase of purple glass with white and gilt flowers, held in narrow upright socket. Low horizontally scrolled frame ornamented with flowers and leaves. 4 spherical feet.

Marks and Dimensions
"MERIDEN B * COMPANY" in circle enclosing shield containing scales, all stamped incuse in circular disk applied to underside. Height: 5½". Length: 4". Width: 1¾".

Maker, Locality, and Date
Meriden Britannia Company (1852–98), Meriden, Connecticut. c. 1882.

Comment
Many late 19th-century Americans depended on the growing industrial complex, working in the factories and aspiring to own their products. Nonetheless, these people often mourned the loss of innocence that was perceived to be a result of the decline of agrarian society. As a result, many factory products were heavily laden with naturalistic ornament, lending a sense of ever-present nature to machine-made amenities.

Hints for Collectors
This combination napkin ring and flower vase is a fairly unusual variant of the everyday napkin ring. Most such objects have lost their original glass attachments. While any marked example that is handsomely designed and well made is desirable, those lacking original parts are worth far less than complete examples.

Victorian electroplated napkin ring

Description
Cylindrical ring divided into 3 segments; outer 2 ornamented
with borders of stylized leaves and flowers; plain central segment
with "EVW" engraved in script.

Marks and Dimensions
Anchor above "0200/N" stamped incuse on inside. Diameter: 1¾".
Height: 1¾".

Maker, Locality, and Date
Gorham Company (1831–present), Providence. 1880–1900.

Comment
The napkin ring was at one time a standard accessory at the
well-appointed dining table, used for both special occasions and
everyday meals. A ring usually had the name or initials of a
household member engraved on it, so that the napkin in it could
be reserved for that particular diner and reused from meal to
meal. Many napkin rings were simple cylinders, but the form
was elaborated on significantly, incorporating sculpted figures
and intricate decoration into the design.

Hints for Collectors
Late 19th- and early 20th-century napkin holders exist in great
quantity. Silver-plated examples are moderately priced, and an
interesting and varied collection can be assembled with relative
ease. Collectors should seek out marked examples and those that
have spirited ornament or fanciful features, because these are of
greater interest and will appreciate in value much more quickly
than unmarked and relatively plain napkin rings.

57 Colonial salt container

Description
Circular form with small shallow depression in top surrounded by molded edge. Curved flared side with gadrooned border at top and bottom and borders of punched dots and designs. "TE" conjoined with "H M" engraved in block letters on side.

Marks and Dimensions
"ITE", the T and E conjoined, in oval; stamped in shallow top depression. Height: 2½". Diameter: 3⅜".

Maker, Locality, and Date
Jacob Ten Eyck (1705–93), Albany, New York. 1730–50.

Comment
Salt, which was an expensive commodity before the 18th century, was used ceremoniously at the table and dispensed from elaborate containers. Large examples were for communal use, while small salts like the one shown here were more frequently for individuals. The shallow depression of this example held the salt, which was scattered with the fingers. By the late 18th century small spoons had been developed to accompany saltcellars. This Colonial example was owned by its maker's uncle and aunt, Hendrick and Margarita Ten Eyck of Albany, New York.

Hints for Collectors
Since salt blackens and pits silver badly, signs of corrosion are to be expected on an antique salt container. If these signs are absent, the object should be closely examined to determine if the area meant to contain the salt has been restored.

Early Victorian salt dish

Description
Circular bowl with narrow rim, Greek-key border, and 3
flattened loop handles. Tapered sides with wide border of engine
turning and 3 plain circular reserves. Narrow circular foot
supported by 3 sphinxes on rectangular plinths.

Marks and Dimensions
"410"; lion; anchor; "G"; and "COIN"; all stamped incuse on bottom
of bowl. Height: 2³⁄₁₆″. Diameter: 3⁵⁄₈″.

Maker, Locality, and Date
Gorham Company (1831–present), Providence. 1848–68.

Comment
Open dishes were the most common type of container for salt
until the popularization of the salt shaker in about the middle of
the 19th century. The diminutive salt dish pictured here, one of a
pair, is highly unusual because of the sphinx supports. Such
Egyptian motifs experienced a limited revival in architecture and
the decorative arts (in the so-called Empire style) after
Napoleon's military campaign in Egypt in 1798. However, the
Egyptian style seems never to have achieved widespread
acceptance in the United States because of the popular
association of ancient Egypt with death rites and mortuary art.

Hints for Collectors
Salt dishes are readily obtainable and easily displayed. The most
desirable ones are unusual interpretations of the form, as
exemplified by the design shown here. The strong iconographic
elements, innovative design features such as the hinged loop
handles, and good workmanship would make this salt dish a
notable addition to any collection.

59 Victorian salt or pepper shakers

Description
Domed, pierced, circular lids with urn-shaped finials. Left:
Bulbous body having tall tapered neck with gadrooned collar. 3
legs with paw feet and lion heads. "R" engraved on body. Right:
Urn-shaped body with tall tapered neck. Flared circular
pedestal. Body decorated with engine turning and foliate
cartouche enclosing "PQS" in script.

Marks and Dimensions
Left: "GORHAM/STERLING/37"; lion; and "G"; each in clipped-corner
rectangle; and anchor in shield; all stamped incuse on underside.
Height: 4¾". Diameter: 2⅝". Right: "TIFFANY & C⁰/STERLING/386 M
7998" with the M in a circle, stamped incuse on underside. Height:
5⅞". Diameter: 2".

Maker, Locality, and Date
Left: Gorham Company (1831–present), Providence. 1870–1900.
Right: Tiffany & Company (1853–present), New York City.
1869–91.

Comment
Prior to the invention of refrigeration, condiments and spices
served not only to flavor food but also to help mask the tainted
taste of perishables on the verge of spoiling. Although most early
containers for salt were small open bowls, the contents of which
were pinched or spooned out, the caster, or shaker, evolved as
the most satisfactory way to disperse seasonings evenly.

Hints for Collectors
Small silver objects for table use were made in large numbers
during the 19th century, and are thus commonly available and
inexpensive. Though less often sought by advanced collectors,
well-designed examples are recommended to beginners or
collectors of modest means.

Early Colonial mustard pot

Description
Upright egg-shaped vessel with lid having small knopped finial
encircled by ornamental leaf tips, and a cutout in edge for spoon.
Small thumbpiece hinged to simple S-shaped handle. Stepped
molded pedestal with borders of rope molding at neck and leaves
and gadrooning at base.

Marks and Dimensions
"V" over "PD" in trefoil stamped below lip of body near handle.
Height: 5⅛". Diameter (base): 3⅜".

Maker, Locality, and Date
Peter Van Dyck (1684–1751), New York City. 1705–15.

Comment
Most condiment containers of this period are either open, like
saltcellars, or have pierced lids for sprinkling the contents onto
food. This diminutive vessel, meant to be used with a spoon, is a
rare exception. At present this pot is the only American example
known, although there are closely related Dutch mustard pots of
the same date. This similarity is not surprising in light of the
large number of Dutch settlers in New York.

Hints for Collectors
This small mustard pot had a spout added to it at one time,
converting it to a pouring vessel, but the spout has subsequently
been removed. Normally such alterations adversely affect the
price and desirability of an object. However, the rarity and
unusual character of this mustard pot are such that it remains
exceptionally appealing in spite of having been altered.

Late Colonial pepperbox

Description
Octagonal domed lid with variously shaped holes and small
knopped finial; fitted over body. Straight-sided, tapered,
octagonal body, flared slightly at base, with molded foot rim.
Simple molded border at top and bottom of body. Simple,
straplike, S-shaped handle. "IL" engraved on underside and "1744/
1764/1877/1909" on side.

Marks and Dimensions
"CW" with pellet above each letter, all in conforming outline.
Height: 3¾". Diameter: 2¼".

Maker, Locality, and Date
Attributed to Charles Whiting (1725–65), Norwich, Connecticut.
1750–65.

Comment
Octagonal, or "8-square," American silver objects from the early
18th century are rare. Of the few early objects made in this
design, pepperboxes are the most common. The body of such a
box was formed of wrought sheet metal, the vertical seam of
which was usually concealed under the handle. Most pepperboxes
have a lid pierced with simple circular holes; this example,
having variously shaped piercing, is better than average.

Hints for Collectors
The most vulnerable parts of these small containers are the
handles and finials, which were always found on the original
boxes, but have sometimes been lost. An original handle and
finial should closely match the body and lid in color and amount of
wear; they should be neatly soldered to the pot. At the place
where it joins the body, an original lid will show signs of wear
appropriate to the box's age and use. The loss of a handle, finial,
lid, or other element detracts from an object's value.

Description
High domed cover with complex multiknopped finial surrounded by border of chased floral swags and numerous holes of different shapes; molded and gadrooned rim with 2 flat irregular tabs. Cylindrical body with narrow fillet around midsection; widely flared and gadrooned molded foot.

Marks and Dimensions
"BLR" in oval, the L and R conjoined, stamped twice on underside. Height: 8". Diameter: 3¾".

Maker, Locality, and Date
Bartholomew le Roux (c. 1663–1713), New York City. 1690–1700.

Comment
The caster, so called because it was used to cast spices over food, was for many years the preferred receptacle for all sorts of seasonings. Only a few casters were as large as this example, and all but one of them were made in New York. Large casters required a secure juncture for the cap, provided here by 2 small tabs that fit over projecting ribs around the vessel's lip.

Hints for Collectors
Early casters of monumental size were usually made singly and are almost impossible to find; later examples, however, are more readily available. By the mid-18th century, casters came to be made in sets, sometimes with as many as 7 vessels, which were often fitted into a frame. The body of a caster was usually made, at least in part, of seamed hammered sheet silver. In some examples, the lower portion of the body was wrought, with a seamed sheet-metal neck added. Although collectors of early silver generally avoid vertically seamed vessels from before about 1780, casters are an exception.

Victorian electroplated pickle caster

Description
Slender upright handle with pierced stylized flower ornament at top and wings pierced with flowers at base. Side of handle with small curved hook from which hang U-shaped tongs, with oval ornaments and hand-shaped tips. Curved circular base decorated with flowers and butterflies. Yellow cylindrical cut-glass bottle; removable electroplated lid with bird finial and border of flowers and butterflies.

Marks and Dimensions
"DERBY SILVER CO. QUADRUPLE PLATE" in circle enclosing anchor over crown, all stamped incuse on underside; "115" stamped incuse on underside of lid. Height: 11¼". Diameter (base): 4".

Maker, Locality, and Date
Derby Silver Company (1873–98), Derby, Connecticut. c. 1883.

Comment
Specially designed to contain and dispense pickles, pickle casters were derived from the caster sets used on American tables since the 18th century. By the 1800s, when the form reached the zenith of its popularity, examples were produced incorporating a wealth of fanciful decoration, such as the hand-shaped tongs accompanying this caster.

Hints for Collectors
Pickle casters are in great demand among those interested in late 19th-century Americana. Most examples are electroplated and have glass containers. Examine any potential purchase for appropriate signs of wear, maker's marks, and quality of design and fabrication in order to make certain your example is not one of many 20th-century reproductions. These are often lacking in detail, having coarse, poorly designed decoration and sloppy finishing.

Victorian liquor frame

Description
Low 4-lobed pedestal with 2 uprights in the form of grotesque animal heads. Vertical loop handle has oval medallion on each side containing relief profile of man. 2 guilloche-decorated rings hold cut-glass decanters with stopper. Base with guilloche border; engraved "George Peabody to Cyrus W. Field" on one side and "New York. 24th Nov. 1866." on other; crest (of Field family) engraved at center of base.

Marks and Dimensions
"S & M" and "60" stamped incuse; 3 pseudohallmarks (lion; anchor; and Gothic "G", each in cut-corner rectangle), all on underside. Height: 13½". Length: 10". Width: 6¾".

Maker, Locality, and Date
Gorham Company (1831–present), Providence. c. 1866. Retailed by Starr & Marcus, New York City.

Comment
This elaborate liquor frame was presented to Cyrus W. Field (1819–92), who successfully masterminded the laying of the first transatlantic telegraph cable in 1866. Its selection to commemorate so significant an event suggests the importance of both silver and liquor to Americans of the late 19th century.

Hints for Collectors
Applied portrait medallions experienced a brief vogue during the late 19th century. Most show profiles of anonymous men or women in ancient Roman garb. This bottle frame, depicting George Peabody and Cyrus Field, is an exception and thus of unusual interest to collectors. It is likely to cost substantially more than a typical example.

Description
Boat-shaped basket at top with borders of stylized leaves and
narrow parallel holes and beaded edge; fitted with glass bowl.
Open wirework shaft with 4 S-shaped arms, each fitted with
shallow circular basket. Long boat-shaped tray below with
beaded edge, pierced parallel holes, and loop handles at each
end. 4 flat semicircular feet. Tray contains wire framework fitted
with 8 cut-glass condiment bottles having silver tops and
handles. Circular, flared, and molded pedestal. Sides of top
basket engraved with crest (of Thomas and Johnson families of
Maryland).

Marks and Dimensions
Unmarked. Height: 17″. Length: 16³⁄₁₆″. Width: 10″.

Maker, Locality, and Date
Unknown. England. 1780–90.

Comment
Epergnes were large ornamental centerpieces, often laden with
fruits and sweets or, on occasion, condiment bottles. The most
expensive epergnes were made of silver, and were very
fashionable on the tables of the well-to-do in 18th-century
England. Fashion-conscious Americans followed suit, but
documented examples made or owned by Americans are rare.

Hints for Collectors
Objects composed of many parts, like this epergne, often lose
elements over the course of time, particularly when those
elements are removable or made of glass. This epergne, for
example, is missing a ninth bottle and the glass liners for the 4
small pierced baskets.

Late Federal bottle frame

Description
Spread-eagle finial atop cannon barrel and American shield. Knopped shaft with foliate borders. Rotating frame of 7 circular rings of varying diameters, each fitted with cut-glass bottle, 2 with silver cap. 3 flared foliate legs standing on slightly domed circular base with gadrooned edge. 3 winged human feet in sandals.

Marks and Dimensions
"GALE & MOSELEY" in rectangle; male bust in oval; and spread eagle in circle; all stamped on underside of frame. "W•W&T•B" in rectangle; lion in shield; male bust in oval; and "d" under crown within shield; all stamped on cap of front bottle. Height: 11⅜". Diameter: 8".

Maker, Locality, and Date
Frame: William Gale & Joseph Moseley (1828–33), New York City. 1828–33. Bottle caps: William Watson & Thomas Bradbury (dates unknown), Sheffield, England. 1828.

Comment
Casters used for salt and spices were made in America as early as the late 17th century. However, American silver frames for these bottles were uncommon before the 1850s, when table manners began to be sufficiently codified to encourage a proliferation of specialized utensils. This is one of relatively few earlier examples known.

Hints for Collectors
Most 18th- and early 19th-century frames were originally fitted with 2 to 10 English cut-glass bottles. Many subsequently lost their bottles, and some have been refitted with inappropriate late 19th-century bottles with acid-etched decoration.

67 English George III fused-plated cruet frame

Description
Low rectangular platform with gadrooned edge, feather-decorated corners, and 4 spherical feet. 4 loop-shaped wire supports on 2 sides, topped with leaf ornaments fitted to framework of 5 horizontal circles. Erect loop handle in center. 5 cut-glass bottles, 3 with silver-plated cap and 2 with glass stopper. "John & Sarah Ruckman/March 31st 1802" engraved in script on top of platform.

Marks and Dimensions
Unmarked. Height: 6¾". Length: 6¼". Width: 5".

Maker, Locality, and Date
Unknown. England. c. 1802.

Comment
Since Americans were unable to produce fused-plated objects commercially in the 18th and early 19th centuries, they imported English fused-plated wares in considerable quantity. Although modest, this small cruet frame shows the type of English wares bought by Americans at the time. The bottles, also English, are original to the frame.

Hints for Collectors
Because of its modest size and lack of elaborate ornament, this cruet frame would not command a high price. Highly ornamented examples that include naturalistic motifs are more in demand and are priced accordingly. To avoid overpaying for an acquisition, collectors must learn the relative desirability of different objects and of related pieces within a given category. Certain forms are much more widely collected than others; for instance, candlesticks are in greater demand than cruet frames.

Description

Frame of 2 parallel triangular elements, each pierced and scroll-decorated; connected at top by knotted-rope loop handle and joined at base by 2 similar parallel bars. Wheel at center supports 3 pairs of free-swinging, pierced wire baskets that rotate vertically around axis. Each basket fitted with glass bottle; 3 bottles have silver-plated caps.

Marks and Dimensions

Unmarked. Height: 15″. Length: 7¾″. Width: 7¼″.

Maker, Locality, and Date

Attributed to Meriden Britannia Company (1852–98), Meriden, Connecticut. c. 1861.

Comment

This cruet frame is one of the most fanciful pieces of dining-table equipment made during the late 19th century. Whereas most cruet frames had few or no moving parts, this example has a revolving framework with freely swinging baskets for each bottle. Although unmarked, it is identical to one pictured in a catalogue published by the Meriden Britannia Company and is therefore attributable to that firm.

Hints for Collectors

Victorian Americans valued elaborate ceremony and ornate objects. Collectors seeking the finest works made during the second half of the 19th century should thus bear in mind that the objects that best capture the spirit of this era incorporate quixotic features that appealed to the Victorians' sense of play and their desire to be surrounded by a rich panoply of ornament. This revolving cruet frame cleverly evokes those values and, as such, is a very desirable piece of Victoriana.

Description
Rectangular tubular frame with 5 vertical boxlike ribs. 2 small rings at one end hold removable, mushroom-shaped salt-and-pepper shakers. Loop-shaped handle at other end supports urn-shaped egg cup with gilt interior and circular flared pedestal. 4 legs, 2 with ball feet. Shakers and egg cup engraved with script initials "C A B".

Marks and Dimensions
"WHW" all conjoined; "STERLING BLACK, STARR & FROST"; all stamped incuse on bottom of rack. Length: 7¼". Height: 4¾". Width: 2¼".

Maker, Locality, and Date
Unknown. Probably United States. Retailed by Black, Starr & Frost (1876–1929), New York City. 1876–1929.

Comment
The combined egg cup and toast rack was popular at English breakfast tables, particularly during the 19th century, and was found far less frequently at American tables. Victorians ate a substantial breakfast, consuming eggs in prodigious quantity. This cup might have been used to hold as many as half a dozen eggs, each fitting inside the empty shell of the previous one.

Hints for Collectors
Toast racks and egg cups may have fallen into disuse even among fastidious breakfasters, but collectors are often eager to acquire them, especially the rare American examples. A marked toast rack offered as American should be carefully authenticated before being purchased; compare any marks on such objects with accepted examples.

Description
Oval serpentine frame with foliate design on upper surface. 7 graduated, radiating vertical arches, center with loop handle. 4 ball feet.

Marks and Dimensions
"AEW" in script in clipped-corner rectangle; 3 hallmarks (Maryland shield; "D"; and male profile, each in clipped-corner square), all stamped on underside. Length: 8½". Height: 7½". Width: 4¼".

Maker, Locality, and Date
Andrew E. Warner, Sr. (1786–1870), Baltimore. 1818.

Comment
Before modern times, bread was toasted in iron racks held close to a fire, and was transferred to the table on a plate. But in more genteel or well-to-do households, a silver toast rack such as this was used. The toast rack seems not to have become a part of dining-room equipage until the 19th century. Most antique examples are English; only a few, including this example, are documented as American.

Hints for Collectors
Be careful when considering the purchase of a supposedly American silver toast rack, since common and inexpensive English objects are often altered and passed off to unwary purchasers as more valuable American articles. Be wary of pieces with smudged areas, which may indicate that an English maker's mark was removed with intent to deceive. In addition, American makers' marks have been extensively faked on these objects. Such deception is particularly tricky to detect on toast racks because their small, narrow surfaces do not register a complete mark.

71 Early Victorian egg coddler

Description
Straight-sided octagonal box with 2 hinged lids and 2 loop handles; sides and lids with chased foliate decoration. Conforming base has 4 S-shaped foliate legs with shell feet that support frame for removable spirit lamp with single wick. Removable wire frame with foliate loop handle and rings to hold 12 eggs. "HLP" engraved in script on side of box.

Marks and Dimensions
"BALL, TOMPKINS & BLACK" in arc, "SUCCESSORS TO" in rectangle, "MARQUAND & CO." in arc, "NEW-YORK" and "FORBES" each in rectangle, all stamped on underside of spirit lamp. Height: 13⅛". Width: 7¾". Depth: 5⅜".

Maker, Locality, and Date
William Forbes (1799–c. 1864), New York City. Retailed by Ball, Tompkins & Black (1839–51), New York City. 1839–51.

Comment
Egg coddlers, used to boil eggs at the table, became popular during the 19th century. Most were made in England of silver plate, though occasionally they were made of japanned sheet iron or tin. The small spirit lamp in the base heated water in the lidded container, which cooked the eggs. Some coddlers were made for only one egg; this example cooks a dozen and is the largest size made for domestic use.

Hints for Collectors
Carefully examine coddlers, since they are composed of many separate parts and slender elements. If the internal rack or spirit burner is missing, the object should be avoided or bought at a substantial reduction; if parts are sloppily repaired with silver or lead solder, caution is advised. All parts should be original, but this may be hard to tell when only one of them is marked.

72 English Victorian electroplated coffee percolator

Description
Spherical bottle with tapered neck and leaf-decorated loop handle with ivory ferrules; bottle fitted with screw-on cap having 2 arms tipped with ivory spheres. Arched tube, with disk-shaped filter at one end, leads from bottle cap to a tapered cup. Bottle supported on 2 slender uprights with knurled knops that allow it to swing freely. Under bottle sits low circular spirit lamp with incurved sides, loop handle, and pierced holes. All supported on long low platform with curved beaded edge and 5 triangular scrolled feet. Bottle and cup engraved with foliate scrolls and series of borders.

Marks and Dimensions
Unmarked. Height: 13¼". Length: 12". Width: 5¼".

Maker, Locality, and Date
Unknown. England. 1830–60.

Comment
A coffee percolator is a rare form in plated wares. Coffee was popular in the 19th century, but the devices used to brew it were generally straightforward, functional, and relegated to the kitchen. The silver plating, ivory ferrules, and elegant embellishments of this object indicate that it was intended to be seen by guests. Although it looks more elaborate, it functions on the same principle as percolators used today.

Hints for Collectors
Adventurous collectors seek out unusual and rarely encountered objects, such as this percolator. Despite their rarity, many are relatively inexpensive, and because of their historical interest, they help build a comprehensive collection.

73 English George III fused-plated dish warmer

Description
Flat, oval, hinged lid with pierced concentric borders of leaves and arches and reeded edge. Shallow body with pierced straight sides. Paired S-shaped bracket at each end, connected by turned wooden handle. 4 oval trumpet-shaped legs on large spool-shaped wooden feet. Tinned sheet-iron bottom.

Marks and Dimensions
Unmarked. Length: 12″. Width: 6″. Height: 3⅜″.

Maker, Locality, and Date
Unknown. England. 1780–1800.

Comment
This low oval stand was originally fitted with a covered vegetable dish, also made of fused-plated copper. The stand was filled with hot coals to keep vegetables warm at the table through a second serving. The decorative piercing in the lid and sides provided a draft to keep the coals lit, while the wooden handles and feet provided insulation. On such objects, only the metal surfaces that showed were silvered. The inside and underside, if coated at all, were tinned.

Hints for Collectors
Even though fused-plated wares were produced in great quantity during the late 18th and early 19th centuries, they are not in abundant supply today. High-quality objects in good condition are hard to find. Collectors of early fused-plated wares will therefore find it much more difficult to assemble a fine collection than will collectors of silver.

Colonial brazier

Description
Shallow bowl with flat flared rim having 3 equidistant scrolled
projections; elaborate pierced border of stylized foliate motifs.
Pierced, flat, circular pan bolted to bottom of bowl. Turned
wooden handle attached to cylindrical socket affixed to one
projection. Simple narrow border of piercing encircles base. 3
legs extend down from rim projections and end in C-scrolls and
large ball-shaped wooden feet.

Marks and Dimensions
"I:POTWINE" in shaped rectangle, stamped on underside. Length:
11¾". Diameter: 6¼". Height: 3⅜".

Maker, Locality, and Date
John Potwine (1698–1792), Boston. 1720–37.

Comment
Braziers, or chafing dishes, were used on the dining table to keep
food warm. Their elaborately pierced sides, which allowed air to
pass over the hot embers within, involved extensive work; each
hole had to be cut out individually by hand with a tiny jeweler's
saw. Because this technique was very time-consuming and
expensive, little early American silver bears pierced decoration.

Hints for Collectors
The wooden balls and handles, which were necessary on braziers
to prevent burning the table or hands, have often been lost or
become worn out. Before making a purchase, it is a good idea to
make sure that these parts are original on any potential
acquisition. Look for heavy wear on the bottom of the feet and
for shrinkage cracks, scorching, and other signs of age. Also
make certain that the separate pierced pan that is fitted into an
early brazier is original.

Early Colonial skillet

Description
Circular, molded, flat-topped lid with spool-shaped finial and flared overhanging lip. Moderately deep, straight-sided bowl with rounded bottom. Tapered S-shaped handle with shield-shaped terminal attached to side. 3 short scrolled feet. Lid engraved with overlapping acanthus leaves radiating from finial. Coat of arms and crest (of Foster family of Boston) engraved on top of finial and on side of body opposite handle.

Marks and Dimensions
"W•R" in shield-shaped outline, stamped on edge of lid and on body under lip near handle. Height: 4⅝″. Width: 6½″.

Maker, Locality, and Date
William Rouse (1639–1705), Boston. 1690–1700.

Comment
Silver skillets, which are very rare today, are related to porringers and were used for serving food at the table. Their popularity seems to have dwindled at the close of the 17th century, whereas porringers continued to be made and used in great quantity. Some skillet lids have a finial, like the one seen here, while others have a flat, pierced, tabular handle attached at the rim; these tabular-handle lids could also be used as porringers. The few known American examples of the form originated in Boston or New York.

Hints for Collectors
Because skillets are so rare, a collector might fail to recognize an example that comes to light at a public auction or in an antiques shop. But by keeping abreast of current literature and the contents of public collections, enthusiastic collectors will stand a better chance of making the most of the unanticipated opportunities that come their way.

Late Colonial saucepan

Description
Squat pear-shaped cup with flared molded lip. Triangular spout with 2 graduated drops below. Cylindrical socket with shield-shaped escutcheon and baluster-shaped wooden handle; attached obliquely under lip at 90° to spout.

Marks and Dimensions
"TA" in rectangle, stamped twice on underside. Height (base of pan to top of handle): 7½". Width (base to projection of handle): 10¼". Diameter: 5".

Maker, Locality, and Date
Thomas Arnold (1734–1828), Newport, Rhode Island. 1759–80.

Comment
Silver saucepans, or brandy warmers, were not meant for cooking like their base-metal counterparts, but for warming liquor over a small open flame. Most examples have wooden handles, since silver conducts heat very quickly. Nonetheless, a few saucepans with original silver handles are known. Most examples were made during the 18th century, when the form seems to have experienced its greatest popularity. Saucepans were made with or without spouts and lids.

Hints for Collectors
The handles of these saucepans are always attached with silver solder just under the lip, and most have a reinforcement in the form of a decorative escutcheon. This solder joint is the weakest area of the object, so that many handles have been separated and reattached or replaced. When examining a saucepan, check to see that the handle and its soldered joint are original.

Description
Drum-shaped form with incurved side; extensively pierced with elaborate stylized foliate design arranged in 3 parallel horizontal rows. Heart-shaped reserve in center of middle border contains engraved script initials "SSC".

Marks and Dimensions
"Myers" in script in conforming outline, stamped twice on side. Diameter: 8⅞". Height: 4⁵⁄₁₆".

Maker, Locality, and Date
Myer Myers (1723–95), New York City. 1760–70.

Comment
Dish rings were used to protect wooden tabletops from hot dishes. Although this example is the only American silver dish ring now known to exist, such silver rings were common in Ireland, and plated examples were imported into America from Ireland and England in the 18th century. The production of these objects was tedious and time-consuming, since each hole had to be made carefully by hand.

Hints for Collectors
While few collectors can ever hope to own an 18th-century American silver dish ring, that does not lessen the interest or enjoyment that this singular example provides. The knowledge that such an exotic form was made in the American Colonies, and that it is equal in workmanship and design to those produced in Ireland and England, should give the enthusiast of American silver a greater appreciation of the exemplary history of the craft in this country. Imported dish rings from Ireland do come up for sale fairly regularly, and some of these will be of interest to American collectors, especially examples that have had a long history in this country.

Late Colonial dish cross

Description
4 rectangular bars forming a large X; joined at center with pierced disk-shaped element with beaded edge. End of each bar terminates in simple rosette. Sliding box with pierced sides fitted around each bar, topped by curved arm with pierced shell end; below, C-shaped leg with pierced shell foot.

Marks and Dimensions
"Myers" in script in conforming outline, stamped on each foot and on one shell-shaped support. Length: 10¾". Height: 3¹⁄₁₆".

Maker, Locality, and Date
Myer Myers (1723–95), New York City. 1765–75.

Comment
Dish crosses were normally fitted with a spirit or alcohol burner to keep food warm on the table. The supports can be adjusted along the length of the arm to accommodate dishes of different sizes, and the arms can be moved laterally to hold dishes of different shapes. English plated examples are quite common, but American silver examples are found infrequently. Most dish crosses date from the late 18th or early 19th century, indicating that their popularity was short-lived. This example is among the finest because of its pierced shell supports and feet.

Hints for Collectors
Dish crosses are often used today to display porcelain bowls; consequently they are popular with both silver and porcelain collectors. The English law requiring all English-made silver objects to be fully marked was not uniformly enforced. Thus with a form such as this, which was relatively common in England but rare in America, it is important to examine a prospective purchase very carefully.

Tureens, Vegetable Dishes, Sugar Bowls, and Related Objects

The vessels in this group were almost all designed to accommodate a matching lid. These pieces were varied in function, and in some cases, their purpose cannot be positively identified. One such container, made from the shell of a coconut, has 3 silver legs and a silver lid and may have been used as a drinking vessel or for storage. Composite objects like this one, however, are unusual and lie outside the mainstream of domestic routine and social custom.

Tureens and Related Dishes

With a few exceptions, most of these objects serve a recognizable purpose, although not necessarily a popular one today. Among the commonest are 2 types of tureens, one for soups and smaller ones for sauces. Most of these basically similar forms have some kind of ornament covering part or all of their bodies and lids. Tureens were usually decorated in the popular style of their day; some, for instance, have clusters of grapes and leaves encircling the body and handles in the shape of gnarled vines. This type of naturalistic ornament is found on many silver objects, regardless of shape or function. Others have ornament that was part of an elaborate symbolic language once widely used and understood but today obscure. Still others have ornament that indicates the intended contents of the object, such as the parsnips on top of a tureen for vegetable soup, or a cow on the lid of a butter dish.

Old-fashioned Specialties

Tureens are still in use, but other objects in this group, such as the tea caddy or the large domed lid for roasts, are obsolete today. Developed to meet the demands of elaborate table etiquette, these pieces represent an increasingly complex and formal life-style. Some aspects of an object testify to the value of its contents. For example, the Colonial tea caddy included in this section has a locking lid and key, illustrating that at the time when the object was made, tea was an expensive and controversial commodity.

One very unusual and rare form in this group is the Colonial sugar or sweetmeat box. The 17th-century view of sugar held that it "nourishes the body, generates good blood, cherishes the spirits, makes people prolific [and] strengthens children in the womb." As if to glorify this precious substance, these boxes are among the most elaborately decorated of early American silver, some employing an encyclopedic range of human, animal, and plant motifs.

79 English Victorian electroplated meat cover

Description
Large, high, oval dome with removable loop handle decorated with beading, leaves, and scrolls and set on low domed base. Cover engraved with wide foliate border enclosing 4 oval reserves depicting animals; fifth reserve with crest and motto (of Gillespie family), "QUI ME TANGIT POENITEBIT" (Touch not the cat without the glove); sixth reserve with coat of arms, crest, motto "HONI SOIT QUI MAL Y PENSE" (Evil to he who evil thinks) and "DIEU ET MON DROIT" (God and my right) of the royal family (Queen Victoria of the Hanover line), and "30TH JULY 1858." Base with flared lip and beaded border.

Marks and Dimensions
Unmarked. Height: 13″. Length: 20¼″. Width: 15⅞″.

Maker, Locality, and Date
Unknown. Probably London. c. 1858.

Comment
This large cover, probably originally accompanied by a matching tray, was used to bring a large meat course to the table and help it retain its heat. Like most plated wares, it bears no maker's mark. Since, unlike silver, the principal material of which it was made had little intrinsic value, no regulation or system of marking was required. This example was a trophy presented by Queen Victoria to Sir John Gillespie, a member of the Royal Company of Archers.

Hints for Collectors
America was not capable of producing electroplated objects commercially until the mid-19th century. Early English plated wares are of interest to American collectors because large quantities were imported to America and influenced the design of American silver.

English George IV fused-plated vegetable dish

Description

Rectangular lid with bulbous rounded corners and applied foliate molding on top. Removable, scrolled, foliate loop handle. Removable inner tray has flared overhanging rim with applied foliate decoration. Dish with removable pierced strainer, 2 arched loop handles, and leaf-decorated scrolled feet. Lid has inset silver rectangle on each side, one with engraved crest and motto "ME MINERVA TENET" (Minerva is my strength).

Marks and Dimensions

Bell in oval with striped ground stamped on underside of lid handle, on edge of removable tray, and underside of dish. "1" stamped incuse on underside of lid handle; "4" stamped incuse on edge of both lid and dish. Gothic "G" stamped incuse on underside of lid handle, lid, and removable tray. A cross in circle on underside of dish. Height: 7½". Length: 14". Width: 9¼".

Maker, Locality, and Date

Samuel Roberts & Company (1784–1848), Sheffield, England. 1820–40.

Comment

Vegetable dishes were often made as part of a set; the stamped numbers on this example suggest it belonged to a set of at least 4. Fused-plating predated electroplating and was popular principally from the 1730s to the 1830s.

Hints for Collectors

Years of use and polishing have exposed varying amounts of the copper base of fused-plated objects. Although collectors like to have as little copper exposed as possible, fused-plated objects should not be restored by electroplating.

Colonial/Federal silver-mounted coconut

Description
Double-domed lid with incised rings and pineapple finial. Fitted to hollow coconut shell with ribbed and scalloped silver ring on top edge. 3 scrolled feet with shell tops and hoof feet. Coconut carved with series of circular flowers. "WEAB" engraved in script on lid.

Marks and Dimensions
"T•H" in rectangle stamped on lip of cup and on underside of lid. Height: 6¾". Diameter (at lip): 3⅜".

Maker, Locality, and Date
Attributed to Thomas Hammersley (1727–81), New York City. 1750–80.

Comment
Silver-mounted coconut shells or ostrich eggs are extremely rare and must be regarded as whimsies, of marginal practical value. These shells are often said to have been carved by sailors who journeyed to the tropics. The silver mounts, however, were undoubtedly fabricated and applied by professional silversmiths, as is clearly evident in the competent design and careful execution of this example.

Hints for Collectors
Many mounted shells, whether made in Europe or America, had either no maker's mark or were marked only with initials. Therefore, assigning one of these objects to a silversmith is problematic if not impossible. Because such curiosities seem to have been made very infrequently in this country, collectors are best advised to be circumspect in accepting an American attribution for such an object.

Victorian butter dish

Description
Domed circular lid with recumbent cow finial on low pedestal; side of lid has engine-turned borders and 3 equidistant circular stylized foliate reserves, 2 containing a helmeted male profile. Low circular dish with removable pierced liner and beaded rim. 3 scrolled legs with leaf-shaped tops.

Marks and Dimensions
"AC" stamped vertically in a diamond, flanked by spread eagle and male bust, each in an oval on underside. Height: 5¾". Diameter: 6⅝".

Maker, Locality, and Date
Albert Coles (d. 1886), New York City. 1836–76.

Comment
The mid-19th century saw a proliferation of silversmithing machinery. Some machines were used for fabrication, others for decoration. One of the most popular was the engine lathe, which could quickly engrave a pattern of lines over the entire surface of an object. This device saved much time and labor.

Hints for Collectors
Before the Civil War, American silver was almost never marked "sterling," even though it was approximately of that purity. As a result, beginning collectors may easily mistake an early American silver object bearing only a maker's mark for silver plate. To avoid this, study early silver markings, particularly since the difference in value between a silver object and its silver-plated counterpart is considerable. Silver plate sometimes reveals a difference in color in areas of heavy wear, such as the bottoms of feet, where the plating has worn through. In general —but by no means always— plated objects are heavier than their silver counterparts.

83 Early Colonial sweetmeat box

Description

Hinged, stepped, and domed oval lid; open, scrolled, foliate finial surrounded by concentric borders of leaf moldings and gadrooning. Hinged, circular hasp depicting swordsman on galloping horse. Squat, bulbous body with wide border of gadrooning interrupted alternately by acanthus leaves and oval reserves depicting equestrian figures. 4 scrolled feet. Engraved on bottom "O/DE donum W.P. 1702."

Marks and Dimensions

"EW" over fleur-de-lis in 3-lobed shield, stamped twice on rim of body, and "EW" in 3-lobed shield-shaped outline stamped twice on rim of lid. Height: 5½". Length: 7½". Width: 5¼".

Maker, Locality, and Date

Edward Winslow (1669–1753), Boston. c. 1702.

Comment

Sweetmeat boxes, originally known as sugar boxes, are one of the rarest forms in American silver. Only 9 are known, and all were made in or near Boston. Because they were made to hold sweetmeats, a candy made largely or wholly of sugar, which was quite expensive in the 18th century, such boxes were luxuries.

Hints for Collectors

Although beyond the reach of most collectors, this rare box may serve as a standard against which to measure potential acquisitions. Its fine, elaborate decoration, carefully integrated into the overall design, makes this a classic example of American silver. Not all American silver is found in the United States; this box, for example, was purchased in England in 1937, having been taken there during the American Revolution by a descendant of the original owner.

84 Victorian electroplated vegetable dish

Description
Oval low-domed lid with multiple conjoined borders of flowers and leaves; topped by low loop handle with lobed and scrolled motifs. Oval dish with flared lip and multiple borders of flowers and leaves. 2 scrolled horn-shaped handles with cylindrical knopped grips. 4 short wide feet with shells and scrolls. Removable enameled-iron liner. Gothic "R" engraved on lid.

Marks and Dimensions
"X MERIDEN B. COMPANY X" within circle also framing scale within a shield, and "PAT<u>D</u> FEB 9. 1869/87" below circle, all stamped incuse on underside of dish. Height: 6¾". Length: 12½". Width: 7¼".

Maker, Locality, and Date
Meriden Britannia Company (1852–98), Meriden, Connecticut. 1887–98.

Comment
Lidded tureens for vegetables, sauces, meats, and soups, popular in 19th-century America, were richly decorated with cast, chased, and engraved ornament. The vegetable dish shown here is a good example. It is fitted with a separate enameled-iron dish in which the food was cooked.

Hints for Collectors
Much of this vessel's silver has worn off, exposing the britannia metal underneath. While collectors abhor electroplating objects that were originally fused-plated, most do not object to reelectroplating wares originally silvered in that manner. Many objects of the late 19th century bear patent dates; these usually refer to an actual or alleged patent for some facet of the design rather than for a manufacturing innovation. An object cannot be dated specifically to the patent year it bears because it may have been produced much later.

Victorian tureen

Description
High, domed oval lid decorated with cabbage leaves, 2 parsnips, and rope border; small cutout in one end for ladle. Deep oval bowl with 2 large buffalo-head handles; echinus border at shoulder and cabbage leaves on body. Flared oval pedestal with cabbage leaves above plain base. Crest of rampant lion holding a dagger engraved on edge of lid.

Marks and Dimensions
"TIFFANY & CO." and "550 BROADWAY" in opposed arcs; "ENGLISH STERLING/925-1000" in double rectangle; "1054/6965"; "M" in oval stamped twice; all on underside. Height: 12½". Length: 17¼". Width: 10".

Maker, Locality, and Date
Tiffany & Company (1853–present), New York City. 1869–91.

Comment
Large silver objects have adorned elegant dining tables throughout history. Among the most popular of these were epergnes, plateaus, nefs, and tureens; only the last were made by American silversmiths with any great frequency. While the other 3 types of objects are showy forms with little functional value, the tureen is as useful as it is decorative. Tureens may be round or oval; they have lids and are usually on pedestals, although a few have legs. Most American examples date from the 19th century.

Hints for Collectors
The best large soup tureens have an abundance of realistic and fine, hand-finished animal, vegetable, floral, and sometimes even human motifs, pleasingly arranged and logically organized. Look for examples with as many of these features as possible. Generally, the heavier the tureen, the more desirable it is.

Victorian parcel-gilt tureen

Description
Domed oval lid with intertwined vine-shaped loop handle; grapevine-decorated edge. Oval bellied body with 2 intertwined vine-shaped loop handles. Low, domed oval pedestal with grapevine-ornamented edge. Lid, body, and pedestal decorated with repoussé grape clusters, vines, and leaves; "C. A. F. Rondeau" engraved in Gothic lettering on one side of body. Gilt interior.

Marks and Dimensions
"A. H./N. O." stamped incuse and "WARRANTED/PURE COIN" in anthemia-ended rectangle, all on underside. Height: 11¾". Length: 15½". Width: 10".

Maker, Locality, and Date
Adolphe Himmel (d. 1877), New Orleans. 1861–77.

Comment
In shape and decoration this tureen from New Orleans is closely related to those made in and around New York about a decade earlier. Close trade ties existed between New York and New Orleans silversmiths, resulting in similarities between their products, particularly in the use of repoussé grape clusters and leaves and naturalistic vine-shaped handles.

Hints for Collectors
Much New York-made silver of this era was retailed in New Orleans, so be careful in assigning a place of origin to any object marked "New Orleans." While Adolphe Himmel did market silver and silver plate from New York, the fact that he was a working silversmith allows collectors to conclude that objects bearing his mark were probably made in New Orleans. Failure to recognize any New Orleans Victorian silver would be unfortunate, since it is rapidly becoming very desirable.

Description
Domed oval lid with fruit-cluster finial and small cutout in edge for ladle. Oval boat-shaped body with leaf-tip border near lip. 2 arched loop handles with leaf-and-berry-cluster ends and knop at center. High molded pedestal with leaf-tip border at neck and bottom. Low oval tray with narrow molded brim having leaf-tip border.

Marks and Dimensions
"T. FLETCHER. PHILA." in oval stamped on underside of tureen; "T. FLETCHER." and "PHILA." each in rectangle stamped on underside of tray. Tureen height: 7½"; length: 8"; width: 4½". Tray length: 9⅜"; width: 5¼"; height: ½".

Maker, Locality, and Date
Thomas Fletcher (1787–1866), Philadelphia. 1825–35.

Comment
Tureens, particularly small ones, are among the rarer forms made in American silver before the Victorian period. While large tureens were made to hold soup, smaller examples like this one were for sauces and gravies. The ornament of this piece, though spare, is typical of its era, when the severe style of classical Greece was esteemed.

Hints for Collectors
This tureen and tray have heavy, thick walls; the hammer marks on their hidden surfaces were created when the objects were made. The lid, which is made of rolled sheet metal, is thinner and lighter in weight and has no hammer marks. This combination of manufacturing styles was fairly common during the early 19th century, an era marked by change from traditional handwork to mass production in factories.

Description
Oval, stepped, domed lid with flared lip and large leaf-and-pomegranate finial. Deep oval body with reeded lip and wide leaf-and-pomegranate border. Curved loop handle at each end. Low flared pedestal. Matching oval tray. Crest (unidentified) engraved on lid, body, and tray.

Marks and Dimensions
"J LOWNES" in script in conforming outline stamped twice, 4 fleurs-de-lis stamped incuse, leaf stamped incuse, and square with 4 semicircular projections each containing a dot, all on underside of tureen. "J•LOWNES" in script in conforming outline stamped twice and "PHILADELPHIA" in circular outline on underside of tray. Tureen height: 12"; length: 13¾"; width: 9¼".

Maker, Locality, and Date
Joseph Lownes (1758–1820), Philadelphia. 1800–10.

Comment
This unusually exuberant example of early American silver has a large pomegranate finial and engraved pomegranate borders. This fruit traditionally symbolized purity and the comforts of civilization, and eating it was thought to purge the system of envy and malice. The lid also fits the tray, converting it to a vegetable dish.

Hints for Collectors
Engraved on the lid, body, and tray is an unidentified heraldic crest—a mermaid with comb and mirror. Knowing the identity of the tureen's original owner would add considerably to its historic interest, though not necessarily to its value. Collectors should always seek out and record such information.

Federal tea caddy

Description
Hinged, molded, rectangular lid with dome and rounded sides
and corners; urn-shaped finial. Bulbous oval body with wide
engraved foliate border just below lip. Keyhole and lock in front
center; small pierced key. Below keyhole, engraved square with
canted corners suspended from foliate swag and engraved "CSH"
in script.

Marks and Dimensions
"W.G. Forbes" in conforming outline stamped on underside.
Height: 6¼". Length: 6½". Width: 4⅝".

Maker, Locality, and Date
William Garret Forbes (1751–1840), New York City. 1800–10.

Comment
Tea caddies, in which tea was stored prior to its use, were made
in many materials, including wood, pewter, earthenware,
porcelain, and plated ware. Silver tea caddies were among the
most expensive; most of these had locks, evidence of the value of
their contents. Although the interior of the caddy shown here is
undivided, many were sectioned for storing several varieties of
tea. The maker of this example was one of several in the Forbes
family who practiced silversmithing in New York City.

Hints for Collectors
William Forbes was identified decades ago as the maker of this
tea caddy, but until about 10 years ago, scholars and historians
believed his middle name to have been Graham. The discovery in
such recent times that his name was actually William Garret
Forbes shows the value of and continuing need for research.

Description
Low domed lid with low cylindrical molded ring on top. Bowl tapers from flared lip to low, cylindrical, molded foot rim. Lid and body engraved with circle containing entwined script initials "EC".

Marks and Dimensions
"SS" in rectangle, stamped on bottom and inside molded ring on top. Height: 4³⁄₁₆″. Diameter: 4¹¹⁄₁₆″.

Maker, Locality, and Date
Simeon Soumain (1685–1750), New York City. 1736–45.

Comment
The clean lines and unembellished surfaces of this bowl are in direct imitation of those of the Chinese porcelain bowls that were popular imports in Europe and America at the time this object was made. The great vogue for Chinese objects of every kind, from silks and tea to porcelain and lacquer, was clearly manifested in the shapes and decoration of stylish 18th-century silver, of which this bowl is a paramount example. The engraved script initials, those of Elizabeth Harris Cruger, are difficult to read because they are intertwined with their mirror images. This bowl was acquired at or after the time of her marriage in 1736 to Henry Cruger of Jamaica, New York.

Hints for Collectors
The lid of this sugar bowl can be inverted for use as a shallow bowl or saucer. Sugar bowls of this period, whether straight-sided or with a flared lip, originally had a lid. However, many examples have lost their lids and are therefore less valuable. So even though a lidless sugar bowl may retain great visual appeal, a collector should purchase it only if its price reflects this incompleteness.

91 Victorian butter dish

Description
Hemispherical lid with finial shaped like a recumbent sheep; 4
equidistant circular medallions, each with a human profile,
flanked by flowers and leaf clusters. Low, flared circular bowl
with stylized leaf-tip edge. Low, flared circular foot rim
decorated with border of leaves and pointed arches. Bowl has
removable pierced silver liner. Lid engraved in script, "Helen/
Dec. 1, 1870/from T L B".

Marks and Dimensions
"C. H. ZIMMERMAN" and "NEW ORLEANS" flanking a crescent moon
with a face; all stamped incuse on underside. Height: 4¾".
Diameter: 5⅞".

Maker, Locality, and Date
Charles H. Zimmerman (d. 1870), New Orleans. c. 1870.

Comment
Butter dishes were typically fitted with a separate, decoratively
pierced liner; a small amount of ice or ice water in the dish
beneath the liner helped keep the butter from melting.

Hints for Collectors
When contemplating the purchase of objects such as this butter
dish, collectors should check that all the original parts are
present. Butter-dish liners have sometimes become separated
from the containers; a collector should not assume that a
particular butter dish never had a liner. Similarly, it is vital to
examine all parts of an object to ensure that they are original.
This determination can be made by comparing fit, decoration,
and construction.

Late Colonial sugar bowl

Description
Multidomed lid with pineapple finial. Double-bellied body on molded circular pedestal. Body and lid ornamented with encircling border of flowers and leaves. "C/D M" (for Daniel and Mary Cannon of Charleston, South Carolina) engraved on side of bowl.

Marks and Dimensions
"T•Y" in rectangle, stamped 3 times on underside. Height: 6½". Diameter: 4½".

Maker, Locality, and Date
Thomas You (d. 1786), Charleston, South Carolina. 1760–70.

Comment
Thomas You is believed to have been the son of Daniel You, a silversmith from Charleston, South Carolina. Thomas You worked in that city around the time of the Revolution, producing many fine, elaborate, and expensive objects—including tankards, punch bowls, coffeepots, ladles, and strainers—for a sophisticated clientele. He also made engraved copperplate views of local landmarks, which he sold to residents of the city.

Hints for Collectors
Although Thomas You apparently enjoyed an extensive business, little of his silver is known today. Its rarity, coupled with a southern origin, makes it very desirable. Collectors should familiarize themselves with current specialized books and articles that discuss southern silver, so that they will be equipped to appreciate and evaluate examples that appear on the market.

Late Federal wine cooler

Description
Removable low domed cover with large center hole and stylized
leaf-and-shell edge. Circular urn with high flared neck encircled
by acorns and leaves. Squat bulbous midsection encircled by
grape clusters and leaves; 2 curved reeded loop handles with
leaf-shaped terminals. Circular, knopped, molded pedestal with 3
egg-and-dart borders. "EKH" engraved in script on side under lip.

Marks and Dimensions
5 pseudohallmarks ("T"; "F"; and "P"; each in shield with striped
background; male bust and eagle, each in circle) all stamped
twice on outside rim of base. Height: 12⅛″. Width: 9½″.
Diameter: 9¼″.

Maker, Locality, and Date
Thomas Fletcher (1787–1866), Philadelphia. 1828–35.

Comment
Many objects have been made to further the enjoyment of wine.
The wine cooler, meant to keep a bottle of wine cool at the table,
is elegantly represented by this example. It is modeled after a
type of ancient Greek vase known as a calyx krater, in which
wine and water were mixed in a predetermined ratio.

Hints for Collectors
American silver wine coolers are very rare, although many
European examples were made of silver or silver plate. This
example is very closely related to an English prototype, and is
distinguishable from it primarily by its marks. While these and
other American marks were imitative of English ones, they
should never be confused with them; English marks were rigidly
regulated by law and always consistent, but American marks
were chosen by makers and tended to vary a great deal.

Victorian 2-handled cup

Description
Deep conical body with applied beading on flared lip. 2 tapered
loop handles with spur at top. Body decorated with strapwork
and foliate clusters surrounding shield-shaped reserves; 4
freestanding leaves serve as brackets below. Low, flared,
circular pedestal. "DLR & JCR" engraved in script on one side of
body and "SCC & SC" on other.

Marks and Dimensions
Lion and "G" each in clipped-corner square, flanking anchor in
shield; "10/COIN/OLD SILVER"; all stamped incuse on underside.
Height: 8½". Width: 6⅞". Diameter: 4¾".

Maker, Locality, and Date
Gorham Company (1831–present), Providence. 1870–1900.

Comment
2-handled cups or vases have been a standard, though not
common, form in American silver since the 17th century.
Suitable for use as everyday drinking vessels or as singular
presentation trophies, these cups were especially popular during
the late 19th century, when they were made in all sizes and
shapes. One of the most famous, more than 8' tall and weighing
several hundred pounds, was presented to Admiral George
Dewey for his decisive role at the battle of Manila Bay in 1898.

Hints for Collectors
Always try to determine if the initials engraved on a silver object
are original. Many objects have had original initials erased, while
others have been engraved or reengraved long after they were
made. Unaltered original initials are preferable; later deletions
or alterations generally lower an object's value.

Porringers, Bowls, Cake Baskets, and Related Objects

 Among the most varied and numerous silver forms are those used to contain, display, and serve food. While all of the containers in this section are related generally by their function, they differ significantly in appearance.

Meals in Early America
For the most part, dining in 17th-century America was fairly simple. Only a few sophisticated residents of Boston, New York, Williamsburg, Virginia, Charleston, South Carolina, and other urban centers had the necessary accoutrements for elaborate table ceremony. Through the 18th and into the 19th centuries, dining became more and more elaborate, as did the manners of an ever-widening segment of the population. This change was accompanied by a growing and increasingly complex array of vessels used to carry and dispense food.

Among the most common items of 17th-century tableware was the porringer, a moderately deep bowl with a single tabular handle at the lip. These bowls, usually accompanied by a porringer spoon, were often used by children. Another early, much rarer, form was the sweetmeat dish. Sometimes made in pairs, always with lobed sides, they held sweetmeats—any sugared food such as nuts, fruits, or even flowers, which were mixed in granular sugar or in a thick sugary syrup.

Festive Occasions and Elaborate Dining
Paneled bowls were rich in appearance and had a ceremonial function. They were typically made in New York and often had 2 handles. On special occasions they were used to hold spiced foods and drinks.

Similar but much larger were the monteiths and punch bowls of a later date. Monteiths experienced a relatively brief period of popularity during the 18th century; the most striking feature of the form is a deeply scalloped lip, from which wine glasses were suspended in cold water to chill them properly. Monteiths sometimes had removable rims so they could double as punch bowls. Numerous monumental and elaborate punch bowls date from the late 19th century. These were typically accompanied by a ladle, several cups, and a tray.

A profusion of specialized table objects, represented in this group by cake baskets and compotes, appeared in the early 19th century. Both of these forms were used to hold carefully arranged fruits or cakes. Great ceremony often accompanied the display and use of these objects and the delicacies they contained. Most American silver cake baskets and compotes had solid bodies, but a few were made of open, interlaced wirework. As the close of the 19th century drew near, large numbers of these dishes were made with elaborate multicolored, ruffled glass bowls.

These forms were accompanied by a host of other highly specialized vessels, such as nut bowls, olive dishes, and the like. The purpose of these little containers was often made manifest by the ornament; a nut bowl might have a squirrel or small still life of silver nuts placed strategically on it; an olive dish might be fashioned in imitation of the fruit it was meant to contain.

Silver and silver-plated bowls have continued to be made in the 20th century, but they usually lack the degree of ornament or specialization so popular during the previous century. Instead, they are characterized by uncluttered lines and undecorated surfaces. Though simple in comparison with their Victorian counterparts, they have great visual appeal and are eminently useful as well as popular with collectors.

95 Late Colonial bowl

Description
Circular tapered body divided into 6 vertical panels, each with
stylized flower enclosed in irregular outline. 2 large S-shaped
handles, each with graduated beading along sides and female
head at top. Bottom of inside decorated with stylized rosette.
Low straight-sided foot rim with flared bottom edge. "W/EE"
engraved on side under lip.

Marks and Dimensions
"I•TE" (the T and E conjoined) within oval, stamped twice on side
under lip. Diameter: 7½". Height: 3¾". Width: 10⅞".

Maker, Locality, and Date
Jacob Ten Eyck (1705–93), Albany, New York. 1726–50.

Comment
6-paneled bowls with elaborately cast handles seem to have been
made only in New York and only during the late 17th and early
18th centuries. With its 6 equal segments, this example is
typical. Similar bowls of a much smaller diameter often had
handles made of twisted silver wire. This bowl bears the
engraved initials of Evert and Engeltie Wendell of Albany, who
were married in 1710. It was certainly not executed at the time
of their marriage, since its maker was then only a child.

Hints for Collectors
Early paneled bowls are quite uncommon, and their rarity
coupled with their distinctive character make them very
valuable. When considering one, check that its handles are
original; these bowls were occasionally made without handles,
which were added in the early 20th century to enhance their
value. Also examine the foot rim to ensure its originality.

Late Colonial keyhole-handle porringer

Description
Moderately deep bowl with convex side, narrow flared rim, and low boss in bottom. Irregularly pierced flat handle attached at rim; "M M" engraved in block letters on top of handle.

Marks and Dimensions
"W. BURT" in rectangle, stamped on top of handle and inside bottom of bowl. Diameter: 5″. Height: 2″. Length: 7¾″.

Maker, Locality, and Date
William Burt (1726–51), Boston. 1746–51.

Comment
Porringers were probably the most common type of silver objects made in America during the 18th century, except for spoons. The form derives from English prototypes and invariably has a bellied bowl with a central boss, or dome, in the bottom. While there were many handle variants, the so-called keyhole type, found on porringers made from Boston to south of Philadelphia, was by far the most common after 1720. These handles were always cast and then soldered to the lip of the wrought bowl.

Hints for Collectors
Carefully examine porringers for makers' marks, which may be found on the top or bottom of the handle, on the inside bottom, under the bowl, or sometimes on the side of the bowl's edge. Check the rim of the bowl near the handle for damage, since this area sometimes tears from use and may require restoration. If existing repairs are small, collectors can be reasonably certain they are legitimate; but if solder encompasses the entire area around the handle, the handle may be a replacement, in which case the porringer should be avoided.

Late Colonial sweetmeat dish

Description
Shallow circular form with slightly flared side having evenly
spaced short ribs and scalloped edge. "P" over "PM" engraved on
underside.

Marks and Dimensions
"GR" in cut-corner rectangle, stamped 4 times on underside.
Diameter: 5³⁄₁₆". Height: ⅞".

Maker, Locality, and Date
George Ridout (dates unknown), New York City. 1745–55.

Comment
Sweetmeats, popular confections made mostly of sugar, were
held in great esteem in the 17th and 18th centuries, sometimes
having special silver vessels made to hold them. Shallow fluted
bowls of either silver or pewter, derived from earlier similar
Dutch and English forms, were used to serve one kind of
sweetmeat, fruit preserved in a thick sugary syrup. Though
relatively simple in character and easily made, such dishes are
rare, perhaps reflecting the infrequency with which such sweets
were available.

Hints for Collectors
This dish is stamped 4 times on the underside with the initial
touchmark of its maker; such multiple stampings are atypical of
American silver. The presence of 4 strikes of the touchmark
often indicates, as it does here, that the craftsman was a recent
immigrant who had been trained in England, where 4 marks
were required on all silver objects. In England, however, each of
these marks was different, while this bowl has 4 of the same
mark—a clue, for the astute collector, that the object is
American.

Modern silver bowl

Description
Low flattened hemisphere with hammer marks over entire
surface; 6 equidistant vertical ribs. Molded lip. Low, circular,
molded pedestal.

Marks and Dimensions
"C"; "S"; and "CO" each in conjoined segments of a circle; "HAND/
WROUGHT/STERLING/270"; all stamped incuse on underside.
Diameter: 9½". Height: 3½".

Maker, Locality, and Date
Chicago Silver Company (1923–45), Chicago. 1923–45.

Comment
The Chicago Silver Company was founded by Knut Gustafson,
who was born and trained in Stockholm. He immigrated to
Bridgeport, Connecticut, in 1906, but moved to Chicago about
1910. After working with several metal shops in the Chicago
area, he organized the Chicago Silver Company in 1923. This
enterprise, which combined handcrafting, a limited amount of
labor-saving machinery, and aggressive marketing, proved to be
quite successful. In 1945 Gustafson sold this company and formed
another, Gustafson Craft, which remained in business until
destroyed by a fire in 1965.

Hints for Collectors
Silver made in the Chicago area during the late 19th and early
20th centuries is drawing increasing attention from serious
collectors. It is generally well designed and of good quality and
fine workmanship. The earliest and most influential of the
Chicago firms producing handcrafted silver was the Kalo shop,
founded by Clara Welles. Among the more respected Chicago
makers were Robert Jarvie, Julius O. Randahl, Jessie Preston,
George H. Trautmann, J. Myer Lebolt, and Edmund Boker.

Colonial monteith

Description
Large circular bowl with deeply scalloped rim ornamented with urns, scrolled architectural volutes, cherub heads, and leaf-and-flower clusters, all on stylized leafy ground. Hinged knopped bail handles hang from mouths of 2 large lion masks below rim. Belly of bowl fluted; 3 dotted borders below. Circular molded pedestal with gadrooned border near base. Coat of arms (of Coleman family of Boston) within foliate mantling engraved inside bowl and "TB" engraved on underside.

Marks and Dimensions
"IC" above fleur-de-lis, all in heart-shaped outline, stamped on underside and on bottom of foot rim. Diameter: 10¾". Height: 8⅝".

Maker, Locality, and Date
John Coney (1656–1722), Boston. 1700–10.

Comment
Because of its scalloped rim, this type of large bowl is called a monteith, reputedly after a 17th-century Scotsman who wore a cloak with a scalloped hem. Wine or punch glasses were hung inside the rim of the bowl, which was filled with cold water to chill them before they were used. Only 3 American monteiths are known, all made in Boston in the 18th century. This one is nearly identical to contemporary London-made monteiths.

Hints for Collectors
One of the most notable and vibrant silver objects made in America, this monteith demands close study. Its surface has been completely worked with a wide variety of silversmithing techniques. Serious collectors should scrutinize this wealth of detail to increase their understanding and appreciation of the "art and mystery" of 18th-century silversmithing.

100 Victorian electroplated punch bowl, tray, cups, and ladle

Description
Deep hemispherical bowl with scalloped rim ornamented with foliate scrolls; 6 cup hooks hang from these on outside. Gilt interior. Border of grape clusters and leaves encircles body, which fits into molded ring pierced with flowers, leaves, and scrolls. Large, flat, circular tray with raised flared foliate rim. 6 circular cups with gilt interior, grapevine border, C-shaped handle, and low foot rim. Ladle with deep hemispherical bowl decorated with leaves and flowers; long, tapered, foliate handle.

Marks and Dimensions
"MERIDEN B * COMPANY" and "QUADRUPLE PLATE" (each in circle), "16"; and "U.S.A."; all stamped incuse on underside of tray and each cup. Bowl diameter: 16½"; height: 11½". Tray diameter: 20½".

Maker, Locality, and Date
Meriden Britannia Company (1852–98), Meriden, Connecticut. c. 1896.

Comment
Large punch sets—complete with tray, ladle and bowls, cups, or goblets—reached the height of their popularity during the last 2 decades of the 19th century. Most have an abundance of ornament, usually grapevines or other motifs related to their intended contents.

Hints for Collectors
Complete punch sets are not common today, particularly not those, like this one, with their silver plating intact. When found, however, they are usually moderately priced. Naturally those in good condition and bearing a maker's mark are the most desirable.

Modern bowl and ladle

Description
Circular bowl with curved side and flared rim. Low circular and convex pedestal. Ladle has curved rectangular wooden handle riveted to short rectangular silver shaft with shallow oval bowl.

Marks and Dimensions
"ALLAN ADLER/STERLING" stamped incuse on underside of bowl; "ALLAN ADLER/HANDMADE/STERLING" stamped incuse on back of ladle. Bowl diameter: 6⅞"; height: 3⅛". Ladle length: 7"; width: 2⅜".

Maker, Locality, and Date
Allan Adler (b. 1916), Hollywood, California. c. 1950.

Comment
Not until after the discovery of large amounts of gold and silver ore in the Far West during the mid-19th century did silver craftsmen begin to settle there. As a result, early western silver, other than religious objects and jewelry made by native Americans, is quite uncommon. Allan Adler's work, which is widely available today, is evidence that the tradition for good-quality handwrought silver objects eventually established in the West continues to the present.

Hints for Collectors
The comparative rarity of California-made silver makes this bowl and ladle of special interest. More important, however, is the maker's mastery of metalsmithing and his fine sense of design. The clarity achieved in the clean, smooth lines and unblemished surfaces is the result of years of study and practice. Because Adler's work is readily available, collectors should pay no more of a premium for it than they would for handwrought silver from the East Coast.

Federal bowl

Description
Circular, flared, scalloped lip; inside of rim engraved with
meandering vine border. Body tapered to rounded bottom. Low
flared and molded pedestal. Engraved in script on side:
"Elizabeth Codwise./and/Major Ezra Starr./Married, April 24,
1781." "EC" engraved on underside.

Marks and Dimensions
"W. Gilbert" and "NEW YORK" each in rectangle, both stamped on
underside. Diameter: 5⅞". Height: 3⅛".

Maker, Locality, and Date
William Gilbert (1746–1818), New York City. 1781–1818.

Comment
This small bowl is part of the long tradition of giving silver in
celebration of a marriage. While silver was frequently given to a
couple at the time of their wedding, it could also be given after
the event. For instance, although this bowl is engraved 1781, it
may have been given or engraved at a considerably later date,
even after the end of William Gilbert's career in 1818. Its
scalloped and engraved rim is quite unusual; most bowls have a
simple molded edge. Bowls of this size and shape were often part
of a tea or coffee set, serving as slop bowls. With its unusual rim,
however, this bowl was intended to be used individually.

Hints for Collectors
Bowls of this size are readily available, but examples as
distinctive as this one are rare and very desirable. Collectors
should expect to pay more for a bowl with detailed decoration
than for a simple piece, but only if such decoration is well-
executed; pleasing line and proportion are equally important.

Description
Shallow, circular bowl with naturalistic grapevine border applied
to rim. 2 horizontal loop handles with foliate, shell, and
gadrooned ornament. Large flower on inside bottom. Flared,
circular pedestal with leaf-decorated collar and foot.

Marks and Dimensions
"PHIL^A" in rectangle and "FLETCHER & GARDINER"; all in circle,
stamped on underside. Diameter: 10½″. Height: 4¼″. Width: 13″.

Maker, Locality, and Date
Thomas Fletcher & Sidney Gardiner (1808–27), Philadelphia.
1817–30.

Comment
Compotes, although related to tazzas, are an unknown form in
18th-century American silver. While they were frequently used
in fashionable mid- to late-19th-century American households,
only a few, including this pair, are known to have been made
during the early 19th century. The vigorous, realistic grapevine
border seen here—applied to a lip conforming to its outline and
serving as the actual edge of the compotes, rather than as a
decorative adjunct—anticipates the ornamental exuberance
characteristic of mid-19th-century American silver.

Thomas Fletcher and Sidney Gardiner were among the most
notable American silversmiths and entrepreneurs during the
early 19th century. These men were acclaimed for their
monumental presentation silver, which included large vases that
were commissioned for heroes of the War of 1812. The quality of

Fletcher & Gardiner's work, coupled with skillful merchandising, helped the partners build the reputation of their silver manufactory as one of the finest in the United States. They produced and marketed fine silver not only to Philadelphians, but also to style-conscious Americans from New Hampshire to Louisiana. Although Sidney Gardiner died in 1827, Thomas Fletcher continued to use the partnership mark until about 1830.

Hints for Collectors

While all work by Fletcher & Gardiner is desirable, some pieces are sought more than others. Their silver objects are usually fairly heavy and almost always of superb design and quality. But those that have animal, human, and mythological ornament generally command a substantially higher price than those decorated with leaves, flowers, fruit, and other similar vegetation. Nonetheless, these compotes are very desirable because they are forward-looking in both form and ornament. The grapevine border presages the voluptuous naturalistic ornament of the mid-19th century, while the form anticipates the growth in popularity of the shallow bowl-on-pedestal. Their other assets include their substantial weight, workmanlike fabrication, and well-conceived and executed details

Federal cake basket

Description
Circular body with solid curved side. Wide horizontal rim with narrow foliate borders flanking wide pierced border of flowers, leafy scrolls, and anthemia. Hinged semicircular handle tapered at ends and decorated with pierced flowers, leaves, anthemia, and birds; "MSR" engraved on applied hexagonal plaque on center of handle. Narrow border of leaf tips at base of bowl. Circular molded pedestal with border of stars near base.

Marks and Dimensions
"H•LEWIS" in rectangle, stamped twice on underside; "HARVEY. LEWIS" in rectangle, stamped inside foot rim. Diameter: 10¼". Height: 10".

Maker, Locality, and Date
Harvey Lewis (d. 1835), Philadelphia. 1805–20.

Comment
Cake or fruit baskets came into fashion late in the 18th century and experienced their greatest popularity during the first half of the 19th century. Because most were rectangular or oblong, this circular example is unusual; its pierced border is also uncommon. By the date when this cake basket was made, most ornamental borders were beginning to be machine-produced. The primary border on this example, however, was made in the traditional way—cast in segments that were then placed end to end around the edge.

Hints for Collectors
Cake baskets were very elegant additions to dining-room silver and remain so today. The best are of substantial weight, often with profuse foliate or animal ornament, and with a superior finish. Documentation about the original owner also adds to an object's appeal.

Federal cake basket

Description
Rectangular body with rounded corners and curved sides. Widely flared molded lip. Hinged, tapered, U-shaped bail handle. Slightly flared oblong pedestal with molded edge. "SSB" engraved on inner rim at one end and "HAACB" on opposite; engraved coat of arms and crest (unidentified) on side.

Marks and Dimensions
"WISHART" in rectangle, stamped on underside and on handle; "S. Richard fecit" (S. Richard made this) engraved on underside. Length: 13⅜". Width: 10⅜". Height (to rim): 5".

Maker, Locality, and Date
Stephen Richard (dates unknown), New York City. 1810–15.

Comment
Before the 19th century the only way to become a silversmith was by apprenticing oneself to a master. Many smiths had apprentices who, after learning basic techniques, were trusted with increasingly difficult tasks. Apprentices made parts or entire objects, yet their work was rarely acknowledged. This basket, a rare exception, is marked by both the apprentice Stephen Richard and his master Hugh Wishart, as maker and shop owner respectively.

Hints for Collectors
Although day-to-day activities in large silversmithing establishments were rarely recorded, collectors need to be sensitive to apprentice-master relationships in order to fully understand the silver they collect. This can sometimes be done by close and critical examination of the objects, which may bear traces of an apprentice's name or initials.

106 Modern bowl

Description
Rectangular body with straight flared sides curving outward to horizontal rim with molded edge and rounded corners. Long sides have raised panels extending from lip to base. Low molded pedestal of conforming shape.

Marks and Dimensions
"P" in circle and "PETER MÜLLER-MUNK/HANDWROUGHT/STERLING-SILVER/925/1000"; all stamped incuse on underside. Length: 7⁷⁄₁₆″. Width: 5¹⁄₁₆″. Height: 2⁷⁄₈″.

Maker, Locality, and Date
Peter Müller-Munk (1904–67), New York City. 1925–35.

Comment
The emphasis on mass production during the 19th century discouraged many people from becoming silversmiths; only a small number of craftsmen continued to produce silver objects for those individuals willing to pay the premium handwrought pieces brought over machine-made wares. The 20th century has seen a notable revival of interest in the craft of silversmithing. This bowl's visual appeal lies in its simple but strong lines and its textured surface.

Hints for Collectors
Peter Müller-Munk's work, especially notable for its excellent design and workmanship, is rare and likely to be expensive. Any silver object made in America during this century, whether by an individual craftsman or in a factory, must be marked "sterling." Collectors should always check for this mark on modern work; if it is not present, the object is most likely not silver. Objects made prior to the Civil War, however, were very rarely so marked.

Modern pierced bowl

Description
Low, oval, boat-shaped form. Rim ornamented with C-scrolls; widely flared ends decorated with stylized shells. Sides pierced overall with geometric shapes and floral motifs.

Marks and Dimensions
Lion and "G" each in clipped-corner square; anchor in rectangle; "STERLING/A 1998"; all stamped incuse on underside. Length: 8¼". Width: 5⅜". Height: 2½".

Maker, Locality, and Date
Gorham Company (1831–present), Providence. 1933–50.

Comment
Decorative piercing on early silver was relatively uncommon because each hole had to be laboriously cut out by hand using a tiny jeweler's saw. Thus, piercing was usually employed only when necessary, as on the top of a sugar or spice caster, in a brazier, or on any other object requiring holes. It was not until the mid-19th century, when fast and inexpensive machine stamping was perfected, that large quantities of silver objects were given pierced patterns solely for ornamental purposes.

Hints for Collectors
Late 19th- and 20th-century pierced silver baskets, bowls, dishes, compotes, and other forms are readily available for reasonable prices and make very interesting decorative objects for table or sideboard use. The most desirable pieces are elaborately pierced, marked by a well-known and respected silver company, and of substantial weight.

Victorian olive dish

Description
Low irregular oval form with textured curved sides. Leaf cluster atop one end.

Marks and Dimensions
Lion; anchor; "G"; "515 STERLING"; and cross in square; all stamped incuse on underside. Length: 6″. Width: 3½″. Height: 2″.

Maker, Locality, and Date
Gorham Company (1831–present), Providence. 1886.

Comment
Because silver can be polished to a brilliant reflective surface, silver objects are usually expected to appear smooth and shiny. Yet throughout history many other ways of finishing the metal—including gilding, blackening, and texturing—have created a variety of contrasting surfaces. The textured surface of this olive dish is a good illustration of this variety.

Hints for Collectors
At first glance, a neophyte collector might conclude that this olive dish has been severely battered and disfigured. Closer examination, however, makes it obvious that the bowl was intended to look as it does, its rough surface resembling that of the olives it was meant to contain. This is confirmed by a picture of the dish in the manufacturer's trade catalogue. Many silver objects of this period have textured or colored areas, which collectors should always take care to recognize, since misguided attempts to remove dents or to polish the surface would destroy the value of such a piece.

Victorian electroplated nut bowl

Description
Deep oval body with angled scalloped rim. Squirrel eating a nut seated on tree branch at higher end. Exterior of bowl ornamented with leafy boughs above single row of medallions and wave pattern below. Gilt interior.

Marks and Dimensions
"QUADRUPLE PLATE MERIDEN CONN." in circle surrounding "WILCOX SILVER PLATE C^O" in another circle enclosing 2 crossed hammers, all stamped incuse on underside. Height: 9¾". Length: 8¹³⁄₁₆". Width: 7¼".

Maker, Locality, and Date
Wilcox Silver Plate Company (1867–98), Meriden, Connecticut. c. 1880.

Comment
Late 19th-century nut bowls were usually designed so that their form and ornament provided clear indications of their intended contents. They were typically in the shape of a coconut shell, oak-tree log, or acorn, and frequently had applied decoration such as oak leaves, acorns, squirrels, or other appropriate motifs. Generally, realistic and sprightly ornament, such as the squirrel atop this bowl, makes an object more desirable.

Hints for Collectors
Because salted nuts have long been popular and salt is very corrosive, the interior of most nut bowls—like salt dishes themselves—were gilded to retard damage. Gilding that has completely worn away can be replaced by a competent restorer, but the pitting caused by salt is a more serious problem and an expensive one to remedy. If used, nut dishes should be thoroughly cleaned with warm water and mild dishwashing soap to remove salt residue.

110 Colonial footed cup or bowl

Description
Circular vessel with straight side and slightly flared rim. Convex
gadrooning around midsection; wider border of convex and
concave gadrooning at base. 3 scrolled legs with paw feet. "The
Gift of the Honorable Judge Davenport & was Formerly
belonging to the Honorable Mr. Secretary Addington October 18
1731" and "A. Cutler/1771" engraved on side, with unidentified
crest engraved twice.

Marks and Dimensions
"I•C" with fleur-de-lis below, all in shield-shaped outline, stamped
on outside under rim and on underside. Diameter: 3⅜″. Height:
2½″.

Maker, Locality, and Date
John Coney (1656–1722), Boston. 1700–10.

Comment
This small footed cup is a very unusual form for early American
silver, for while most cups have a curved flared side and a central
pedestal or foot rim, this example has a straight side and 3-toed
paws at the base of each scroll.

Hints for Collectors
John Coney, the maker of this small bowl, died in 1722, long
before its engraving was added. A silver object was often later
engraved to record ownership or the object's history. After
completing an object, a silversmith frequently scratched its
weight in an inconspicuous place. The original weight of this cup
—7 ounces 4 hundredweight—is engraved on the underside, yet
its present weight is 3 ounces 5 hundredweight. This loss can be
explained only in part by the friction of polishing and the later
engraving. Most of the difference might be attributable to the
loss of a lid.

111 Late Federal/early Victorian wirework cake or fruit basket

Description
Oval body with interlaced, outward-flared wirework sides; applied border of overlapping grape clusters, leaves, and tendrils on upper edge. Shallow, molded base with 2 narrow borders of undulating vines with grape clusters and leaves. 4 large pierced feet with flower-and-leaf decoration.

Marks and Dimensions
"B•GARDINER" and "NEW YORK" each in serrated arc; 3 pseudohallmarks (male bust in profile; "G"; and rampant lion), each in clipped-corner rectangle; all stamped under base. Length: 11¾". Width: 9⅞". Height: 4¾".

Maker, Locality, and Date
Baldwin Gardiner (dates unknown), New York City. 1827–46.

Comment
Cake or fruit baskets were very popular in the United States during the 19th century. While most had solid sides, a few were made with interlaced wirework sides to copy English models. Almost all wirework examples were made in New York City. Cake baskets were usually elaborately decorated with lush ornamental borders, most often grapevines. The lavishness and large number of these baskets indicate they occupied a prominent place on the American dining table.

Hints for Collectors
These baskets are readily available, so do not be satisfied with an average example having solid sides, a moderate amount of uninteresting decoration, and modest weight, or with one by a common maker. Seek out an unusual, finely made basket, such as this example.

Victorian electroplated fruit basket

Description
Large wire loop handle topped by stylized pierced foliage; connected to circular ring with curved side and floral decoration. Glass basket with undulating ruffled edge and orange foliate decoration on white background. 4 curved foliate feet.

Marks and Dimensions
"THE MERIDEN SILVER PLATE CO. QUADRUPLE PLATE" in circle enclosing lion holding urn, all stamped incuse on applied circular disk on underside. Height: 12¾". Diameter: 12".

Maker, Locality, and Date
Meriden Silver Plate Company (1869–98), Meriden, Connecticut. c. 1896.

Comment
The well-dressed late 19th-century dining room always had a fruit basket. The favorite type was made of silver, but if that was beyond the means of a household, electroplated examples were acceptable substitutes. As the century progressed, these amenities grew more elaborate, often having an abundance of naturalistic or stylized ornament added to a complex shape. Many incorporated multicolored ruffled glass baskets for even greater elegance.

Hints for Collectors
The glass baskets in silver or silver-plated frames were often broken, but collectors can purchase reproduction glass parts. While a frame with a modern glass basket is preferable to one without a basket, do not mistake a reproduction for a completely original piece, since it is less valuable. If a basket fits badly, is poorly decorated, and lacks wear, it is probably a reproduction.

113 Victorian electroplated fruit bowl

Description
Shallow circular frame with 3 clusters of birds and flowers. Baluster shaft having flared molded foot with knop below; 3 horizontal swags extend from knop to 3 cherubs serving as base. Figures wear gilt loincloths and hold gilt chain. Frame supports ribbed glass bowl with undulating ruffled lip; interior red, exterior white with border of gilt leaves and flowers. Cherub framed by foliage and holding book inscribed "For You" engraved on stand under glass bowl.

Marks and Dimensions
"QUADRUPLE PLATE MERIDEN, CONN." in circle surrounding "WILCOX SILVER PLATE C⁰" in another circle enclosing 2 crossed hammers and "2684"; all stamped incuse on underside. Height: 9¾". Diameter: 8¾".

Maker, Locality, and Date
Wilcox Silver Plate Company (1867–98), Meriden, Connecticut. c. 1886.

Comment
Fruit bowls and baskets symbolized plenty during an era of agricultural and industrial abundance. The most ornate have glass bowls that were frosted, engraved, or painted.

Hints for Collectors
This unusually ambitious fruit bowl is remarkable for its sculpted figures, contrasting gilding, and polychrome glass bowl. Because its vital design and excellent workmanship represent the best of the Victorian era, this object would complement any collection. The silver-plated stand is itself worthy of note, but the glass adds significantly to its value. Original glass bowls of this type are very difficult to replace because they are hard to fit; most modern copies are thick-walled and relatively coarse.

Victorian electroplated fruit bowl

Description
Low bowl-shaped frame composed of swag-shaped elements and stylized leaves and flowers; narrow fluted rim. 2 arched angular loop handles. Shallow circular bowl of cut and frosted glass. Supported by tapered molded shaft in center with 3 surrounding winged female monopodes. Low, circular, molded base with "CEK" engraved in script.

Marks and Dimensions
"SIMPSON, HALL, MILLER & CO." in circle surrounding "TREBLE/ PLATE" all in stamped raised letters on circular plaque applied to underside; "404" stamped incuse on underside. Height: 8¾". Width: 12". Diameter: 9¼".

Maker, Locality, and Date
Simpson, Hall, Miller & Company (1866–98), Wallingford, Connecticut. 1866–98.

Comment
The Victorian dining room, central to many a social occasion, was often used for the conspicuous display of wealth through luxurious table objects. During the late 19th century, dining rooms of the affluent overflowed with an abundance that was perhaps symbolized by the objects placed on the sideboard. Principal among them was the cake or fruit basket, always replete with food.

Hints for Collectors
Late 19th-century plated wares were made in great quantity, and stylish examples in good condition are readily available today. The serious collector can, with a moderate amount of study, assemble an impressive and varied collection.

Victorian electroplated butter dish and knife

Description
Spherical covered dish in frame. Cover engraved with bird in bough and encircling border; opens by swiveling down around bottom half. Removable colorless glass liner inside. Frame has arched loop handle ornamented with flowers; elaborate hinge pins for rotating lid; 2 hooks for knife. 2 curved triangular supports ornamented with flowers and leaves; lower ends have foliate brackets and meet in a small sphere. Low domed base with foliate border. Butter knife has wedge-shaped handle with stylized foliate decoration.

Marks and Dimensions
"MERIDEN B* COMPANY" in circle enclosing shield containing scales; "4978"; all stamped incuse on underside of base. Height: 12″. Width (including hooks): 10⅝″. Diameter: 5¾″.

Maker, Locality, and Date
Meriden Britannia Company (1852–98), Meriden, Connecticut. c. 1882.

Comment
Butter dishes varied from simple low receptacles to complex enclosed vessels like the one shown here. The most elaborate had stands with large quantities of ornament in the form of leaves, flowers, and animals, especially cows. These dishes were frequently fitted with a swiveling lid to keep flies away. Some were fitted with their own matching butter knife.

Hints for Collectors
Although the function of these vessels was fairly simple, the best of them were quite complex and made of many parts. Carefully compare the decoration and method of fabrication on all parts. Rough unfinished areas may indicate that a part has broken off.

Federal bowl and French stand

Description
Circular low-domed lid with spherical finial. Circular container with straight upper portion and tapered lower portion. Supported in framework of 3 horizontal rings and topped by hinged pierced bail handle; 3 long incurved legs terminating in cloven hooves below acanthus leaves. Stand ornamented with 9 decorative mounts including female nudes on dolphins, satyr masks, and winged cupids holding doves.

Marks and Dimensions
"E. LOWNES" in rectangle and incuse fleur-de-lis, stamped on underside of bowl. Height (to finial): 7⁹⁄₁₆″. Diameter: 6⅛″.

Maker, Locality, and Date
Bowl: Edward Lownes (1792–1834), Philadelphia. 1817–34.
Stand: Unknown. Paris. 1815–25.

Comment
19th-century American silversmiths imported large quantities of European objects for their customers. This object's elaborate frame, though unmarked, is French. It probably held a glass bowl when Lownes acquired it for his shop inventory, but he replaced this with a silver container. His bowl is absolutely plain, relying on the exquisitely detailed mounts of the framework for visual accent.

Hints for Collectors
At a quick glance this bowl and stand might both be attributed to Edward Lownes. Close examination, however, reveals that the stand is unlike anything known to have been made by American silversmiths. The exceptionally high quality and minute detail of the ornamental mounts, as well as the frame's light weight, indicate a French origin. American examples were invariably heavier and less detailed.

117 Victorian electroplated cake basket

Description
Shallow oval bowl with low straight-sided edge tapered inward.
Flat horizontal lip with 8 equidistant pegs, 2 supporting narrow,
semicircular, hinged handle with dog's head on top, and 2
supporting small bird. Bowl interior ornamented with 4 foliate
panels. Pedestal of 4 straight flared legs with stretchers, each leg
topped with male bust and foliate rosette; free-swinging loop
with bird suspended from center. 4 hairy paw feet.

Marks and Dimensions
"MF'D & PLATED BY/REED & BARTON" stamped incuse on bottom of
one foot, "DESIGN/MARCH 30, 1869" on another, and "2514" on
another. Height: 13¾". Length: 11¼". Width: 8⅝".

Maker, Locality, and Date
Reed & Barton (1840–present), Taunton, Massachusetts. c. 1869.

Comment
Mass production allowed for the fulfillment of the demands for
fashionable goods by the growing, affluent middle class. Many of
the objects displayed disparate combinations of ornament on
unusual forms, as seen in this cake basket, with its dog's head,
perched birds, classical busts, and paw feet.

Hints for Collectors
Most late 19th-century plated wares are not marked. Those that
do bear a maker's mark often have an applied disk on which the
name is impressed. This basket is atypically marked on the
underside of the feet, which should caution collectors to carefully
examine every part of an object for markings. Most makers used
standard types of marks and placed them in common locations on
an object, but exceptions do occur.

Teapots, Coffeepots, Pitchers, and Related Objects

For centuries silver has proven itself particularly suitable for household objects that are both functional and ornamental. Silver's plastic nature allows it to be worked into a limitless range of shapes; its brilliant reflective surface, its ability to accept many kinds of ornament, and the universal respect it commands have all combined to make it the preferred metal for affluent and fashion-conscious householders.

Teapots and Coffeepots

Perhaps no other drinkable liquids are served as often in silver pouring vessels as tea and coffee. These beverages were introduced in Europe and America during the 17th century, and the vessels used for them have not changed substantially in the 300 years since they first evolved. The drinking of tea became a polite art early on, one that involved an elaborate etiquette and an extensive array of objects. Coffee drinking also required numerous utensils and serving pieces, which were often made of silver.

Before the Revolution, the great expense of both tea and silver was reflected in the typically small size of teapots and the limited number of companion objects used with them. After the war, teapots and coffeepots began to be made in sets with matching sugar bowls, cream pots, slop bowls, and other items. Very expensive sets included a kettle-on-stand with a burner, which supplied extra hot water as needed. The vogue for large, highly decorated ensembles—sometimes with a matching tray measuring as much as a yard across—reached its zenith during the late 19th century.

Pitchers, Jugs, and Other Vessels

Silver and silver-plated vessels were also used for cold liquids. In the 18th century the few such containers were usually called cider or beer jugs. Made in increasing quantities in the 19th century, they proved suitable for a wide variety of beverages. These objects frequently served as presentation pieces to mark events ranging from horse races to retirement. By the late 19th century, tilting ice-water pitchers had become popular; these were fitted into elaborate frames that allowed the pitcher to swivel easily and pour forth its contents.

Other silver pouring vessels were made for highly specialized purposes and are thus considerably less common than teapots, coffeepots, and pitchers. Among these are pap boats, made for infants, and spout cups, made for invalids; both types had specially designed spouts that made it easier for the user to drink food or medicine. Sauce or gravy boats, sometimes called butter boats in the 18th century, were usually made in pairs. 19th- and 20th-century examples were generally accompanied by a ladle, even though the form always had a spout and a tray to catch the drippings.

Although silver has been less commonly used for tableware since the Second World War, domestic silver objects are still being produced by talented and sensitive craftsmen. These works continue to point out the metal's beguiling nature and sensuous visual appeal.

Late Colonial/Federal sauceboat

Description
Bulbous oval body with incurved neck, flared scalloped rim, and arched spout. Freestanding double-C-shaped handle with acanthus leaf at top. 3 C-shaped legs with scallop shells at juncture with body and as feet. "TSC" engraved in script on side.

Marks and Dimensions
"I•DAVID" in rectangle stamped on underside. Height: 4⅝″. Length: 7″. Width: 3½″.

Maker, Locality, and Date
John David (1736–94), Philadelphia. 1760–80.

Comment
Sauceboats were sometimes called butter boats in the 18th century because they held melted butter as well as sauces or gravies. The example shown here, one of a pair, was made for Thomas and Sarah Cooch of Cooch's Bridge, Delaware. Like this family, many Americans who lived in out-of-the-way places wanted fashionable silver; they often sought the services of a silversmith in the nearest major city. Urban centers, with a relatively large proportion of inhabitants receptive to the latest fashions, provided the best setting in which silversmiths could pursue their careers and develop new styles.

Hints for Collectors
Sauceboats were made in all major silversmithing centers during the 18th and 19th centuries, and their popularity in the past makes it easy for collectors to find good examples today. However, sauceboats made in areas other than the Northeast are difficult to find and generally more expensive.

119 Late Colonial sauceboat

Description
Deep oval body with outwardly curved scalloped lip and flared spout. S-shaped handle with scrolled spurs. 3 cabriole legs with shell-shaped ends. "M/I M" (for James and Molly Murdaugh) engraved in block letters on underside.

Marks and Dimensions
"I•M" in rectangle stamped 3 times on underside. Height: 4½". Length: 7". Width: 4⅟₁₆".

Maker, Locality, and Date
James Murphree (d. 1782), Norfolk, Virginia. 1758–75.

Comment
James Murphree worked in Norfolk, Virginia, during the late 18th century. Although only a small amount of his silver is known today, these objects testify to his considerable ability. In spite of the large clientele he had during his lifetime, Murphree was not discovered by modern scholars until the 1970s.

Hints for Collectors
Collectors should always seek to unravel an object's history. This is made difficult, however, by the fact that many silversmiths who worked in this country in earlier centuries have not yet been identified. Do not blithely ascribe a mark, such as the "I•M" on this example, to a well-known and frequently published silversmith, such as John McMullin or Joseph Moulton; when you explore the possibilities, you may discover that the mark belongs to a previously unknown craftsman. At the same time, be careful of buying objects that a dealer has assigned to an otherwise unknown maker; such attributions may lead to paying higher prices than necessary.

Description
Sauceboat: Low oval body with incurved neck and undulating, flared lip. Arched, outward-curved spout. C-shaped handle. Rectangular foot scrolled and lobed. Body entirely covered with hammered facets and ornamented with shells, leaves, fish, and seaweed. Tray: Irregular rectangle with shallow well and wide brim. Ornamented with shells, fish, and seaweed on hammered background. "CGG" in script and "1911" engraved on underside of sauceboat and tray.

Marks and Dimensions
"Martelé" over 3 pseudohallmarks (lion and "G"; each in an octagon; anchor in shield topped by spread eagle), ".9584/LKF" (".9584/LKG" on tray)/SPAULDING & CO./CHICAGO."; all stamped incuse on underside of sauceboat and tray. Sauceboat height: 5¾"; length: 8¾"; width: 5". Tray length: 9½"; width: 7¼"; height: ⅞".

Maker, Locality, and Date
Gorham Company (1831–present), Providence. 1911. Retailed by Spaulding & Company, Chicago.

Comment
Martelé was a select line of silver objects produced by Gorham in the early 20th century. These objects, although utilitarian, were perceived by the company as artwork, and fewer than 5000 pieces were made. They were characterized by sinuous outlines, undulating, hand-hammered surfaces, and naturalistic ornament.

Hints for Collectors
Martelé, always finely executed and heavy in weight, is among the most desirable American silver from the early part of this century. Objects in this pattern are unusually high in silver content, having 950 parts per 1000, rather than 925.

Victorian pap boat

Description
Low oval body with bellied sides and rolled rim. Long flared
spout. Small, S-shaped handle. Repoussé border of alternating
flowers and leaf clusters around sides; oval reserve under spout.

Marks and Dimensions
"BAILEY & Co." stamped incuse and 3 pseudohallmarks (lion in
rectangle, stamped 3 times; "S" in oval; and American shield), all
on underside. Length: 6½". Width: 3¼". Height: 1¾".

Maker, Locality, and Date
Bailey & Company (1846–78), Philadelphia. 1846–78.

Comment
Pap, or bread softened with milk, was fed to infants and invalids.
Pap boats, also referred to as "sick cups," were popular from
about the mid-18th through the mid-19th centuries. Made by a
number of noted silversmiths from Boston to New Orleans, they
were usually quite simple and undecorated, although there is a
known example with 3 short cabriole legs, and another with an
ornamented spoonlike handle. The example shown here is typical
except for its repoussé ornament, which was popular on mid-
19th-century American silver.

Hints for Collectors
The oval reserve on the side of this pap boat would normally
contain the engraved initials of the original owner. If a reserve is
empty, the initials have probably been erased; you can tell this
by looking for a slight depression and thinning of the metal in
that area, as well as smearing, excessive shininess, or partial
erasure of the ornament around the reserve. Since none of these
signs is present on this pap boat, the object was most likely
never engraved.

Late Colonial/Federal cream pot on pedestal

Description
Circular double-bellied body with tapered neck and flared gadrooned lip. Arched flared spout. S-shaped, asymmetrically scrolled handle. Circular molded pedestal with worn gadrooning on foot rim. "EE" engraved in script on side; "T/IS" engraved in block letters under pedestal.

Marks and Dimensions
"Myers" in script in conforming outline, stamped twice on underside. Height: 4⅞". Width: 4⅛". Diameter: 1⅛".

Maker, Locality, and Date
Myer Myers (1723–95), New York City. 1750–85.

Comment
Pyriform, or double-bellied, silver vessels for serving tea and coffee were very popular in America during the 1760s and 1770s. Although coffeepots, teapots, sugar bowls, and cream pots were often similar in shape, these objects were rarely made in matching sets. This cream pot is typical, with its one-piece body and its added pedestal, handle, and gadrooned borders. A few New England cream pots of this general type also have added spouts. The handle on this example, a complex sculpted composition of scrolls, is exceptional, since most handles were a simple S-shaped strap.

Hints for Collectors
Cream pots are readily available, and there are many interesting varieties. The most desirable are those made by a recognized craftsman, especially those with unusual, expertly worked features, such as the asymmetrical rococo handle and double belly of the example shown here.

123 Modern Art Nouveau electroplated pitcher

Description
Bulbous body with outward-flared lip and spout, sinuous floral ornament, and incurved neck and base. C-shaped handle ornamented with abstract foliage. Flared circular foot rim with molded edge.

Marks and Dimensions
"DERBY SILVER COMPANY" in circle enclosing anchor over crown; "PAT. JUN. 14/1904"; all stamped incuse on underside. Height: 8¾". Width: 7⅝". Diameter: 6¼".

Maker, Locality, and Date
Derby Silver Company (1873–98), Derby, Connecticut. c. 1904.

Comment
The increasing complexity and elaboration of late 19th-century household objects eventually spawned a reaction against ornamentation among some artisans and tastemakers. By the turn of the century, a simplified, elegant style, known as Art Nouveau, began to prevail. Regardless of material, all Art Nouveau objects have smooth, flowing lines, and many are sparingly ornamented with sinuous, naturalistic plant forms. The Derby Silver Company, which joined International Silver in 1898, maintained its factory in Derby, Connecticut until 1933; the mark that appears on this object was used from about 1900 to 1904.

Hints for Collectors
Art Nouveau was short-lived in America, and relatively few silver examples of the style were made. Plated wares are especially scarce. Do not be dissuaded from acquiring an example with badly worn plating, as long as the price reflects its poor condition.

Victorian pitcher

Description

Pear-shaped body with arched flared spout. Slender, tapered, S-shaped handle. Low, domed, circular pedestal. Ornamented with repoussé vines, flowers, and leaves. Engraved in Hebrew "This cup is a gift sent to the man who in his generosity has done a thousand favors"; and in English script "Presented/Mr. B. M. Bettman, G.N.A./by the Brothers of Gan Eden Lodge, No. 24. I.O.B.B./New Orleans/as a token of Respect, Brotherly Love and Harmony./January 22, 1856. (5616)"; all in a reserve opposite handle. Also in English script "PRESENTED TO HIS/FIRST GRANDSON/JEOFFREY BETTMAN/FROM HIS GRANDPA/CINCINNATI JUNE 26TH 1888" under spout.

Marks and Dimensions

"A. RASCH" in rectangle stamped on underside. Height: 11".
Width: 8¼". Diameter: 5".

Maker, Locality, and Date

Anthony Rasch (born c. 1778–1858), New Orleans. c. 1856.

Comment

Rasch was an accomplished Bavarian silversmith who lived and worked in Philadelphia until about 1821, when he moved to New Orleans, residing there until his death. Like many silversmiths who moved south, he apparently retained his northern ties, importing northern silver for resale and making objects in the same style in his workshop.

Hints for Collectors

Although Rasch worked in New Orleans for about 35 years, little of his silver is known. The few objects documented to his time in Philadelphia are extremely fine. This pitcher is of particular interest because it was made in New Orleans, and also because of its Hebrew inscription, unusual in American silver.

Victorian ewer

Description
Tall pear-shaped body with arched, flared lip. Loop handle with leaf decoration and spur at top. Flared circular pedestal. Lip, body, and pedestal decorated with clusters of leaves and flowers.

Marks and Dimensions
"GARNER & WINCHESTER" and "LEX. KY." each in a rectangle, stamped on outer rim of base. Height: 12⅜". Width: 7½". Diameter: 6".

Maker, Locality, and Date
Eli C. Garner & Daniel F. Winchester (1842–62), Lexington, Kentucky. 1842–62.

Comment
American silversmithing first became established along the Atlantic Coast, and some northeastern cities still retain their importance as major silversmithing centers. During the 19th century, however, other cities in the South and Midwest joined the ranks as important silvermaking centers, among them New Orleans and, somewhat later, Chicago. Besides Garner & Winchester, Lexington boasted several much-admired silversmiths, including Asa Blanchard and George W. Stewart. Garner & Winchester made many large pitchers, some of which were used as thoroughbred racing trophies.

Hints for Collectors
Ewers made in Lexington were usually marked on the outer rim of the base, unlike those made in the Northeast, which were marked under the base. Garner & Winchester's large ewers are very desirable because of their high quality and their southern origin. They generally cost more than common examples from the Northeast.

Early Victorian ewer

Description
Slender urn-shaped body with incurved neck and arched,
outward-flared spout. Applied scrolled border on lip; body
decorated with landscape scene of houses amid trees, shrubs, and
rocks. Elaborate C-shaped handle with foliate spurs at top and
along length. Tall circular pedestal with molded foliate borders
and floral clusters. Reserve under spout engraved "NYSAS/
Awarded to/H.T.E. Foster, Lakeland/1ˢᵗ Premium on Farms/
January/1849."

Marks and Dimensions
"G&H" in rectangle, "G&H" vertically in oval, and "1849" in
diamond, all stamped on underside. Height: 12⅝″. Width: 7⅝″.
Diameter: 5¾″.

Maker, Locality, and Date
William Gale & Nathaniel Hayden (1847–50), New York City.
c. 1849.

Comment
The New York State Agricultural Society presented this ewer to
Henry Ten Eyck Foster for having the best-tended farm. The
agricultural and mercantile societies that flourished during the
19th century were devoted to the encouragement of excellence in
farming and manufacturing. They sponsored fairs and
expositions and juried exhibitions of livestock, produce,
furniture, clothing, and other objects. Even whole farms could be
submitted for consideration.

Hints for Collectors
Presentation silver could be of great size and value, but awards
presented for more modest purposes were frequently in the form
of household objects that were customized by their inscriptions.

127 Victorian toby jug

Description
Vessel in shape of man from waist up, with tricornered hat, shoulderlength hair, and cape; right hand holds cup against chest. Tapered loop handle attached at back of head and small of back. "To Susan Dows/Dec. 9, 1886/from Enoch Pratt of Baltimore" engraved in script on underside.

Marks and Dimensions
"A. E. WARNER" and "112" each in rectangle stamped on underside. Height: 5¾". Width: 5⅜".

Maker, Locality, and Date
Andrew E. Warner, Jr. (1813–96), Baltimore. c. 1886.

Comment
Toby jugs, usually in the form of a stout man, were popular in England and the United States in the 19th century. Examples were made by numerous American potteries and were typically earthenware with a mottled brown glaze. While silver, a precious metal with fashionable overtones, usually inspired craftsmen working in other media, in this instance the reverse seems to have been true. Enoch Pratt was a well-known merchant and philanthropist, 1886 marked the opening of his famous Free Library in Baltimore.

Hints for Collectors
This silver toby jug is an excellent example of an object specially commissioned by an individual who knew what he wanted. As such, it reflects both the abilities of the maker and the character of the merchant who ordered it. Some people might shy away from such an unusual object, but perceptive collectors will take the time to discover the merits of out-of-the-ordinary articles.

128 Federal presentation pitcher

Description
Upright bulbous body with tapered ends slightly flared at lip and base. Triangular spout at lip opposite C-shaped handle. Engraved on side "PRESENTED/to the/Rev.ᵈ Joseph McKean./by a number of his Friends/&/late Parishioners of/MILTON,/as a testimonial of their affection,/and to hold in remembrance how deeply/they regret his separation/from them./1804."

Marks and Dimensions
"REVERE" in rectangle stamped twice on underside. Height: 6½". Width: 7¼". Diameter: 4⅛".

Maker, Locality, and Date
Paul Revere, Jr. (1735–1818), Boston. c. 1804.

Comment
Silver has traditionally been considered the ideal medium for objects commemorating notable events or expressing thanks to individuals. The sizes and purposes of these presentation pieces varied greatly: National heroes received monumental urns and vases underwritten by the public, while schoolchildren received small silver medallions for excelling in their studies. Such objects are generally inscribed with the names of those who commissioned them and those for whom they were made, the event they commemorate, and a date. This pitcher clearly notes the sense of loss felt by a group of parishioners at the departure of their minister.

Hints for Collectors
Presentation silver objects are historically valuable documents that deserve the same care and consideration given a rare and fragile manuscript. Engraved inscriptions should therefore never be removed or altered for any reason.

Victorian pitcher

Description
Removable low-domed lid with acorn finial and spout cover. Low pear-shaped body. Tapered triangular spout. C-shaped handle with spur at top and 2 ivory ferrules.

Marks and Dimensions
"GALE & WILLIS/447 BROOME ST/NEW-YORK/925 STERLING"; "G&W" vertically in rectangle; circle; and "1859" in diamond; all stamped incuse on underside. Height: 5¼". Width: 7". Diameter: 5⅛".

Maker, Locality, and Date
William Gale & John R. Willis (1859–62), New York City. c. 1859.

Comment
Silver was frequently made into serving vessels for hot food and drink. Since the metal conducts heat very quickly, the parts of an object that were handled had to be insulated. In the 18th century, wooden handles and finials protected the hands; in the 19th century, silver handles became common and ivory ferrules were used as insulators.

Hints for Collectors
Collectors generally prefer to pay higher prices for decorated rather than plain objects; and ordinarily, a simple silver pitcher like this one would be fairly modestly priced. However, the example shown here has several interesting features. One of these is the removable lid with spout cover; lids were normally hinged to vessels. The incorporation of a date in the mark is typical of this maker but otherwise uncommon. Astute collectors are aware that simple objects, when as well made and pleasing as this pitcher, have much to recommend them.

Colonial spout cup

Description
Circular, molded, high-domed lid with belted knopped finial. Circular pear-shaped body. Slender, tapered, S-shaped handle with volute terminals, row of tapered beading along length, and spur on spine. Tapered S-shaped spout affixed to body at 90° angle to handle. Low circular pedestal molded and flared. "MC" engraved in script on body, and "SM" in block letters under base.

Marks and Dimensions
"IE" with crown above and cross below, all stamped in shield-shaped outline on side between handle and spout. Height: 4¾". Width: 3¾". Diameter (base): 2¹⁄₁₆".

Maker, Locality, and Date
John Edwards (1671–1746), Boston. 1699–1725.

Comment
Spout cups are named for the long slender spout at the base, through which sick and bedridden people could easily sip medicinal fluids. The handle was always at a right angle to the spout for ease in manipulating the cup. The few known early examples lack elaborate decoration, befitting their use at a private sickbed. This cup was originally owned by Sarah Marshall, whose initials are engraved on the underside. It was used for several generations, as evidenced by the initials of Mary Cushing, her granddaughter, on its side.

Hints for Collectors
Spout cups were usually fitted with lids to prevent spillage, but many lids have been lost. The conformation of a cup's lip will tell you if an example originally had a lid: Those intended for a lid have a straight-sided neck, usually with a molded edge, while uncovered ones have a flared lip.

Federal tankard

Description
Hinged, molded, domed lid; thumbpiece pierced with scrolls and shells. Tapered double-C-shaped handle with shield-shaped terminal. Circular pear-shaped body. Short triangular spout. Circular pedestal flared and molded. "M•NEWBOLD" engraved in block letters on handle.

Marks and Dimensions
"I•NR" in rectangle, the N and R conjoined, stamped twice on underside. Height: 8¹¹⁄₁₆". Width: 7¾". Diameter: 6⅝".

Maker, Locality, and Date
Joseph Richardson, Jr. & Nathaniel Richardson (1777–1790), Philadelphia. c. 1787.

Comment
For women as well as men, the tankard was one of the most popular drinking vessels in 18th-century America, as indicated by this bellied example originally owned by Martha Newbold. The form fell from favor about 1800, and tankards were made infrequently after that time. During the 19th century, many earlier tankards were destroyed to be remade into more up-to-date objects, and others, like this example, were converted from drinking to pouring vessels with the addition of a spout.

Hints for Collectors
Be cautious when considering the purchase of an 18th-century American silver tankard. Many that were converted to pitchers in the 19th century have since been restored to their original function by removing the spout—creating the impression that the tankard was never altered. That restoration, often cleverly disguised by careful soldering and sometimes by electroplating, will substantially lower the cost of a tankard.

Description
Circular, molded, domed lid with naturalistic leaf-shaped thumbpiece. Elaborate S-shaped handle with stylized naturalistic volutes, molding, and leafage. Elongated pear-shaped body. Long, curved, covered spout. Circular base stepped and molded. Side of body engraved with coat of arms and crest (of Clarkson family of New York) within foliate mantling.

Marks and Dimensions
"Myers" in script within conforming outline stamped on underside. Height: 11¾". Width: 11". Diameter: 7¾".

Maker, Locality, and Date
Myer Myers (1723–95), New York City. c. 1765.

Comment
Large silver vessels specifically for pouring liquids were not common in America until after the Revolution. Examples from the 18th century, such as cream pots, are typically small and sparsely decorated. Even though large ewers, called ale or beer jugs, were made in quantity in England before the Colonies' independence, they were not as popular here until the 19th century. The few pre-Revolutionary American examples, church flagons excepted, all seem to have originated in or around the New York area.

Hints for Collectors
Although quite rare, large ewers were occasionally made in America as early as the mid-18th century. Because of their great value, such objects should be carefully scrutinized to certify authenticity. The large size, ambitious form, elaborate ornament, documentation to original owner, as well as rarity would make this ewer a very desirable addition to any collection of American silver objects.

133 Late Colonial coffeepot

Description
Circular domed lid with turned finial; shell- and scroll-shaped hinge socket. C-shaped wooden handle with spur at top. Tall bellied body. Tapered S-shaped spout decorated with stylized acanthus leaves. Low, molded, circular foot rim. "D. Ravenel./ 1776" engraved in script on underside.

Marks and Dimensions
"AP" in rectangle stamped 4 times on underside. Height: 11″. Width: 8⅝″. Diameter: 4⅜″.

Maker, Locality, and Date
Alexander Petrie (d. 1768), Charleston, South Carolina. c. 1767.

Comment
Alexander Petrie was a very fine craftsman, and like many 18th-century goldsmiths, he amassed a comfortable estate for retirement through discipline, frugality, and wise investments. At the time of his death, his obituary stated that he "had acquired a handsome fortune . . . and had some time ago retired from business." Even though men like Petrie were thoroughly trained in a proud tradition, many saw the objects they made primarily as the means to achieving a gentlemanly retirement.

Hints for Collectors
This coffeepot, an excellent example of early American silver, has added appeal because the name of its original owner is engraved on the underside. Although the handle has been restored, this pot would command a premium if it were available for purchase. Its southern origin, widely respected maker, documented original owner, and visual appeal contribute to its desirability and value.

Federal rococo coffeepot

Description
Hinged, circular, molded lid with high dome and gadrooned edge; large flower-shaped finial. Tall, double-bellied body. Tapered S-shaped spout with leaf-and-shell ornament. Double-C-shaped wooden handle with spur at top, fitted into silver sockets decorated with shells and scrolls. Circular pedestal flared and molded with gadrooned border. "MM" in script on side of body.

Marks and Dimensions
"JA" in script in rectangle stamped 3 times under base. Height: 12¾". Width: 10". Diameter: 5".

Maker, Locality, and Date
Joseph Anthony (1762–1814), Philadelphia. 1783–1800.

Comment
During the late 18th century, American silver objects were almost always made with a preponderance of curved lines, following the rococo style of the period. It was believed at this time that any object had to incorporate one or more S-shaped lines—called the line of beauty—to be visually appealing. This coffeepot, with its S-shaped spout, double-bellied body, double-C-shaped handle, and molded lid and base, is among the most elaborate examples of this rococo style. Such pots reached the zenith of their popularity during the 1760s.

Hints for Collectors
Double-bellied Philadelphia coffeepots are among the most desirable objects of 18th-century American hollowware. The form derives closely from English and Irish prototypes, and sometimes the only differences between American and European examples are the makers' marks. Examine such coffeepots carefully, since American examples are much more valuable.

Victorian repoussé teapot

Description
Hinged circular lid with low dome, stylized foliate ornament, and asymmetrical leafy finial. Tall baluster-shaped body covered with repoussé ornament, including leaves, people, animals, and buildings, as well as vermicelli patterning. Square handle with foliate decoration, ivory ferrules, and ram's head at top. Tapered S-shaped spout with foliate ornament. Circular flared pedestal with foliate ornament. Crest (of Pratt family of Maryland) engraved in reserve on one side; "To Isaac Pratt Jr., from the Weymouth Iron Co. June 26th 1854" in script under pedestal.

Marks and Dimensions
"S.KIRK & SON" incuse and "11.OZ" in rectangle stamped on edge of pedestal. Height: 11¼". Width: 9". Diameter: 4⅝".

Maker, Locality, and Date
Samuel Kirk & Son (1815–1979), Baltimore. c. 1854.

Comment
The so-called repoussé pattern has become synonymous with the name of Samuel Kirk. This style of decoration, which enjoyed a brief heyday in the mid-18th century, again became popular in the early 19th century. While many silversmiths made repoussé objects, Kirk was the principal producer of them, making huge quantities throughout the 19th and 20th centuries. The pattern is still favored by both the general public and collectors of antique silver.

Hints for Collectors
While most repoussé decoration depicts generic leaves and flowers, some variants include specific plants. A few objects were decorated with landscapes; those containing Oriental figures are of special interest to collectors.

Late Colonial repoussé kettle-on-stand

Description
Large, double-bellied tapered kettle-on-stand. Hinged bail handle with foliate scrolls, wooden insulator, and scrolled foliate mounts. Low domed lid with flared edge and artichoke finial. Body and S-shaped spout decorated with asymmetrical repoussé scrolls, leaves, shells, flowers, and animals; tip of spout in shape of bird's head. Low circular foot ring fits into circular base with 3 S-shaped leaf-decorated legs having shell feet; 3 pendant aprons pierced and elaborately ornamented. Lower framework supporting removable spirit lamp. Coat of arms and crest (of Plumstead family of Philadelphia) engraved on both sides of pot.

Marks and Dimensions
"IR" stamped in rectangle; leafy scroll stamped incuse; both appear twice on underside of kettle and once on underside of spirit lamp. Kettle height: 11¹¹⁄₁₆″; width: 11⅛″; diameter: 8⅝″. Stand height: 4¼″; diameter: 5⅝″.

Maker, Locality, and Date
Joseph Richardson, Sr. (1711–84), Philadelphia. 1745–55.

Comment
This complex, finely detailed kettle-on-stand is one of the most exemplary pieces of American silver. A veritable encyclopedia of silversmithing techniques, it incorporates the most ambitious cast, chased, engraved, and repoussé ornament. Only one other comparable American example is known.

Hints for Collectors
Ambitious and elaborate objects such as this kettle-on-stand provide a wealth of information for the student of American silver. Although silver of this quality is not often found, it is an excellent reference for comparison with other pieces.

137

English George III fused-plated hot-water urns

Description
Oval domed lid with spherical finial. Oval urn-shaped container with ribbed rim and incurved upper section above Greek-key border. 2 female heads near top, each surrounded by hinged loop handle. Curved cylindrical spigot with ivory-tipped petcock near narrow base. Slender tapered pedestal above rectangular molded base with incurved sides. 4 spherical feet. Engraved foliate wreath above spigot enclosing script initials "WJL" (of William and Julia Ludlow of New York). Interior fitted with removable tube of tinned sheet iron with separate cover holding solid iron rod.

Marks and Dimensions
Unmarked. Left height: 18¾"; length: 12½"; width: 11⅝". Right height: 13½"; length: 8¾"; width: 8⅛".

Maker, Locality, and Date
Unknown. England. 1800–10.

Comment
A hot-water urn was a fashionable accoutrement for the tea table. A heated iron rod was placed inside, providing a ready and long-lasting supply of hot water for tea. No plated American examples from before the mid-19th century are known, and although many English urns of the period were imported, few can be documented to original American ownership.

Hints for Collectors
These 2 urns, employing neoclassical motifs, are fine examples of their type. Even more interesting is the fact that the initials of the original owners are engraved on the urns. These urns still remain in the family, so their full history is known, a rare occurrence that adds to the interest and desirability of any piece.

Federal tea and coffee set

Description
Left to right: Bulbous slop bowl with ram's head at each side, on triangular plinth. Lidded hemispherical sugar bowl with 3 cast ram's heads, one atop each of 3 long, curved legs, set on triangular plinth with seated dog. Bulbous cream pot with flared spout and curved handle tapered to point at top, on triangular plinth. Coffeepot (and teapot, not shown) with hinged, circular, incurved lid with flat top; finial shaped like bunch of berries. Bulbous body slightly tapered in center; border of grape clusters and leaf swags on shoulder above border of interlocking ovals, stars, and leaves. Cylindrical, tapered, curved spout with animal-head tip. Wooden handle either angular (coffeepot) or C-shaped (teapot), with acanthus leaf at top; fitted into scrolled leafy silver sockets. Flared circular pedestal set on triangular plinth with incurved sides and engraved leafy border. 3 spherical feet. Bodies of all engraved with matching ornamental borders and crest and motto "LUX VENIT AB ALTO" (Light comes from on high) of Dallas family of Philadelphia.

Marks and Dimensions
"CHAUDRON'S & RASCH" and "STER•AMERI•MAN" each in S-shaped outline stamped on underside of plinths. Slop bowl height: 6¼"; diameter: 6¼". Sugar bowl height: 10¾"; diameter: 5⅞". Cream pot height: 7¼"; width: 5½"; diameter: 3⅝". Coffeepot height: 10"; width: 12⅝"; diameter: 6⅜". Teapot height: 9¾"; width: 10⅞"; diameter: 6".

Maker, Locality, and Date
Simon Chaudron & Anthony Rasch (1809–12), Philadelphia. 1809–12.

Comment
This 5-piece tea and coffee set is one of the most exotic of its period. The sugar bowl, derived from ancient Roman long-legged

censers, is particularly interesting, and the elaborate, realistic animal heads stem from the same source. During the first 2 decades of the 19th century, Philadelphia was the United States' largest and most cosmopolitan city, and some of the most vital and exuberant neoclassical American silver was made there.

Hints for Collectors

Clarity of outline and finely executed ornament—desirable features in any object—combine to make this set a strong, evocative expression of the tastes and values of its makers and original owners. When made in sets, teapots and coffeepots were almost always very much alike. Keeping this in mind, a careful comparison of the wooden handles on these 2 pots revealed that the teapot's handle was broken or lost, and replaced without any concern for accuracy. This unfortunate oversight lowers the value of this otherwise exceptional set.

Numerous East Coast centers—notably Boston, New York, and especially Philadelphia—made fine and ambitious neoclassical silver. Today, collectors of neoclassical American silver seek out objects that employ a great deal of specific animal, human, and mythological ornamentation. Objects with a great quantity of lion monopodes, eagle finials, human-mask handles, and similar motifs are generally more desirable, and collectors should be prepared to pay substantial premiums for silver of this type. Examples that have only stylized leaf and plant decoration, while also appealing, are not nearly so desirable.

Federal tea and coffee set

Description
Left to right: Straight-sided oval hot-water pot (and matching teapot, not shown) with pierced gallery, pineapple finial, straight spout, and carved wooden handle. Urn-shaped slop bowl with square plinth. Urn-shaped sugar bowl with removable lid has urn-shaped finial, pierced gallery, and square plinth. Coffeepot has oval arched lid with incurved sides and pineapple finial. Oval urn-shaped body with incurved beaded shoulder and pierced gallery encircling lip. Tapered S-shaped spout with beaded borders along top and bottom. Tapered C-shaped wooden handle with carved acanthus leaf at top; fitted into cylindrical silver sockets. Circular flared pedestal with beaded border and low square platform. "AE" engraved in script in foliate mantle on side. Urn-shaped cream pot with flared spout, curved strap handle, and square plinth. Not shown: U-shaped sugar tongs with tapered flat arms and oval tips. Set of 12 teaspoons with rounded handles.

Marks and Dimensions
"J•R" in rectangle stamped on underside of hollowware and on back of flatware. Hot-water pot height: 5⅞"; length: 11½"; width: 4¼". Teapot height: 5¼"; length: 10¾"; width: 3⅞". Slop bowl height: 5¾"; diameter: 6⅜". Sugar bowl height: 10½"; diameter: 4⅜". Coffeepot height: 13"; length: 12½"; width: 4½". Cream pot height: 7"; length: 5"; width: 2¾". Sugar tongs length: 6"; width: 2¼". Teaspoon length: 5⅝".

Maker, Locality, and Date
Joseph Richardson, Jr. (1752–1831), Philadelphia. c. 1795.

Comment
By the late 18th century, drinking tea had been codified to the extent that utensils were made in complete matching sets. Late

18th-century examples were usually urn-shaped, loosely reflecting ancient Greek and Roman styles. Some had fluted bodies, but most were plain with ornamented borders. Pierced borders were occasionally used, principally in the Delaware Valley. Despite regional variations, tea sets from this era were generally very similar.

Hints for Collectors

Tea and coffee sets were often quite large; this set, for example, consists of 19 objects. Unfortunately, many sets have been broken up. While the separate elements of tea services are often collected in their own right, these objects are of greater historical interest and monetary value when they remain together. An interesting feature of this unusually large tea service—and one that would not be discernible had its parts been separated—is that the maker used 2 stamps of different sizes to mark the various objects. Joseph Richardson, Jr., and other silversmithing members of his family are particularly well known and popular with collectors. As a result, many fakes have been made in this century that bear imitations of the Richardsons' marks. Become familiar with the genuine marks, and exercise extreme caution when examining an object purported to have been made by a Richardson. This advice holds true for the work of other well-known, popular makers such as Paul Revere, Philip Syng, Myer Myers, and John Coney.

Colonial pear-shaped octagonal teapot

Description
Octagonal pear-shaped vessel with wooden handle. Octagonal domed lid with molded edge and midband; knopped finial. Body with molding at shoulder. Tapered S-shaped wooden handle with spur at top; fitted into 2 cylindrical sockets. Tapered, octagonal, S-shaped spout has notched molded tip. Low, molded, octagonal foot rim.

Marks and Dimensions
"P•V•D" in oval stamped under lip near handle. Height: 7⅛". Width: 7⅞". Diameter: 4¼".

Maker, Locality, and Date
Peter Van Dyck (1684–1751), New York City. 1720–35.

Comment
The strong S curves evident in this teapot's profile were much admired in the 18th century. Today this shape is routinely associated with what is called the Queen Anne style. At the time this teapot was made, numerous silversmiths in all the major Colonial American cities, as well as some in smaller towns, fashioned teapots similar to this pear-shaped example. But this teapot is the only octagonal version known today.

Hints for Collectors
Like many teapots and coffeepots from this era, this example has a replaced wooden handle. Because the original handles often wear out and break, the loss of such a part is unfortunate but not unexpected. For this reason, collectors should not be overly critical of a pot with a replaced wooden handle, so long as the handle is well made and in keeping with the style of the teapot itself. The handle seen here, while a bit heavy, does not seriously detract from the value of the object.

Federal octagonal teapot

Description
Hinged rectangular lid with flat-sided dome and squirrel finial.
Octagonal bowl-shaped body with narrow border of stylized
anthemia at lip, wider border of roses and leaves on mat ground
at shoulder, and wide border of waterleafs and oak leaves at
bottom. S-shaped spout with faceted lower section and animal-
head tip. Ribbed C-shaped wooden handle with acanthus leaf at
top; fitted into animal head socket (top) and leaf socket (bottom).
Octagonal molded pedestal with narrow neck; flat base with
anthemia border. 4 paw feet with acanthus caps. "DMH" engraved
in script on side of body.

Marks and Dimensions
"E.T. WEAVER" in rectangle stamped on underside of bottom.
Height: 9½". Width: 13". Diameter: 4¾".

Maker, Locality, and Date
Emmor T. Weaver (dates unknown), Philadelphia. 1805–20.

Comment
Early 18th-century American silversmiths produced a limited
number of octagonal objects, which they called "8-square."
Octagonal silver objects were made again in the last years of the
18th and beginning of the 19th centuries, most notably in New
York. This Philadelphia teapot, with its pedestal and animal feet,
is a typical early 19th-century example.

Hints for Collectors
Because silver began to be factory-produced at the start of the
19th century, the work of the relatively few well-known
silversmiths of this period is costly and in great demand.
However, there were still many lesser-known silversmiths like
Weaver working at this time, and their wares are often
considerably less expensive today.

Late Colonial pear-shaped teapot

Description
Hinged, circular, domed lid with pineapple finial. Double-bellied body with chased shell-and-leaf decoration encircling upper portion and lid. Tapered S-shaped spout decorated with shells and leaves. C-shaped wooden handle with spur at top, fitted into cylindrical silver sockets. Flared, molded circular pedestal. Engraved "LD to ER/1757" in block letters on underside, "ES to ER" in block letters under lid, and "ER" in script on each side of body.

Marks and Dimensions
"S•E" with crown above and fleur-de-lis below stamped on underside. Height: 5½″. Width: 9⅛″. Diameter: 5⅜″.

Maker, Locality, and Date
Samuel Edwards (1705–62), Boston. c. 1750.

Comment
Popular during the third quarter of the 18th century, most inverted pear-shaped teapots of this type had engraved decoration spanning the juncture of the lid and body. The teapot shown here, with its repoussé ornament, is unusual. While the body and lid of these teapots were always wrought, all the appendages—spout, foot, handle sockets, and finial—were cast separately and applied.

Hints for Collectors
Teapots like this one require very careful examination. Unlike most 18th-century hollowware, these teapots usually have a separate bottom fitted into the body. While the presence of a separate bottom bearing the mark would normally suggest that the vessel had been altered or upgraded, the separate bottom was routine for these small, difficult-to-make teapots. Even so, you should scrutinize the maker's mark carefully.

Modern teapot

Description
Hinged low domed lid with tall wooden finial that is straight-sided and tapered. Spherical body. Tapered, slightly curved triangular spout with notched tip. C-shaped, tapered, triangular wooden handle with silver handle sockets. Low, flared, square pedestal with rounded corners.

Marks and Dimensions
"STERLING/ENTIRELY HAND/WROUGHT" in block letters; "Reino J. Martin" in script; all stamped incuse on underside. Height: 5⅝". Width: 8". Diameter: 3⅞".

Maker, Locality, and Date
Reino J. Martin (b. 1923), Gloucester, Massachusetts. 1955–60.

Comment
Although this teapot is visually simple, creating it from a single piece of metal was a difficult task, the work of an expert silversmith who has years of experience and total control of his medium. Because this form lends itself well to continual experimentation in design, there are intriguing and pleasing variations from every era of American history.

Hints for Collectors
Because this teapot is a fresh, original interpretation of a classic form, it will always have the approval of serious collectors and students of silver. Moreover, it is superbly made, with a textured but smooth spherical surface that is especially appealing. The exceptional quality and special allure of this example should be sought in any potential acquisition, whether antique or modern.

Modern coffeepot

Description
Hinged lid slightly concave and flush with lip of tapered oval body. Flared spout. Tapered wooden handle set upright into lid.

Marks and Dimensions
"HJC/HAND MADE/STERLING/21" stamped incuse on underside. Height: 9⅝". Length: 6⅝". Width: 5⅜".

Maker, Locality, and Date
Hans Christensen (1924–83), Rochester, New York. c. 1960.

Comment
20th-century designers created smooth, clean-lined compositions that exploited silver's natural depth and reflectivity. "Form follows function" became the catch phrase to describe the manner in which modern objects have been designed according to their practical purpose. As a result, many modern examples are devoid of superfluous embellishment. This coffeepot is a superb example; its maker apprenticed in the Danish shop of Georg Jensen before immigrating to the United States in 1954.

Hints for Collectors
Collectors of silver esteem ornament, frequently judging an object's desirability on the basis of how much ornament it has. This superb coffeepot refutes this way of thinking. Its sensuous clean lines and practicality make it a classic; it will always be one of the standards against which other objects of its era are measured. Although coffeepots of this caliber are not encountered every day, energetic collectors may find similar articles at crafts fairs, or they can even commission work from an artist. Any collector who owns such an object is fortunate indeed, for it will undoubtedly increase in both artistic and monetary value.

Modern double-spout coffeepot

Description
Tall trapezoidal body with 2 wide bowed sides. Flat top has 2 flush hinged lids. 2 small curved spouts. Straight triangular wooden handle mounted horizontally on side.

Marks and Dimensions
"E" over square containing "SKMS" (one letter in each corner), and triangular device; rectangle below containing "925S"; all stamped incuse on bottom edge. Height: 7¹⁵⁄₁₆″. Width: 4½″.

Maker, Locality, and Date
Robert W. Ebendorf (b. 1938), New Paltz, New York. 1965.

Comment
Although Americans use silver objects less frequently today than in previous centuries, talented silversmiths still practice their craft, fabricating sensitively designed and skillfully wrought objects. Few silversmiths can earn a living working solely for private clients, so many capable ones divide their time between making objects for sale and teaching metalworking. Ebendorf made this coffeepot while teaching and studying in Oslo, Norway.

Hints for Collectors
This silver coffeepot represents the best in recent American craftsmanship and design. It has clean lines and a superbly finished surface; it is also eminently practical, as both left-handed and right-handed people can manipulate it. Collectors of works by contemporary craftsmen always run the risk that these objects will not stand the test of time. However, carefully wrought objects that are functional and yet designed with a vital, fresh, and innovative approach will most likely be highly esteemed and increasingly valuable in the future.

146 Modern Art Deco coffee set

Description
Coffee service of polished, gilt, and oxidized burgundy silver in irregular pattern of triangles. Coffeepot has peaked lid with obelisk-shaped finial; tapered body of interlocking triangles; angular loop handle with ivory ferrules; tapered, triangular spout. Sugar bowl has peaked lid and obelisk-shaped finial; short body tapered and faceted, with 2 angular loop handles. Cream pot has short, tapered, faceted body, triangular spout, and angular loop handle.

Marks and Dimensions
"EM" conjoined; "GORHAM 28 STERLING"; lion; anchor; and "G" all stamped incuse; "DESIGNED AND EXECUTED/BY/ERIK MAGNUSSEN" engraved; all on underside of each. Coffeepot height: 9½"; width: 9⅜"; diameter: 4⅝". Sugar bowl height: 6¾"; width: 7⅝"; diameter: 4⅜". Cream pot height: 4⅜"; width: 6⅜"; diameter: 4¼".

Maker, Locality, and Date
Erik Magnussen (1884–1961), Providence. 1927.

Comment
The Art Deco style had its first exposure to general public scrutiny at the Exposition Internationale des Arts Décoratifs et Industriels Modernes (from which the term Art Deco was later coined) in Paris in 1925. It emphasized streamlined geometric shapes and developed from abstract versions of Art Nouveau. Other sources of inspiration included the Cubism of Paul Cézanne and Pablo Picasso, and designs made for Diaghilev's Ballets Russes. The Gorham Company, long interested in art silver,

included Art Deco objects in its production beginning about 1925, when it hired the well-known Danish designer Erik Magnussen. Prior to his arrival in the United States, Magnussen had become familiar with the modern silver movement as it was being formulated in shops like that of Georg Jensen. At the age of 14, Magnussen worked as an apprentice in his uncle's art gallery; he studied sculpture, worked as a chaser, and by 1909 was making his own silver in Denmark, where he received wide acclaim. The fact that Gorham sought out his talents as a designer and silversmith testifies to the company's vital interest in current design. The work done by Magnussen while he was at Gorham is representative of the fine design and excellent craftsmanship being produced by the company's artisans at the time.

Hints for Collectors
This coffee set represents the acme of American Art Deco silver. Its design is daring, and its use of color innovative. While it is unlikely that many examples with the vitality of this coffee set will come on the market, collectors should be sensitive to the merits of the style, especially in the imaginative use of color and texture. Much silver made in America between the Civil War and the Second World War was patinated and textured; collectors should not unwittingly polish away these surfaces.

Late Colonial coffeepot

Description
Hinged, circular, double-domed, molded lid; knopped finial.
Circular, tapered, straight-sided body. Tapered S-shaped spout
with scrolled tip and knopped drops at base. C-shaped wooden
handle with spur at top and cylindrical silver sockets. Molded
foot rim. "EP" engraved in block letters on underside; coat of
arms and crest (of Clarke family of Massachusetts) on side.

Marks and Dimensions
"HURD" in rectangle stamped below rim next to handle. Height:
9⅞″. Width: 8⅝″. Diameter: 5¼″.

Maker, Locality, and Date
Jacob Hurd (1702–58), Boston. c. 1750.

Comment
While tea was undoubtedly the most popular fashionable drink
during the 18th century, coffee was a close second. Coffeepots
were typically taller than teapots and rarely had a strainer at the
base of the spout. Most 18th-century examples had a wooden
handle, although in Europe the handles were occasionally made
of ivory. As seen in this coffeepot, smooth, highly polished
surfaces were greatly esteemed during this period.

Hints for Collectors
Early 18th-century coffeepots are very uncommon, and those
made in the late 18th century usually had bellied rather than
straight sides. Therefore, fine examples command very high
prices. Become familiar with the techniques by which fakes are
created: Some are made completely new; others are less
expensive English examples altered to appear American, and
still others are genuine unmarked objects given fake marks.

Victorian electroplated ice-water pitcher

Description
Hinged circular lid, domed and molded, with swan finial. Straight-sided tapered body with molded lip. Curved triangular spout with foliate base and closing valve. C-shaped handle in form of tree limb. On front and back, oval medallion containing man and woman and surrounded by stylized foliate ornament. Molded foot rim. Interior lined with enameled sheet iron.

Marks and Dimensions
"LYMAN'S PATENT/JUNE 8, 1850/8" stamped incuse on underside. Height: 12″. Width: 7⅜″. Diameter: 5¾″.

Maker, Locality, and Date
Meriden Britannia Company (1852–98), Meriden, Connecticut. c. 1867.

Comment
Before the advent of electricity and refrigeration, ice-water pitchers like this one were popular household objects. One of the first patents for such a pitcher was granted in 1854; the patent was for a double wall, similar to that found in vacuum bottles today. Made in profusion until the turn of the century, ice-water pitchers often had a stand that allowed them to tilt and pour; other, simpler ones, like this example, had a patented closable valve in the spout to keep the water cool.

Hints for Collectors
Because ice-water pitchers are large and somewhat difficult to handle, many have dents and misshapen areas. Repairing this damage can be very difficult because of the vacuum container within, so do not purchase dented examples. Similarly, try to avoid those that have lost major portions of their electroplating, although replating is feasible.

149 Victorian electroplated tilting ice-water pitcher

Description
Hinged, circular, low-domed lid with finial of bust of Cleopatra. Cylindrical body with borders of stylized leaves and flowers at top, narrow vertical panels below. Tapered loop handle with male head at top and stylized Egyptian designs. Curved triangular spout ornamented with male face flanked by wings, leaves, and flowers. Molded foot rim. 2 small lugs on sides allow pitcher to swing in frame. Interior lined with enameled sheet iron. Frame with 2 triangular uprights ornamented like pitcher. Hinged brass loop handle topped by symmetrical leafy scrolls with male heads. Elliptical base. "Sybil/from/Father" engraved in script on lid.

Marks and Dimensions
"ROGERS, SMITH & CO. CONN." in circle surrounding "NEW/HAVEN"; all stamped incuse on disk applied to underside of pitcher; "PAT$^{\underline{D}}$ JUNE 13, 1868/PAT$^{\underline{D}}$ NOV. 3$^{\underline{D}}$ 1868/16" stamped incuse on underside of pitcher. "ROGERS, SMITH & CO. CONN." in circle enclosing "NEW/ HAVEN" and "1b" all stamped incuse on underside of frame. Height: 19¾". Frame length: 14⅜"; width: 10".

Maker, Locality, and Date
Rogers, Smith & Company (1857–98), New Haven, Connecticut. c. 1868.

Comment
This is a rich example of the Egyptian style, which, like the Greek and Roman styles, experienced a surge in popularity during the 19th century.

Hints for Collectors
This pitcher is made of relatively soft metal and is liable to extensive damage. Fortunately, such electroplated objects were made in quantity, so collectors can pass over poor examples.

150 Victorian electroplated tilting ice-water set

Description
Circular hinged lid with tall pierced foliate finial. C-shaped pierced handle with leaf-and-fish design. Fish-head spout. Body has pink porcelain sleeve at center ornamented with branches and flowers; metal borders at top and base decorated with camels, pyramids, and palm trees. Sides have 2 small lugs on metal strap to support pitcher. Interior lined with enameled sheet iron. Frame with hinged floral loop handle; 2 triangular pierced uprights with female figure flanked by floral panels. Molded rectangular platform with ornamental borders; at one end, 2 circular trays supported by pierced leafy brackets; at opposite end, circular tray with squat vase.

Marks and Dimensions
"SIMPSON, HALL, MILLER & Cᴼ" around a circle, enclosing "QUADRUPLE/PLATE" with fleur-de-lis; "400"; all stamped incuse on underside of pitcher and frame. Height: 23¾". Length: 12⅛". Width: 10⅛".

Maker, Locality, and Date
Simpson, Hall, Miller & Company (1866–98), Wallingford, Connecticut. c. 1891.

Comment
Ice-water pitchers were made in great quantity and variety, and the manufacturer of this example alone offered 51 designs. All were ornately decorated and fitted with an enameled insert that insulated the contents.

Hints for Collectors
This set, in a pattern known as "Denizen," is quite unusual because of the porcelain sleeve covering the body. Though it is missing a pair of goblets, its excellent condition adds greatly to its value.

Mugs, Cups, Chalices, and Beakers

Silver and silver-plated drinking vessels are all basically similar, having a cylindrical body and a smooth lip. They may have one handle, several, or none at all. Those with lids may have hinges, or the lids may be removable. Some drinking vessels rest directly on the table, while others are fitted with a short or tall pedestal; a few even have multiple supports in the form of animal or human feet. While such vessels are typically made simply of silver or silver plate, some examples also incorporate other materials, such as porcelain or animal horn.

The Fashion in Drinking Vessels
Lidded drinking vessels, called tankards, reached their greatest popularity during the 17th and 18th centuries. After that time, they seem to have been made less and less frequently, and the form has virtually not been used in this century. Lidless forms, specifically beakers, mugs, and goblets or chalices, have retained their usefulness; however, none of these forms is made of silver today as often as it was in the past. Multiple-handled drinking vessels, which are rather uncommon today, were often used communally in the past. Today, one of the few uses for such vessels is in church communion ceremonies, where other chalices without handles are also used.

Types of Decoration
While most drinking vessels are very plain, having their entire surface highly polished, others bear a wide range of ornament—a fact that points out the metal's receptivity to a great variety of decoration. Some cups are textured with hammer facets or a regular pattern of machine-made ornament, and still others have an impressive array of chased, engraved, hammered, or applied decoration. The quality and degree of decoration depended on how much a purchaser was willing or able to pay. However, various types of ornament have experienced different periods of vogue. The most consistently popular decoration—not only on these vessels, but on all silver or silver-plated objects—is derived from plants and flowers. This type of decoration usually consists of leaves, flowers, vines, and scrolls in a variety of patterns. Some of this decoration is highly stylized and quite general in character, but some objects bear ornament that is as realistic as a leaf plucked from a tree.

Animal and human motifs are much less common types of decoration. They appear to have had limited popularity as ornament on silver drinking vessels from the 17th century right through to the present. Such instances as women who emblazoned 17th-century caudle cups and the leering ram's head on late 19th-century tankards were very graphic and easily recognizable. The skill required in representing realistic animal and human figures presumably explains the infrequency with which such motifs have traditionally been used.

Some vessels included in this section have decoration that is extraordinarily explicit but unrelated to the object's function. This sort of ornament provides insight into times and personalities of the past. One diminutive beaker shows a vitriolic vision of the Devil marching into the mouth of Hell; this scenario is accompanied by 3 couplets venting rage toward the Pope and Catholic Pretender to the Throne of England (the son of James II); this anger is understandable in light of knowledge that the maker fled from Switzerland under pain of death for heretical activities against the Roman Catholic Church. This kind of ornament sheds light on the values, attitudes, and feelings of earlier generations.

Victorian mug

Description
Hourglass-shaped body, hammered overall. Ribbed loop handle. Narrow foot rim. "Mary Brinsmade de Camp" engraved in script on underside.

Marks and Dimensions
"TIFFANY & C⁰/4831 M 821/STERLING-SILVER" stamped incuse on underside. Height: 3⅞". Width: 3⅞". Diameter: 2⅞".

Maker, Locality, and Date
Tiffany & Company (1853–present), New York City. 1869–91.

Comment
Silver objects made before the Industrial Revolution always bore hammer marks; these were considered unsightly, and every attempt was made to minimize their presence. Later, machines allowed for the production of smooth objects that had no trace of hammer facets. In the late 19th century, however, a small group of designers, influenced by the Arts and Crafts Movement, lauded hammer marks as evidence of hand-craftsmanship and aesthetic merit. As a result, some machine-made silver pieces, like this mug, were purposely given pronounced hammer facets. Such objects may be of greater interest—although not of greater value—than objects without such markings.

Hints for Collectors
Hammer marks should always be evident on a handwrought silver object. On those fashioned from the 17th through the early 19th centuries, planishing, polishing, and wear have minimized the visibility of the facets. On more recently made objects, such marks have relatively less wear and are more obvious. Being familiar with these subtle differences will help collectors distinguish very worn 18th-century hammered objects from late 19th-century hammered examples that have less wear.

Description
Pear-shaped body with flared molded rim. Double-C-shaped handle with spur at top. Low flared and molded foot rim. Engraved on body opposite handle: coat of arms and crest (of Badlam family of Massachusetts) in foliate mantling.

Marks and Dimensions
"J. COBURN" in rectangle stamped on underside. Height: 5¼". Width: 5⁹⁄₁₆". Diameter: 4¼".

Maker, Locality, and Date
John Coburn (1724–1803), Boston. 1760–70.

Comment
18th-century drinking vessels with bellied bodies were called canns; this term distinguishes them from mugs, which are straight-sided. This example is typical of many made in major American cities as well as in numerous outlying areas. Canns made between 1740 and 1760 usually have a plain C-shaped handle; this one has a complex double-C-shaped handle that was more common later, between 1760 and 1780. The drinker's thumb rested against the spur at the top of the handle; more expensive examples have an acanthus leaf atop the handle instead.

Hints for Collectors
This cann has "S Badlam" scratched lightly on the underside. Badlam, a cabinetmaker in Lower Dorchester Mills, Massachusetts, is thought to have been the original owner of this object, which was passed through succeeding generations of his family into this century. Such information rarely survives with antique silver, but when it does it adds greatly to the object's interest, though not necessarily to its value unless the original owner was a person of note.

153 English George III French-plated paktong cann

Description
Pear-shaped body with flared lip having narrow serrated border. S-shaped handle with volute and spur at upper end. Narrow molded foot rim. Engraved on body opposite handle: shield suspended from bowknot and flanked by leafy boughs; intertwined initials "RBB" engraved in shield.

Marks and Dimensions
Unmarked. Height: 3⅞". Width: 4". Diameter: 2⅝".

Maker, Locality, and Date
Unknown. England. 1760–90.

Comment
This small half-pint cann was originally silver plated inside and out, but only traces of the silvering remain in recessed and protected areas. The bulk of the silver plate has been worn and polished away, leaving the paktong (a copper alloy) body exposed. The technique by which the silver was applied to this cann was known as French plating. It was accomplished by applying extremely thin, heated sheets of silver to an object; these sheets were then burnished or rubbed with steel- or agate-tipped tools, causing the silver to affix itself to the base metal. This laborious process was eventually discarded after the development of fused plating.

Hints for Collectors
While small silver canns and mugs are relatively common, silver-plated examples are scarce. Often they are not recognized, because most or all of their plating has worn away. Such plated vessels usually lack the careful finishing and detailing of silver ones. But the diminutive cann shown here is an exception; its graceful form and fine engraving would make it a fine addition to any collection.

Description
Cylindrical body with tapered side and molded lip. Slender
C-shaped handle with stylized acanthus leaf at top. Narrow
foliate foot rim. Body engraved with cluster of leaves and flowers
around shield-shaped reserve enclosing "H.A. DUP."

Marks and Dimensions
"BAILEY & KITCHEN" in rectangle; 3 pseudohallmarks (eagle in
clipped-corner square; thistle; and hibernia; each in rectangle),
all stamped on underside. Height: 2⅞". Width: 3½". Diameter:
2⅝".

Maker, Locality, and Date
Joseph T. Bailey & Andrew B. Kitchen (1833–46), Philadelphia.
1833–46.

Comment
The history of the present-day firm of Bailey, Banks & Biddle in
Philadelphia extends back to the partnership that Joseph T.
Bailey and Andrew B. Kitchen formed in the mid-19th century.
Although several name changes have taken place during the
interim, the firm has continued to supply fine silver to the
residents of Philadelphia and surrounding communities.

Hints for Collectors
Most American mugs made after the Revolution were fabricated
from sheets of machine-flattened silver. The bottom was soldered
into a hollow cylindrical body that was seamed vertically, usually
under the handle. Ornamental borders at the lip and base were
also machine-made. Always examine an object carefully for these
signs of machine manufacture. Although often very decorative
and certainly desirable, 19th-century mugs made in this fashion
are not as valuable as pre-Revolutionary handwrought examples.
This small mug was probably a christening gift.

155 Early Colonial mug

Description
Cylindrical body with flared side and lip. Slender C-shaped handle with spiraled upper terminal and 3-lobed lower terminal. Molded foot rim. "T/I*R" engraved on underside.

Marks and Dimensions
"w•r" with star above, in shield-shaped outline and stamped twice on underside. Height: 3″. Width: 4½″. Diameter: 2⅞″.

Maker, Locality, and Date
William Rouse (1639–1705), Boston. 1695–1705.

Comment
Small cups with handles, usually referred to as mugs, have been popular in America since the founding of the Colonies. While large examples of a pint capacity or more were used by adults, smaller ones, such as the mug shown here, were often reserved for children.

Hints for Collectors
William Rouse was an accomplished silversmith who produced high-quality work, only about a dozen examples of which are known today. For the collector, this means that any newly discovered Rouse objects will be eagerly sought and therefore expensive. Mugs of this type were made by other silversmiths with great frequency and remain readily available today, so that collectors can afford to be discriminating. Avoid the purchase of common and cheaply made examples; mugs with distinguishing ornament, an engraved name or inscription, and substantial weight are preferable. It is also important to recognize a mug that has lost its handle at some time in the past, since such a vessel may be offered as a beaker.

Victorian presentation mug

Description
Straight-sided cylinder with beaded and molded edges at top and bottom. Angular, scrolled, foliate loop handle. Body decorated with engine turning and 3 ornate oval reserves, 2 containing engraved genre scenes, the third engraved "Presented by the/ Vestry of Trinity Church/Newark, N.J./To Mr. Phillip Moore./on his retiring/from the office of Sexton./as an emblem of their Appreciation/of his Faithful Services./for nearly a Quarter of a Century/Christmas Day, 1859."

Marks and Dimensions
"W&H" in rectangle; "1 X"; all stamped incuse on underside. Height: 4⅝". Width: 5¼". Diameter: 3½".

Maker, Locality, and Date
Henry Wood & Dixon G. Hughes (1845–99), New York City. c. 1859.

Comment
Many a long and successful working career has been commemorated with a gift of silver—a watch, tray, bowl, or similar object engraved with the record of the person who was retiring. In the last century, a great variety of objects were given to individuals, with the size and lavishness of the present determined by the person's status and value to the institution.

Hints for Collectors
Because they reflect the history of a particular person, organization, place, time, and event, presentation objects are of greater interest and value than comparable pieces having no such record. Many mass-produced presentation mugs, thin-walled and lightweight, are modestly priced. More unusual examples are more desirable; this mug, for instance, boasts highly decorative landscape scenes and a superbly detailed inscription.

157 Victorian parcel-gilt mug

Description
Tapered form in shape of hooped barrel. Flat-topped loop handle.
"H. F. K." applied on side opposite handle; "Hamilton Fish Kean
2nd/March 1st 1925/from/Hamilton Fish Kean/from/HamiltonFish/
May 1862" engraved in script on underside. Gilt interior.

Marks and Dimensions
"TIFFANY & CO." in arc; "QUALITY/925–1000" in rectangle; "M" in
oval; "825/8344"; all stamped incuse on underside. Height: 4⅛".
Width: 4¼". Diameter: 3¼".

Maker, Locality, and Date
Tiffany & Company (1853–present), New York City. c. 1862.

Comment
Being an expensive and coveted material, silver was often
imitated. It is somewhat surprising, however, that silver was
fashioned after less revered materials, but the whims of fashion
have led to silver imitations of porcelain, earthenware, bronze,
rope, and even wood, as seen in this mug. Silver was sometimes
even made to look like fruit, vegetables, and animals.

Hints for Collectors
The applied initials on this mug are quite unusual, since silver
was more commonly personalized with engraved initials. The
initials, along with the interesting wood-textured body, make
this a most desirable object. The mug's history, traced through
several generations by the engraving, adds to its appeal. If the
original owners of an object were persons of prominence—as
were the members of the Fish family of New York mentioned
here—the interest and value is likely to be still greater.

Federal pint tankard

Description
Circular lid with concentric rings. Upright thumbpiece with series of narrow vertical loops. Angular double C-shaped handle. Straight-sided cylindrical body with 2 bands of narrow encircling rings.

Marks and Dimensions
"I•LOWNES" in script in conforming rectangle, stamped on underside. Height: 5⅜". Width: 5½". Diameter: 3½".

Maker, Locality, and Date
Joseph Lownes (1754–1820), Philadelphia. 1790–1810.

Comment
Prior to the American Revolution, tankards were invariably wrought from a single piece of metal. However, examples that date from the last decade of the 18th century and the early years of the 19th were fabricated almost completely of sheet metal that was seamed along one side to form the body; the bottom was a separate piece that was soldered in. This technique is clearly evidenced by the flat character of this tankard's thumbpiece, hinge, and barrel.

Hints for Collectors
Although sheet-metal tankards are not as popular with collectors as earlier wrought examples, they are nonetheless interesting for their use of a new fabrication technique to make what was considered an old-fashioned form. The small pint size of this example is noteworthy, as is the hooped barrel. When considering the purchase of a tankard, look for examples with unusual features like these. As with other forms of silver, the substantial weight, excellent condition, and respected silversmith's name present in this example are all factors that contribute to the tankard's value.

Colonial quart mug

Description
Slightly tapered cylindrical body with molded lip. Tapered
S-shaped handle with spur at top and shield-shaped terminal.
Flared molded foot rim. "P + S" engraved in block letters on back
of handle.

Marks and Dimensions
"FR" in shield-shaped outline under crown, stamped on back of
handle. Height: 5¹¹⁄₁₆". Width: 6¾". Diameter: 4½".

Maker, Locality, and Date
Francis Richardson (1681–1729), Philadelphia. 1727–29.

Comment
Quart-size mugs were among the most popular drinking vessels
in 18th-century America and were used by men and women alike
for both alcoholic and nonalcoholic beverages. This example
bears the initials of its original owner, Phoebe Sharples of
Chester County, Pennsylvania, who, like most rural residents,
had to seek the services of a nearby urban silversmith for stylish
goods. The original ownership of this mug is documented,
disproving the common assumption that all mugs were owned
by men.

Hints for Collectors
While it is not unusual to find owners' initials on the handles of
mugs, canns, and tankards, silversmiths' marks are almost never
placed there; instead they are usually stamped on the barrel or
underside. This mug is a rare exception. Fortunately, it is well
documented to its original owner through her descendants,
providing reassuring evidence of its authenticity.

160 Late Colonial tankard

Description
Circular, molded, double-domed lid, with stylized urn-and-flame finial. Scrolled reeded thumbpiece hinged to S-shaped tapered handle, with applied molded ornament at top and grotesque mask terminal at bottom. Straight-sided tapered body with molded lip. Band encircling body above lower handle juncture. Flared molded base. "The Gift of/Mary Bartlett, Widow of Eph^m Bartlett./to the third Church in Brookfield./1768" engraved in script opposite handle.

Marks and Dimensions
"•REVERE" in rectangle stamped under lip near handle. Height: 8⁵⁄₁₆″. Width: 6¹¹⁄₁₆″. Diameter: 5⁷⁄₈″.

Maker, Locality, and Date
Paul Revere, Jr. (1735–1818), Boston. 1768–72.

Comment
The silver for this tankard was willed to the Third Church in Brookfield, Massachusetts, to be fashioned into a set of communion vessels. A common practice among all Protestant denominations in America, communicants sometimes also willed household silver to their churches. This tankard is from a set of 6 that was ordered in 1768 but not completed until 1772.

Hints for Collectors
The tankard is one of the most sought-after forms of American silver, and collectors must exercise considerable caution when buying one. Many have had the lid replaced or a spout added and later removed. Also, numerous English examples have had their marks replaced with spurious American ones.

Description
Circular flat-domed lid with flared edge and engraved scalloped lip. Scrolled thumbpiece hinged to tapered S-shaped handle with leaf tip and lion on its spine and child's face on shaped tab at lower terminal. Straight-sided tapered body with molded lip, lower border of leaf tips, and complex molded base. Top of lid has engraved circle of leaf tips enclosing "RJS"; "S/R∗J" on mid-handle; on body, coat of arms and crest (probably of Sill family of Connecticut) within foliate mantling.

Marks and Dimensions
"CK" in rectangle stamped once on lid and twice on barrel under lip at each side of handle. Height: 7½". Width: 7⅝". Diameter: 5½".

Maker, Locality, and Date
Cornelius Kierstede (1675–1757), New York City. 1710–40.

Comment
This very fine tankard has many features typical of the best early designs from New York, including a flat-topped lid, scrolled thumbpiece, scalloped lip, and applied human, animal, and foliate devices on the handle. The lid and barrel are floridly engraved with the owner's initials and personal insignia, while the base rim has leaf tips known as cut-card work.

Hints for Collectors
Because ownership of tankards was evidence of wealth and good taste, many were personalized with engraved coats of arms, initials, or presentation inscriptions. If original engraving has been removed, the object is generally less interesting and less valuable than an unaltered one.

162 Late Victorian silver-and-porcelain tankard

Description
Silver domed lid with molded edge. Fleur-de-lis thumbpiece with strapwork support hinged to silver strap around top of loop handle. Cylindrical, slightly tapered porcelain body with molded base; decorated with sepia figure of friar with upraised glass standing by barrel.

Marks and Dimensions
Lion; anchor; Gothic "G"; "STERLING"; "C2543"; and triangular device, all stamped incuse on edge of silver lid. "CAC" within wreath above "LENOX" in lavender on underside. Height: 5½". Width: 5¼". Diameter: 3⅞".

Maker, Locality, and Date
Silver: Gorham Company (1831–present), Providence. 1898. Porcelain: Lenox China Company (1894–present), Trenton. 1894–96.

Comment
Because of its value, silver is not often used with other materials that have no significant innate worth. Drinking vessels, however, along with condiment vessels and cruet frames from the 18th and 19th centuries, are exceptions. As early as the 12th century, wooden bowls and coconut shells were made with silver edges and bases. The silver portion of this tankard is relatively nondescript. It typifies turn-of-the-century machine-stamped and lathe-spun silver at its most straightforward.

Hints for Collectors
Because its metal portion is not the primary visual element, silver collectors might overlook this tankard. Yet it is of interest because the silver is well marked, including the company symbol, and because of the purity of the metal, the date mark (the triangular device), and the pattern number.

163 Victorian tankard of parcel-gilt silver, horn, and porcelain

Description
Low hinged lid with urn-shaped finial, wide foliate border, and curved tabular thumbpiece. S-shaped handle fitted with animal horn in form of goat's head. Bulbous body with repoussé foliate ornament and 6 blue-and-white porcelain medallions of women's heads. Low bulbous foot with scrolled border. Gilt interior.

Marks and Dimensions
Lion and "G" each in clipped-corner square flanking anchor in shield; "PATENTED/STERLING/3⅝ PINTS" and trident; all stamped incuse; "XIX Century/heirloom/1893–1900" in rectangular cartouche with mat ground; all on underside. Height: 9¾". Width: 8¼". Diameter: 5¾".

Maker, Locality, and Date
Gorham Company (1831–present), Providence. 1897.

Comment
About 1800, perhaps because refinement in table manners prompted a move away from the use of communal drinking vessels, tankards suddenly ceased to be used. Drinking vessels with handles continued to be made, but they almost never had a hinged lid, so this Victorian example is quite interesting.

Hints for Collectors
The rarity of 19th- and 20th-century American silver tankards recommends them to collectors. When a late tankard, such as this one, features a vigorous design and an innovative use of materials, it is even more desirable. The mark on this example stating that it was intended as a "19th-century heirloom" is not recorded elsewhere and enhances the interest of the piece.

Federal mug with lid

Description
Low-domed lid with ball finial. Tapered barrel body with simple molding at lip and base. Freestanding S-shaped handle attached near lip, with stylized acanthus leaf at top. Engraved in script opposite handle: "The Gift of/C. Gayton Pickman,/to/William S. Wetmore./1845."

Marks and Dimensions
"BALDWIN & JONES" in scrolled banner stamped on underside. Height: 5". Width: 5½". Diameter: 3¾".

Maker, Locality, and Date
Jabez Baldwin & John B. Jones (c. 1813–19), Boston. 1815–19.

Comment
Although mugs were among the most common silver American drinking vessels throughout the Colonial and early Federal periods, lidded examples are uncommon. The type of handle on this mug, with its unattached upper end, was usually reserved for sauce boats and, rarely, cream pots. Also of interest is the engraved presentation inscription, which is dated some 25 years after the mug was made.

Hints for Collectors
Because this lidded mug with its unusual handle deviates significantly from the norm, collectors might be skeptical of its authenticity and desirability. However, some eccentric creations are worthy of special attention, since their individuality provides a refreshing relief from more standard pieces. If such an object is closely examined to ensure its authenticity, there is every reason to look upon it as an interesting addition to a collection.

Early Colonial 2-handled covered cup

Description
Circular stepped lid with central dome, 3 scrolled finials near flared lip, and leafy scroll and floral ornamentation. Deep body with curved side and wide border of leaves near base. 2 double-C-shaped handles with spur at top and leaf decoration. Low, circular, flared foot rim. "C/I*E" engraved in block initials on side of body; coat of arms with crest (of Philipse family of New York) amid leafy mantling on other side.

Marks and Dimensions
"IB" with 4 conjoined circles below, all in square, stamped once on rim of lid and twice on body near lip. Height: 5⅝". Width: 9". Diameter: 5⅝".

Maker, Locality, and Date
Jurian Blanck, Jr. (c. 1645–1714), New York City. 1666–99.

Comment
Only 3 of these elaborately decorated 2-handled covered cups are known. They have cast handles, repoussé acanthus leaves, and richly engraved coats of arms, and may have been wedding gifts. All originated in New York during the late 17th century, although several larger related examples from a later date are known to have been made in Massachusetts.

Hints for Collectors
This cup and its mates, all in museums, are well worth close study, since they exemplify early American silversmithing at its best. They are quite similar to English and Dutch pieces of the same era, and it is probable that another example will be found in the United States or Europe, so study existing examples carefully.

Early Colonial caudle cup

Description
Squat pear-shaped body with flared rim. 2 S-shaped handles with
volute ends, stylized leafage, and bust of woman on each. Wide
engraved border on convex lower half of cup between handles on
front and back; scene depicts turkey flanked by long-stemmed
flowers. "S/T A" engraved in block letters on underside.

Marks and Dimensions
"RS" under sunburst, all in conforming outline and stamped twice
on underside. Height: 5″. Width: 7⅝″. Diameter: 5¾″.

Maker, Locality, and Date
Robert Sanderson (1608–93), Boston. 1656–76.

Comment
Fewer than a dozen American 2-handled cups of this type are
known today, and all date from before the mid-18th century.
Although they could have held a variety of liquids, they are
believed to have been used principally for caudle, a thin porridge
mixed with wine or ale and flavored with spices, which served as
an elixir for the sick. The original owners of this example, the
Reverend Thomas and Ann Shepherd, of Charlestown,
Massachusetts, had their initials engraved on the underside.

Hints for Collectors
It is unlikely today that a collector will be fortunate enough to
acquire an object this rare, although early 2-handled cups do
appear on occasion. It is equally unlikely that an object of this
age will have survived intact and undamaged. Collectors
contemplating the purchase of such a valuable piece should
therefore check carefully that its parts are genuine. The
replacement of a handle, for instance, although not an
unreasonable repair, would significantly lower the value of
this cup.

167 Modern silver-and-porcelain broth cup, demitasse, and saucers

Description
Left: Deep, ivory-colored porcelain bowl with flared gilt lip. Conforming silver base has hammered surface, undulating flower-decorated lip, 2 opposed loop handles, and scrolled molded foot; "SCW" in cartouche on side. Matching circular saucer with scrolled, molded, flower-decorated brim. From set of 12. Right: Deep, ivory-colored porcelain cup decorated with narrow blue and a wider gold border at flared lip. Conforming silver base has hammered surface, undulating flower-decorated lip, loop handle, and scrolled molded foot; "SEW" in cartouche on side. Matching circular saucer with scrolled, molded, flower-decorated brim. From set of 12.

Marks and Dimensions
Both: "Martelé"; lion; and "G" flanking anchor under spread eagle; ".9584"; all stamped incuse on foot of cup base and underside of saucer. Left: "PVT" on cup and "PVU" on saucer. Cup height: 2¼"; width: 5¼"; diameter: 3½". Saucer height: ⅞"; diameter: 5". Right: "PVR" on cup and "PVS" on saucer. Cup height: 2½"; width: 3"; diameter: 1⅞". Saucer height: ½"; diameter: 3½".

Maker, Locality, and Date
Silver: Gorham Company (1831–present), Providence. 1908. Porcelain: Lenox China Company (1894–present), Trenton. c. 1908.

Comment
Before the mid-19th century, when the large-scale industrial production of silver began, individual silversmiths were responsible for the style and functional design of silver objects. After factories assumed the principal role, the corporate name replaced the individual's name in all respects. While most factory-made silver wares were purely functional, some pieces

fashioned during the decades around 1900, such as those made by Gorham in the style called Martelé, were also intended to be appreciated as works of art. Gorham made fewer than 5000 objects in this style at the turn of the century. Martelé pieces contain a higher silver content—950 parts per 1000—than do most typical sterling objects, which meet a standard of 925 parts of silver per 1000.

In general, silver objects made by companies such as Tiffany, Gorham, International, and Kirk are among the most sought-after of modern silver products; they are regarded as the 20th-century equivalents of the fine silver produced in much earlier eras by individual silversmiths like Revere, Richardson, Ten Eyck, and You.

Hints for Collectors

Gorham's Martelé is today among the most desirable of American art silver. Any silver object bearing this name should be expected to be very well made, heavy, hammered over its entire surface, and expensive. While entire sets of 12 objects are rarely found today, pairs or groups of half a dozen or so are easier to acquire. A collector who is lucky enough to encounter a single Martelé cup and saucer should buy it, if it is appealing and the price is right.

Victorian cup and saucer

Description
Tapered, belted, circular cup set on shallow flared pedestal. Slender tapered loop handle. Oval medallion encloses child's head and is flanked by engraved scrolls and flowers. "J. Israel" engraved on handle and "M" on body. Foot rim of saucer decorated with guilloche.

Marks and Dimensions
"A. B. GRISWOLD & CO." over "N.O.-H"; all stamped incuse on underside of saucer. Cup height: 2⅝"; width: 3³⁄₁₆". Saucer diameter: 4½".

Maker, Locality, and Date
Arthur B. Griswold & Company (1865–1906), New Orleans. 1865–77.

Comment
Cups and saucers were occasionally used for cold drinks in the 19th century. Apparently, however, the custom did not prove popular, because references to it in the literature of the last century are infrequent. In its day, Griswold & Company was one of the leading silver manufacturers in New Orleans, but the firm also retailed much silver and silver plate made by the Gorham Company of Providence. It is thus possible that this cup and saucer were made by Gorham and sold by Griswold & Company.

Hints for Collectors
Objects in the so-called medallion pattern, featuring applied oval or circular reserves containing the profile of an adult, were quite popular during the third quarter of the 19th century. This cup is unusual, however, because the medallion shows a child in three-quarter view.

Federal tumbler

Description
Low circular body curving in to small base. Engraved skull and crossbones in front of 2 candlesticks, one with lit candle and the other just snuffed, all under motto "Sic transit Gloria/MUNDI" (Thus passes away the glory of this world). Engraved in script around remainder of body: "Magdalen Swift died 27ᵗʰ March 1790-aged 67."

Marks and Dimensons
"I•NR" in rectangle, the N and R conjoined, stamped twice on underside. Height: 2¾". Diameter: 3½".

Maker, Locality, and Date
Joseph Richardson, Jr. & Nathaniel Richardson (1777–90), Philadelphia. c. 1790.

Comment
Small drinking vessels without handles were fairly common in 18th- and 19th-century America. They were made of pewter, horn, wood, ceramic, and, less often, silver. This tumbler is typical of silver examples, except for its engraving, which records the death of its presumed owner.

Hints for Collectors
Though many people would consider it morbid, this small tumbler is quite desirable. Its makers, Joseph Richardson, Jr., and Nathaniel Richardson, were members of the most respected and long-standing silversmithing shop in Philadelphia. The engraving is visually superlative and serves as graphic testimony to the frank attitude of 18th-century America toward death— manifested more often in memorial church silver than in its domestic counterpart.

Federal beaker

Description
Circular vessel with slightly bellied body, flared and molded lip, and flared base. Initials "AMC" engraved in script on side of body.

Marks and Dimensions
"HUTTON" in rectangle and eagle in oval, all stamped on underside. Height: 3⅞". Diameter: 3⁵⁄₁₆".

Maker, Locality, and Date
Isaac Hutton (1766–1855), Albany, New York. 1790–1815.

Comment
Small drinking vessels were popular throughout the 18th and 19th centuries. 18th-century examples usually have handles, while those made in the 19th century seem to occur with and without them in equal numbers. This beaker is gracefully shaped in a baluster form, which is less common than the straight-sided variety. Like most such objects created at the time, this beaker was made from a rolled sheet of silver and seamed vertically up its side. In contrast, most earlier examples from the 18th century were hammered into shape from a single disk of silver, and do not have a seam.

Hints for Collectors
Good-quality examples of typical forms are always welcome additions to a collection; unusual variations are equally desirable. The graceful bellied shape of this beaker makes it somewhat unusual and more difficult to manufacture than its straight-sided counterpart.

Late Colonial beaker

Description
Circular body flared out to molded lip. Low, molded, circular foot rim. Engraved fanciful scene of monstrous head identified as "Hell," the Devil holding chain that passes through gate of "DEATH" to Pope, who holds a rope that passes under gallows labeled "DANGER" to neck of figure identified as Pretender to British throne. Encircling lip is engraved verse, "THREE MORTAL ENEMIES REMEMBER/THE DEVIL POPE AND PRETENDER; MOST WICKED DAMNABLE AND EVIL/THE POPE PRETENDER AND THE DEVIL; I WISH THEY WERE ALL HANG'D IN A ROPE/THE PRETENDER DEVIL AND THE POPE." Inscribed above foot: "This gift is to my son R Samuel by his father Samuel Samuel N. York 14 March/1778." "D/IM" engraved on underside.

Marks and Dimensions
"DCF" in oval and "N:YORK" in shaped outline, all stamped on underside. Height: 3⅛". Diameter: 3⅜".

Maker, Locality, and Date
Daniel Christian Fueter (d. 1785), New York City. 1754–69.

Comment
This fairly typical beaker is engraved with a highly charged political commentary denouncing the presumed enemies of the British crown. The unusual decoration, probably copied from a satiric 18th-century print, illustrates the strength of political opinions on the eve of the American Revolution.

Hints for Collectors
This beaker sheds light on 18th-century silversmithing techniques, since it was made of sheet metal flattened by rollers, shaped, and seamed, rather than wrought from a disk, the more traditional technique at the time.

Victorian beaker or julep cup

Description
Tapered cylindrical vessel with molded lip and base.

Marks and Dimensions
"P.L. KRIDER/STANDARD/PHILAD^A" and "JOHN B. AKIN/DANVILLE/
KY." stamped incuse on underside. Height: 3⅝". Diameter: 3¼".

Maker, Locality, and Date
Peter L. Krider (dates unknown), Philadelphia. Retailed by John
B. Akin (dates unknown), Danville, Kentucky. 1850–60.

Comment
Beakers of this sort, made in great quantity during the mid-19th
century, seem to have experienced their greatest vogue in
Kentucky, Tennessee, Alabama, Louisiana, and nearby states,
where they were generally known as julep cups. While most
were made by local silversmiths, many, including this example,
were imported from large northeastern manufacturers. Such
cups were usually relatively plain, although some have elaborate
ornamental borders. This particular example is marked with the
names of both its northern manufacturer and its southern
retailer.

Hints for Collectors
Since beakers or cups of this type are not hard to obtain,
collectors should seek out especially interesting or unusual
examples. Be sure that any potential purchase is indeed a beaker
and not a mug that has lost its handle, as small mugs of
approximately the same size and shape were made during this
period. Such damaged mugs are, of course, less valuable.

173 Early Colonial beaker

Description
Tall body with flared side and outcurved lip. Sectional foliate
border engraved under lip; below, 3 oval reserves surrounded by
bound foliate boughs, one containing a vase of flowers, and 2 with
scenes of animals; near base, 3 scenes of animals and a skeleton.
Molded base band with diapered border and scalloped upper
edge. "Robbert Sandersen/1685" engraved on one side; "RS"
under a cross on bottom.

Marks and Dimensions
"CV" over "B" in heart stamped on underside. Height: 8".
Diameter: 4¹³⁄₁₆".

Maker, Locality, and Date
Cornelius van der Burch (c. 1653–99), New York City. c. 1685.

Comment
This type of beaker, while usually identified with early New
York, was also made in New England. Most examples were used
in churches to hold the Eucharist, but this particular beaker was
made for domestic use. Of all such beakers, this is perhaps the
most interesting, being fully decorated with moralistic scenes in
which human vices and virtues are represented by animals: The
ermine stands for integrity, the goose for industry.

Hints for Collectors
Magnificent beakers such as this are among the most impressive
of early American silver objects, and are thus very desirable and
expensive. Because such beakers have been frequently faked, do
not contemplate buying one unless you have studied early silver
extensively.

Victorian parcel-gilt goblet

Description
Deep circular body encircled by bamboo branches; border of triangles at lip. 2 slender, upright, flared handles in shape of bamboo; each attached to body with 3 struts. Flared circular pedestal with border of triangles at base. "L.G.T./FROM/K.E.T./1877" engraved on base. Gilt interior.

Marks and Dimensions
"TIFFANY & C⁰/UNION-SQUARE/3591/3322" stamped incuse; "QUALITY/ 925-1000" in rectangle; "M" in oval; all on underside. Height: 5⅞". Width: 5⅛". Diameter: 3⅛".

Maker, Locality, and Date
Tiffany & Company (1853–present), New York City. c. 1877.

Comment
During the last half of the 19th century there was a great vogue for the Oriental style in the United States, influenced by political involvement in the Far East, artistic interest in the Orient, and the importation of Chinese and Japanese objects. The style that grew from this fashion, known as Japonisme or Japonica, was particularly evident in silver. Although most silver objects like this cup were basically Western in form, their ornament had a distinct Oriental flavor.

Hints for Collectors
The Oriental style of late 19th-century American silver was quite strong and unmistakable, though it never became common. The relative rarity and unusual character of Oriental-style objects recommend them to collectors, especially those pieces made by Tiffany & Company or Gorham Company, both forerunners in that artistic movement.

Federal presentation cup

Description
Circular cup with deep flared bowl. Base of bowl with wide border of alternating acanthus leaves and anthemia in ovals; small leaf tips between ovals, and narrow border of stylized flowerets below. Short circular pedestal with gadrooned collar and narrow border of stylized leaves at base. Engraved in oval reserve on side of cup: "Francis Fred^k McFarland/to/Dr Hamilton/as a token of Gratitude," with banner below enclosing "Erin go Bragh."

Marks and Dimensions
"ANT.^{Y} RASCH" in rectangle stamped twice on underside. Height: 5⅝". Diameter: 4½".

Maker, Locality, and Date
Anthony Rasch (born c. 1778–1858), Philadelphia. 1812–18.

Comment
This small footed cup is a fine example of the numerous 19th-century silver objects made to commemorate a special occasion or honor an individual. Such presentation silver could vary greatly from large urns costing, at the time, thousands of dollars to small medals valued at only a dollar or so. This cup is an example of a moderately priced, though handsomely decorated, personal gift.

Hints for Collectors
Inscriptions of any kind deserve special attention and should never be removed from a silver object. They record important information about an object's history, including the reason it was made. Some inscriptions are evidence of the complex mix of national and ethnic types that constitute American culture; this cup, for instance, bears a Gaelic expression of good will.

176 Victorian repoussé goblet

Description
Inverted bell-shaped cup with undulating intertwined vine at lip. Exterior covered with repoussé grapevines, leaves, and grape clusters. Tall pedestal with flared, molded, circular foot and small knop; grapevine encircles knop and foot.

Marks and Dimensions
"HYDE & GOODRICH" in rectangle stamped on underside. Height: 8¹/₁₆". Diameter: 4¼".

Maker, Locality, and Date
Hyde & Goodrich (1829–c. 1864), New Orleans. 1850–55.

Comment
The firm of Hyde & Goodrich, founded in 1829, operated under a series of partnerships involving James N. Hyde (d. 1838), his son Edward G. Hyde, Charles W. Goodrich (d. 1849), his son William McLeary Goodrich, Henry Thomas, Jr., and Arthur B. Griswold. It was the largest firm of its type in mid-19th-century New Orleans, selling silver objects made locally and in other American cities, as well as other fancy wares.

Hints for Collectors
The 1850s saw a revival of naturalistic ornament on domestic silver. Perhaps the most popular manifestation of this trend was the grapevine, typical examples of which are seen on this goblet. While footed cups of this type were traditionally used in churches, they became common household objects during this era. Since many such cups are available today, collectors should be discriminating, seeking only well-made examples that are of substantial weight and bear a maker's mark.

Victorian presentation goblet

Description
Inverted bell-shaped cup with beaded lip. Decorated with scene
of men amid barrels of tobacco on one side; wreath of tobacco
leaves on other side enclosing engraved inscription: "PRESENTED/
by the Ky. State Agl Society and/SPRATT BOURNE & C°/May 25th
1859." Tall circular pedestal decorated with tobacco leaves.

Marks and Dimensions
Unmarked. Height: 6½". Diameter: 3⅝".

Maker, Locality, and Date
Unknown. Probably Kentucky. c. 1859.

Comment
In the 19th century many states sponsored annual agricultural
fairs, where farmers competed in a number of categories, from
the largest cow to the best-kept farm. The awards, usually
silver, were often in the form of a teaspoon or medal, but
sometimes larger objects like this goblet were given. They were
typically engraved with the name of the event being
commemorated, the name of the winner, and the date.

Hints for Collectors
Although this goblet bears no maker's mark, it was almost
certainly made in Kentucky, where numerous silversmiths were
working at the time. The repoussé decoration depicting 2 men
standing next to barrels of tobacco, an important crop in that
state, is singular. It adds a significant point of interest to the
goblet, which, because unmarked, would otherwise be
unexceptional. The presentation inscription, documenting the
cup's southern origin, further contributes to the interest and
value of this object.

178 Early Colonial chalice

Description
Circular cup with tapered side, flared lip, and slightly rounded
bottom. Stem with one large knop and several smaller ones. Low
conical base with molded edge. "Capt. Willets' donation to/ye.
Ch: of Rehoboth, 1674" engraved on side of cup under lip.

Marks and Dimensions
"RS" under a rose in conforming outline; "IH" under pellets in
conforming outline; both stamped on side of cup. Height: 7⁵⁄₁₆".
Diameter: 4¼".

Maker, Locality, and Date
John Hull & Robert Sanderson (c. 1650–83), Boston. c. 1674.

Comment
This standing cup, or chalice, is one of.9 known examples made
by Hull and Sanderson. Such cups were used in households and
churches, and were sometimes bequeathed to the latter.
Communion vessels left to American Protestant churches were
often conspicuously engraved with the name of the donor and the
date of the gift. Thomas Willet stipulated in his will, probated in
1674, that he would leave "unto the church att Rehoboth
[Massachusetts] five pounds to be disposed of as [the church]
shall see most convenient." His gift, in the form of silver coin,
was given by the church to Hull and Sanderson for conversion
into this chalice.

Hints for Collectors
Hull and Sanderson are the earliest American silversmiths whose
works survive. This fact, together with the engraved inscription
and reliably documented history of this chalice, make it highly
desirable. 18th- and 19th-century church and household chalices,
though not common, are easier to find than 17th-century
examples.

179 Federal parcel-gilt goblet

Description
Urn-shaped cup on circular flared pedestal with narrow beaded border at top and bottom. Low square base. Gilt interior. "T" engraved in script on side.

Marks and Dimensions
"R•SWAN" in rectangle, stamped twice on underside. Height: 6½". Diameter: 3¾".

Maker, Locality, and Date
Robert Swan (c. 1748–1832), Philadelphia. 1799–1810.

Comment
Although goblets have been made in America since the 17th century, the form remains rather uncommon in American silver. Most were intended for use in churches; however, in the 19th century many were made for domestic purposes. Domestic goblets, such as this example, were ornamented with owners' initials, names, or more lengthy inscriptions. Both chalices and domestic goblets were sometimes elaborately decorated with cast, die-stamped, engraved, or repoussé ornament.

Hints for Collectors
Like most goblets, the example shown here is lined with gold. Although the gilt is often largely worn away, traces should be visible. Most goblets of this type are marked on the interior or exterior of the base. Some 19th-century pieces, however, are marked on the underside of the cup, which has been covered by the stem; since the stem is hollow, the mark may be seen by carefully looking up through the base.

Candlesticks, Lamps, and Related Objects

Until the mid-19th century, candles were the principal source of artificial light in the home. Candle holders were fashioned from many materials, including wood, pottery, porcelain, copper, brass, iron, pewter and, less commonly, silver. Since their basic shape was dictated by the simple cylindrical form of the candle, they remained virtually unchanged for centuries.

Candlesticks, Chamber Sticks, and Candelabra

The early 19th century brought with it the advent of the woven wick, stearine (a highly refined animal fat), and paraffin. Prior to this time, candles had been made of tallow (animal fat) or wax (vegetable fat). They usually burned inefficiently and guttered often, resulting in messy drippings. Therefore candlesticks almost invariably had saucerlike disks, called drip pans or bobeches, to catch the melted wax for reuse. At first these wax catchers were located at or near the base, but by about 1800 they were always placed at the top and were often removable. Candlesticks made primarily for stationary use on tables are typically 6″ to 12″ tall. They were often made in pairs, although the wealthy sometimes had sets of 4 and more. Chamber sticks, a more portable variety, are under 5″ high and have an unusually wide saucerlike base, which caught dripping wax as the stick was carried from one room to the next. Most have a finger loop for easy transport.

When greater amounts of light were needed, several candle holders could be clustered around a single shaft; this arrangement is called a candelabrum. Candelabra are typically quite elaborate; some late examples even have pierced shades and spring-loaded holders to raise the candles as they burn.

Lamps

Like candles, fuel-burning lamps have been used since ancient times. However, they only became common in America in the 19th century. Before the advent of kerosene during the third quarter of the 19th century, most stylish examples were imported from Europe. By the close of the Civil War, however, up-to-date American lighting fixtures had supplanted foreign-made examples.

Although lamps were fueled by a considerable variety of fluids, the lamps themselves were of 2 basic types. The simpler had a wick that absorbed fuel by capillary action, while the more sophisticated type had the font above the wick; gravity helped saturate the wick, producing more constant and brighter light. Early lamps had relatively simple woven wicks similar to those used in candles. During the early 19th century, sophisticated examples used tubular wicks, which created a draft for brighter light. Most 19th-century lamps required cylindrical glass chimneys to allow them to burn efficiently.

Ornamentation and Weighting

Many American candlesticks and lamps were ornamented. The ornament might consist of a simple series of knops and rings or faceted sections along the shaft, or of far more extensive and elaborate decoration, such as plant motifs, or, infrequently, animal and human ornament.

Many lighting devices, especially those that were fairly tall, had their bases weighted with a piece of iron or pitch to keep them stable. This was especially common on silver-plated models, not only because candlesticks are fairly lightweight, but also because the weighted filling prevented the thin metal of plated examples from being disfigured or otherwise damaged.

180 English George III fused-plated chamber sticks

Description
Left: Circular, urn-shaped candle cup; removable rectangular bobeche with rounded corners and gadrooned edge. Knopped tapered shaft and dished rectangular pan with rounded corners and gadrooned edge. Ring-shaped finger hole on side. Small square receptacle holding conical douter with knopped tip and molded bottom edge. Right: Rectangular urn-shaped candle cup with rounded corners; removable bobeche with flat molded lip. Short shaft connected to dished rectangular pan with rounded corners and gadrooned edge. Ring-shaped finger hole topped by oval disk on side. Small square receptacle holding conical loop-tipped douter.

Marks and Dimensions
Unmarked. Left height: 2¾"; length: 3¹⁵/₁₆"; width: 3¹¹/₁₆". Right height: 2¹/₁₆"; length: 3⅝"; width: 3¼".

Maker, Locality, and Date
Unknown. England. 1795–1810.

Comment
Chamber sticks varied in size; their saucers ranged from 2" to 5" wide. The smaller sticks, with candles inadequate to read by, were used to take a fire from one room to another; they were frequently fitted with a snuffer.

Hints for Collectors
Although these candlesticks retain their separate bobeches and snuffers, many do not. It is important to recognize when an element is missing, because lost parts reduce the value of an object. The bobeche is missing if the top of the candle cup is unfinished or lacks ornament. Snuffers were held in place with a small rectangular socket; if a socket is empty, the snuffer is missing.

Colonial candlesticks

Description
Circular molded candle cup. Knopped shaft, faceted baluster.
Molded, dished octagonal base; base engraved with coat of arms
of Fanueil family of Boston, and crest and motto "Deo Duce
Ferro Comitante" (God my leader, my sword, my companion) of
Caulfield family of Boston.

Marks and Dimensions
"NM" in rectangle stamped on edge of base. Height: 6¼".
Width: 3⅞".

Maker, Locality, and Date
Nathaniel Morse (c. 1685–1748), Boston. 1710–30.

Comment
American-made candlesticks of the 17th and 18th centuries are
quite rare, especially silver examples. This unusually pleasing
pair was originally owned by the merchant Peter Fanueil and
later became the property of the Caulfield family, probably
through marriage. While some early silver has remained in the
same family since it was made, most has passed into the hands of
others. Silver was often bought and sold at estate auctions, or
vendues, as they were called in the 18th century.

Hints for Collectors
Before the 19th century, the shafts of almost all American silver
candlesticks were cast in halves, silver-soldered together, and
then soldered into a separately cast base. 2 vertical seams
opposite each other should be visible along the length of the
shaft. The underside of the base was then lathe-turned to remove
excess silver and smooth the surface; shallow concentric rings
created in this process should usually be visible. If these features
are absent, the object is probably a modern reproduction.

182 English Victorian electroplated candlesticks

Description
Cylindrical candle cup with removable shaped bobeche decorated with wide flutes and anthemia. Shaft has square flared knop with anthemion on each corner over slender, fluted baluster; cylindrical knop below. Stepped, molded, square base, with shaped sides and anthemia on corners.

Marks and Dimensions
"ELKINGTON & Cº" and "A" stamped incuse on one side of base; "R" and 5 pseudohallmarks on another side; "E & Cº" under crown in shield; "E"; "&"; "Cº" in Gothic script; and "C"; (each in square), all stamped on third side. Height: 11⅝". Width: 5¼".

Maker, Locality, and Date
Elkington & Company (1841–1963), Birmingham, England. 1841–55.

Comment
Although most plated wares were unmarked, these electroplated German-silver candlesticks, closely related to silver examples of the era, bear numerous manufacturer's marks. Elkington pioneered the use of electroplating in about 1840. This fast and inexpensive process allowed complex shapes and convoluted surfaces to be easily plated, making all other methods obsolete.

Hints for Collectors
These candlesticks are in very good condition, but many plated objects have not fared as well. Those from the late 19th and early 20th centuries were made of metal that easily bent and split. Also, on earlier pieces, the silver strips, or edges, placed at points of greatest wear to prevent the base metal from showing, have often been polished through or have broken off. Examples damaged in these ways should be avoided, since they are virtually impossible to restore.

Federal candlesticks

Description
Circular candle cup with alternating anthemia and flowers; removable bobeche with flared cupped lip and wide knurled border. Tapered spool-shaped support below candle cup and above drum-shaped section, with beaded and anthemia borders. Long, tapered, faceted shaft on radiating paw feet. Large, circular, molded base with beaded and anthemia borders; "UPL" engraved in script on top.

Marks and Dimensions
"CHAUDRON'S & RASCH" and "STER•AMERI•MAN•" each in S-shaped outline, stamped on outside edge of base. Height: 12⅛". Diameter: 5⅝".

Maker, Locality, and Date
Simon Chaudron & Anthony Rasch (1809–1812), Philadelphia. 1809–12.

Comment
Many Continental craftsmen immigrated to the United States during the early 19th century, bringing current fashions with them. Simon Chaudron, a Frenchman, and Anthony Rasch, a German, were among the most important of these, since the silver they made during their short partnership had a great impact on American silversmiths. For example, these exotic candlesticks, almost identical to the finest made in Paris, have prominent paw feet and anthemia borders, elements used on virtually all stylish American silver of the next 2 decades.

Hints for Collectors
Although most work by these makers is excellently designed and well made, on occasion objects of inferior quality were produced. Collectors should thus evaluate an object not only by the renown of its maker but also by the merit of its design and execution.

184 English George III fused-plated candlesticks

Description
Candle cup in form of acanthus-leaf capital; removable bobeche with scalloped and gadrooned flat edge. Shaft made of clustered columns with narrow horizontal bands. Square base with incurved sides bordered by bound laurel leaves above and below, and with foliate scrolls flanking oval medallion or urn in center. Pitch filling in base with tinned sheet iron at bottom.

Marks and Dimensions
Unmarked. Height: 12⅜". Width: 5⅛".

Maker, Locality, and Date
Unknown. England. 1765–85.

Comment
In the late 18th century, special gravity-operated presses were developed in England to stamp decoration onto fashionable metalware. Prior to assembly, the parts of an object could have ornament impressed into them quickly and inexpensively. These candlesticks are a fine example of this process: The bases were stamped with foliate borders and urns, and the shafts were stamped in halves and soldered together.

Hints for Collectors
Many English fused-plated candlesticks are available today at moderate prices, so check their condition carefully. Most candlesticks from the late 18th century have been repaired, but if competently and sensitively executed, such repairs do not decrease the value of a piece. In many examples, the pitch filling in the base has become brittle and may break, causing the candlestick to become misshapen. Avoid examples in which the juncture of the shaft and base has been repaired with heavy, grayish lead solder.

Victorian candlesticks

Description
Leaf-decorated flared candle cup; removable bobeche with flared gadrooned edge. Cylindrical shaft ornamented on top half with flowers, ferns, and leaves; reeding and leafy baluster below. Square molded base with flowers and leaves; wooden insert under base.

Marks and Dimensions
"TIFFANY & CO. STERLING" stamped incuse on outer edge of base; "TIFFANY & C^O 7822 M 7627 STERLING-SILVER" stamped incuse under base. Height: 11″. Width: 4⅜″.

Maker, Locality, and Date
Tiffany & Company (1853–present), New York City. 1873–91.

Comment
An essential feature of European and American life for centuries, candlesticks have been made in a tremendous variety of shapes and materials. Silver, however, has remained the most desirable material. Even after the advent of electric lighting, silver candlesticks continued to be made for fashionable interiors. During the last few decades of the 19th century, silver candlesticks were used chiefly in the dining room, suggesting that by then they were considered decorative rather than functional.

Hints for Collectors
These candlesticks are pleasingly designed with the exuberant decoration typical of their era. They are also well marked and heavy—important features to look for when considering a purchase. Thin-walled, lightweight silver objects are less desirable, since they are more susceptible to damage.

Description
Cylindrical candle cup with molded borders; shallow circular
bobeche with molded edge; swiveling S-shaped arm. Flat circular
backplate with triangular projection at top and attached vertical
cylindrical element to hold arm; acorn-shaped pendant. Plate
nailed to bottom of wooden frame containing ornamental
quillwork composition of wax figures, paper flowers, and leaves
under glass. "RR/1720" engraved in block letters on underside of
one bobeche.

Marks and Dimensions
"K•Leverett" in shaped rectangle stamped twice on each circular
backplate. Height (sconces only): 4½″. Diameter: 3¼″.

Maker, Locality, and Date
Knight Leverett (1703–53), Boston. c. 1720.

Comment
These candle arms, a rare form in American silver, were made to
illuminate the elaborate floral picture under glass to which they
are attached. Most 18th-century American silver lighting devices
were table candlesticks. Chandeliers from the period are
virtually unknown, while the few early wall sconces known today
appear to have originated in New England, and all were made to
light quillwork (paper filigree). This pair bears the initials of its
first owner, Ruth Read of Boston.

Hints for Collectors
Because the quillwork they illuminated is fragile, few sconces
have survived. Yet, periodically, unrecorded examples do
appear. Evaluate the condition, genuineness, and American
origin of such pieces. Be prepared to pay handsomely for them
and then to take great care to ensure their safekeeping.

187 Federal candelabrum

Description
Cylindrical, knopped central shaft with encircling oak-leaf
borders; topped by removable candle cup with flared lip into
which is fitted cap with stylized flame. 2 slender curved arms
with stylized acanthus-leaf knops and candle cups with flared
lips. Stepped and molded circular base decorated with stylized
oak leaves.

Marks and Dimensions
"I•OWEN" in rectangle stamped on outer edge of base. Height:
15½". Width: 17¼".

Maker, Locality, and Date
John Owen (dates unknown), Philadelphia. 1815–31.

Comment
This candelabrum, one of a pair, is typical of the few made of
silver in this country before the Civil War. Its central shaft is
topped with a flame-shaped finial that can be removed to expose
another candle cup if additional light is needed. Usually placed on
dining tables today, candelabra were more often used on
sideboards in the 19th century

Hints for Collectors
Because they are uncommon, candelabra from this early date are
in demand and command a premium. Their slender, spidery
arms have often been broken and have sometimes been poorly
repaired. Examine such pieces for broken arms or shafts as
well as missing bobeches. Instead of separate bobeches, some
examples, like this one, have flared rims.

Victorian electroplated candelabrum

Description
Knopped, baluster-shaped central shaft with ribbed candle cup and removable shell-and-scroll-decorated bobeche. 3 radiating S-shaped arms decorated with leaves; each topped with candle cup and bobeche similar to central ones. Candle cups fitted with spring-loaded, simulated candles made of cellulose nitrate. Removable conical shades made of isinglass, red paper, and cover with pierced decoration. Circular molded base with wavy edge and stylized decoration of shell-and-leaf scroll.

Marks and Dimensions
"GORHAM ELECTROPLATE/0294"; anchor in shield; and sickle, all stamped incuse on underside. Anchor in shield; "GORHAM & CO. 015"; and crescent; all stamped incuse on inside of each shade. Height: 21⅛". Diameter: 16".

Maker, Locality, and Date
Gorham Company (1831–present), Providence. Candelabrum: 1899. Shades: 1895.

Comment
By the time this candelabrum was made, electric lamps were widely used. Even so, candles remained an important part of the dining table decoration. This elaborate example has spring-loaded tubes simulating candles. Real candles were placed into the tubes; when lit, they produced a dramatic effect through the colorful red shades.

Hints for Collectors
Make certain that a plated object of this type is made of heavy metal, is substantially plated, and has no loose or broken joints. Also, the internal pitch filling, added for strength, should not be broken and loose inside the object.

English George III fused-plated Argand lamp

Description
Fluted column with stylized leafy capital surmounted by square stepped plinth. Oval fluted font above plinth, with guilloche border and leafy bud finial. 2 fluted horizontal arms extend from plinth. Fluted vertical cylinder attached to each arm; pierced at lower end and topped by colorless glass tube supported by wire frame attached to arm and column. Square plinthlike base with incurved sides, chamfered corners, and beaded and guilloche borders. 4 small acorn-shaped feet. Pitch filling in base with tinned sheet iron at bottom.

Marks and Dimensions
"ARGAND & CO. PATENT" stamped in raised letters in oval disk on plinth between burners; "BOULTON" stamped incuse on side of base. Height: 24¼". Width: 11¼". Depth: 6½".

Maker, Locality, and Date
Matthew Boulton (1728–1809), Birmingham, England. 1787–1809.

Comment
Beginning about the 1790s, extensive experimentation took place to develop more efficient lighting devices. A Frenchman, Ami Argand, invented an oil lamp with a tubular wick. On the typical lamp, the oil was held in a font; below it was a horizontal arm to which the wick and burner were attached; thus, gravity fed oil to the wick. Made in great variety, these lamps proved very popular because the light they emitted, though not bright by today's standards, was far brighter than that of a candle.

Hints for Collectors
Much has been written about Boulton, one of the most celebrated English makers of silver and base-metal objects. His fine, innovative wares are quite expensive today.

English George III fused-plated oil lamp

Description
Spherical font; removable upper portion topped by spherical finial. 2 cylindrical, tapered arms curving from one side of font. Curved vertical reflector with double-arched top. Cylindrical flared column has square base with incurved molded sides. Stylized leafy borders on font, column capital, and base.

Marks and Dimensions
Unmarked. Height: 16⅛". Width: 4¼". Depth: 5⅛".

Maker, Locality, and Date
Unknown. England. 1800–25.

Comment
During the late 18th and early 19th centuries, interest in ancient Greece and Rome was pervasive. Virtually every category of household object incorporated decorative elements derived from antique sources. Though lacking a Greek or Roman prototype, this lamp has a columnar support reminiscent of classical buildings and stylized borders of leaf tips that also recall ancient ornament.

Hints for Collectors
Although this lamp was originally completely silvered, its copper has become exposed in several places, the inevitable result of handling and polishing an object that has only a thin silver coating. The coating should not be restored by electroplating, a technique that is vastly different from the fused-plating process; such a restoration would compromise the integrity of the object and reduce its value.

191 English George III fused-plated Argand lamp

Description
Flattened, oval, upright font with inset mirror on one side; pierced finial with arches and scrolls. Cylindrical knopped shaft with reeded base. Flared molded foot rim. Reeded horizontal arm supports upright cylinder with thumbscrew mechanism and urn-shaped, engraved, colorless glass chimney above, and pierced inverted bell below.

Marks and Dimensions
Unmarked. Height: 19⅞". Width: 5". Depth: 7½".

Maker, Locality, and Date
Unknown. England. 1790–1810.

Comment
Argand lamps were among the most popular and fashionable lighting devices of the late 18th and early 19th centuries. Most were made of brass, but some were made of fused-plated silver. Both single- and double-arm examples were made, usually with strong architectural elements. All had a cylindrical glass chimney that created a forced draft, resulting in a large flame and a comparatively bright light.

Hints for Collectors
Argand lamps are plentiful. Most, however, have been altered, usually around the burner, for conversion to kerosene or electricity. Since it is almost impossible to find a lamp that has not been tampered with in some way, collectors should acquire only those lamps that have been sensitively converted. If you are fortunate enough to find an Argand lamp that is intact, do not alter it.

English George III fused-plated oil lamps

Description
Octagonal urn-shaped font with chased foliate border and swags. Brass burner with cylindrical brass thumbscrew. Cylindrical frosted and engraved glass chimney; truncated conical copper shade (silver plate almost entirely worn off). Slender, flared, pierced circular pedestal with leafy border near base.

Marks and Dimensions
Unmarked. Height: 13″. Diameter: 5¹⁄₁₆″.

Maker, Locality, and Date
Unknown. England. 1790–1815.

Comment
The remarkable interest in Greece and Rome during the late 18th and early 19th centuries prompted many connoisseurs to collect antique artifacts and to purchase new objects that were patterned after classical styles. The urn was perhaps the most popular classical motif for domestic objects at this time; everything, from lamps like this pair to knife boxes, tea sets, and wine cisterns, was fabricated in this shape or decorated with painted or inlaid urns.

Hints for Collectors
These lamps are very fine examples of the stylish urn shape so prevalent when they were made. They are unusual because they have remained a pair, and because they retain most of their original silvering (except on the shades). Moreover, since these lamps have not been converted for electricity, their burners are original and unaltered, a particularly rare feature collectors should always look for. All these qualities would make this pair a most desirable addition to any collection.

Victorian electroplated kerosene lamp

Description
Pierced, circular brass burner with colorless glass chimney and 3 brass arms supporting painted hemispherical glass shade. Hammer-textured globular font with 2 applied, vinelike flower-and-leaf-decorated loop handles and ornament. Molded foot rim with 4 tabular feet decorated with applied rosettes.

Marks and Dimensions
"The Solar E & M Co." in raised letters on wick elevator knob. Height: 19½". Diameter: 7½".

Maker, Locality, and Date
Meriden Britannia Company (1852–98), Meriden, Connecticut. c. 1882.

Comment
Kerosene was the most popular lighting fuel between about 1870 and 1900 because it burned cleanly and provided efficient, inexpensive, and bright light. Most kerosene lamps were simple forms in nickel-plated brass or glass, but a few, like this example, were decorated with the floral motifs and landscapes popular at the time.

Hints for Collectors
This lamp is unusual because the applied handles and flower-and-leaf ornament have been patinated to contrast with the brightly polished surface of the hammer-textured font. In such lamps the condition and integrity of the metal parts are most important; although an original shade and chimney are desirable, most are replacements and acceptable to collectors. Since many lamps were assembled from parts made by various companies, you may find the name of a different manufacturer on each component. In this example, the attribution to Meriden Britannia is supported by information in one of the firm's old pattern books.

Boxes and Other Containers

The silver and silver-plated boxes in this group are varied not only in shape, size, and decoration, but also in purpose. Some are very practical, serving to protect fragile eyeglasses, while others reflect social customs such as the use of snuff or tobacco. Some, like cosmetics cases, are meant for the exclusive use of one owner, while others are representative of public occasions or ceremonies.

Ornament and Style

Many of these boxes have been engraved with the name, initials, or other insignia of the owner. Others bear more generalized decoration, sometimes alluding to the contents, as with cigar or cigarette cases depicting a rapturous figure clouded by swirling smoke. Most, however, bear the stylistic motifs popular during the era in which they were made. The elaborate naturalistic flowers and scrolls popular during the mid-18th century stand in strong contrast to the clean, uncluttered surfaces of early 20th-century boxes.

While most boxes are straightforward in shape—square, rectangular, circular, or oval—others are elaborately designed and constructed. Some boxes are specialized, having the interior custom-fitted with compartments to house distinct items, from toothpicks to facial rouge. For example, the etui is a form that contained a variety of personal objects. Some etuis held professional articles, such as drafting instruments, but most were meant to contain little tools used in personal hygiene, such as scissors and tweezers. Such etuis are comparable to present-day manicure sets.

Other silver boxes in this group have elaborate exteriors; some are even fitted with ornate and complex mechanisms for opening and closing. Most such boxes are fabricated exclusively of silver, but a few freely integrate other materials, such as tortoiseshell or enamel, for decorative effect. In some examples, only the lid, the part that showed, is made of silver or silver plate, and the rest of the box is of inexpensive, undecorated base metal.

The Social Life of the Time

From the 17th century to the present, silver boxes of all sizes and shapes have performed a useful function in American daily life. Each example reflects the life-style of an era and the forces at work in the creation of such a box.

Nowhere is this fact more evident than with calling-card cases. These tiny boxes were popular between the Civil War and the First World War, when the elaborate social rituals of the time included paying obligatory visits to acquaintances and leaving a card behind. The function of most boxes can be fairly readily interpreted by an informed examination. Occasionally, their function remains obscure because of its highly specialized and now outmoded purpose. This is especially true of boxes like vinaigrettes, which were used to contain aromatic spirits and are infrequently encountered today. Small boxes of this type were relatively common in 17th- and 18th-century Europe and England, where the use of smelling salts was commonplace, but seem to have been made and used with much less frequency in this country.

Late Colonial repoussé snuffbox

Description
Oval box with flat back. Hinged flat lid with elaborate repoussé composition of shells, scrolls, flowers, leaves, and diapering. Shallow container with slightly concave sides.

Marks and Dimensions
"IR" in rectangle; leafy scroll stamped incuse; both on inside bottom. Length: 3¼₆". Width: 2⁵⁄₁₆". Height: ⁹⁄₁₆".

Maker, Locality, and Date
Joseph Richardson, Sr. (1711–84), Philadelphia. 1750–70.

Comment
The term rococo is generally applied to the popular 18th-century style that involved elaborate, often asymmetrical, naturalistic designs. While true asymmetry is rarely found in American rococo silver, this diminutive snuffbox has a genuinely asymmetrical pattern of shells, fruits, and flowers, and is thus of considerable interest.

Hints for Collectors
Most American silversmiths' marks are fairly simple, usually consisting of the maker's initials or his first initial and full surname. However, supplementary marks, not yet fully understood, were occasionally used on silver made prior to the mid-19th century. The leafy scroll stamped inside this box, for example, seems to have been used exclusively in Philadelphia during the last half of the 18th century, and is believed to be a mark of quality, assuring purchasers they were buying silver that equaled the English sterling standard. Such a mark does not necessarily increase the value of an object, but it certainly adds historical interest.

Colonial silver-and-tortoiseshell tobacco box

Description
Hinged, flat oval lid elaborately pierced and engraved with leafy scrolls and animals surrounding coat of arms (of Welstead family of Boston); backed with tortoiseshell. Shallow, straight-sided oval box lined with tortoiseshell. Conjoined initials "ww" engraved on bottom.

Marks and Dimensions
"I•G" with crown above and fleur-de-lis below, all within shield stamped on underside. Length: 4¼". Width: 3⅛". Height: 1¹⁄₁₆".

Maker, Locality, and Date
Joseph Goldthwaite (1706–80), Boston. 1730–40.

Comment
Silver tobacco boxes were popular in 18th-century America, and numerous examples were made in all major East Coast cities. Most are simple oval boxes with hinged lids. This elaborate example, with its tortoiseshell lining and pierced lid, is an unusual variant. While most boxes of this type have engraved ornament on the lid, the rabbits and squirrels depicted here are uncommon. Ownership of these boxes was not restricted to men; women often carried their own tobacco in such containers.

Hints for Collectors
Because tobacco boxes were used daily, collectors should expect them to have sustained great wear. The delicate pierced lid of this example has been broken and repaired in numerous places, and its hinge, originally soldered to the box, is now held on with screws. Collectors should seek out unusual boxes with spirited ornament; in addition, the condition and possibly the provenance will contribute significantly to their worth.

Late Federal snuffbox

Description
Circular low domed lid engraved with coat of arms and crest
(of Lloyd family of Boston) featuring rampant lion in shield
surmounted by helmet and bird in nest. Lid fits over plain
shallow circular container.

Marks and Dimensions
"FLETCHER & GARDINER" in circular outline, also enclosing
"PHIL^A" in rectangle, stamped on bottom of container. Diameter:
3⅜". Height: ½".

Maker, Locality, and Date
Thomas Fletcher & Sidney Gardiner (1808–27), Philadelphia.
1820–30.

Comment
This shallow box, well designed for pocket use, may have held
snuff, though it is somewhat larger than most such containers.
Its most striking feature is the coat of arms and crest engraved
on the lid. Such devices were pictographs, each element having a
specific meaning. In combination, the arms, crest, and motto—
the last of which is not included here—were assigned to one
family. In Europe the right to such heraldic devices was rigidly
regulated by law, but in America these aristocratic devices were
adopted and used more freely. The meaning of a coat of arms on
an object was as clear and understandable as any signature.

Hints for Collectors
Though small, this spectacular box would make a notable
acquisition for any discriminating collector. Moreover, its coat
of arms, identifying the original owner, provides useful
documentation about the box's history and thus enhances
its value.

Federal fused-plated box

Description
Shallow circular lid ornamented on top with central spread eagle having shield-shaped body and clutching arrows and an olive branch in its talons; tapered ribs radiating from eagle. Fitted over shallow cylindrical container of tinned sheet iron.

Marks and Dimensions
Unmarked. Diameter: 3½". Height: 1⁵⁄₁₆".

Maker, Locality, and Date
Unknown. United States or England. 1810–40.

Comment
The purpose of this box is not known, but the presence of the eagle used in the Great Seal of the United States indicates that it may have been intended for governmental purposes. The box is unusual because it combines silver-plated copper and tinned sheet iron. The decoration on the lid was stamped in a 2-part steel die, a technique for decorating silver that was widely used during the 19th century.

Hints for Collectors
American silver-plated objects dating from the early 19th century are quite rare. Because of the Federal-style eagle that is its sole ornament, this box might be tentatively attributed to an American maker. The manufacturing techniques and talent to make such a box were certainly to be found in America at the time. But collectors should bear in mind that much fused plate tailored to the American market was imported from England during this period.

Description
Circular lid with molded edge enclosing embossed spread eagle
with shield-shaped body, its talons clutching an olive bough and
cluster of arrows. Above, group of stars and banner inscribed
"E PLURIBUS UNUM" (One out of many) within a cloud border.
Shallow container holding red wax seal with same design as lid.
Left: Border of stars around rim. Right: 2 silver-wire tassels
suspended from side.

Marks and Dimensions
Unmarked. Left diameter: 5″; height: ½″. Right diameter: 5″;
height: 1¼″.

Maker, Locality, and Date
Both attributed to Seraphim Masi (active c. 1822–50), Charles A.
Burnett (1760–1849), or Jacob Leonard (dates unknown),
Washington, D.C. 1815–71.

Comment
Skippets held the ceremonial wax seals used to indicate official
approval on important United States government documents.
Such boxes were attached by woven silver cords to most
American treaties and were used from the War of 1812 until
1871. The covers of these silver, gold, or silver-gilt pendant
boxes bore the impressive national emblem, known as the Great
Seal of the United States.

Hints for Collectors
Although most American skippets are unmarked, Federal
records indicate that only 3 silversmiths, located in the
Washington area, were contracted to make them, which narrows
down their attribution. Handle a skippet gently because the wax
seal enclosed within is fragile. If you find a skippet still attached
to its treaty, never separate the two.

Modern cosmetic case

Description
Hinged cylindrical box decorated with alternating plain and
striped panels, and "A A J" in small rectangular reserve. Woven
silk loop at one end, tassel at other. Interior has 3 hinged lids;
one with mirror, another engraved "Alwilda Althea Josephs" in
script.

Marks and Dimensions
"E.A.M./STERLING/78281" stamped incuse twice on interior. Length:
3¼". Diameter: 1½".

Maker, Locality, and Date
Elgin-American Manufacturing Company (1887–1950), Elgin,
Illinois. 1900–40.

Comment
Silver has traditionally been a desirable material for personal
articles such as jewelry, purses, cosmetic cases, and other small
objects. These silver objects not only were a sign of wealth but
also provided a discreet way for women to carry the necessities
of genteel life. The example shown here is meant to hang from
the wrist; earlier small cosmetic containers were simple boxes
that could be tucked away in a pocket.

Hints for Collectors
Most silver purses and cosmetic cases originally had parts made
of fabric; in many cases, the fabric has been lost, detracting from
the object's interest and value. Complete and intact examples are
preferable if all other factors, such as the presence of a maker's
mark and condition of the metal parts, are equal. Of course,
fabric parts can be restored and a lost mirror replaced, but not
without additional expense and sometimes extensive research,
which should be taken into account when considering a purchase.

Federal case and spectacles

Description
Long flat-sided box with rounded ends; one end hinged to form lid having flat raised lip. Contains pair of spectacles with oval eyepieces and arched bridge. Hinged bows with thin, flat, adjustable extensions. "Dr. Didier" engraved in script on edge of lid and on outside of one bow.

Marks and Dimensions
"HJP" in rectangle stamped on one bow of spectacles. Box length: 5¹⁄₁₆"; width: 1½".

Maker, Locality, and Date
Henry J. Pepper (c. 1790–1853), Wilmington, Delaware. 1813–26.

Comment
Making eyeglasses and other small personal objects, along with repair work such as tightening the hinge on a tankard or soldering a tear in the side of a beaker, was the mainstay of the silversmith's business. Spectacles always came in a case, usually made of tinned sheet iron, papier-mâché, or brass; the silver case seen here is less common. The sliding extensions of the bows made the spectacles adjustable. Lenses were sometimes made of bifocal glass; some spectacles had shaded lenses hinged to the frame for light-sensitive eyes.

Hints for Collectors
Because Pepper worked in both Wilmington and later in Philadelphia, it is often difficult to assign his work to one of these cities and a time span narrower than 1813–50. Collectors often attribute their own Pepper objects to his Wilmington period because the Wilmington work is rarer and more desirable. Fortunately, these spectacles and case are documented as having been owned by Dr. Pierre Didier, a Wilmington physician.

Modern spectacles case

Description
Flat rectangular case with rounded ends and hinged lid. Engine-turned decoration on surfaces, and borders of stylized foliate design. Raised central boss decorated with leaf tips surrounding engraved script initials "W J K." "Presented to/Prof. W. J. Kaup/by the /Machine Construction Class/of Pratt Institute/1911" engraved on underside.

Marks and Dimensions
"MADE FOR TIFFANY & CO. STERLING 20"; "LF" in heptagon; all stamped incuse on edge of lid. Length: 4⅜". Width: 2".

Maker, Locality, and Date
La Secla, Fried & Company (c. 1909–22), Newark, New Jersey. Retailed by Tiffany & Company (1853–present), New York City. c. 1911.

Comment
Although eyeglasses originated in medieval Europe, they came to be made with great frequency only after Benjamin Franklin's invention of bifocals. Eyeglass frames were usually made of gold or silver, but the cases were usually made from more humble materials. Silver spectacles cases are quite uncommon and usually lack any decoration except for the owner's initials.

Hints for Collectors
Silver spectacles cases, while not common, can be acquired for fairly modest prices. On the whole, eyeglass cases are small, straightforward, and rather plain, but unusual examples such as this one do occasionally turn up. This box is elaborately decorated with engine turning and has an unusually shaped domed lid. The presentation inscription, which nicely documents the original owner, lends additional interest. These features make this spectacles case more valuable than most.

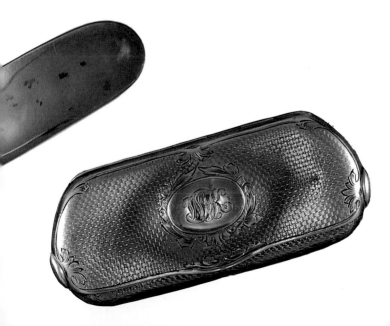

Description

Flat, slightly tapered, oval box with hinged domed lid and spring latch. Narrow borders of stylized foliate ornament at top of lid, juncture of lid and container, and base. Side engraved with crown and bound laurel boughs encircling "This/MEMORIAL/was bequeathed/by the best of/MOTHERS/to her son/John/DeLancey"; opposite side engraved with draped urn enclosing "Eliz.^{h} DeLancey/ob.^{t} 23 Sept.^{r}/1784/A et. 64." Underside engraved in script "When you Receive this Token/The Parent who gives it/ Will no longer be here on Earth./Let us live so as to hope to meet/in Heaven." Fitted interior holds steel scissors, ivory and tortoiseshell notebooks, compass, knife, and corkscrew.

Marks and Dimensions

Unmarked. Height: 4″. Width: 1⁹/₁₆″.

Maker, Locality, and Date

Attributed to William Garret Forbes (1751–1840), New York City. 1780–84.

Comment

An etui is a small box meant to contain personal articles, usually for sewing. This fine example was one of 5 that Elizabeth DeLancey commissioned in her will to be made for her sons as posthumous gifts. Etuis were more frequently made of brass than silver.

Hints for Collectors

Many etuis have lost some or all of their tools; this example, for instance, originally had 8. Although unmarked, this etui can be tentatively assigned to Forbes because one of its marked companion pieces still exists, as does the will stating their commission. This piece is of only moderate value but has considerable historical interest.

English and American Victorian calling-card cases

Description
Shallow rectangular box with narrow hinged lid edged with scrolls. Flowers, scrolls, and leaves surrounding main scene. Left: Philadelphia Waterworks on front; foliate scrolls on back; "MBP/TO/AC" engraved on side of lid. Right: Houses of Parliament on front; "JGN" engraved on back.

Marks and Dimensions
Left: Unmarked. Height: 3½". Width: 2½". Depth: ¼". Right: 4 hallmarks ("N•M"; lion; "U"; and anchor), each in clipped-corner square, and female profile in oval, all stamped on bezel of body. Height: 3⅜". Width: 2⅜". Depth: ⅝".

Maker, Locality, and Date
Left: Unknown. Probably Philadelphia. 1860–1900. Right: Nathaniel Mills (dates unknown), Birmingham, England. 1894–95.

Comment
Calling cards experienced a great vogue from the late 19th century until about the First World War, and calling-card cases were made of a great variety of materials, including mother-of-pearl, papier-mâché, wood, brass, leather, and silver. These 2 silver cases bear typical scrolled foliate ornament, but their decoration is unusual.

Hints for Collectors
Although the use of calling cards has virtually disappeared, cases are in ample supply and popular with collectors. Most silver ones are unmarked. The unusual decoration of these 2 examples—identifiable buildings—adds considerably to their appeal and value. American collectors would probably pay more for the case depicting the Philadelphia Waterworks, since this famous landmark indicates that the object is most likely American.

204 Modern cigarette case and match safe

Description
Top: Curved rectangular cigarette case with rounded corners; hinged at one end; spring-loaded catch with steel spring. One side decorated with narrow stripes and rectangle enclosing "1919"; other side engraved "JMK" in script. Bottom: Flat rectangular match safe with rounded corners; hinged at one end; small loop and snap catch. Decorated like cigarette case.

Marks and Dimensions
Top: "G" in clipped-corner square; "H" and "F" each in chevron-shaped outline; and "STERLING"; all stamped incuse on bezel on interior. Length: 4¼". Width: 3¼". Bottom: Unmarked. Length: 2⅝". Width: 1⅞".

Maker, Locality, and Date
Top: G. H. French & Company (c. 1919–35), North Attleboro, Massachusetts. c. 1919. Bottom: Attributed to same firm.

Comment
Silver boxes to hold cigars, cigarettes, and matches were made in considerable quantity during the 19th and 20th centuries. Some were extraordinarily fanciful, shaped, for instance, in the form of a clenched fist or a rolled newspaper, or imaginatively decorated with stamped, engraved, or enameled scenes. However, most were fairly straightforward and, like these examples, decorated with simple engraving and the owner's initials.

Hints for Collectors
While fanciful and imaginative boxes are more sought after than plainer articles, any potential acquisition should be in good condition. The hinge and latch should be operative, as should the internal spring-loaded mechanism of a cigarette case. The striking surface of a match safe should be intact.

Modern Art Nouveau cigar case

Description
Shallow rectangular box with rounded corners. Hinged on one long side, pressure-operated latch on other. Decorated with head of a woman smoking a cigarette amid swirling smoke, die-stamped on both sides.

Marks and Dimensions
Circle with "925 FINE STERLING" around edge, enclosing conjoined initials "UB"; all incuse. Length: 5″. Width: 3¾″.

Maker, Locality, and Date
Unger Brothers (1878–1914), Newark, New Jersey. 1901–10.

Comment
This small box is a fine example of the French style known as Art Nouveau, which enjoyed a short-lived popularity in the United States during the first decade of this century. The Unger Brothers' catalogue of 1904 shows that this image of a woman surrounded by swirling cigarette smoke embellished cigarette cases, ashtrays, match holders, and even unrelated objects like tape measures. The sinuously curved lines and naturalistic features are characteristic of Art Nouveau.

Hints for Collectors
The output of the Unger Brothers firm was considerable. The striking and appealing style of the company's objects was greatly influenced by contemporary French design. Since many of the company's products are small personal artifacts, they are generally less expensive than the large dining-room objects made by other firms at the time. Collectors with a limited budget would do well to familiarize themselves with this manufacturer's products; the best made by the Unger Brothers will provide years of enjoyment and continue to increase in value.

Description
Hinged, rectangular, slightly domed lid with rounded corners; embossed with the word "Solace." Interior gold-washed. Inscription in block letters "COMPLIMENTS OF/JOHN ANDERSON & CO." stamped inside lid.

Marks and Dimensions
"GORHAM MFG. CO./STERLING"; lion; anchor; Gothic "G"; and rooster, all stamped incuse inside lid. Length: 3½". Width: 2⅜". Height: 1".

Maker, Locality, and Date
Gorham Company (1831–present), Providence. 1890.

Comment
Small silver boxes have traditionally been used to contain a great variety of objects, from personal items such as jewelry or beauty spots to amenities such as tobacco. While many boxes are decorated, few provide specific information about the exact purpose for which they were originally intended. This example is one of the few that allows a reasonable hypothesis; the inscription "Solace" suggests that it was meant to contain medicines.

Hints for Collectors
Small silver objects have universal appeal to both serious collectors and those with only a casual interest. Boxes such as this example are usually utilitarian as well as decorative, and because they are small, they are often inexpensive. Smaller silver objects are much less often faked than are larger, rarer objects. But even so, you should examine them carefully.

Federal vinaigrette

Description
Hinged, flat, rectangular lid with rounded edges and corners. Top decorated with engine turning and oval reserve with stylized foliate border containing script initials "F. St." Shallow container with sides and bottom ornamented with engine turning. Gilt interior fitted with sliding cover with pierced flowers and scrolls.

Marks and Dimensions
"W. Ball" in rectangle stamped on inside bottom. Length: 1⁵⁄₁₆″. Width: ¹³⁄₁₆″. Height: ½″.

Maker, Locality, and Date
William Ball (1763–1815), Baltimore. 1810–15.

Comment
Vinaigrettes are small, portable containers that held a sponge containing aromatic vinegar, which was used to mask offensive smells. With the development of plumbing, deodorants, and higher standards of cleanliness, the need for such boxes was eventually obviated. The inner lid, which held the sponge in place, was pierced to allow the aroma to escape, and slid open so the sponge could be removed and replenished with spirits. The gilding helped to prevent the silver from being tarnished by the acidic contents.

Hints for Collectors
This box is ornamented with engine turning, which came into vogue during the third quarter of the 19th century. Its presence on this box, whose maker died in 1815, suggests that the engraving was a later addition. Much silver was updated in this way, so always examine any ornamentation to determine if it is original. Such alterations may lower the price of an object substantially.

Modern enameled box

Description
Rectangular hinged lid with border of applied ribbed oval reserves and small spheres, surrounding a rectangular, slightly convex enameled plaque depicting a bird amid flowers and leaves in red, purple, green, and yellow. Moderately deep body, with sides similar to lid. 4 small spherical feet.

Marks and Dimensions
"EC" applied on edge of underside. Length: 6⅝". Width: 5¾". Height: 3⅜".

Maker, Locality, and Date
Elizabeth Copeland (dates unknown), Boston. 1907–16.

Comment
Enameling on silver is a decorative technique that has been used for centuries in both Oriental and Western art. Its great appeal derives from the freedom it gives a craftsman to experiment with design and also from its brightly colored and boldly or delicately patterned results. The technique of filling compartments with colored glass through several carefully controlled firings is time-consuming and requires much patience.

Hints for Collectors
This very desirable box, which is both utilitarian and highly decorative, is covered by bold, simple, colorful patterns that are fine examples of enamelwork. Its maker signed it in a most unusual manner, applying her initials rather than stamping them into the underside, and this feature adds to the box's interest. An enameled object should be handled carefully, since dropping or jarring it would result in the breakage and probable loss of enameling, decreasing its value considerably.

Victorian electroplated jewel casket

Description
Frame: Stylized leafy arch above 3 birds on branch; 2 flat triangular ends with pierced leafy design, topped with pierced anthemia; triangular pieces joined by cylindrical rod at top, 2 rods at base. Rectangular box suspended from frame; sides pierced in guilloche pattern; foliate device hanging from bottom of front. Curved, pierced, foliate arm connects lid of box to arch of frame; rotating arch lifts lid to reveal cloth-lined interior.

Marks and Dimensions
"MERIDEN B*COMPANY" in circle enclosing shield containing scales; "QUADRUPLE PLATE/106" directly below circle; all stamped incuse on underside of box. Height: 9¾". Length: 6¼". Width: 4".

Maker, Locality, and Date
Meriden Britannia Company (1852–98), Meriden, Connecticut. c. 1886.

Comment
Silver-plated boudoir accessories became very popular during the late 19th century. Inexpensive manufacturing techniques provided elaborate and valuable-looking objects, including jewelry boxes. Many incorporated novelty features, such as hinged handles that automatically opened the lid.

Hints for Collectors
Jewelry boxes are almost always lined with fabric, which often becomes faded or stained. If the fabric is so badly soiled that it needs replacement, be sure to restore the interior to its original appearance by choosing an appropriate material. If damaged, novelty features such as lids that open automatically should also be carefully and properly repaired.

Sewing and Desk Accessories and Other Personal Objects

Perhaps nowhere is the versatility and appeal of American silver and silver plate more apparent than in the many diverse household and personal articles that have been fashioned over the past 300 years. Although relatively few Americans have ever owned large numbers of silver objects, most aspired to possess something made of silver. Often this desire resulted in the acquisition of small personal articles, such as sewing equipment, toiletries, or objects for the desk or study. The less affluent made do with silver-plated counterparts.

An Abundance of Silver
The discovery of the extraordinarily rich and seemingly bottomless silver mines in California and Nevada during the 1850s, '60s, and '70s had a profound effect on the ownership of silver. Annual production totaling millions of ounces made silver affordable, and a great number of small personal objects, such as ashtrays, hair curlers, hairbrushes, and noisemakers, were made for Americans at this time.

Jewelry, buttons, buckles, and other objects of personal adornment are the most popular and well-cared-for articles of this type. The interest and value of other small silver objects—especially those of humble purpose and inconsequential character, such as sewing accoutrements or toilet articles—have often been discounted by owners and heirs. As a result, relatively few such objects have survived from previous centuries.

Many such artifacts are whimsies, eccentric complements to the lives of individuals. These tiny silver objects capture a certain freedom of expression, without regard for public opinion, and provide a fascinating insight into private taste and fancy. Representative are a small lamp in the shape of a man-in-the-moon, fish-shaped needle holders, a lighter built around an animal's horn, and a chatelaine embellished with a tiny and very realistic landscape.

Social Customs
Small personal artifacts also reflect the great variety of social activities that people pursued. Many, like small swords, were part and parcel of accepted custom; too small and lightweight to be effective weapons, they were usually worn to indicate social status, and can be seen in many portraits executed before the American Revolution. Similarly, some symbols of membership in private organizations, such as the Order of Freemasons, were often made of silver; such organizational tokens are usually laden with secret symbolism. Agricultural and mechanics societies also used silver to promote or commemorate their activities. Annual competitions were held to encourage art and industry, and craftsmen, farmers, and others received objects made of silver in recognition of their achievements.

A great variety of silver objects were also part of the business of households. Silver inkstands, paper clips, and other items were useful in letter-writing or attending to everyday affairs. And even children partook of the general abundance of silver items—whistles and teething toys were often fashioned of silver for the infants of the well-to-do. Large, ostentatious silver objects, such as tea services or tureens, may or may not accurately reflect the lives of their owners. But small articles—whether formal or casual, personal or public—provide valuable insight into the details of daily life in earlier times and reveal silver's central role in it.

Victorian pincushion holder

Description
Wide cylindrical ring pierced with pattern of stylized scrolls and anthemia. Beaded upper border and molded foot rim. Applied symmetrical cartouche of scrolls and leaves engraved with "F" in script. High-domed lid padded and removable. Fitted with pink silk interior.

Marks and Dimensions
Deer head; Gothic "R.W.&S"; "STERLING"; and "57"; all stamped incuse on underside. Height: 2⅞". Diameter: 3¼".

Maker, Locality, and Date
Robert Wallace & Sons (1871–1956), Wallingford, Connecticut. 1871–1920.

Comment
After the advent of the sewing machine in the 19th century, sewing by hand became something of a genteel art in many households, and a profusion of silver implements was developed for it. This large, elegant pincushion has a removable lid padded to receive straight pins, and a pierced silver container, lined with silk, to hold a thimble, needles, spools of thread, and the like. Its materials and decoration attest to the owner's good taste and affluence.

Hints for Collectors
Most late 19th- and 20th-century factories marked their silver products with symbols rather than full names, so that identifying a maker is often difficult. The fragile fabric on pieces like this is often badly soiled or tattered; if it is suitably replaced with material similar to the original, the value of the object will be little affected. Any loss or change in the silver portion, however, would render the article substantially less desirable.

Federal knitting-needle holders

Description
Left: Flat, slightly convex, heart-shaped form. Tube soldered to back has 4 small loops attaching it to fabric swatch. Imbricated scale pattern on front surrounds central heart enclosing "JRM" engraved in script. Right: Fish-shaped form, slightly convex on one side. Slender tube soldered along length of back. Engraved fins and features; loop at tail. 6 small holes along edges for attaching to fabric swatch. "AR" engraved in script under eye.

Marks and Dimensions
Unmarked. Left length: 1⅝"; width: 1". Right length: 2¼"; width: ¾".

Maker, Locality, and Date
Unknown. Probably Philadelphia area. Left: 1790–1820. Right: 1800–20.

Comment
These small devices were also made in leaf and urn shapes. They were sewn to a fabric swatch that was pinned to the waist of a knitter's skirt. The slender tube held a knitting needle, against which the other needle could be manipulated, thereby freeing one hand for keeping the yarn untangled and feeding it to the needles. Although these small personal artifacts were almost never marked, surviving records suggest that most were made in the Philadelphia area during the late 18th and early 19th centuries.

Hints for Collectors
Needle holders are easy to overlook because of their small size and outmoded purpose. If the original fabric swatch is attached, it should not be removed, regardless of its condition, for it makes evident the function of these rare objects.

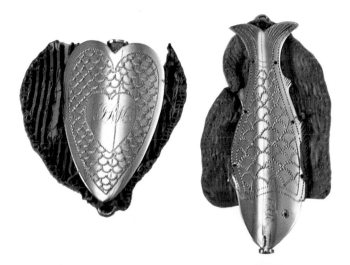

Victorian/modern letter clip

Description
2 shield-shaped sides joined back to back by spring-loaded clasp with steel spring. Upper side engraved with narrow border encircling crossed boughs enframing "MFC" in script.

Marks and Dimensions
"S. C. & L. CO./STERLING" stamped incuse on inside of bottom half. Length: 3″. Width: 2½″. Height: 1″.

Maker, Locality, and Date
Shreve, Crump & Low (1869–present), Boston. 1869–1920.

Comment
Letter writing was widely practiced in earlier centuries and fostered a large array of objects, including writing instruments, blotters, sanders, seals, and sealing wax, as well as letter clips. The engraved leaves and stylized border that decorate this clip were more popular during the late 18th century than during the late 19th and early 20th centuries, when this object was produced.

Hints for Collectors
Pay careful attention to the maker's mark to determine the age of an object. For example, the ornamentation of this clip, with its strong resemblance to 18th-century decoration, might lead a collector to assume that it is much older than it actually is. An understanding of the various forms of silver is also very helpful; this form, as far as is known, did not exist in the 18th century. This sort of knowledge will help collectors avoid paying too high a price for an object, mistakenly thinking it dates from an earlier era than it does.

Victorian classical presentation medal

Description
Disk embossed in front with scene glorifying knowledge.
Woman, seated amid classical emblems, holds laurel wreath over
standing child with book. Group of children with objects
symbolizing arts and sciences. Background includes steamboat,
rising sun, columned building on mountaintop, and winged angel
with horn. Inscribed above, "MECHANICS INSTITUTE"; below,
"NEW-YORK/FURST.F." Reverse inscribed in script "Awarded to/J.
Hague/for an Improvement in/Ever Pointed Pencils/Sep 1839"
surrounded by boughs under "KNOWLEDGE IS POWER."

Marks and Dimensions
"FURST.F." (for "Furst made this") stamped in raised letters on
front. Diameter: 2″.

Maker, Locality, and Date
Moritz Furst (b. 1782), Philadelphia. c. 1839.

Comment
The Mechanics Institute in New York was one of many 19th-
century American societies devoted to encouraging the arts and
sciences. These sponsored annual competitions for everything
from livestock to household furnishings, often giving silver
awards to the winners. This award was presented for an
improvement in the mechanical pencil, a significant invention in
its day.

Hints for Collectors
Presentation silver, especially from the 19th century, is readily
available from dealers, auctions, and sometimes even flea
markets. It is of interest for its documentary content and for the
insights that it provides into the values of an era. Objects that
incorporate flamboyant decoration are considerably more
desirable and valuable than undecorated ones.

Description
Disk with small loop attached at center of back. Left: Front with narrow gadrooned edge and simple flower in center. Center: Front has "TD" engraved in foliate script. Right: "TG" engraved in foliate script.

Marks and Dimensions
Left: "TS" in conforming outline stamped twice on back. Center: "PG" stamped in rectangle on back. Right: "LH" stamped in rectangle on back. Diameter: 1³⁄₁₆″ (left); 1″ (right and center).

Maker, Locality, and Date
Left: Attributed to Thomas Skinner (1712–61), Marblehead, Massachusetts. 1750–61. Center: Peter Getz (1764–1809), Lancaster, Pennsylvania. 1784–1809. Right: Lewis Heck (1755–1817), Lancaster, Pennsylvania. 1778–1817.

Comment
18th-century portraits of wealthy men show that silver buttons were used on costly, fashionable greatcoats and, sometimes, on waistcoats. A greatcoat, extending to the knee, was usually worn over a waistcoat, which reached only to the thigh; together they bore as many as 2 dozen buttons on the front, pockets, and sleeves. Most buttons were pewter, brass, or gilt copper; fabric-covered ones were occasionally used. Silver buttons, reserved for the most expensive coats, were often engraved with the initials of their owners.

Hints for Collectors
Although most buttons of this type were discarded or lost, a number of them have survived. If heavily tarnished and mixed in with other objects, they may be overlooked easily by collectors. Since most buttons are not marked, those that are can be worth 2 to 20 times as much as comparable unmarked buttons.

English George III shoe buckle

Description
Arched rectangular brass frame, faced with silver, with cut corners and beaded border. At midpoints of opposite sides, 2 beaded oval reserves enclose profile busts identified as George Washington. Rectangular, hinged steel chape and tongue.

Marks and Dimensions
"HUGHES" stamped incuse on chape. Length: 2¹¹⁄₁₆″. Width: 3¼″.

Maker, Locality, and Date
Hughes (first name and dates unknown), probably England. 1795–1805.

Comment
Silver buckles were popular accessories in a gentleman's wardrobe, serving both functional and, as seen by this example, decorative purposes. They were used not only on shoes, but also to fasten breeches at the knee and to keep stocks, or neckerchiefs, in place. Whereas buckles for breeches and stocks were fairly small, those for shoes were often of considerable size. The buckle shown here, bearing portrait profiles of George Washington, is exceptional; it illustrates the ability of British merchants to cater to the newly created American market.

Hints for Collectors
Lively trade continued to exist between England and America after the Revolution. Because English objects played an important part in American life of the times, they have appeal for American collectors, especially if they can be documented to an original American owner. Pairs of buckles are preferable to a single example. Naturally, silver buckles command higher prices than those made of pewter, brass, paste, or steel, but any example with a depiction of George Washington will be of some interest and historical value.

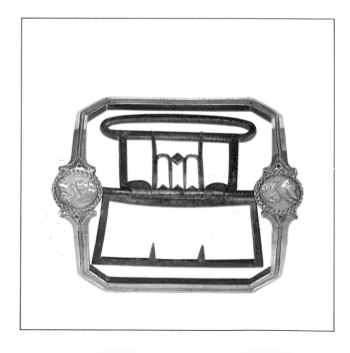

216

Colonial/Federal parcel-gilt Masonic medal

Description
Flat triangular form with shaped edges. Small hinged loop at upper corner. Front engraved with narrow ornamental border enclosing Masonic symbols, including sun partially obscured by clouds, open book inscribed "CHAP/VII," 3 lighted candles in candlesticks, 2 columns, a pick, and 3 obliquely conjoined blocks. "N⁰ 283/Sam.!Orrs" engraved in florid script on back.

Marks and Dimensions
"WH" in script in serrated rectangle stamped on back. Height: 2¹³/₁₆″. Width: 4⅛″.

Maker, Locality, and Date
William Hollingshead (dates unknown), Philadelphia. 1754–85.

Comment
Freemasons belong to a secret fraternity, the origins of which are said to date back to antiquity. During the 18th century, membership became widespread in Europe and America and included such notables as George Washington and Benjamin Franklin. The ceremonial nature of the organization encouraged the development of a large and rich body of regalia, including personal membership devices that, like this medal, were often made of silver.

Hints for Collectors
The secret nature of the society of Free and Accepted Masons has discouraged public familiarity with the fraternity's inner workings and the objects associated with its rituals. Masonic materials, occasionally available as antiques, are of considerable interest as historical evidence of this widespread benevolent society. Some collectors, Masons themselves, specialize in antiques of Masonic interest and are often willing to pay a premium for them.

Victorian boatswain's pipe

Description
Tapered and curved hollow tube with narrow rim at one end. At
other end, hollow ball with boss on 2 sides and hole under end of
tube. Ball and tube connected to flat conforming strip with
reinforcing flange at outer edge; strip pierced by loose ring
attached to flat woven cord.

Marks and Dimensions
Spread eagle; "L"; "BOSTON"; and "COIN"; stamped incuse on side.
Length: 5″. Width: 1⅛″.

Maker, Locality, and Date
Vincent LaForme (1823–93), Boston. 1850–70.

Comment
The boatswain is a ship's officer whose duties include summoning
the crew to assigned tasks. His principal tool is the boatswain's
pipe, which has remained unchanged for centuries. A number of
calls can be sounded on it, depending upon the job needing to be
done. Silversmiths in most coastal towns made these pipes for
use on both naval and merchant ships.

Hints for Collectors
Since this pipe is simple and utilitarian and has no ornamental
features, it might not have immediate appeal to collectors. But it
provides an insight into the great variety of objects American
silversmiths were asked to supply, and also into the importance
of maritime activity in early America. This example is of
particular interest because, unlike most such pipes, it bears a
maker's mark.

Victorian Purim noisemaker

Description

Cylindrical tube with bulbous whistle at end; small loop and flat pear-shaped tab at other end. One side of tab is pierced; base of tab encloses steel spring that rotates against serrated ring to create clicking noise.

Marks and Dimensions

"D&H" in rectangle; circle; "1878" in diamond; and "STERLING"; all stamped incuse on shaft. Length: 4¾". Width: 2⅛". Depth: ⅝".

Maker, Locality, and Date

H. Blanchard Dominick & Leroy B. Haff (1867–1928), Newark, New Jersey. 1878–89.

Comment

Part of the charm of silver is its suitability to widely different purposes. This noisemaker and whistle, created for use during the Jewish holiday of Purim, is a fine example. Celebrated near the close of winter, Purim commemorates the deliverance of the Persian Jews from death at the hands of Haman, minister to King Ahasuerus (Xerxes), as recorded in the Book of Esther. This kind of noisemaker has traditionally been used as part of the general merrymaking of Purim.

Hints for Collectors

Because this form of Judaica was rarely marked by American silversmiths, this noisemaker would be a valuable addition to any collection. Collectors are advised to keep their eyes open for other unusual objects from various cultural traditions. If you encounter a noisemaker, take care that the vibrating steel clicker is intact. Although such an object is still of interest without the mechanism, the value of an inoperable article is always somewhat diminished.

Colonial silver-and-coral baby's toy

Description
Whistle with small ring loosely attached. Below, square knop from which 4 bells are suspended; 4 additional bells around shaft below. Cylindrical tube with fillet and scalloped end, into which a tapered freeform piece of coral is fitted.

Marks and Dimensions
"I•R" in rectangle stamped on underside of whistle. Length: 5⅝". Width: 1⅞".

Maker, Locality, and Date
Joseph Richardson, Sr. (1711–84), Philadelphia. 1734–50.

Comment
The whistle and bells on this toy served as noisemakers that entertained a baby, who could also teethe on its coral tip. Many children of well-to-do families in the 17th and 18th centuries had toys like this; those from very wealthy families sometimes had gold ones. Portraits show such toys loosely hung around children's necks. The maker of this example recorded many of these toys in his order book, referring to them variously as "coral & bells," "socket & bells with a corell," or "wisel & bells."

Hints for Collectors
Since toys for babies were heavily used, the few that have survived are often badly battered. Nonetheless, their rarity makes them desirable even if they have a whistle that has become disfigured from chewing, a replaced piece of coral, or even a few missing bells. Because these toys provided the silversmith with few areas large enough to stamp his mark, examine any marked example carefully. Make sure that the mark has not been cut out of another object and then inserted into the toy, or stamped by a modern die.

Victorian chatelaine

Description
Circular plate with square projections on sides, flat hook on back, and molded border. Central disk engraved with bright-cut ornament. Landscape of bird amid flowers and leaves applied in silver, copper, and gold. 3 link chains suspended from fixed angular bail. Disk-shaped pincushion, penknife, and ivory-leaved notebook hang from chains; "MPF" in interlocked script engraved on notebook cover.

Marks and Dimensions
"TIFFANY & C?/3047/STERLING/1320/UNION-SQUARE" stamped incuse, and Gothic "M" in an oval, all on back of hook. Length: 9¼". Width: 3¼".

Maker, Locality, and Date
Tiffany & Company (1853–present), New York City. 1870–75.

Comment
First used in ancient Rome, chatelaines were hung at the waist and held a variety of small personal objects, such as perfume bottles, toiletries, keys, and sewing equipment. This silver example is notable for its ornamental use of other metals— applied gold and copper—to highlight the landscape on the plate.

Hints for Collectors
Executing applied ornament on silver objects with diverse materials was done by a number of large silversmithing firms during the late 19th and early 20th centuries. This technique never achieved wide popularity and is rarely encountered today. Consequently, even a small object thus embellished, such as this chatelaine, is quite valuable.

European filigree posy holder

Description
Conical wirework body with angular lip. 3 spring-loaded wirework legs terminating in leaf tips. Pin, circular ring, and hexagonal ring attached to 3 chains suspended from body. "J. L./ to/M. E. W./Septr 25th/1845" engraved in script on oval applied to body.

Marks and Dimensions
Unmarked. Height: 5⅞". Diameter: 3".

Maker, Locality, and Date
Unknown. Probably northern Europe or possibly United States. c. 1845.

Comment
Decorative or utilitarian objects made of fine silver wire soldered together were made in Europe long before the American colonies were founded. The technique seems to have been most popular during the 19th century, when wirework boxes, vases, jewelry, picture frames, miniatures, and other kinds of objects were made using this time-consuming process. This posy holder could stand on a table, or it could be pinned to a dress or held in the hand when its spring-loaded legs were closed.

Hints for Collectors
Filigree or wirework objects were rarely marked, there usually being no convenient area large enough to stamp a maker's name, though occasionally a small silver plate with this information was inconspicuously soldered on. Most wirework was made on the European continent, or in India, so collectors should be careful in assigning an American origin to any unmarked example. This intriguing posy holder is a good case in point; its English inscription might suggest an American origin. But the piece could easily have been imported from Europe and personalized here.

Modern vase

Description
Baluster-shaped body forming cluster of leaves and long-stemmed flowers. Gilt interior. Flared circular base with owner's initials (illegible) on bottom edge.

Marks and Dimensions
"BLACK, STARR & FROST/STERLING/108" stamped incuse on underside. Height: 5⅞". Diameter: 2¼".

Maker, Locality, and Date
Unknown. Retailed by Black, Starr & Frost (1876–1929), New York City. 1910–29.

Comment
The hundreds of flower varieties that have been cultivated and hybridized for use in and around homes have generated almost as many types of containers for their display. While most vases are made of ceramic or glass, bud vases or containers for small clusters of flowers are sometimes silver. The flowers and leaves that decorate this vase, though complex and realistically depicted, are successfully integrated with the shape of the object and nicely complement its function. Collectors should seek out this type of carefully thought-out design; silver objects like this one are much preferable to more elaborate but awkwardly conceived pieces.

Hints for Collectors
Like many pieces of mid- to late 19th-century American silver, this vase bears a retailer's mark but not that of the manufacturer. Collectors should not mistake the retailer of a silver object for its maker. An object marked only with the name of the retailer is likely to be worth more than a similar article bearing no mark at all.

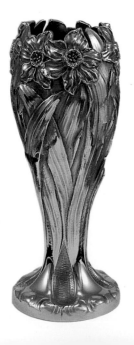

Late Victorian silver-mounted perfume bottle

Description
Squat circular glass bottle with short upright neck and flared lip. Mushroom-shaped stopper. Bottle and stopper covered with silver, pierced and engraved with pattern of scrolled flowers and leaves. "ARF" engraved in script on bottle reserve; "1900" engraved on stopper.

Marks and Dimensions
Anchor; lion; Gothic "G"; and "S197J" stamped incuse in scrollwork on side of bottle. Height: 5″. Diameter: 3¾″.

Maker, Locality, and Date
Gorham Company (1831–present), Providence. c. 1900.

Comment
A vogue for objects made of silver and glass occurred during the late 19th and early 20th centuries. The materials were combined in 2 ways: Silver-deposit wares have the silver chemically or electrolytically bonded to a glass vessel to create a decorative pattern; silver-mounted wares, such as this perfume bottle, have pierced sheets of silver fitted to the glass. These types can be readily distinguished by the thickness of their silver mantle: Deposited silver is quite thin and clearly bonded to the glass, while mounted silver is relatively thick and does not appear to be bonded to the vessel it encloses.

Hints for Collectors
The manufacturer's marks on silver-mounted vessels were frequently placed inconspicuously amid the ornament, so such pieces should be examined carefully. While much silver bears owners' initials, the identity of these owners is usually unknown. This perfume bottle belonged to Anne Fell Ruchman of Lahaska, Pennsylvania, a fact that adds to the interest, though not necessarily to the value, of the object.

Victorian parcel-gilt flask

Description
Flat oval vessel decorated with radiating stylized foliate design on both sides. Hinged, screw-on, mushroom-shaped lid at end. Gilt interior.

Marks and Dimensions
"TIFFANY & C⁰ 4705 MAKERS 4793 STERLING SILVER 925-1000 M 1 GILL" all stamped incuse on bottom. Length: 5″. Width: 3″. Depth: 1″.

Maker, Locality, and Date
Tiffany & Company (1853–present), New York City. 1869–91.

Comment
Some like to have liquor on hand when traveling, and silver is well suited for flasks because it does not break and because it imparts no flavor to its contents. Flasks of this type are almost always fairly flat and compact. Metal flasks usually have screw caps; the cap on this example, however, is also hinged and has a leather washer to prevent leaking.

Hints for Collectors
Although this flask does not now have a leather case, many 19th-century examples did. An original case will add to the value of a flask. There is no prohibition against using a silver flask as it was originally intended, so long as you take care to avoid denting, misshaping, or scratching it. Collectors are well advised to avoid a potential purchase that has such flaws. Because dents are difficult to remove from a vessel with a small opening, it would prove troublesome to find a conservator capable of restoring a dented flask to its original condition.

Victorian/modern military hairbrush

Description
Oval low-domed back with beaded border. Engraved foliate script initials "LPBF." Natural bristles set in ivory.

Marks and Dimensions
"STERLING"; "C1354M"; ewer; and 3 pseudohallmarks (anchor in shield; lion; and Gothic "G"; each in clipped-corner square), all stamped incuse on edge of silver back. Length: 5″. Width: 3″. Height: 1⅞″.

Maker, Locality, and Date
Gorham Company (1831–present), Providence. 1903.

Comment
Because silver became increasingly available in the late 19th and early 20th centuries, it was used for a wide variety of new forms, such as dresser sets. These sets frequently included a hand mirror, nail file, scissors, shoehorn, buttonhook, hair comb, hair box, clothes brush, and lint brush, all made *en suite* and often decoratively engraved with the initials of their owner. Military hairbrushes—oval, handleless, and always in a pair—were an integral part of such sets.

Hints for Collectors
The silver backs of articles in dresser sets were often very thin, making them prone to splitting or disfigurement. Such damage may be easily overlooked if the silver is elaborately decorated. Avoid imperfect examples, since such objects are readily available. Dresser sets were made either of silver or silver plate, so look for the word "sterling" on each piece of a set that is supposed to be silver.

Late Colonial dirk

Description
Tapered, turned and molded wooden handle with silver tip and
base. Narrow tapered finger guards. Long tapered steel blade
with molded sides and one sharp edge.

Marks and Dimensions
"PS" in script in conforming outline, and leafy scroll, both
stamped twice on finger guards. Length: 18″. Width: 3¾″.

Maker, Locality, and Date
Philip Syng, Jr. (1703–89), Philadelphia. 1750–89.

Comment
Many bladed weapons made from the 17th to the 19th century
had silver hilts. Usually owned by military officers or gentlemen,
they were often carefully made, elaborately decorated, and finely
finished. Since they were intended not only for dress use but also
for combat, many such weapons were destroyed over the years,
and few antique examples are available today. Most are found in
specialized collections of weapons, since general silver collectors
tend not to acquire swords or firearms.

Hints for Collectors
Silver collectors should not shun silver-mounted weapons, which
were an important part of any soldier's or gentleman's trappings
in earlier centuries. A potential acquisition should be carefully
scrutinized and, if possible, examined by an antique-weapons
expert to ensure its authenticity. In particular such a specialist
must verify that both the blade and the hilt are original parts of
the object.

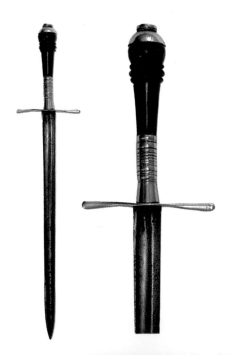

Federal small sword and scabbard

Description
Left: Hilt with bulbous silver-wire-wrapped handle (grip) above curved projection *(quillon)*; 2 open loops *(pas d'âne)*, and 2 convex oval lobes (counterguards); slender C-shaped loop (knuckle bow) at left and spherical terminal (pommel) above. Slender tapered steel blade with ridge on one side and trough on other; inlaid brass flower and leaves near base. Right: Leather-covered wooden scabbard encircled by silver bands at both ends and in middle; center band with circular loop; "I S/Lott" engraved on band at top.

Marks and Dimensions
Unmarked. Length: 35¾″. Width: 3¾″. Depth: 2½″.

Maker, Locality, and Date
Unknown. New York City. 1780–1800.

Comment
This lightweight weapon, known as a small sword, was not intended for heavy fighting, but for dress use by a gentleman or military officer. While European examples were often quite elaborate, American examples showed greater restraint. Although this sword bears no maker's mark, it is similar to examples made and marked by John Coney of Boston, Jacob Ten Eyck of Albany, Timothy Bontecou, Jr., of New Haven, Joseph Draper of Wilmington, and others.

Hints for Collectors
While this sword retains its original scabbard, unfortunately most examples do not because the leather is so fragile. The silver hilts of these swords are usually in good condition, but the blades, being iron, are often poorly preserved. The braided silver wire originally wrapped around a grip was frequently replaced with plain silver wire at a later date.

228 English George III close-plated candle snuffer

Description
Long cylindrical shaft with oval scissors-like finger grips attached at right angle to one end. Opposite end with 2 overlapping tabs at right angle to shaft; one tab has 5-sided box, pointed at bottom; other tab is flat and fits into box; tabs activated by finger grips at other end. Box engraved with unidentified crest.

Marks and Dimensions
4 pseudohallmarks ("Y"; "J"; and eagle, each in square with striped background; and "S" in plain square), all stamped on tab. Length: 9½".

Maker, Locality, and Date
Unknown. England. 1760–1800.

Comment
To prevent the flame of a candle from being extinguished by drafts, a number of devices were invented, including the hurricane shade. This tall glass tube, placed over the entire candlestick, required a special snuffer able to reach far down into the shade. The example pictured here, except for its long shaft, is typical of the scissors-type snuffers used throughout the 18th and early 19th centuries.

Hints for Collectors
Candle snuffers were often made of iron plated with silver for decorative purposes. If the silver cracks or wears away in places, the exposed iron rusts, and iron-oxide bubbles form under the adjacent silver plating, eventually causing it to flake off. Carefully examine a close-plated iron object for bubbles, because if they are widespread over the entire surface, the object should probably not be purchased.

Federal snuffer and tray

Description
Scissors-shaped snuffer with 2 overlapping flat arms: Long arm with hexagonal box and pointed tip; short arm with upright rectangular tab that fits into box. Double C-scroll handles with oval finger grips. 3 short baluster-shaped feet. Applied oval disk on top of box engraved with "DH" in script. Narrow octagonal tray with flared sides, molded edge, and "DH" engraved in script in center.

Marks and Dimensions
"CARREL" in rounded rectangle, stamped twice on underside of tray and once on snuffer box tab. Tray height: 1"; length: 8⅞"; width: 3½". Snuffer height: 1¾"; length: 6½"; width: 3".

Maker, Locality, and Date
Daniel Carrel (dates unknown), Philadelphia or Charleston, South Carolina. 1785–1805.

Comment
Although candles were the principal source of artificial light in the 18th century, American-made silver snuffers are surprisingly rare. When fitted with legs, like this pair, they always rested on an accompanying tray, while those without legs usually fit vertically into a stand. Carrell advertised his talents in Philadelphia in 1784–85, but by 1790 he had moved to Charleston, where he produced silverware, jewelry, and silver-handled "Philadelphia-made whips." He returned to Philadelphia by 1806, apparently disillusioned with the southern market.

Hints for Collectors
Many snuffers have become separated from their trays or stands. Those examples retaining their supporting elements are always more valuable.

Victorian curling iron and stand

Description
Rectangular font with rounded ends and serpentine sides; flower-and-leaf-decorated upper edge. Knurled screw cap at one end. 2 flat pierced triangular supports hinged to top; these hold scissors-shaped steel curling iron with leaf-and-bead-decorated silver handles. "EILLA" engraved in script on top of screw cap.

Marks and Dimensions
"TIFFANY & CO./4/STERLING/PAT'D 89." and 3 small conjoined outlines: Rectangle containing "925"; circle; and diamond containing "1891"; all stamped incuse on bottom of stand. "STERLING" in raised letters on each curler handle. "GERMANY" stamped incuse on curling iron. Stand height: 2¼"; length: 7⅛".

Maker, Locality, and Date
Curler handles and stand: H. Blanchard Dominick & Leroy B. Haff (1867–1928), Newark, New Jersey. c. 1891. Curling iron: Unknown. Germany. c. 1891. Retailed by Tiffany & Company (1853–present), New York City.

Comment
Like clothing styles, hair fashions change often and rapidly. Many implements have been made to manipulate, style, or regiment the hair, but few are made of silver.

Hints for Collectors
This highly specialized object is as interesting an artifact for the collector of silver as would be a 17th-century posset pot, but far less expensive because of its later date. Collectors should not be confused by the word "Germany" among the marks; only the steel portion of the curler was imported. This is an important distinction, since American-made silver is typically of more interest and value to American collectors than is foreign silver.

English Victorian oil lamp

Description
Body shaped like crescent moon, with small sphere at each tip. Along crescent, caricature of man's face with long nose; slender wick tube in mouth.

Marks and Dimensions
"TIFFANY & C⁰" stamped incuse on underside; 3 hallmarks (lion; uncrowned leopard's head; and "Q"; each in shield) stamped on end. Height: 3″. Length: 4¾″. Width: 1½″.

Maker, Locality, and Date
Unknown. London. 1891. Retailed by Tiffany & Company (1853–present), New York City.

Comment
This whimsical oil lamp, much too small to provide adequate light for reading, was probably used to light cigars or perhaps a pipe. Made in England, it was imported to the United States for retail sale by Tiffany & Company. It has been dated on the basis of its marks—in the hallmarks of English silver, the letter "Q" stands for the year 1891. The use of the alphabet for this purpose was cyclical, with the letters recurring every 20 years or so.

Hints for Collectors
Much 19th-century New York silver bears small marks that inexperienced collectors may easily confuse with English hallmarks. The distinction in this instance is particularly important; the lamp bears the name of Tiffany, which might lead a casual observer to conclude that it was made in New York. Collectors seeking only American-made silver should be on the alert for such marks.

Modern cigarette lighter

Description
Slim rectangular box with hinged rounded lid. Front and back ornamented with narrow striped panels alternating with plain ones; "FMS" engraved in diamond on front. Filler hole with knurled threaded cap near bottom. Lid has spring-loaded mechanism that strikes flint when opened. Inner mechanism made of steel and brass.

Marks and Dimensions
"STERLING NASSAU PAT. DEC. 26, 1905" and a torch behind a banner, stamped incuse on bottom. Height: 2⅜". Width: 1½".

Maker, Locality, and Date
Nassau Lighter Company (c. 1915–22), New York City. 1915–22.

Comment
Small silver objects associated with the use of tobacco date as far back as the initial cultivation of the plant by European colonists. Developed in the late 19th century in various sizes, automatic lighters for cigars and cigarettes had a simple operating mechanism: A steel wheel rubbed against a flint, creating a spark that ignited a wick saturated with a flammable liquid. This example, made by the short-lived Nassau Lighter Company, is an interesting variant—opening the lid automatically produces a spark.

Hints for Collectors
Small silver objects like this lighter are plentiful and usually modestly priced. When collecting a certain type of object, study its various forms and learn about their relative rarity and merits. The most desirable lighters of this type are made of heavy-gauge silver, bear a maker's mark, and are in operable condition. The continued use of an old lighter will not affect its value if it is treated with care.

Victorian silver-and-horn cigar lighter

Description
Pear-shaped leaf-decorated silver font with removable wick holder; snuffer attached by small chain. Font affixed to animal horn on flared octagonal silver pedestal with alternating plain and floral panels. "LSF" engraved in script on side of pedestal.

Marks and Dimensions
Spread eagle under Gothic "M"; "STERLING/36"; all stamped incuse on underside. Length: 8″. Height: 4½″. Width: 2″.

Maker, Locality, and Date
Meriden Britannia Company (1852–98), Meriden, Connecticut. 1870–98.

Comment
During the late 19th century a profusion of exclusively masculine activities spawned a large array of artifacts for the house, public areas, and especially for that inner sanctum of the man's world, the private club. One of the most popular pastimes for the wealthy was big-game hunting. Practitioners of the sport liked to document their prowess with trophies, so numerous artifacts were fabricated as a consequence of their exploits—elephant-foot stools, bear-skin rugs, and horn-handled carving sets. All, including this horn-handled cigar lighter, attest to the masculine sensibilities of the time.

Hints for Collectors
Silver objects that incorporate natural materials are interesting and somewhat rare. When you find such an object, check that the silver parts are securely attached. Natural substances like horn should be closely examined for undue drying, cracking, chipping, or unacceptable wear, any of which would decrease the value of an object.

Modern shell-and-silver ashtray

Description
Oyster shell covered on exterior with roughly textured silver; small silver-covered snail shell on underside and silver-covered barnacle at end. "S.C.Y.C. 1912 WON BY AMINITA IV" engraved inside edge.

Marks and Dimensions
"STERLING/CARL SCHON/BALTIMORE" stamped incuse on applied rectangular plate on underside. Length: 5⅜". Width: 3½". Height: 1⁷⁄₁₆".

Maker, Locality, and Date
Carl Schon (dates unknown), Baltimore. c. 1912.

Comment
Yacht racing became a favorite American sport in the mid-19th century, and from about 1850 to the First World War, most American silver companies were called upon to make yachting trophies. Tiffany was foremost in this field because of the company's fame and its location in the New York–Newport area, where yachting was pursued with particular enthusiasm. Although many yachting trophies were merely ornamental, others were more practical. This fine example, presented by the Seawanhaka Corinthian Yacht Club of Oyster Bay, New York, was made by a little-known silversmith in Maryland.

Hints for Collectors
Although an object such as this shell ashtray cannot be expected to command the price of a large vase, it should not be overlooked. Because of its history and its unusual character, this little trophy has special appeal. Carl Schon was known in his lifetime for his innovative experiments in coating natural artifacts with silver. Good examples of his work are worth seeking, for they are sure to appreciate in value.

Victorian ashtray

Description
Bell-shaped shallow dish; flared rim with beaded edge and beaded double-loop handle. Shallow cutout on flat side of rim; bar extends across well at narrowest part. 4 spherical feet. Engraved "F.S/July 25th 1857." in well.

Marks and Dimensions
"TIFFANY & CO." in arc above "682"; "M" in oval; and "3014"; all stamped incuse on underside. Length: 4½". Width: 2½". Height: 2¼".

Maker, Locality, and Date
Tiffany & Company (1853–present), New York City. c. 1857.

Comment
The use of tobacco requires a number of accoutrements—boxes, lighters, ashtrays, and the like. Most of these are inexpensive and looked upon as conveniences deserving no special attention. However, during the late 19th and early 20th centuries, when silver was relatively inexpensive, an increasing desire for the trappings of luxury caused many of these accessories to be made of this metal. Some objects were personal in nature, such as cigarette lighters bearing their owners' names or initials. Others, like ashtrays, were usually more impersonal, intended for communal use. Because of its engraved inscription, this example is less impersonal than most.

Hints for Collectors
Even small and relatively simple silver objects should be treated with care. For instance, a silver ashtray should not be used for burning cigarettes. Heat and caustic ash will eventually corrode and pit the surface, which in this case might eradicate the engraved initials and date.

236 Victorian electroplated card receiver and flower vase

Description
2-wheeled chariot with tubular frame ornamented with grape clusters and leaves; supports fluted scallop shell having gilt interior, and blue glass cornucopia with gilt and white ornament. Cherub with gilt hat and short leafy skirt sits astride cornucopia, holding reins of hummingbird. Oval platform having sides ornamented with panels of flowers and birds. 4 scrolled feet with semicircular brackets.

Marks and Dimensions
"MERIDEN SILVER PLATE CO. QUADRUPLE PLATE" surrounding lion holding an urn; "1077"; all stamped incuse on underside. Height: 12". Length: 10¾". Width: 4½".

Maker, Locality, and Date
Meriden Silver Plate Company (1869–98), Meriden, Connecticut. c. 1884.

Comment
The use of calling cards spanned most of the 19th century. The most elaborate calling-card receivers were made during the 1880s and literally overflowed with ornament that rarely related to their function. Highly imaginative examples had much realistic ornament as well as glass or porcelain elements.

Hints for Collectors
In spite of their great popularity in the last century, card receivers, especially those highly decorated examples composed of more than one material, are not common today. With its naturalistic ornament and fanciful design, this is as fine an example as any a collector might hope to find. Though collectors should expect to pay a premium for such a fine object, its value will appreciate more quickly than that of a common, plain example.

Victorian electroplated card receiver

Description
Shallow fluted bowl with broad curved rim decorated with engraved foliate and beaded ornament. Narrow border of wave-shaped ornament on underside and 3 equidistant rams' heads from which hang chain swags. Slender baluster shaft tapered and knopped. Flared molded pedestal with engraved "F".

Marks and Dimensions
"ROGERS, SMITH & C⁰ NEW HAVEN, Cᵀ " in circle with beaded border enclosing leafy form and "N⁰ 0/1613"; all in stamped raised letters on plaque applied under base. Height: 5″. Diameter: 6⅞″.

Maker, Locality, and Date
Rogers, Smith & Company (1857–98), New Haven, Connecticut. 1862–77.

Comment
The calling-card stand or receiver, an important object in affluent Victorian households, was placed in the hallway near the door so that a visitor could place a card there on his arrival. Some card receivers were small, simple trays, while more ostentatious designs could be as large as a small table.

Hints for Collectors
This plated receiver was broken, had most of its plating polished away, and had lost its chains. When collectors encounter interesting objects like this one, they should not hesitate to buy them. But try to be sure that such objects can be acquired reasonably and restored in a manner that will not compromise their integrity.

Late Federal/Victorian inkstand

Description
Small urn has flat stepped cover with 3 holes around circumference; urn has knopped pointed base. Supported on 3 C-shaped foliate scrolls, from which emanate leaves and greyhound heads. Hollow-sided, molded, triangular platform fitted with removable, deep, urn-shaped candle cup on circular pedestal. Candle cup ornamented with bowknots, leafy swags, border of leaf tips, and separate bobeche with beaded edge.

Marks and Dimensions
"O. Rich"; "BOSTON"; and "fine"; all stamped incuse on underside. Height: 6¾". Width: 4½".

Maker, Locality, and Date
Obadiah Rich (1809–88), Boston. 1830–40.

Comment
Like most silver of its period, this inkwell is monumental in concept. Most animal motifs on early 19th-century silver were made up of composite mythological images; recognizable creatures like these greyhounds were rarely used. At present, only 3 such inkwells are recorded, including another by Rich.

Hints for Collectors
Silver objects have sometimes been significantly altered long after they were first made, often with little concern for the purpose or integrity of an object. The candle cup in this example, for instance, was added at a later date. This inkwell may originally have had a holder for a taperstick (used to melt sealing wax), in which case the candle cup could be considered a replacement rather than an alteration. Always examine a potential acquisition for evidence of such modifications, because they often reduce the value of an object.

Description
Rectangular tray with rounded corners and grapevine border. Low center platform surrounded by shallow depression. 2 square cut-glass bottles fitted onto platform, with dish-shaped silver-plated covers having border of leaves and scrolls; one cover with large single hole, other with series of small holes. In center of tray, container in form of leaf-decorated Ionic capital, topped by small removable candle cup decorated with leaves, scrolls, and flowers. 4 flat triangular feet decorated with shells and leaves.

Marks and Dimensions
Unmarked. Length: 10¾". Width: 6¼". Height: 3⅜".

Maker, Locality, and Date
Unknown. England. 1820–40.

Comment
This fused-plated standish, or inkstand, once included many accessories needed for writing. One glass vessel contained ink; the other contained blotting sand, which was scattered over the written page to absorb excess ink. The long shallow grooves held pens, and the central container held sealing wax, which was used to close envelopes. Above this container is a cup that held a taperstick, a small candle used to melt the wax.

Hints for Collectors
Few standishes have survived intact, since their many parts often became separated and mismatched. Examine every item very closely to ensure that all are original parts of the same object. Only silver examples seem to have been marked by their makers.

Pewter

Because pewter is so rarely used today, it is difficult to comprehend its importance in daily life prior to the late 19th century. But pewter is an ancient alloy; used in Roman times, it persisted as a mainstay of European domestic life for centuries. Before the American Civil War, pewter was used for literally dozens of household objects at every level of society. Today, other materials such as aluminum, stainless steel, porcelain, glass, and plastic have replaced pewter, so that this metal is rarely encountered in 20th-century daily life.

Early European and American Pewter Making

Beginning in the late Middle Ages, European and English cities had guilds that controlled the production and quality of pewter. In England, the largest and most powerful guild was the Worshipful Company of Pewterers in London. In addition to overseeing the activities and production of pewterers in the city and outlying areas, it required pewterers to place their mark on all objects as a guarantee of quality. Failure to comply was punishable by fine.

Although required to place only their names or initials on their work, many English pewterers added phrases like "SUPERFINE HARD METAL." Slogans like this helped assure purchasers they were buying the best. Some pewterers even used markings imitative of the hallmarks on English silver.

British output exceeded domestic needs and much was exported. The impact of English pewter on early Americans was great; more than 177,828 pounds sterling of finished pewter was sent to America during the decade immediately preceding the Revolution.

In spite of this flood of English pewter into the Colonies, America had its own pewterers. In fact, these metalworkers were among the first to practice their craft after the founding of the Colonies. Like apprentices to silversmiths, those who aspired

Detail of a flagon.

to learn the pewter craft had to work for a pewterer for a period of about 7 years.

In America, the Northeast has traditionally been the area of greatest concentration of pewterers; about 500 of those craftsmen who worked before the mid-19th century have been identified. Many were first-generation immigrants who had learned their trade in their homeland, while others were native born. During the 17th and 18th centuries, demand was sufficient to provide most of these men with enough business to earn a living; but after 1800, a number of pewterers found it more advantageous to move south. Others followed routes west to growing centers like Cincinnati, Ohio.

Throughout the Colonial and Federal eras, virtually every city and most rural areas had men plying the pewtering trade. But most worked in cities, where there was the greatest and most constant demand. The variety of wares needed meant that pewterers had to make a large capital outlay for molds, which were very expensive. However, innovative use of a limited number of molds allowed some pewterers to interchange parts from them to make various objects. A single body mold might be used for a teapot, sugar bowl, and pitcher, with the appropriate spout, lid, or handle being added later. In this way, a pewterer could offer a full range of objects to customers without buying a large number of molds. Such ingenuity helped these early craftsmen to survive and prosper, even in the face of so much competition from England.

Following English precedent, although there was no guild to oversee their work, American pewterers marked most of their wares. The character of their marks generally followed English style. Pre-Revolutionary American marks often included the Tudor rose and crown with the maker's name. Some makers even included the word "LONDON" or "FROM OLD ENGLAND" in their

Detail of a teapot.

marks, because of the high reputation English pewter had at that time. After the Revolution, many American pewterers changed the character of these marks to include the word "LIBERTY" or an American eagle.

Competition with Other Materials

Beginning in the late 18th century, pewterers began to experience increased competition from the makers of silver-plated wares and ceramics, both of which were attractive, inexpensive, and more widely available than in previous centuries. As a result, pewterers improved their product by adding more antimony, making the alloy slightly harder and more silvery. This innovation was first developed by English pewterers, who gave it the patriotic name britannia metal. Yet in spite of innovations in alloy and production, and in spite of extensive advertising, pewter continued to lose place to its competitors. By the time of the Civil War, most objects made of britannia metal—with the exception of spoons—were electroplated. Even in the electroplating process, pewter eventually lost its market in favor of German silver, an alloy of copper, zinc, and nickel, which was harder and whiter. Within the relatively short span of about half a century, pewter all but disappeared from the American household.

Pewter and Changing Fashions

Silver and pewter have always been closely related. In fact, pewter was frequently looked upon as a less expensive substitute for silver. Pewter objects are usually shaped like silver ones, and the metal was brightly polished to achieve a silverlike luster. However, the difference in the way they were made prevented pewter from paralleling silver at its most elaborate. Silver was worked freeform, using hammers both to shape and decorate it. This process allowed silversmiths great freedom to make

Detail of a tankard.

elaborate, extensively decorated objects. Pewterers, on the other hand, usually cast their wares in molds. And once a mold was made, its shape determined the character of everything that was cast in it. Similarly, the use of expensive molds prevented pewterers from changing the character of their objects quickly as style and taste changed. Since silversmiths were limited only by their ability to wield a hammer, they could respond immediately to customers' demands for something new and different. Pewterers had greater difficulty and expense in doing so. Consequently, old styles linger longer in pewter. So while the changes that took place in silver design from the 17th through the 19th centuries have parallels in pewter, the pewter examples were usually made much later than their silver counterparts.

Pewter in the Modern World
The 20th century has seen a limited revival of interest in pewter on the part of craftsmen. While the metal is far from being common in households, a number of artisans have begun to explore its properties, making both decorative and utilitarian objects. Interestingly, modern pewterers avoid the casting process, adopting instead the ancient technique of hammering. Thus, today's pewterers can find the same range of expression that silversmiths have known.

Detail of a teapot stand.

Plates, Porringers, and Related Objects

Next to spoons, plates were the most common form made by American pewterers. They varied in diameter from about 6" to 12"; those over 12" were referred to as dishes. The largest American pewter dish known measures 19", whereas at least one English example survives that measures 36" across. Virtually every American pewterer made plates, but English craftsmen also sent their work to this country by the ton. Export records from England to the principal ports in America show that 3485 pounds of pewter was sent across the Atlantic in 1697 alone. This figure continued to increase annually, reaching a staggering 20,825 pounds in the year 1767.

Plates and Dishes

As far as is known, 17th-century American pewter plates and dishes consisted of 2 basic types, based on the width of the brim. Broad-brim dishes were mostly made before the 18th century. By the 18th century, plates with a multiple-reeded edge had become more common, judging from the number of examples that survive. At this time, the width of the brim became fairly standardized, and close in proportion to that seen today. The more common of these plates have a single, moderately wide molding on the top of the brim at the edge; a much rarer stylistic variant has a completely smooth brim.

Basins

Basins are closely related to plates and were used almost as frequently. Like plates and dishes, they were made in many sizes, as well as in varying depths. Most basins were lidless with a very narrow, flat, molded brim; a few are known to have been fitted with a lid. Very rare examples have a deeply scrolled edge. Basins were used principally for domestic tasks but also functioned as baptismal fonts in both Protestant and Catholic churches. Similarly, plates were used both in the house and as communion patens or collection plates. 18th-century basins were plain and rested directly on the table, but by the 19th century, many began to be made with pedestals, and a few even had reeded or fluted sides.

Porringers

Pewter porringers were also popular vessels and were made in great quantity. The most popular bowl size was between 5" and 6", but some were as small as 2" across. Porringer bowls were all basically the same, with a bulging side and a low dome, called a boss, in the center of the bottom. Almost all American porringers had a single handle; these varied greatly in design. The most popular is known today as the crown handle; other variants are geometric, flower, solid, and dolphin—all named for the principal design motif on the top of the handle. A major variant, produced exclusively in southeastern Pennsylvania, is called the tab-handle porringer.

The elaboration of porringer handles is one of the very few instances of extensive ornament on American pewter, which otherwise is quite plain, decorated only with molding or, sometimes, elaborate shaping. Occasionally, American pewter was engraved, but such engraving typically consisted only of an owner's initials.

English George III teapot stand

Description
Flat oval top with raised rim and molded edge. Top engraved with bright-cut, stylized floral border and central shield with pendant swag and tassels; shield engraved with "PT" in script. 4 low and reeded scroll feet.

Marks and Dimensions
Unmarked. Length: 7¾". Width: 5¾". Height: 1".

Maker, Locality, and Date
Attributed to James Vickers (dates unknown) or Broadhead, Gurney, Spurle & Company (dates unknown), Sheffield, England. 1780–1800.

Comment
This stand, with its delicate bright-cut ornament and fashionable oval shape, is closely related to silver examples. Such oval trays, whether silver or pewter, were used to support teapots, and were either plain like this one or else shaped or fluted. Although this tray is unmarked, its engraved design, which is very unusual for pewter, is similar to that found on cream pots, teapots, ewers, and snuffboxes made and marked by several pewterers in Sheffield, England. Such objects were exported to the United States and sold to those who wanted fashionable objects but were unwilling to pay the cost of silver ones.

Hints for Collectors
In the past, some collectors have assigned an American origin to beautifully engraved pewter objects like this one. Such an attribution, which enhances the value of a piece in the eyes of chauvinistic American collectors, is today seen merely as wishful thinking. These objects can be properly understood only as being made in England for the English or American market.

Colonial/Federal oval dish

Description
Large oval dish with wide flared brim and shallow well.

Marks and Dimensions
4 pseudohallmarks ("HW"; seated female; leopard's head; and rampant lion), each in clipped-corner rectangle; crowned rose within 2 opposed banners, one inscribed "HENRY WILL" and the other "NEW YORK"; crowned "X" stamped incuse; all on underside. Length: 15¼". Width: 11⅝". Height: 1¼".

Maker, Locality, and Date
Henry Will (c. 1734–c. 1802), New York City or Albany, New York. 1761–93.

Comment
Circular pewter dishes, ranging from 6" to 20" in diameter, were made by the tens of thousands during the 17th, 18th, and early 19th centuries. Oval examples were far less common; all of those now known were made by members of the Will family during the second half of the 18th century.

Hints for Collectors
Because circular pewter plates and dishes are readily available, collectors should be quite discriminating in selecting them. It is wise to pass over those that are corroded, heavily worn, split, or repaired, and to seek examples with a good clear mark of a respected maker. However, oval dishes must be judged differently because of their rarity. The opportunity to own an American example occurs so infrequently that an astute collector would make concessions on all these points. Even so, the collector should be absolutely certain that a potential purchase is American by carefully studying its marks and comparing it to documented examples.

Early Colonial broad-brim dish

Description
Large circular plate with wide, slightly dished brim and shallow well.

Marks and Dimensions
"E∗D" above cluster of 4 stars, all in shield-shaped outline, stamped 4 times on front of brim. Diameter: 16⅝". Height: 1⅜".

Maker, Locality, and Date
Edmund Dolbeare (c. 1642–1711), Boston or Salem, Massachusetts. 1671–1711.

Comment
Most pewter was cast in its final shape. This large dish is an exception, since it was cast as a simple flat disk and hammered into shape. The small hammer facets over its entire surface are evidence of this handwork. Its maker, born and trained in England, stamped his mark 4 times, in imitation of the 4 distinct hallmarks required on English silver.

Hints for Collectors
Large dishes like this are the only pieces of 17th-century American pewter that have survived. They are quite rare. Amazingly, most such early broad-brim dishes, some with multiple reeding, are reasonably well preserved. A few, however, have splits at the juncture of brim and well, the weakest point on this large and somewhat cumbersome form. Fewer than a dozen plates by Dolbeare are known, yet the possibility of discovering another one still exists. A lucky and discerning collector may turn up an example selling for very little because it has gone unrecognized, while documented pieces are very expensive and continue to increase in value.

Early Colonial multiple-reeded dish

Description
Large circular plate with shallow well. Slightly dished brim with concentric bands of molding. Block initials "SG" stamped on top of brim.

Marks and Dimensions
"E*D" above cluster of 4 stars, all in shield-shaped outline, stamped 4 times on top of brim. Diameter: 16⅝". Height: 1⁵⁄₁₆".

Maker, Locality, and Date
Edmund Dolbeare (c. 1642–1711), Boston or Salem, Massachusetts. 1671–1711.

Comment
In Europe pewter was used for household artifacts, and immigrants brought this tradition with them to the New World, creating an immediate need for craftsmen who could work the metal into plates, dishes, spoons, tankards, mugs, commodes, and a host of other objects. Like silversmiths, most pewterers settled in the cities, where demand was the greatest. Dishes, among their most popular products, are defined as being 12" or more in diameter (some measure as much as 36" across), and were intended for carrying and serving. Plates, by contrast, measure less than a foot across. This example is today called a multiple-reeded dish because of the concentric bands of molding around its perimeter.

Hints for Collectors
This dish has the initials "SG" stamped on its brim opposite the maker's marks. Such initials, stamped or engraved, belonged to the original owner and should never be mistaken for those of the maker.

Late Colonial/Federal and Colonial smooth-brim plates

Description
Circular plates with shallow wells. Left: Slightly dished brim; incised ring in well and at edge of brim. Right: Flat brim with molding on edge of back.

Marks and Dimesions
Left: "Wm WILL" in serrated rectangle, and incuse "x" with 5 dots above, all stamped on top of brim. Diameter: 5⅝″. Height: 9/16″. Right: "EW:VIRGINIA" cast in raised letters on back edge of brim. Diameter: 9⅟16″. Height: ⅞″.

Maker, Locality, and Date
Left: William Will (1742–98), Philadelphia. 1764–98. Right: Attributed to Edward Willit, Sr. or Jr. (dates unknown), Virginia. 1725–72.

Comment
Although used principally in households and public eating places, plates also served for dispensing the Host or collecting alms in churches. Small 6″ examples were typically used to hold the communion bread, while 8″ to 12″ plates served for collection. Unless a particular plate has remained in a church, is inscribed with the church's name, or is accompanied by its flagon and chalice, it is impossible to know for sure that it was used in a church.

Hints for Collectors
Both these plates are atypical because of the location of their makers' marks. While most 18th- and 19th-century American plates were marked on the underside of the well, the plate on the left is stamped on the top edge of the brim, and the plate on the right has its mark cast into the reverse of the brim. The latter mark is very uncommon because it is cast rather than stamped.

Description
Circular plates, each with flat brim and shallow well with incised ring near perimeter. Left: Molded edge on front of narrow brim. Right: Molded edge on back of brim.

Marks and Dimensions
Left: Circle enclosing "LOVE" and pair of birds under crown; "LONDON" in serrated arc, and "x" under crown stamped incuse; all on underside. Diameter: 6″. Height: 9/16″. Right: Serrated circle enclosing spread eagle clutching arrows and laurel bough in talons; "P.BOYD.PHIL A." above; all stamped on underside. Diameter: 8½″. Height: 7/8″.

Maker, Locality, and Date
Left: Attributed to John Andrew Brunstrom (c. 1753–93), Philadelphia. 1781–93. Right: Parks Boyd (c. 1771–1819), Philadelphia. 1795–1819.

Comment
After spoons, plates were the most frequently made pewter objects from the 17th to early 19th century. While plates in the 8″ range were quite common, 6″ examples were made much less often. Most early American pewter plates had a molded edge on the top of the brim; those with a smooth brim, like the one on the right, were uncommon.

Hints for Collectors
London pewterers had a vast output that was distributed throughout the western world. The high quality of their work made it very desirable, and pewterers in other areas imitated it, even to the extent of marking their wares with the word "LONDON," as on the small plate shown here. Collectors therefore should not assume automatically that this mark indicates an object was made in England.

Federal deep dish

Description
Circular dish with moderately deep well. Slightly dished brim with molded edge on top.

Marks and Dimensions
"8" with upper arc containing "GG" and lower arc "AUGUSTA" all enclosing spread eagle with shield-shaped body and halo of stars, stamped twice on underside. Diameter: 11⅛". Height: 1½".

Maker, Locality, and Date
Giles Griswold (1775–1840), Augusta, Georgia. 1818–20.

Comment
Giles Griswold did not enjoy great success as a pewterer. He began his career in Connecticut but met with intense competition, which forced him to move south, where there were fewer competing pewterers. Griswold eventually settled in Augusta, Georgia, where he pursued pewter making for only a few years. This change of residence earned him the distinction of being the southernmost pewterer who worked in early America. Plates are the only products today known to have been made by Griswold.

Hints for Collectors
Deep dishes have virtually the same shape and form as plates and dishes, but their wells are up to twice as deep. Although deep dishes are relatively plentiful, they are far less common than plates. Because this deep dish was made in Georgia, it would command a considerable premium over its more common counterparts made in the Northeast.

Description
Circular dish with moderately deep well. Curved flared side and narrow flat lip with beaded border.

Marks and Dimensions
2 curved opposed banners connected at center, one containing "Wᵐ WILL" and the other "PHILADELPHIA"; spread eagle on field of stars below curved banner containing "FEDERAL" all in beaded circle and stamped twice; all stamped on underside. Diameter: 10⅝". Height: 1⅝".

Maker, Locality, and Date
William Will (1742–98), Philadelphia. 1782–98.

Comment
Having established his business in Philadelphia, William Will remained there his whole life, producing a large quantity and great variety of forms. In addition, he was active in the American Revolution and held public office in Philadelphia for a number of years.

Hints for Collectors
Basins and deep dishes, ranging from 4" to 20" in diameter, usually had brims, although a few, like this example, did not. Instead of a brim it has an unusual beaded border. The brim of a deep dish typically measures about 1", while that of a basin is narrower, measuring only about ⅜". Because plates, dishes, and basins differ little in appearance, collectors place great weight on makers and geographic origin to determine desirability. This basin is very valuable because its maker, William Will, is greatly respected.

Federal lidded basin

Description
Circular stepped and domed lid; knob-shaped finial. Moderately deep circular body with curved flared side and flat, narrow, molded lip.

Marks and Dimensions
Circle enclosing spread eagle clutching arrows and olive branch on starry ground surrounded by "BOARDMAN WARRANTED" stamped on bottom of interior. Diameter: 14³⁄₁₆″. Height: 8″.

Maker, Locality, and Date
Thomas D. Boardman & Sherman Boardman (c. 1808–60), Hartford. 1820–30.

Comment
American pewter basins are quite common. This very deep Federal example is one of the few that have a cover; most were lidless. It is perhaps not surprising that it bears the mark of 2 members of the Boardman family. The Boardmans were good businessmen; they produced great quantities of high-quality pewter in Hartford, New York City, and Philadelphia, and from the late 18th to the late 19th century, marketed it throughout every state.

Hints for Collectors
Like almost all pewter, this basin was cast; molds were of brass, bronze, or sometimes soapstone. The lid seen here, however, was shaped by being spun over a wooden form on a lathe. This early 19th-century technique proved to be useful in making a few forms, including basin lids. Therefore, do not be suspicious if a basin has a spun lid and a cast body, provided it is from the 19th century. However, an 18th-century basin would never have had a spun lid; if it does, its parts have been deceptively mated.

Description
Circular body with moderately deep, curved, and flared well.
Flat brim with molded, scalloped, filleted edge.

Marks and Dimensions
Crown over rose enclosed within 2 C-scrolls: upper scroll
containing "HENRY WILL" and lower scroll "NEW YORK" (all
stamped twice); crowned "X" incuse and 4 pseudohallmarks
("HW"; Britannia seated; leopard's head; and rampant lion), each
in clipped-corner square; all stamped on top of brim. Diameter:
12¼". Height: 2¾".

Maker, Locality, and Date
Henry Will (c. 1734–c. 1802), New York City or Albany, New
York. 1761–93.

Comment
American pewter basins ranging in diameter from 6" to slightly
over 14" are fairly common, with most measuring 8" to 10". Their
brims are typically quite narrow with a simple molded outside
edge. When marked they usually bear the stamp on the inside or
outside bottom of the well. This example seems to be unique
because of 4 features: its strongly scalloped rim; the prominent
conforming fillet (a simple molded rib applied to both decorate
and strengthen the edge); the location of the maker's marks; and
the unusually wide brim.

Hints for Collectors
All collectors aspire to own something their competitors do not
have. But if an object is unique, they often wonder why there are
no others and if it is a fake. Collectors must use caution based on
extensive experience and on study of both the objects and the
literature about them. At the same time, they should not close
their minds to the merits of something out of the ordinary.

250 Modern mayonnaise set

Description
Circular bowl with curved flared side, molded lip, and low foot rim. Low circular saucer with molded edge and shallow central well. Ladle with shallow circular bowl; tapered curved handle with ribbing and stylized thistle-shaped tip.

Marks and Dimensions
"L. H. VAUGHAN/TAUNTON MASS./PEWTER" and "LH/V" in 2-part square, stamped incuse on underside of bowl and saucer. Bowl diameter: 4$\frac{11}{16}$"; height: 1$\frac{7}{8}$". Saucer diameter: 5$\frac{5}{8}$"; height: $\frac{5}{8}$". Ladle length: 4$\frac{5}{8}$".

Maker, Locality, and Date
Lester Vaughan (dates unknown), Taunton, Massachusetts. c. 1925.

Comment
Even though pewter objects can be decorated with cast, chased, or engraved ornament, most American examples are plain. Before inexpensive electroplating became widely used, it was pewter that competed with silver; it was thus usually finished to a highly reflective silverlike surface. The 20th century has witnessed a limited revival in popularity of new pewter objects; however, modern pewter is often extolled not for a silvery surface but for a softer satiny finish. The maker of this strikingly modern bowl was obviously familiar with early American pewter, since he sometimes used an eagle mark that is closely related to those of pewterers working a century earlier in New England.

Hints for Collectors
Even though Vaughan's work is less than half a century old, it is quite desirable because of its attractive lines and surfaces. His pewter is not intended to be highly polished; to do so would detract from its value.

Federal sugar bowl

Description
Circular double-domed lid with urn-shaped finial and beaded edge; fits into rim of bowl. Circular double-bellied body with row of beading at rim; low, molded, circular foot rim.

Marks and Dimensions
Unmarked. Diameter: 4¾". Height: 4¾".

Maker, Locality, and Date
Attributed to Parks Boyd (c. 1771–1819), Philadelphia. 1795–1819.

Comment
Although American pewter sugar bowls were made as early as the mid-18th century, very few from this period are known today. Virtually all of those recorded were made in Pennsylvania or Connecticut. The double-bellied body of this example relates more closely to the shape of silver tea- and coffeepots than it does to any known pewter teapot. Although unmarked, it has been attributed to Parks Boyd because the lid is virtually identical to the lids of pewter pitchers that bear his mark.

Hints for Collectors
Pewter sugar bowls and cream pots were made to accompany coffee- and teapots before the American Revolution, but apparently they were never made *en suite*. While most 18th- and early 19th-century American pewter sugar bowls originally had lids, many today have lost them and can be easily confused with English broth or soup bowls, which are much more common. But the lip on English broth bowls flares outward at a pronounced angle; on American sugar bowls, the rim is much straighter. In addition, sugar bowls almost always have small nicks in the bottom interior, whereas broth bowls do not.

Description
Circular double-bellied body with beaded rim. Circular molded pedestal.

Marks and Dimensions
Unmarked. Diameter: 2⅝″. Height: 2⅜″.

Maker, Locality, and Date
Attributed to William Will (1742–98), Philadelphia. 1764–98.

Comment
Even though salt dishes, or "salts," are listed in a number of 18th-century American pewterers' shop inventories, this diminutive salt is one of 12 known examples that are the only ones that can be attributed to a maker. In fact, Will's salts are the only documentable early American pewter salts recorded today. Because William Will used the molds for these salts to make parts of larger forms like cream pots and chalices, which he marked, the salts can be safely attributed to him. These late 18th-century salts differ little from 17th-century silver examples, which were also in the form of small open cups. It was not until the mid-19th century that shakers with pierced caps were used for dispensing salt.

Hints for Collectors
Salt dishes resembling the example shown here should not automatically be attributed to William Will, since there are 2 different types that are very similar in size and design. One type has a slightly thicker stem than the other, indicating that it was cast in another mold. Only those with the thin stem seen here are known to have been incorporated into Will's cream pots and chalices and can therefore be attributed to him. The thick-stemmed variety must be assigned to an unidentified Philadelphia craftsman.

Federal footed basin

Description
Circular, moderately deep bowl with tapered convex lobes and narrow molded rim. Circular molded pedestal.

Marks and Dimensions
"CROSSMAN/WEST & LEONARD" stamped incuse on underside. Diameter: 6½". Height: 3⅞".

Maker, Locality, and Date
Crossman, West & Leonard (1829–30), Taunton, Massachusetts. 1829–30.

Comment
Footed basins are commonly called baptismal basins because they were used in churches for the performance of that sacrament. However, footed basins were also used as compotes on the table. Most had a smooth-sided bowl, while a few were fluted. This bowl, with its side shaped into broad, convex reeds, is quite uncommon.

Hints for Collectors
Most collectors of American pewter prefer the metal to be shiny, as it was often kept when originally used. Many therefore remove all traces of corrosion and surface dirt. Such cleaning should not be undertaken without first examining the object for traces of painted decoration, since some early pewter was originally painted, usually in gold on black, but sometimes in bright colors. It is possible that the basin shown here was once painted or japanned, because a very similar example in the Winterthur Museum collection has traces of japanning. Early painted pewter is extremely rare today and any example should be preserved.

Federal crown-handle porringer

Description
Circular bowl with bulbous side, narrow flared rim, and large boss in center of bottom. Flat handle in form of stylized crown over circle flanked by leafy scrolls.

Marks and Dimensions
Spread eagle with shield-shaped body and talons holding olive branch and arrows, surrounded by "BOARDMAN & C⁰ NEW-YORK"; all within bordered circle stamped on top of handle. Diameter: 5″. Height: 1¹³⁄₁₆″.

Maker, Locality, and Date
Boardman & Company (1825–27), Hartford or New York City. 1825–27.

Comment
The flat "crown" handle with foliate scrolls seen on this porringer is by far the most common type used on American pewter porringers. A literal copy of an English prototype, it was produced by at least 22 American pewterers throughout the 1700s and into the 19th century. Although all of these are very similar, there are differences in design and proportion, and in the supporting bracket on the underside. The molds used to cast these porringers and their handles were usually brass and either imported from England or made in America.

Hints for Collectors
Crown-handle porringers are the most readily available examples of this very common form. Many have no mark, and unless direct parallels can be drawn between them and marked American examples through comparison of size and other details, collectors should never assume they are American. Beware of porringers with thin walls and a thin or folded edge, since these are probably later copies or modern fakes.

Federal geometric-handle porringer

Description
Moderately deep bowl with bulbous side, narrow flared rim, and boss in center of bottom. Flat triangular handle with multiple irregularly shaped holes. Attached to rim with shaped, ribbed, triangular bracket.

Marks and Dimensions
"D:M" in rectangle, stamped on top of handle. Diameter: 5¼". Height: 2⅛".

Maker, Locality, and Date
David Melville (1755–93), Newport, Rhode Island. 1779–93.

Comment
Many porringers originally had companion spoons; no such pewter examples are known today, but a few silver ones with original spoons still intact have been recorded. While porringers were used for both eating and drinking, a similar form that bore graduated rings inside the bowl was used for bleeding, a common 18th-century medical procedure.

Hints for Collectors
Porringer bowls made before about 1850 were always cast, never spun. Modern examples were shaped by spinning on a lathe and their walls are invariably thinner than the older pieces. Cast examples were also put on a lathe, but simply to skim off rough spots. The shallow concentric grooves that result from skimming differ from the grooves created in the spinning process. The collector should study the differences between the 2 types of grooves, since they can easily be confused.

Federal flower-handle porringer

Description
Circular bowl with bulbous side, narrow flared lip, and boss in center of bottom. Flat horizontal handle with irregular U-shaped outline and multiple piercings.

Marks and Dimensions
Spread eagle with halo of stars, "E PLURIBUS UNUM" in banner in beak, arrows and olive branch in talons, and "HAMLIN" below, all within circle, stamped on top of handle. Diameter: 4¾″. Height: 2⅛″.

Maker, Locality, and Date
Samuel Hamlin, Sr. (1746–1801), Providence. 1794–1801.

Comment
The porringer was a popular vessel for eating and drinking in England and America throughout the 17th and 18th centuries. Toward the end of this period, its use began to wane in Britain, but Americans continued to import, make, and use the form until well into the second quarter of the 19th century. There are about 2 dozen types of handles on American-made porringers, far more than those found on English products.

Hints for Collectors
The handle is the area on a porringer most likely to sustain damage, but the bowl may also come in for its share of abuse. The bellied portion of the side may become dented, or holes, caused by heat or a sharp object, may appear in the bottom of the bowl. Carefully examine a porringer's bowl for patches and repairs; these are usually revealed through differences in color, wear patterns, and finish. Since there are substantial numbers of porringers on the market, collectors can be selective when making a purchase.

Federal porringer

Description
Circular bowl with bulbous side, flared rim, and boss in center of bottom. Flat 3-lobed handle pierced with symmetrical design of hearts and crescent. Flat triangular support beneath handle at juncture with bowl.

Marks and Dimensions
"R", partially visible, cast in relief and reversed, on back of handle. Diameter: 3⅜". Height: 1¼".

Maker, Locality, and Date
Attributed to Roswell Gleason (1799–1887), Dorchester, Massachusetts. 1822–71; or Richard Lee, Sr. (1747–1823), or Jr. (b. 1775), Springfield, Vermont. 1795–1820.

Comment
Small porringers that have handles pierced with heart and moon shapes are quite common. A few have a portion of the letter "R" cast in relief on the handle; the remainder of the mark is missing, since the handle was poorly designed and the central heart-shaped piercing obliterated the lettering. The configuration of the mark is such that it could only be the initial of the first name; the surname initial was apparently lost when the mold was cut. Because the only New England pewterers at this time with a first name beginning with "R" were Roswell Gleason and the Richard Lees, Sr. and Jr., this porringer is tentatively assigned to one of them.

Hints for Collectors
Many copies of porringers like this one were made in the early 20th century without any attempt to reproduce traditional fabrication techniques or induce artificial wear. If a bowl is spun, a rim folded, or a handle soldered to the bowl, the porringer may have been made in this century.

Late Colonial/Federal porringer

Description
Circular bowl with bulbous side and narrow flared rim. Large boss in center of bottom. Flat 3-lobed handle; circular hole pierced in end. Handle attached to rim of bowl.

Marks and Dimensions
"J:B" in oval, stamped on back of handle. Diameter: 5⅜". Height: 2".

Maker, Locality, and Date
Attributed to Joseph Belcher, Sr. (1729–78), or Jr. (born c. 1751), Newport, Rhode Island, or New London, Connecticut. 1769–87.

Comment
With the single exception of the Pennsylvania tab-handle porringers, the handles of all American porringers were attached to their bowls in the same way. The bowl was cast first, then the handle mold was placed against the rim of the bowl and molten metal poured into it. The molten metal came into direct contact with the bowl, partially melting the area in contact with the handle and thus joining the handle to the bowl. The type of solid porringer handle seen here was peculiar to Rhode Island, except for one example that was probably made in Philadelphia.

Hints for Collectors
From the 17th through the mid-19th century, the pewterer held the bowl with a cloth-tipped tool when attaching a porringer handle. The area adjacent to the handle juncture became impressed with the woven design of the cloth. This "linen mark" indicates that the porringer was made in the traditional manner. Its absence may be a sign of a spurious modern copy.

Federal tab-handle porringer

Description
Basin-shaped bowl with straight flared side, narrow molded rim, and flat bottom. Flat tab handle with curved sides, rounded corners, and large central hole. Handle attached to rim of bowl.

Marks and Dimensions
"ELISHA KIRK" and "YORK•TOWN" each in bordered rectangle, stamped on top of handle. Diameter: 3½". Height: 2⅛".

Maker, Locality, and Date
Elisha Kirk (d. 1790), York, Pennsylvania. 1780–90.

Comment
Tab-handle porringers, with their basin-shaped bowl and flat rectangular handle without decoration, seem to have been made only in Pennsylvania. Their construction is unique because the handle and bowl are cast integrally. Numerous tab-handle examples bear no maker's mark, but many can be attributed to Elisha Kirk or to Samuel Pennock and his son Simon, all from Chester County, Pennsylvania. Although Kirk's and Pennock's porringers are very close in appearance, they do vary in design, size, and proportion, thus allowing a confident attribution of an unmarked example. One half of Pennock's brass porringer mold belongs to the Chester County Historical Society in West Chester, Pennsylvania, and the other half is about 15 miles away in the Henry Francis du Pont Winterthur Museum in Delaware.

Hints for Collectors
Although these porringers are very straightforward and functional, lacking the elaborate separately cast handles of most American pewter porringers, they are very desirable as a unique regional type.

Spoons and Ladles

Pewter's soft nature made it a poor material for forks and knives. But a careful examination of the inventories of early American pewterers will leave little doubt that spoons were in great and constant demand. The 1742 inventory of Philadelphia pewterer Simon Edgell, for example, listed 164 dozen spoons (and only 7 dozen forks). But this number pales by comparison with the production figures of Garry I. Mix & Company of Wallingford, Connecticut; in 1860, this firm made 15,000 gross of pewter spoons. A number of other firms at work in Connecticut at the same time produced spoons in similar quantities.

Shape, Size, and Decoration

Pewter spoons and ladles were made in a fairly large variety of sizes and shapes, and were generally similar to their silver counterparts until the mid-19th century. At that time, however, silver flatware began to be produced in an extraordinary profusion of shapes and patterns, with much decoration. Pewter spoons and ladles, on the other hand, tended to retain their relatively plain character; only occasional exceptions had extensive amounts of ornament.

17th-century spoons generally had a circular or blunt oval bowl. Early in the century, their handles were very simple, straight, and square-ended; by about 1675, many were being made with a flared, 3-lobed tip. English examples often had extensive cast decoration on the front of the handle and the back of the bowl, but very few spoons of this elaborate type have been attributed an American origin. The only documentation that has been made consists of several fragments of spoons, all cast in the same mold, that were excavated at Jamestown, Virginia. Although badly defaced and corroded, the handle ends bear the name Joseph Copeland, the date 1675, and location Chuckatuck, which was about 18 miles south of Jamestown.

For most of the 18th century, designs in silver flatware called for a handle with a rounded end and pointed, oval bowl; contemporaneous pewter spoons followed suit and were largely devoid of ornament. A few urban pewterers cut patterns into their spoon molds to decorate their wares with the fashionable foliate designs of that era, but rural craftsmen rarely did so. Still other pewterers made iron stamps that were used to impress decoration into their spoons, but this type is even less frequently encountered than cast ornament. The most notable examples were made by the eccentric New York pewterer George Coldwell, who lavished patriotic motifs on his handles.

In the early 19th century the bowls of spoons became markedly more pointed, while the handles took on a complex curved profile. These handles resembled those of the so-called fiddle pattern, a remarkably popular shape used for most silver spoon handles from about 1810 to 1860.

Survival Rate

Pewter spoons were fairly short-lived in daily use. Because such spoons were weak, especially at the narrowest point of the handle, early pewterers made the handle thicker from front to back; some examples that survive today are exceptionally thick in this area. In about 1850 pewterers began to implant an iron wire inside the handle. Virtually invisible after the spoon was cast, the wire increased the spoon's strength and longevity.

Of the other pewter flatware forms produced, apparently only ladles have survived. They are reasonably numerous, and marked American examples with both metal and wooden handles are available.

Federal midrib-handle and fiddle-handle teaspoons

Description
Left: Tapered handle with rounded end having midrib and scrolled ornament on front. Oval bowl. Right: Tapered fiddle-pattern handle with gadrooning around wide section. Pointed spurs near shallow oval bowl.

Marks and Dimensions
Left: "R Lee" ("R" and "L" conjoined), cast in script on back of handle. Length: 4¼". Width: ¾". Right: "P/DERR/1820" cast in raised letters on back of handle. Length: 8⁷⁄₁₆". Width: 1½".

Maker, Locality, and Date
Left: Richard Lee, Sr. (1747–1823), or Richard Lee, Jr. (b. 1775), Springfield, Vermont. 1795–1816. Right: Peter Derr (1793–1868), Berks County, Pennsylvania. 1820–40.

Comment
The smaller of these 2 spoons is typical of 18th-century teaspoons, which were considerably smaller than those used today. The larger spoon is in the so-called fiddle pattern, popular for American flatware throughout most of the 19th century. Both these simple spoons are good examples of the skill and style of rural pewterers.

Hints for Collectors
Spoons are an interesting, comparatively inexpensive collecting specialty. Relatively early spoons, such as those pictured here, are somewhat more expensive and difficult to find than later 19th-century spoons, but can be obtained by serious collectors. These 2 examples are of interest because the makers' names are cast, while most marks from this period were stamped. The date 1820 on the spoon at right is a mark that was cut into the mold; the spoon could have been made at a later date, since the same mold was probably used for as long as a generation.

Victorian tablespoon and late Federal/Victorian teaspoon

Description
Left: Teaspoon with long wavy fiddle-shaped handle; shallow bowl. Right: Tablespoon with rounded handle having midrib on front and back and threaded edge on front; pointed bowl with scrolled drop on back.

Marks and Dimensions
Left: "J. WEEKES N.Y." in rectangle stamped on back of handle. Length: 5⅜". Width: 1⅛". Right: "G. I. MIX" in rectangle stamped on back of handle. Length: 8¼". Width: 1½".

Maker, Locality, and Date
Left: James Weekes (dates unknown), New York City. 1820–43. Right: Garry I. Mix (dates unknown), Wallingford or Yalesville, Connecticut. 1845–61.

Comment
Pewter spoons broke easily because of the softness of the metal and the slenderness of the handles. 19th-century makers sought to correct this by thickening the handles or inserting iron-wire reinforcements, the ends of which sometimes project slightly from the sides of a handle. The teaspoon on the left is unusual because it has pockmarks and pitting caused by improper mold temperature. Such disfigured objects were generally returned to the melting pot and recast.

Hints for Collectors
Although 19th-century pewter spoons are relatively rare today, they are not expensive. Makers who marked their spoons invariably stamped the mark into the back of the handle. Occasionally, mid-19th-century spoons have raised, cast patent numbers and dates, which, if worn, can be easily misinterpreted as makers' marks. Pewter objects with casting flaws should cost less than perfect examples.

Description
Downturned handle with rounded end. Narrow oval bowl with raised design of leafy shell on back, with ridge, at juncture with handle. "HFS" engraved on back of handle.

Marks and Dimensions
"Wᵐ WILL/PHILA-/DELPHIA" with eagle's head above and row of dots under maker's name, all in serrated outline and stamped on back of handle. Length: 8½". Width: 1½".

Maker, Locality, and Date
William Will (1742–98), Philadelphia. 1782–98.

Comment
These tablespoons are part of a group of 6, of which 4 are marked. Spoons were the most common form of pewter flatware made in 18th-century America, largely because the metal was much too soft to be used for fork tines or knife blades. Most 18th- and 19th-century pewterers made spoons, yet because of their fragility they are comparatively rare today. For example, records show there were more than 44 gross of pewter teaspoons and 20 dozen pewter tablespoons in William Will's shop at the time of his death, but only 7 spoons bearing his mark are known to us today.

Hints for Collectors
Judging from their condition, these spoons were never used. If they had been, they would probably not exist today. Collectors should expect to find signs of use on antique metalware; in fact, such evidence is helpful in proving its age. Yet, occasionally, antique objects pass from one generation to another and are little or never used. Their excellent condition makes them particularly desirable to collectors and historians.

Federal tablespoons

Description
Downturned handle with rounded end and feathered front edge.
Shallow oval bowl with rounded ridge on back at juncture with
handle. Left: 2 crossed American flags flanking a liberty pole and
cap, all above banner with motto "PEACE & AMITY"; below,
bowknot with pendant leaves. Right: Spread eagle clutching
laurel bough, liberty cap, and pole, all within oval banner
inscribed "FEDERAL * CONSTITUTION"; "LIBERTY" inscribed above
banner; "PEACE" with pendant leaves below banner.

Marks and Dimensions
Left: "G:COLDWELL" in arcaded rectangle stamped on back of
handle. Length: 7¾". Width: 1 9/16". Right: "G.COLDWELL" in
serrated rectangle stamped on back of handle. Length: 7 9/16".
Width: 1 9/16".

Maker, Locality, and Date
George Coldwell (died c. 1811), New York City. 1787–1811.

Comment
American pewter spoons, made in great quantity, were seldom
decorated, and any ornamentation was almost invariably cast.
These spoons, therefore, are significant exceptions, since the
patriotic designs on their handles were stamped with steel dies.
Coldwell made many unusual forms, but his spoons are the most
commonly seen today. He is the only craftsman of his time
known to have made japanned pewter.

Hints for Collectors
The handles of pewter spoons should always be examined closely
for cracks or for irregular discolored areas, indicating the handle
has been broken and resoldered. Cracks or repaired breaks
generally lessen the cost of a spoon, but important examples like
those pictured here would not be significantly devalued.

264 Early Federal slip-ended spoon and early Colonial trifid-handle spoon

Description
Left: Straight, flat, rectangular handle with chamfered edges and raised oval lobe on front near bowl; shallow circular bowl with tapered pointed ridge on back. Right: Straight, flat, tapered handle; baluster-shaped end has 3 projections. Shallow oval bowl with narrow tapered rib on back at juncture with handle. "S/IE" stamped on front of handle and "X" stamped on back.

Marks and Dimensions
Left: "W•E" with star above and fleur-de-lis below, all in serrated circle stamped inside bowl. Length: 7¹⁄₁₆″. Width: 2¼″. Right: "IB" in rectangle stamped on handle back. Length: 8⁵⁄₁₈″. Width: 2″.

Maker, Locality, and Date
Left: Attributed to William Ellsworth (1746–1816), New York City. 1767–98. Right: Unknown. England or America. 1690–1720.

Comment
The slip-ended spoon at left, with its shallow circular bowl and straight unornamented handle, typifies spoons used in 17th-century America. By the early 18th century, many spoons had oval bowls and lobe-shaped handles; however, the earlier slip-ended type continued to be used. Molds were expensive and were not discarded indiscriminately; many pewter designs continued to be used long after styles had changed.

Hints for Collectors
The early form at left was reproduced extensively in the late 19th century. Such reproductions are a dull gray and unusually soft, revealing a high lead content; also, although they are often in excellent condition, many have a crude appearance and coarse finish. The marks on reproductions are usually struck on the tip of the handle front rather than in the bowl.

Federal midrib, wooden-handle, and fiddle-handle ladles

Description
Ladles with deep circular bowls. Left: Handle with rounded upturned end and midrib along front; "AMH" engraved on back. Center: Turned wooden handle with multiple knops and incised rings, fitted into tapered cylindrical pewter socket. Right: Downturned fiddle handle; shaft tapered, with slight shoulders.

Marks and Dimensions
Left: "P•Y" within beaded circle stamped inside bowl. Rose under crown with initials "PY" below, all within arched-top beaded rectangle; and 4 pseudohallmarks (rampant lion; flower; bird; and "PY"), each in square; all stamped on back of handle. Length: 16″. Diameter: 4″. Center: "R•LEE" in serrated rectangle stamped inside bowl. Length: 12″. Diameter: 3½″. Right: "J. H. PALETHORP" in rectangle stamped on back of handle. Length: 13½″. Diameter: 3⅝″.

Maker, Locality, and Date
Left: Peter Young (1749–1813), New York City or Albany, New York. 1775–95. Center: Richard Lee, Sr. (1747–1823), or Richard Lee, Jr. (b. 1775), Springfield, Vermont. 1788–1820. Right: John Harrison Palethorp (dates unknown), Philadelphia. 1820–45.

Comment
Few 18th-century pewter ladles survive; the example at left is noteworthy for its excellent condition and full series of marks. The working relationship of the Lees is not fully understood, so their objects must be assigned to a broad time span.

Hints for Collectors
Always study marks carefully; many American pewter marks are very similar to one another and to English marks.

Teapots, Coffeepots, Pitchers, and Related Objects

From early Colonial times until well into the 19th century, pewter was an immensely popular material for teapots, coffeepots, cream pots, kettles, pitchers, and flagons. Most such vessels made in the Colonies were modeled after imported English examples or related to counterparts from the Continent. The pouring vessels covered in this section range from large flagons to tiny cream pots. All except a few flagons have a pouring rim, spout, or spigot. Most rest on a foot rim or pedestal, which may be quite tall; examples with 3 legs are encountered less often. Rarer still are those that have feet made in the shape of a recognizable decorative element, such as a shell or claw-and-ball.

Teapots and Coffeepots

As early as the 1730s, the popular custom of drinking tea and coffee gave rise to a great demand for pewter teapots and coffeepots, as well as their related accoutrements, cream pots and sugar bowls. Their popularity continued unabated for over a century. Many 18th-century pewter teapots exist, but pewter coffeepots are curiously rare; there are fewer than a dozen American examples known. By the 19th century, pewter teapots were usually accompanied by matching cream pots and sugar bowls. Virtually all 18th century pewter teapots and coffeepots have wooden handles to prevent the hand from being burned. In contrast, almost all 19th-century examples have pewter handles, no doubt requiring the use of a potholder; originally these handles were painted black, although few retain their paint today.

Pitchers and Flagons

Pitchers and flagons, which are closely related to teapots and coffeepots, were used to pour cold liquids. These objects date from both the 18th and 19th centuries, and are either lidless or have hinged covers. Most of the large pitchers known today date from the 19th century and, in contemporary records, were variously referred to as beer, water, or cider pitchers. Their smaller counterparts were used for pouring milk or cream. Pitchers and flagons made after 1800 usually have 2 or more times the capacity of earlier examples, a fact that holds true for teapots, coffeepots, and sugar bowls as well. Flagons are the biggest of all these vessels, since they were often used in the communion services of large church congregations.

Decoration

Most of these pewter objects are plain. Any decoration is usually cast or engraved and characterized by restraint. Only rarely is the entire surface of a pewter object ornamented, but flagons are among those types that may be so embellished. They sometimes have lengthy presentation inscriptions engraved on their bodies, commemorating the communicant who gave the object and naming the church and date.

Pewter was also occasionally decorated with paint in a type of ornament known as japanning, so called because it was executed in imitation of Oriental lacquerwork. Oriental wares were very popular and avidly imported to Europe as early as the 17th century. Today, almost none of the paint remains on the American pewter that was japanned.

English Queen Anne lidless flagon

Description
Tall, circular, straight-sided body with molded lip. Tapered S-shaped handle with flat semicircular terminal. Molding encircling body beneath upper handle juncture. Narrow flared and molded foot rim. "IPSWICH/Second Ch ʰ/1734" engraved in block letters in heart-shaped outline opposite handle.

Marks and Dimensions
"I•K" in shield-shaped outline and "X" stamped on underside; "I•K" in shield-shaped outline stamped once; crowned leopard's head stamped 3 times; all on body under lip. Height: 8¾". Width: 7¾". Diameter: 5⅜".

Maker, Locality, and Date
Unknown. England. 1700–34.

Comment
Although great quantities of English pewter were imported into the American colonies, most pieces bear no documentation concerning their early American ownership. This lidless flagon, used to dispense wine into chalices or cups for communion, is a rare example that retains a record of its very early American owner, the Second Church in Ipswich, Massachusetts. The flagon undoubtedly had served in some other capacity in England or possibly in America prior to its use in the church, since its style indicates it was made about 1700.

Hints for Collectors
This flagon was marked by its maker on both the underside and the body. Despite extensive research, the maker of this object remains unidentified, reminding curious collectors that there are many questions to be answered about the objects they find.

Federal flagon

Description
Hinged, circular, domed and molded lid; upright acanthus-leaf finial and pierced chair-back thumbpiece. Tall, tapered, circular body with molded lip; encircled by molding just above lower handle juncture. Molded S-shaped handle with spurs along its length. Molded flared foot rim. "WS" topped by 2 crowns stamped incuse on body opposite handle.

Marks and Dimensions
4 pseudohallmarks ("P•W"; seated female figure; lion's head; and lamb suspended from a rope, each in clipped-corner square), stamped on inside bottom. Height: 12¾". Width: 7½". Diameter: 5¼".

Maker, Locality, and Date
Philip Will (1738–87), Philadelphia or New York City. 1763–87.

Comment
Philip Will, son of John and brother of William and Henry, is the most elusive member of this famous family of pewterers. Only 2 of his pieces are known, this flagon and a plate. The excellent quality of design and workmanship of this flagon testifies to his abilities; its unusually elaborate finial and handle are closely related to silver patterns.

Hints for Collectors
Many pewter flagons, including this example, were made for American churches during the 18th and 19th centuries. As rural congregations dissolved or urban congregations became more affluent, these pewter objects were often sold, so that many church vessels are available to collectors today. Among the most interesting objects in American pewter, they make notable additions to any collection.

Late Colonial/Federal flagon

Description
Hinged, double-domed, circular lid with chair-back thumbpiece and triangular spout cover. S-shaped tapered handle with ball terminal. Tall cylindrical body with encircling fillet. Notched triangular spout. Flared base. 3 cherub-head feet.

Marks and Dimensions
"•I•C•H•" under crown and "LANCASTER" in rectangle, all stamped on underside. Height: 11½". Width: 7½". Diameter: 6⅜".

Maker, Locality, and Date
Johann Christoph Heyne (1715–81), Lancaster, Pennsylvania. 1766–81.

Comment
Heyne was a devout Moravian who divided his time between pewtering and serving his church. The range of his products consisted mainly of flagons, chalices, ciboria, pyxes, and a few nonreligious items like flasks, which were probably made for the military during the Revolution. The conservative nature of the Moravian communities for whom he produced his wares is evident in the traditional forms and designs of his objects. Heyne's products retained a strong German character, a style he brought with him from his homeland.

Hints for Collectors
Heyne marked most of his products with only his initials, and his marks have been fully researched and published. It is very important to remember that a few other 18th-century American pewterers had the initials ICH, as did many German pewterers, whose objects are probably worth a good deal less in this country. If you are contemplating purchasing an object attributed to Johann Christoph Heyne, be sure that its mark accords with those that have been published.

Description
Circular, molded, multidomed lid with 3-tiered disk finial.
Molded chair-back thumbpiece hinged to tapered S-shaped
handle with bud terminal. Tapered cylindrical body with molded
rim, encircling fillet, and multistepped molded base. Triangular
curved spout.

Marks and Dimensions
Circle enclosing spread eagle with body in form of American
shield, clutching laurel branch and cluster of arrows, with
"BOARDMAN & CO." above and "NEW-YORK" below; "X" struck twice
incuse; all on underside. Height: 9¾". Width: 8". Diameter: 5".

Maker, Locality, and Date
Boardman & Company (1825–27), Hartford or New York City.
1825–27. Retailed in New York City.

Comment
The production of the Boardman family was so prodigious that it
has been estimated that more than half of all surviving American
pewter was made by its members. The Boardman firm in
Hartford, Connecticut, had numerous outlets in other major
cities and an efficient merchandising network. The flagon shown
here was made in quart as well as 2- and 3-quart sizes. Most had
finials with 1, 2, or 3 tiers.

Hints for Collectors
Even though works by the Boardman family are common, their
high quality and fine design make them very desirable. But
because of this popularity, their work has been faked; for
example, the "TD & SB" mark in a rectangle and the "T.D.B."
spread-eagle mark have been found on spurious objects.
Carefully compare the marks on a newly encountered example
with those on authenticated objects.

Federal lidless pitcher

Description
Circular body with straight tapered side and flared lip. Angular
loop handle. Curved triangular spout. Flared molded foot rim.

Marks and Dimensions
"S. S. HERSEY" in scallop-edged rectangle stamped on underside.
Height: 7″. Width: 8⁷⁄₁₆″. Diameter: 6⅛″.

Maker, Locality, and Date
Samuel S. Hersey (b. 1808), Belfast, Maine. 1830–35.

Comment
This pitcher is unusual for several reasons. Most 19th-century
pitchers have bulbous bodies, and cylindrical examples are quite
rare. Pewter made in Maine, which was sparsely populated
during much of the 19th century, is also rare. Unlidded examples
are uncommon probably because of the need to keep insects out
of the vessels in an age before the use of screens on doors and
windows. Large hollowware objects like this were typically made
in major urban areas, where pewterers had the requisite talent
and capital to fabricate items requiring complex molds.
Pewterers in outlying areas usually made only simple forms such
as plates and spoons.

Hints for Collectors
Although this pitcher's rarity and unusual design make it
desirable, most collectors would not pay a substantial premium
for it, primarily because 19th-century pewter is less in demand
than that made a century earlier. However, as earlier pewter
becomes increasingly rare, objects like this pitcher will
undoubtedly assume increased importance for collectors.

Federal lighthouse teapot

Description
Hinged, hemispherical lid; rounded wooden finial with pewter tip. Conical body with engraved foliate border and 4 reeded bands near lip; tapered, S-shaped spout. Curved wooden handle with scrolled spur, fitted into 2 cylindrical pewter sockets.

Marks and Dimensions
"I•TRASK" in rectangle stamped on underside. Height: 11⅜". Width: 9⅝". Diameter: 5⅝".

Maker, Locality, and Date
Israel Trask (1786–1867), Beverly, Massachusetts. 1812–30.

Comment
Lighthouse teapots are made of sheet metal that was flattened in a rolling mill. After being bent to the correct shape, the edges were soldered together, forming a vertical seam along the full length of the body on either the spout or handle side. Although many examples are plain, some are engraved with stylized foliate ornament called "bright-cut" decoration because of the way the facets catch and reflect the light. Israel Trask, his brother Oliver, and his competitor Eben Smith—all of whom worked in Beverly—are the best-known makers of such teapots.

Hints for Collectors
Teapots like this are often called coffeepots because of their height, but they can be identified by the strainer where the spout joins the body. Their wooden handles were originally painted black; traces of black remain on this example, but most have completely lost their paint. Original wooden handles are sometimes lost; if the replacement does not look precisely like the handle shown here, it has been incorrectly restored and will lower the market value of the pot.

272 Late Federal/Victorian baluster-shaped teapot

Description
Hinged, circular, double-domed lid with flared lip; mushroom-shaped finial with wooden insulator. Tall, baluster-shaped body with flared lip and foot rim; incised rings around body. Cylindrical, tapered, S-shaped spout. C-shaped handle with spur at top and simulated handle sockets.

Marks and Dimensions
"BOARDMAN/& HART" in 2 conjoined rectangles of differing lengths; "N-YORK" in another rectangle; all stamped on underside. Height: 10¾". Width: 9⅞". Diameter: 5¼".

Maker, Locality, and Date
Thomas D. Boardman & Lucius Hart (1828–53), Hartford or New York City. 1828–53. Retailed in New York City.

Comment
Although this teapot is similar to many made in America during the early to mid-19th century, it is of special interest because its body was cast in the same mold the firm used to make half-gallon liquid measures. The makers simply adapted the casting by adding a spout, hinged lid, and teapot handle instead of the measure's simple strap handle. Casting objects in molds limited the range of forms pewterers were able to produce, but by combining parts in innovative ways, they were able to overcome this limitation and reduce their costs.

Hints for Collectors
Although this teapot is only one of many objects made from interchangeable parts, it is the only example known to have been made from a measure mold. This makes it more desirable, but not necessarily more valuable, than other teapots.

Description
Hinged, molded, high-domed lid with pointed finial and wooden insulator. Symmetrical baluster-shaped body with flared rim and foot. Octagonal, S-shaped spout tapered and paneled. Tapered S-shaped handle with spur at top, fitted into circular pewter sockets.

Marks and Dimensions
Serrated circle enclosing spread eagle with shield-shaped body holding laurel bough and arrows with "S. KILBURN." above and "BALTIMORE" below, all stamped on inside bottom. Height: 9″. Width: 8½″. Diameter: 5⅜″.

Maker, Locality, and Date
Samuel Kilburn (d. 1839), Baltimore. 1814–30.

Comment
Teapots were perhaps the most common form of pewter hollowware made during the 19th century. Although most have a complex outline, this attractive example is quite simple. Its body was cleverly created by taking 2 castings from the same mold and then attaching them base to base to form a symmetrical unit. Although the handle is now the same color as the rest of the teapot, it was, like almost all teapot handles of this type, originally painted black to imitate the stained-wood handles of the 18th century. Teapots almost identical to this one, but with cylindrical spouts, were made by the Boardman family of Hartford.

Hints for Collectors
This teapot is in excellent condition. Its surface is free from corrosion, pits, and tarnish, and it has no dents or missing pieces. Such damage reduces the value of a teapot, but repairs may be made by a competent pewter restorer.

Victorian teapot

Description
Hinged, circular, molded lid with high dome and flared lip; mushroom-shaped wooden finial. Pear-shaped body with multiple encircling rings. Tapered S-shaped spout with notched tip. Complex scrolled handle painted black with spur at top. Low circular pedestal flared and molded.

Marks and Dimensions
"SAGE & BEEBE." in letters without serifs, stamped incuse on underside. Height: 10⅞". Width: 10¾". Diameter: 6⅛".

Maker, Locality, and Date
Timothy Sage & Beebe (first name unknown; dates unknown), St. Louis. c. 1850.

Comment
Teapots were made in tremendous quantity during the early 19th century. They were usually much larger than their 18th-century counterparts, with the result that they are sometimes mistaken for coffeepots. Most pewter examples were made in Philadelphia, New York, Hartford, and other major East Coast centers, but some, such as this example from St. Louis, were produced elsewhere. This teapot is closely related to and was undoubtedly copied from a teapot made in Hartford or perhaps New York. Such borrowing of designs was a common practice.

Hints for Collectors
Because of the relative rarity of midwestern and southern pewter, it is generally more expensive than its East Coast counterpart, even though quality is comparable. Whereas 18th-century teapots had wooden handles, 19th-century pots almost always had metal handles painted black. Many handles have lost their paint, while others have had the paint restored, but neither condition affects the value of the pot.

English George III coffeepot

Description
Hinged, molded, domed lid with knopped finial. Elongated pear-shaped body with flared lip. Slender S-shaped spout, tapered and paneled, with scalloped base. Tapered C-shaped wooden handle fitted into cylindrical pewter sockets. Circular molded pedestal. Lid, body, spout, and base decorated with bright-cut engraved borders, floral swags, and oval reserves.

Marks and Dimensions
Unmarked. Height: 11¾". Width: 8⅜". Diameter: 3⅞".

Maker, Locality, and Date
Unknown. England. 1780–1800.

Comment
Although tea and coffee were both popular beverages, 18th-century English and American pewter teapots are relatively common, while coffeepots are scarce. Teapots are typically squat and have a strainer at the base of the spout; coffeepots are taller and have a large open hole at the base of the spout. This example, undoubtedly English, is engraved all over, which is rare, and retains its original handle, also rare. Many early pewterers' advertisements and shop inventories included coffeepots, yet very few of these vessels have survived.

Hints for Collectors
Unmarked pewter is fairly common and typically worth about one-third to one-half the value of its marked counterparts. 18th-century pewter coffeepots, however, are rare and relatively expensive, even if unmarked. This example might cost perhaps a third more than a simpler English coffeepot. Because of its rarity and elaborate decoration, this coffeepot would be 20 to 30 times more expensive if it were marked.

Description
Hinged, tall, double-domed lid with 4 beaded borders and ribbed finial. Urn-shaped body with tall incurved neck, molded lip, and beaded border at widest diameter. Tapered S-shaped spout with stylized leaf at tip. Double-C-shaped wooden handle with spur at top, fitted into cylindrical pewter sockets. Flared circular pedestal with beaded border near base; set on low square plinth.

Marks and Dimensions
"Wͫ WILL/PHILA-/DELPHIA" with eagle's head above and row of dots under maker's name, all within serrated outline, stamped twice on outside edge of plinth; "LONDON" (with each N backward) beneath crowned rose flanked by fluted columns, stamped twice on inside edge of plinth. Height: 15⅞". Width: 11⅜". Diameter: 6".

Maker, Locality, and Date
William Will (1742–98), Philadelphia. 1782–98.

Comment
This and the 4 other known coffeepots by Will are among the rarest and most impressive of all American pewter. While this example bears unquestionable marks of William Will, it also has puzzling unknown marks, including "LONDON," which may have been meant to fool a buyer into thinking the object was made there.

Hints for Collectors
It is simply a matter of time until a sixth or seventh companion to this coffeepot appears, since numerous examples were made by Will and other American pewterers. Even if unmarked, an example might be attributed to Will if its dimensions exactly match those of the marked coffeepots, because all the parts were cast in molds and are therefore virtually identical.

Federal flagon

Description
Circular multidomed lid with flat rim, triangular spout cover, and beaded borders. Molded chair-back thumbpiece hinged to tapered S-shaped handle with ball terminal. Urn-shaped body with elongated incurved neck and molded rim. Long triangular spout. Beaded border at shoulder. Circular molded pedestal with beaded borders and square base.

Marks and Dimensions
Unmarked. Height: 13¾". Width: 7¼". Diameter: 6¹⁵⁄₁₆".

Maker, Locality, and Date
Attributed to William Will (1742–98), Philadelphia. c. 1795.

Comment
Since the Middle Ages, Roman Catholic doctrine has maintained that silver and gold were the only substances suitable to hold the Eucharist. This tradition was also maintained by most Protestant denominations. Not every church, however, could afford silver objects, so pewter was deemed a suitable substitute, and many American Protestant churches, especially rural congregations, used pewter flagons in the 18th and 19th centuries. This example was originally owned by a small rural church in central Pennsylvania. It is one of the finest 18th-century American pewter flagons known, being very close in its design to silver examples.

Hints for Collectors
American pewter church flagons are readily available. Most do not have any presentation inscription or even names of the churches that first owned them. Look carefully for clues to the identity of the original owners, not only because such information is historically important, but also because it can confirm whether the objects left the churches legitimately or were stolen.

Late Federal/Victorian coffee urn

Description
Circular lid with faceted finial, pointed dome, and flared lip. Tall double-bellied body with flared lip; 2 faceted loop handles above widest section, and brass spigot below with scrolled, loop-shaped petcock. Circular molded and flared pedestal.

Marks and Dimensions
"R GLEASON" in rectangle stamped on underside. Height: 14″. Width: 7½″. Diameter: 6¾″.

Maker, Locality, and Date
Roswell Gleason (1799–1887), Dorchester, Massachusetts. 1830–70.

Comment
In spite of the great popularity of both coffee and pewter since the early 18th century, very few American pewter coffee urns are known. At present, only 17 examples are recorded, all but one made in New England. Silver-plated coffee urns, by contrast, are much more common. Expensive molds of brass or bronze were required to make pewter. Moreover, the casting process was relatively slow, and the cost of each urn high compared to that of electroplated wares fabricated in England.

Hints for Collectors
Large pewter urns like this are desirable because they are some of the rare instances in which pewter was used in combination with another metal. Despite the rarity of pewter coffee urns, a lucky and persistent collector has a good chance of finding one, and at an affordable price. Make certain that the area around the spigot has not become weakened, and that the spigot has not become loose or separated from the urn. The pedestal and handles should also be closely examined, for they may have become disfigured from abusive handling.

279 Late Federal flagon on pedestal

Description
Hinged, molded, double-domed lid with widely flared lip and knopped finial with reeded umbrella-shaped top. S-shaped thumbpiece. Tapered S-shaped handle with Z-shaped terminal. Urn-shaped body with tall straight-sided upper section flared to molded lip; squat, bulbous lower section. Large, triangular, curved spout with scrolled top. Tall pedestal circular and molded, with narrow neck encircled by fillet. "St. John Church/New London/1830" scratched lightly under pedestal.

Marks and Dimensions
"H•YALE" and "WALLINGFORD"; each in form of opposed arcs enclosing "& CO"; all stamped incuse on underside of pedestal. Height: 14⅝". Width: 10". Diameter: 5¾".

Maker, Locality, and Date
Hiram Yale (1799–1831), Wallingford, Connecticut. 1817–31.

Comment
Although 19th-century American pewter flagons are common, only a few were made with pedestals to match the chalices they were used with. Hiram Yale made 2 slightly different types of flagons on pedestals. The type shown here, more attenuated than his other variety, is of special interest because of its unusual Z-shaped handle terminal.

Hints for Collectors
Interesting information about pewter objects is sometimes found on the objects themselves. The lightly engraved inscription on this example, documenting it to its original church, is an excellent case in point. Such engraving is easily overlooked, so carefully scrutinize every surface of an object for information that may have been recorded on it.

Late Colonial/Federal cream pot on pedestal

Description
Circular double-bellied body with long tapered upper section and beaded lip. Flared, curved spout. Double-C-shaped handle with spur on back and volutes at top and bottom. Circular molded pedestal with beaded foot rim.

Marks and Dimensions
Unmarked. Height: 5½″. Width: 5″. Diameter: 3″.

Maker, Locality, and Date
Attributed to William Will (1742–98), Philadelphia. 1764–98.

Comment
This cream pot illustrates the ingenuity of American pewterers in creating a variety of objects using a limited number of molds. The lower portion of this cream pot was cast in a mold for open salt containers. Its maker, instead of investing in another expensive mold for casting cream pots, simply used the salt container and attached a cream pot body, spout, and handle to it. This mixing and matching of parts allowed the innovative pewterer to offer his clientele a variety of forms at the minimum expense.

Hints for Collectors
Most cream pots of this design are unmarked. A few have the mark of William Will—the letter "x" with 5 small dots in a line over it—stamped on the inside bottom, often making it difficult to see. Persistent collectors who have committed this form to memory may be rewarded with discovering an inexpensive example at a flea market or local auction.

Late Colonial/Federal tripod cream pot

Description
Pear-shaped body with scalloped lip. Flared, creased, and pointed spout. Double-C-shaped handle with spur at top. 3 double-C-shaped legs with shell-shaped tops and feet.

Marks and Dimensions
"x" with 5 dots in line above, all stamped incuse inside bottom. Height: 3⅞". Width: 4⅜". Diameter: 3".

Maker, Locality, and Date
William Will (1742–98), Philadelphia. 1764–98.

Comment
This little cream pot bears a strong resemblance to examples of fine Philadelphia silver, from which it is derived. Its scalloped lip, curvilinear profile, complex double-C-shaped handle, and shell-decorated feet are all features of the rococo style popular for fashionable silver during the third quarter of the 18th century. This cream pot differs significantly from its silver counterparts, however, in its lack of engraved, chased, or repoussé ornament. While silver lent itself readily to elaborate naturalistic decoration, pewter was only occasionally engraved.

Hints for Collectors
Because pewter wares are soft, they are easily damaged, especially objects with slender feet and delicate handles. Examine any potential acquisition to determine if these appendages have been altered. Absence of wear on the underside of a foot or sloppy soldering at the juncture between the body and a leg or handle might indicate that an element has been replaced or repaired, which would lower the object's value.

Late Federal/Victorian pitcher

Description
Hinged circular lid, stepped and domed; upright molded finial.
Large pear-shaped body with flared lip. Faceted S-shaped handle
with spur at top. Curved triangular spout. Flared and molded
foot rim.

Marks and Dimensions
"ROSWELL GLEASON" stamped incuse on underside. Height:
12³⁄₁₆". Width: 12¼". Diameter: 10⅜".

Maker, Locality, and Date
Roswell Gleason (1799–1887), Dorchester, Massachusetts.
1830–50.

Comment
Large pitchers with or without lids were made in a variety of
sizes by numerous pewterers during the mid-19th century. Their
popularity, however, seems to have been short-lived, since
virtually all date from the second or third quarter of the 19th
century. They were advertised as cider pitchers, although they
were undoubtedly used for a variety of potables served cold or at
room temperature. Although made by a substantial number of
pewterers in the northeastern United States, these pitchers vary
little in design.

Hints for Collectors
Pitchers of this type are relatively common and quite similar in
overall shape, so pay particular attention to proportion and
pleasingly designed handles, finials, and spouts. Avoid examples
with heavy corrosion or pitting. Corrosion is very difficult to
remove; never buff pewter to alleviate corrosion because that
creates a smeared appearance and obliterates details such as
engraving or molded borders. It is best to have an expert
remove heavy corrosion with lye or acid.

Late Federal/Victorian pitcher

Description
Hinged, circular, bell-shaped lid with disk-shaped edge; knopped finial with fluted umbrella-shaped insulator. Bulbous body with short straight-sided neck and narrow encircling fillet at widest dimension. Narrow curved spout. Curvilinear handle resembling number "7" with short spur at top.

Marks and Dimensions
"G. RICHARDSON" in rectangle; "GLENNORE Cº" and "CRANSTON. R. I." each in serrated arc; spread eagle in rounded square; "Nº" in serrated square and "1" incuse; all stamped on underside. Height: 9¾". Width: 8½". Diameter: 6¾".

Maker, Locality, and Date
George Richardson (c. 1782–1848), Cranston, Rhode Island. 1830–45.

Comment
Pewter pitchers, varying in capacity from 1 to 6 quarts, were produced in large quantities in the 19th century. They were made with and without lids, and almost all were very similar in design. This example is somewhat unusual because its neck is straight-sided instead of curved and flared. Although collectors are familiar with Richardson's work, not much is known about his life or about the meaning of "Glennore Company," found stamped on most of his objects. The number "1" undoubtedly refers to a pattern number given in a catalogue.

Hints for Collectors
Early 19th-century pewter pitchers are readily available, so purchase only those that are in good condition. Most have a pear-shaped body with a thick, outward-curved neck. This pitcher has an inverted pear-shaped body and a short straight neck; these unusual features make it more desirable and valuable.

Victorian octagonal tea set

Description

Teapot (center): Hinged, octagonal, pointed lid with curved sides and flared lip; elaborate sculpted finial of grapes and leaves. Tall, pear-shaped, octagonal body. Long, octagonal, double-C-shaped spout. Double-C-shaped handle with spur at top and flat, domed attachments to body. Low, octagonal, molded base. Left: Matching octagonal cream pot with short triangular spout. Right: Matching octagonal sugar bowl with 2 double-C-shaped handles.

Marks and Dimensions

"4800/ROSWELL GLEASON/10" stamped incuse on underside of each piece. Teapot height: 11¹³⁄₁₆"; width: 10"; diameter: 5¾". Cream pot height: 6¹³⁄₁₆"; width: 6⅜"; diameter: 3⅞". Sugar bowl height: 7¹³⁄₁₆"; width: 7¹¹⁄₁₆"; diameter: 4¾".

Maker, Locality, and Date

Roswell Gleason (1799–1887), Dorchester, Massachusetts. 1835–65.

Comment

The pieces in this tea set are complex and quite unusual interpretations of common forms. While octagonal silver objects are found with some frequency, these are among the few octagonal pewter pieces known. The shape is uncommon because of the difficulty in designing a multipart mold from which pewter pieces can be extracted easily, without damaging them. The problem was circumvented in this instance, since the bodies of these vessels are made of sheet-metal panels soldered together. The finials, handles, and spouts, however, were cast in the traditional manner.

Hints for Collectors

With its complex profile and paneled surface, this pewter tea set was designed in direct imitation of the then-fashionable style in domestic silver. Compared to contemporary silver examples, however, these objects are relatively simple; but they are still interesting testimony to Roswell Gleason's attempts at updating pewter design even as the popularity of that metal for household objects was declining.

Gleason was a very successful pewterer who, after taking over his master's business in 1822, earned a reputation and won well-advertised acclaim for the fine quality of his teapots. By the time this tea set was made, in the middle of the 19th century, the same forms were being widely produced in inexpensive, attractive ceramic and silver-plated versions that were surpassing pewter in appeal. In fact, Gleason's own factory was among those that helped pioneer electroplating in this country. Today, however, the pewter objects shown here are desirable because they are unusual: Their bodies were not cast, allowing for the handsome octagonal design that distinguishes them. Furthermore, they have remained together as a set. These are the sorts of factors that enhance the interest and value of objects such as these. In fact, any one of the 3 objects would be an interesting addition to a pewter collection.

285 Early Victorian teapot

Description
Hinged, circular, stepped lid with incurved conical side and flared lip; small button finial with disk-shaped wooden insulator. Compressed body with convex side, stepped incurved upper and lower sections, and flared lip. Tapered S-shaped spout with flat back. Faceted, compressed, double-C-shaped handle with voluted spur at top; leaf-and-volute-decorated handle sockets. Circular flared pedestal.

Marks and Dimensions
"HALL/BOARDMAN/&CO." in rectangle with indented corners, and "PHILAD" in rectangle; all stamped on underside. Height: 8⁵⁄₁₆". Width: 10⅛". Diameter: 7¼".

Maker, Locality, and Date
Franklin D. Hall & Henry S. Boardman (c. 1843–60), Philadelphia. 1846–48.

Comment
Short, bulbous teapots of this general type were common during the early to mid-19th century. The body was usually made of 2 castings from the same mold, one of which was inverted, thus forming a perfectly symmetrical shape from lip to foot. The leaf-decorated sockets on this example are unusual, since most sockets had no ornament. The Boardman family were among the most successful of all American pewterers for 4 generations.

Hints for Collectors
Since teapots of this type are readily available, look for the subtle differences that make one example preferable to another. For instance, the attractive decorated handle sockets seen here are an unusual feature that sets this pot apart from most made at about the same time.

Late Federal teapot

Description
Hinged circular lid with incurved conical side and flared lip; short mushroom-shaped finial with wooden insulator. Squat drum-shaped body with broad ogee-shaped shoulder, incurved neck, and flared lip. Tapered S-shaped spout with flat back. Compressed double-C-shaped handle with spur at top and simulated cylindrical handle sockets. Circular, flared, and molded pedestal.

Marks and Dimensions
"D.CURTISS" in 8-shaped banner stamped on underside. Height: 8⅞". Width: 10¾". Diameter: 5⅞".

Maker, Locality, and Date
Daniel Curtiss (c. 1799–1872), Albany, New York. 1830–40.

Comment
Albany had been an important center for the production of fine silver and pewter from early in the 18th century until well into the 19th. Daniel Curtiss, one of the city's later pewterers, seems to have specialized in pitchers and plates. This teapot, which bears Curtiss' interesting banner-shaped mark, is a type that, with minor variations, was made in all the East Coast centers. Other pewterers made similar teapots in taller shapes or in very small 1- or 2-cup varieties.

Hints for Collectors
Collectors can assemble a large and varied collection of 19th-century pewter teapots with relative ease and modest expense. Because such pots are common, collectors can afford to be selective. Avoid examples that are heavily corroded, battered, worn, partially melted from being placed on hot stoves, or indistinctly marked.

Description
Hinged, circular, high-domed lid with encircling fillet and flared molded lip; tall knopped finial with wooden insulator. Pear-shaped body with flared molded lip and encircling fillet above convex lower section. Tapered S-shaped spout. S-shaped wooden handle with spur at top, fitted into cylindrical pewter sockets. 3 short carbiole legs with hoof feet.

Marks and Dimensions
Crown over rose flanked by fluted columns with "CORNELIUS" in arc above and "BRADFORD" in rectangle below; "x" incuse; all stamped on inside bottom. Height: 7¼″. Width: 8½″. Diameter: 3⅞″.

Maker, Locality, and Date
Cornelius Bradford (1729–86), New York City or Philadelphia. 1752–85.

Comment
The pear shape was the most popular form for teapots during the mid-18th century. Bradford was one of the very few American pewterers to have applied legs to his pear-shaped teapots. The teapot shown here could have been made in New York City or Philadelphia, since Bradford worked in both cities, and this pot is quite close in appearance to English examples that were imported to both centers.

Hints for Collectors
Pewter teapots are often heavily corroded inside with black encrustation. Such tarnish can effectively obscure makers' marks, which were generally stamped on the inside rather than the outside of 18th-century pewter teapots. A close examination of a potential acquisition might reveal an indistinct but well-respected name.

Late Colonial/Federal teapot

Description
Hinged, circular, domed lid with knopped finial and molded border. Pear-shaped body with molding near neck. Tapered S-shaped spout. S-shaped wooden handle with spur at top, fitted into cylindrical sockets. 3 curved legs with claw-and-ball feet.

Marks and Dimensions
"W^M WILL" in serrated rectangle stamped on inside bottom. Height: 8″. Width: 8⅛″. Diameter: 5¼″.

Maker, Locality, and Date
William Will (1742–98), Philadelphia. 1764–98.

Comment
Pewter objects from the 18th century were closely related in design to their silver counterparts. Many of the features that became popular in silver were quickly incorporated into pewter, although the pewter versions tended to be somewhat simpler in interpretation. Because decoration—whether cast, chased, or engraved—was costly, there was usually little of it on American pewter, which was meant to be inexpensive.

Hints for Collectors
Pear-shaped 18th-century pewter teapots are not as common as silver ones, probably because the softness of the metal caused many to wear out quickly. Pewter teapots with feet are quite rare—most rest directly on a tabletop—and William Will is the only American pewterer now known to have used claw-and-ball feet. For this reason, and also because of Will's highly respected name, his claw-and-ball footed teapots are considerably more expensive than the teapots of his contemporaries.

English George II teapot

Description
Hinged circular lid domed and molded; stepped pointed finial
with wooden insulator. Squat pear-shaped body encircled by
molding at shoulder. S-shaped paneled spout with affixed lid.
Tapered S-shaped wooden handle with spur at top, fitted into
cylindrical pewter sockets. Narrow foot rim under base.

Marks and Dimensions
2 leafy scrolls, upper one containing "IOHN" and lower
"TOWNSEND" with "1748" between, all encircling oval containing
lamb and dove with olive branch in its beak, and all on stippled
ground; "X" crowned and "LONDON" in serrated rectangle; all
stamped on underside. Height: 6⅜". Width: 7⅝". Diameter: 3⅞".

Maker, Locality, and Date
John Townsend (c. 1728–1801), London. 1748–66.

Comment
England produced vast quantities of pewter for the American
market, and much of it was copied by American pewterers. This
teapot, for instance, is very similar to many American examples.
Although no one has proved that it was imported to America in
the 18th century, others just like it were.

Hints for Collectors
Although chauvinism directs most collectors toward American-
made objects, English pewter has a place in their collections. It
was used in this country from the beginnings of European
settlement, and there are close stylistic ties between it and
American pewter. Another important factor is cost: This English
teapot would be much less expensive than its American
counterpart.

Late Colonial/Federal egg-shaped teapot

Description
Hinged circular lid low and molded; knopped finial with wooden
insulator. Egg-shaped body with engraved borders near lip and
at widest diameter. Small, tapered, S-shaped spout. S-shaped
wooden handle with spur at top, fitted into cylindrical pewter
sockets. Low flared and molded base.

Marks and Dimensions
Rampant lion flanked by "F" and "B"; all in serrated circle
stamped on inside bottom. Height: 6⅜″. Width: 8″.
Diameter: 4⅞″.

Maker, Locality, and Date
Attributed to Frederick Bassett (c. 1740–1800), New York City
or Hartford. 1761–99.

Comment
This teapot is a very early and fine example of American pewter.
Like most 18th-century teapots, it is of fairly small capacity, able
to dispense about 2 modern-day cupfuls; it would have served
more cups at the time it was made because teacups were also
small in size, reflecting the high price of tea. Apparently made
exclusively in the New York area, the egg-shaped body is
unusual; most pewter teapots of this date were pear-shaped or
cylindrical.

Hints for Collectors
The maker of this teapot was one of several men in the same
family with the same name or initials and similar marks. There
are also other instances of this potentially confusing
phenomenon. To properly identify the maker of an object in a
case like this, collectors should refer to the table of marks in the
appendix as well as to other current reference books for the most
up-to-date information.

European japanned kettle-on-stand

Description
Removable circular lid with low dome and knopped finial.
Flattened globe-shaped body with 2 circular tabs at top into
which is hinged scrolled loop handle with wooden baluster shape
at center. Tapered S-shaped spout. Separate bowl-shaped stand
with flared side, 3 shell-shaped tabs rising above lip, 2 hinged
loop handles, shaped skirt, and 3 scrolled feet. Painted black
overall with gilt foliate ornament.

Marks and Dimensions
Illegible. Height: 13⅞". Width: 10⅛". Diameter: 8¼".

Maker, Locality, and Date
Unknown. Holland or England. 1750–80.

Comment
Pewter was usually left quite plain, but some was ornamented
with cast, chased, or engraved decoration. A very small amount
was japanned, using a painting technique imitative of Oriental
lacquerwork. Most japanned pieces were painted black with gilt
ornament, although some were painted red, yellow, or blue.
Japanned pewter was most popular during the late 18th century.
European japanned pewter objects far outnumber American
examples, which are quite rare.

Hints for Collectors
Since the japanned surfaces on pewter are extremely fragile,
very few pieces have survived with their original ornament
intact. Closely examine a darkened piece of pewter to determine
whether it is heavily tarnished or japanned. Great care should be
taken to preserve any japanned piece for future generations of
collectors. Japanned objects with their original ornament intact
are worth 2 or 3 times as much as those objects that have lost it.

Federal drum-shaped teapot

Description
Hinged, circular, flat lid with small dome and beaded edge; knopped beaded finial. Tapered cylindrical body with short neck, beaded border at shoulder, and molded foot rim. Straight, tapered, cylindrical spout. C-shaped wooden handle with spur at top, fitted into cylindrical pewter sockets.

Marks and Dimensions
"W.ᵐ WILL/PHILA-/DELPHIA" with eagle's head above and row of dots under maker's name, all within serrated outline stamped on inside bottom. Height: 6³⁄₁₆". Width: 10⅛". Diameter: 4¾".

Maker, Locality, and Date
William Will (1742–98), Philadelphia. 1782–98.

Comment
Drum-shaped pewter teapots from the 18th century, which are quite rare, imitate silver examples and seem to have been made only in Philadelphia. Although Will was working in Philadelphia as early as 1764, this teapot can be reliably dated to the last 2 decades of the century because its drumlike shape, straight spout, and beaded borders did not become popular until after the Revolution. The eagle's-head motif in the maker's mark confirms this estimate, as the eagle was adopted as the national symbol only after American independence.

Hints for Collectors
The juncture of the body and spout of this pot has obviously been repaired, since the solder is crude and awkward. Amateur repairs can drastically lower the value of an object. Fortunately, the spout and body were not damaged or melted when this repair was made, so this teapot can be repaired again by an expert restorer.

Mugs, Chalices, Beakers, and Related Objects

From the 17th century through the early part of the 19th, pewter was widely used to make various types of drinking vessels. Until the 18th century, Americans employed both lidded vessels (tankards) and lidless beakers and mugs. Both seem to have been popular, but those without lids were much more common because they were less expensive than tankards. Although no writer of earlier times has recorded precisely why tankards existed, it is likely that they were valued for sanitary reasons—the lid kept insects and debris from the contents.

Capacity and Function

Tankards were made in pint, quart, 3-pint, and gallon capacities. The quart size seems to have been most useful, judging from antique examples. Mugs that have survived seem to be largely of the pint and quart size, although there are some half-pint examples. Beakers, which may be made with or without handles, typically had a slightly greater range of sizes, but were usually of smaller capacity than mugs. Most known antique examples are fairly small, ranging from a gill (half a cup) to a pint.

Chalices, or standing cups, form the other major category of American drinking vessels. Usually made without handles and lids, chalices were the exclusive province of Christian churches that practiced the sacrament of communion. Tankards, mugs, and beakers were found principally in the home or tavern, but they were also used in churches, as evidenced by numbers of examples that bear presentation inscriptions and others that still remain in use in some early churches.

Shape and Decoration

Most drinking vessels have fairly uniform shapes and are usually straight sided. Beakers generally have a slight or sometimes pronounced outward flare, while mugs become narrower toward the lip. During the mid- to late 18th century, a number of examples were made that had tulip-shaped or bellied bodies; bellied mugs were known as canns. Drinking vessels of this shape usually had a handle that was more complex in profile and decoration than that found on straight-sided examples.

These vessels were sometimes decorated with engraving, but the majority—like most pewter objects from this country—were absolutely plain. Whereas mugs and beakers are still made today, albeit in other materials, tankards quickly fell from popularity around 1800, and examples from the 19th and 20th centuries are virtually nonexistent.

Measures

Pewter seems to have been the most popular metal for measures, which were used to regulate beer and other strong beverages in inns and taverns. Measures were typically made in sets, which could have as many as 13 vessels ranging in capacity from one twenty-fourth of a pint to one gallon. However, one rarely encounters antique American pewter measures in sets of more than 4 or 5. While almost every major early American pewterer made and offered measures, presumably largely for tavern use, very few that survive date from before the mid-19th century.

Drinking vessels were sometimes adapted for other uses. On some, spouts were added to convert them into pouring vessels. Still others were adapted for sickbed use by adding a removable lid with a flexible tube and holes in the handle; such infusion pots, as they were known, were used by invalids to inhale medicinal vapors, much as a vaporizer is used in this century.

Description
Circular pear-shaped body with flared lip. Double-C-shaped handle with acanthus leaf and volute at top and scrolled terminal at bottom. Molding encircling body at widest point. Flared molded foot rim.

Marks and Dimensions
"ww" with foliate device above and below, all in serrated circle, stamped on bottom of interior. Height: 6⁷⁄₁₆″. Width: 6⅜″. Diameter: 5⅜″.

Maker, Locality, and Date
William Will (1742–98), Philadelphia. 1764–98.

Comment
Tulip-shaped or bellied pewter mugs were usually referred to as canns. They are much less common than their straight-sided counterparts. The same can be said for the double-C-shaped handles. Most handles were of a straightforward S shape, having a simple ball terminal and rudimentary spur at top. Only a very few are more elaborate, most notably those made by John Will, a New York pewterer, and his son William, who worked in Philadelphia.

Hints for Collectors
This mug is exceptional because of its bellied shape and because its handle is decorated with an acanthus leaf. Bellied pewter mugs and tankards mostly date from the late 18th century, and seem to have been most popular in Philadelphia. Their rarity and visual appeal makes them more desirable with collectors than their straight-sided counterparts. The fact that this example bears William Will's mark makes it worth even more to the discerning collector.

Description
Circular double-domed lid. Pierced chair-back thumbpiece hinged
to double-C-shaped handle, with acanthus leaf and volute at top,
ribs along length, and scrolled terminal at bottom. Pear-shaped
body with flared lip. Molded circular foot rim.

Marks and Dimensions
"JOHN*WILL" in rectangle stamped under lip near handle. Height:
7¾". Width: 6½". Diameter: 5⅜".

Maker, Locality, and Date
John Will (c. 1696–1774), New York City. 1752–74.

Comment
New York pewterers and silversmiths produced many tankards
during the 18th century, usually with straight sides, a flat-topped
lid, and a relatively simple S-shaped handle. This unusual
example has a bellied body, domed lid, and a complex handle
with an acanthus-leaf decoration. The acanthus leaf is interesting
because of the rarity of cast ornament on American pewter
objects. Another unusual feature is the placement of the maker's
mark just under the lip beside the handle, since most American
pewter tankards were marked on the inside bottom. The
placement of the mark on this example is similar to that of
makers' marks on silver tankards.

Hints for Collectors
The tankard is one of the most desirable of all forms for
collectors of American pewter. While pewter tankards are not
especially rare, their great popularity with collectors has made
them quite expensive. This particular tankard would command
an exceptional premium because of its well-respected maker, fine
workmanship, and pleasing design. Despite its very high price,
such a piece will undoubtedly continue to appreciate in value.

Description
Elongated pear-shaped body with straight-sided flared lip and flared base. Incised lines at lip, mid-body, and base. Tapered S-shaped handle with flat platform at top.

Marks and Dimensions
"T B & C⁰" in serrated rectangle and "N-YORK" in rectangle, all stamped under base. "I.P.S." and "1827" stamped incuse on lip next to handle. Height: 9⅛". Width: 7½". Diameter: 4¾".

Maker, Locality, and Date
Timothy Boardman & Company (1822–25), New York City. c. 1827.

Comment
Pewter measures for dispensing wine and beer were mandated by law in America as early as the 17th century, and vessels with distinctive shapes were created for that purpose. Very few examples survive, the most common being in the shape of this half-gallon specimen. All are marked or attributed to the Boardman family of pewterers. Most bear the stamped initials of the inspector of weights and measures of New York City, as well as the date of inspection, on the lip near the handle. In this unusual case, the measure was not inspected until 2 years after the maker's death.

Hints for Collectors
American measures like the one shown here are almost identical to English baluster measures of the same period or earlier. If a measure is unmarked, it is dangerous to assign it an American attribution unless you know what to look for. In this instance, the narrow molding at the top edge of the lip, the flat platform on the handle, and the diamond-shaped attachment at the lower handle juncture would substantiate an American attribution.

Federal pint mug

Description
Circular barrel-shaped body with molded lip. Tapered S-shaped handle with spur at top and ball-shaped terminal. Multiple rings encircling body. Flared molded foot rim.

Marks and Dimensions
"R•PALETHORP J^R/PHILAD^A" in conforming scalloped outline, stamped on inside bottom. Height: 4¼". Width: 5". Diameter: 3⅝".

Maker, Locality, and Date
Robert Palethorp, Jr. (1797–1822), Philadelphia. 1817–22.

Comment
Unlike tankards, mugs retained their popularity as drinking vessels from the 18th through 20th centuries. They were typically made in pint or quart sizes, and usually had straight sides. Variations were not common, but are found in the type of handle used, the presence and placement of encircling bands, and sometimes in the shape of the body. This is a notable example, having been fashioned in the shape of a barrel with encircling hoops.

Hints for Collectors
This mug is noteworthy because of its pint size; most American mugs, canns, and tankards are of the larger quart variety. Also important is the shape, for most mugs were straight-sided, and only a very few with a barrel shape and simulated hoops are known today. Palethorp died while quite young, and as a consequence, his pewter is very rare. Such features make a great difference to collectors, resulting in a three- or fourfold increase in value over more common examples.

Description
Circular vessel with side flared out toward base. Lip and base reeded. 2 simple, rounded, rectangular handles set vertically under lip. Simple, flared, molded foot rim.

Marks and Dimensions
"H. YALE" and "WALLINGFORD" each in form of opposed arcs enclosing "& CO"; all stamped incuse on inside bottom. Height: 6½". Width: 6¾". Diameter: 5⅞".

Maker, Locality, and Date
Hiram Yale (1799–1831), Wallingford, Connecticut. 1825–31.

Comment
Although American pewter mugs of the 18th and 19th centuries are quite common, most examples have a single handle; 2 handles were typically reserved for footed vessels such as chalices. However, by the late 19th century, mugs with 2 handles became more prevalent. Known as loving cups, these later examples sometimes have glass bottoms—a feature never found on earlier pieces. The form has been frequently reproduced and was popular for athletic trophies in the late 19th century.

Hints for Collectors
This mug is interesting because it has 2 handles, a rather rare feature on a mug of this date. However, the simple handles seen here do not compare favorably with the more curvilinear types of a century or so earlier. As a result, collectors seem less willing to pay a premium for mugs with handles like these, proving that while rarity is important, fashions and collectors' preferences, often based on visual factors, can be just as decisive in determining desirability and price.

Late Colonial/Federal strap-handle mug

Description
Circular body with straight tapered side and molded lip. Thin, tapered, S-shaped handle with stylized shell at top and flat circular terminal at bottom. Narrow molding encircling body. Flared molded foot rim.

Marks and Dimensions
"N•AUSTIN" in cast raised letters around perimeter of handle end. Height: 5¹³⁄₁₆″. Width: 6¼″. Diameter: 5¼″.

Maker, Locality, and Date
Nathaniel Austin (c. 1741–1816), Charlestown, Massachusetts. 1763–1807.

Comment
Mugs were among the most popular drinking vessels during the 18th century. They were usually straight-sided and simple in shape with a minimum of ornament and were made in quart, pint, and, less commonly, half-pint sizes. Most handles on pewter mugs and tankards were made separately and soldered to the body. But some handles were cast, like porringer handles, in a technique known as burning on. In this process, the mold was held directly against the vessel, allowing molten metal to come into direct contact with the side, partially melting it and forming a permanent joint between the body and the handle.

Hints for Collectors
While a mug by any American maker would be a desirable addition to a pewter collection, this one is particularly noteworthy and valuable. It is very unusual because the maker's name is cast on the handle terminal, and because of the solid strap handle, an early substitute for a hollow handle.

Description
Circular body with tapered side and molded lip. Tapered S-shaped handle with spur and fishtail terminal. Molding around body above lower handle juncture. Flared molded foot rim.

Marks and Dimensions
"FB" with star above and below, all enclosed in rope-edged circle and stamped on inside bottom. Height: 4¾". Width: 5⅝". Diameter: 4¾".

Maker, Locality, and Date
Frederick Bassett (c. 1740–1800), New York City. 1761–1800.

Comment
The Bassetts, a major pewtering family, were active in New York City for almost a century. John and Francis Bassett, who were first cousins, were the earliest pewterers in the family and worked for most of the early 18th century. John's oldest son, also called Francis, and his youngest son, Frederick, were pewterers as well. However, the younger was apparently much more prolific. His work is found in most major collections, while Francis' is quite rare. Frederick's impressive range of products included 11 sizes of plates and dishes.

Hints for Collectors
Mug handles most often have a ball terminal; variants like this fishtail terminal are relatively uncommon. Serious collectors are frequently willing to pay a premium for such unusual features.

Federal infusion pot

Description
Circular body with tapered straight side. Flat lid has beaded edge, hinged pierced tab covering shallow pocket, and short cylindrical projection at center, into which is fitted coiled iron spring covered with leather and having ivory tip. Body has narrow encircling band just above lower handle juncture. Tapered S-shaped handle with 3 holes and spur at top and ball terminal. Molded foot rim.

Marks and Dimensions
"R. PALETHORP J^R / PHILA^D " in 2 conjoined arcaded rectangles. Height (not including tube): 4⅞". Width: 5¾". Diameter: 4⅜".

Maker, Locality, and Date
Robert Palethorp, Jr. (1797–1822), Philadelphia. 1817–21.

Comment
Early Americans frequently looked upon home remedies and herbal brews as the only cures for dreaded diseases. Infusion pots such as this one were often used by sick persons, who inhaled medicinal vapors through the flexible tube at the top.

Hints for Collectors
This infusion pot, a modified mug, is one of only a few such items known to exist today. Although the leather-covered tube is tattered and unsightly, it is an important record of the materials used in early medical practices. Its presence adds not only to the pot's historical significance but also to its value.

Late Colonial engraved tankard

Description
Circular lid with low dome, flat top, and crenate lip. Molded
scrolled thumbpiece hinged to tapered S-shaped handle with
fishtail terminal. Tapered cylindrical body with molded foot rim.
"SC" engraved in script within foliate circle on lid; "SC" also
engraved normally and in reverse amid elaborate foliate mantling
on body opposite handle.

Marks and Dimensions
"WB" with fleur-de-lis above and below, all in circle and stamped
on inside bottom. Height: 7 1/16". Width: 7 5/8". Diameter: 5 1/4".

Maker, Locality, and Date
William Bradford, Jr. (1688–1759), New York City. 1740–58.

Comment
This flat-topped tankard is fairly typical of those made by New
York City pewterers throughout the 18th century. However, it
has 2 quite unusual features, the fishtail terminal and the
engraved initials within the foliate enclosures. While American
pewter was sometimes decoratively engraved, the ornament on
this tankard relates more closely to that on silver objects of the
same date.

Hints for Collectors
This tankard is in relatively poor condition, showing evidence of
heavy corrosion and extensive repairs, including a lid and handle
that were broken off and restored. In spite of this, it is very
desirable because of its extraordinary engraving, unusual fishtail
terminal, and uncommon maker. In general, the more unusual an
object, the more repairs and restoration serious collectors will
accept. However, there are always limits to the amount of
damage that careful collectors will tolerate, even on the rarest
pieces.

Federal tankard

Description
Circular double-domed lid with flared molded lip. Chair-back thumbpiece with inverted teardrop-shaped hole, hinged to tapered S-shaped handle with flat back and spherical terminal at bottom. Cylindrical body with molded lip. Narrow fillet encircling body at lower handle juncture. Molded foot rim. Beaded ring on lid and foot rim.

Marks and Dimensions
"x" with crown above; "I•BRUNSTROM" in serrated arc; and 3 pseudohallmarks (upright lion in diamond struck 3 times), all stamped on inside bottom. Height: 7⅜". Width: 6½". Diameter: 5¼".

Maker, Locality, and Date
John Andrew Brunstrom (c. 1753–93), Philadelphia. 1781–93.

Comment
John Brunstrom was a Swedish immigrant who worked in Philadelphia for only a short time, but the inventory of his shop indicates he was a prolific pewterer. Yet only 2 objects that bear his name—this tankard and a quart mug—are known today. The tankard is of high quality, and the unusual flattened disk surrounded by a beaded circle on its lid is a design probably derived from Swedish silver tankards.

Hints for Collectors
Even though there are only 2 known pewter objects stamped "I•BRUNSTROM," the secondary marks—a crowned "x" and 3 lions —occur with great frequency on Pennsylvania pewter, thus allowing some objects to be tentatively attributed to Brunstrom.

303 Colonial and Federal beakers

Description
Tall circular body with straight side flared at lip. Molded foot rim. Right beaker with 2 incised rings just below center.

Marks and Dimensions
Left: Crown over rose flanked by "RB"; all in circle; "x" with crown above stamped incuse; all on inside bottom. Height: 5¼". Diameter: 3⅝". Right: "TB & C⁰" in serrated rectangle; "x" stamped incuse; all on underside. Height: 5¼". Diameter: 3½".

Maker, Locality, and Date
Left: Robert Bonynge (dates unknown), Boston. 1731–63. Right: Timothy Boardman & Company (1822–25), New York City. 1822–25.

Comment
Tall cylindrical beakers have been popular in America since the 17th century, and numerous 18th-century silversmiths and pewterers made them. The silver examples from this period seem to have been predominantly for church use, while their pewter counterparts, lacking the elaborate pictorial decoration and inscriptions present on the silver ones, could just as well have been used in homes or taverns.

Hints for Collectors
Beakers of this type are relatively plentiful. Pairs are more desirable than single examples and command a premium. Even though examples by different pewterers may be virtually indistinguishable, their prices can vary greatly depending on their makers.

Modern beakers

Description
Cylindrical body with slightly tapered side and flared lip; exterior surface shows pronounced hammer facets.

Marks and Dimensions
Hammer flanked by "FD"; stamped incuse on underside. Height: 4½". Diameter: 3⅛".

Maker, Locality, and Date
Fred Dodson (b. 1921), Acworth, New Hampshire. 1969.

Comment
Until the late 19th century, when the use of pewter ceased almost entirely, cast pewter objects of all sorts were popular household commodities. As early as the 1930s, a few craftsmen rediscovered the metal and began to make handwrought objects. The softness of pewter lends itself readily to making objects in this manner, and the textured surface of a handwrought article contrasts dramatically with the smooth polished surface of a cast object.

Hints for Collectors
These beakers are a fine interpretation of a traditional form. Their clean lines echo the designs of cast examples made more than a century earlier, while their richly textured surfaces reflect the innovation of a talented contemporary craftsman. The combination bespeaks a creative approach to design and commends the objects to the sensitive collector. In this instance, the hammer marks indicate the method in which the objects were made. Sometimes hammer marks have been added to machine-fabricated objects to give them a handmade appearance. Collectors should study the surfaces of these and similar objects to distinguish genuine handwrought hammer facets from marks that have been added to machine-made articles.

Federal beakers

Description
Left: Circular, slightly tapered body encircled by 3 pairs of incised rings. Low molded foot rim. Right: Circular body with curved flared side; incised ring on lip. Low foot rim.

Marks and Dimensions
Left: "E.S." below 3-masted ship stamped on underside. Height: 4⅜". Diameter: 3¹¹⁄₁₆". Right: "J. WEEKES N. Y." in rectangle stamped on underside. Height: 3½". Diameter: 2¹⁵⁄₁₆".

Maker, Locality, and Date
Left: Ebenezer Southmayd (1775–1831), Castleton, Vermont. 1802–20. Right: James Weekes (dates unknown), New York City. 1820–35.

Comment
While silver beakers typically had engraved names, inscriptions, pictorial scenes, and other decoration, pewter examples are usually devoid of ornament other than simple incised rings. Like most pewter objects, beakers were cast in molds; therefore all examples from the same mold are identical in size and shape. But since pewterers could add a touch of variety to their products in finishing, such details as the shape of the foot rim or the placement of encircling rings often vary from one beaker to the next.

Hints for Collectors
Because American pewter beakers show only slight variations in size, shape, or detail, a new collector might mistakenly assume that their prices would be fairly consistent. Yet factors such as condition, age, rarity, and the popularity of the maker cause prices to vary widely.

Victorian cup with handle

Description
Moderately deep circular body with flared curved side and
molded lip. Tapered S-shaped handle with spur at top. Molded
foot rim.

Marks and Dimensions
"CALDER" in serrated rectangle stamped on inside bottom.
Height: 2¹³⁄₁₆". Width: 4⁵⁄₁₆". Diameter: 3⅛".

Maker, Locality, and Date
William Calder (1792–1856), Providence. 1830–56.

Comment
Small, handled cups, generally used for drinking hot liquids, are
typically made of some type of ceramic material. Metal cups
cannot serve this purpose because they conduct heat too readily;
their contents, whether alcoholic or nonalcoholic, must be cold.
Cups of this type from before the mid-18th century were often
fitted with 2 handles, while most dating after that time have only
a single handle.

Hints for Collectors
American pewter or silver cups with handles are quite rare
today, not only because few were made, but also because many
of these have since lost their handles. Carefully examine any
beaker under consideration to ensure that it was not originally a
cup that has lost its handle. Much late 19th-century pewter was
decorated with cast, die-stamped, or engraved ornament and was
originally silver-plated. For this reason many collectors do not
acknowledge such objects as pewter and avoid them, although
they are relatively common and sought by collectors of
Victoriana.

Description
Deep cylindrical cup with flared lip and 2 double-C-shaped handles. Short stem with circular molded pedestal.

Marks and Dimensions
Unmarked. Height: 6¼". Width: 7⅛". Diameter: 3⅜".

Maker, Locality, and Date
Attributed to Thomas D. Boardman & Sherman Boardman (c. 1808–1860), New York City. 1810–27.

Comment
American chalices with handles are rare and seem to have been most frequently used in Presbyterian churches. This example, however, with its mate and a matching flagon, was used in the First German Baptist Church in Wilmington, Delaware. Very often churches lost their congregations through attrition, so that many sold their communion vessels, as happened with this chalice in 1898.

Hints for Collectors
While communion vessels have been sold by many American churches, they have been stolen from others. Collectors should always seek out the history of any church object, whether to determine which church owned it or to discover if the object has been stolen. Chalices with handles are rarer and therefore more valuable than those without. Carefully study the design, wear, solder joints, and color of handles to ensure that they are compatible with and original to the vessel. Chalices that have lost their handles may have irregular areas on the surface of the cup where the handles were originally placed.

Description
Left: Circular, molded, domed lid with knopped finial. Deep circular cup with flared straight side and ring encircling center. Large knopped stem and domed molded pedestal. Right: Deep circular cup with flared curved side and incised ring around lip. Slender multiknopped stem and domed molded pedestal.

Marks and Dimensions
Left: Unmarked. Height: 10¹¹⁄₁₆″. Diameter: 4⅜″. Right: "PY" in serrated circle stamped on inside bottom. Height: 8½″. Diameter: 4¼″.

Maker, Locality, and Date
Left: Johann Christoph Heyne (1715–81), Lancaster, Pennsylvania. 1756–80. Right: Peter Young (1749–1813), New York City or Albany, New York. 1775–95.

Comment
The chalice has always been the central liturgical object for most Christian denominations. Silver was the preferred material for it, but many churches, particularly American Protestant ones, turned to pewter as an acceptable, less costly substitute for chalices and accompanying flagons. Chalice cups were typically large, since they were intended to serve the entire congregation, and the stem was always knopped for easy handling. Lidded examples could serve as either a chalice for wine or a ciborium for the communion wafers.

Hints for Collectors
American 18th-century pewter chalices are fairly rare. Although many are not marked, their makers may still be identified because the chalice parts were cast in molds. All parts from the same mold are identical, so an unmarked example can be attributed to a maker if its parts match those of a marked one.

Candlesticks, Lamps, and Related Objects

Between 1792 and 1862, the United States granted more than 600 patents for improvements in candles, candle holders, lamps and lamp fluids, and gas and gas-burning devices for home use. Still more patents were given for kerosene burners and related equipment made for commercial or public purposes. An extensive array of these lighting devices was made of pewter, since this metal was relatively easy to work and fairly inexpensive.

Candlesticks
17th- and 18th-century shop records and advertisements indicate that pewterers routinely made and sold candlesticks, which are also mentioned in household inventories of the period. Despite this, no pewter household candlestick from before the 19th century has yet been positively assigned an American origin. In the beginning of the 19th century, candles continued to be America's chief source of artificial illumination. Refinements were made in wick designs and in waxes. Candles were increasingly made with spermaceti, since it burned cleanly and with a bright flame. The candlesticks themselves reveal a number of simple stylistic variations.

Lamps
Throughout the 19th century, lamps assumed increasing importance. Extensive experimentation led to the discovery of new lamp fuels and the means to derive greater amounts of light from them. Burning fluid, a mixture of turpentine and alcohol that burned very brightly, was developed. But because of this fuel's unstable nature, even the use of long flaring wick tubes did not always keep lamps filled with burning fluid from exploding. Innovations took place not only with fuel but also with the lamps themselves. In some, a magnifying glass amplified the flame; in others, multiple wicks provided greater light. In one type, the font was set in a swiveling gimbal, allowing the burner to remain upright whether placed on a table, hung from a wall, or knocked to the floor. In another type, the wick was hollow, creating a central draft through the lamp's glass chimney.

Decoration
Unlike silver, silver-plated, or brass lighting devices, pewter examples were almost never elaborately decorated. Most were quite severe, relying on shape and color for decorative effect. When ornament was incorporated into their design, it invariably took the form of molded rings, simple beaded borders, or an occasional series of gadrooned moldings. This was in keeping with the traditional simplicity of American pewter.

Competition among pewterers was intense in the 19th century. There was constant borrowing—usually without permission—of new ideas and products. Consequently, lamps and candlesticks marked by different makers who were geographically distant sometimes appear virtually identical in size, shape, and detail. Pewterers also sometimes used a single mold to make a part that could be incorporated into either a lamp or a candlestick, thereby cutting manufacturing costs.

309 Federal or English George III candlesticks

Description
Cylindrical shaft with multiple encircling moldings. Flared and dished candle cup with flat bobeche. Circular, stepped, molded base. Candlestick at left has multiple recessed rings on shaft; at right, single raised rings.

Marks and Dimensions
Unmarked. Height: 5⅝″. Diameter: 3¹⁵⁄₁₆″.

Maker, Locality, and Date
Unknown. England or United States. 1780–1800.

Comment
Although numerous 18th-century American pewterers advertised candlesticks, the only documented examples known today dating from before the 19th century are 4 large altar candlesticks made in Lancaster, Pennsylvania. By contrast, many 18th-century English brass candlesticks survive, as do some American silver examples and marked 18th-century pewter candlesticks from England and the Continent. It is likely that the American pewter candlesticks of the time were similar to their brass and silver counterparts, and that American examples will eventually be discovered.

Hints for Collectors
Many varieties of 18th-century candlesticks were made, from very simple examples to complex ones complete with a special ejector, like the push rod that runs through the shaft of each of the sticks shown here, which removed candle stubs. The ribbed borders seen here are similar to those found on documented pewter objects from Philadelphia, which has encouraged one scholar to assign them an American origin. Until documented American examples are discovered, collectors should be cautious, assuming that 18th-century candlesticks are probably English.

310 Victorian chamber stick

Description
Cylindrical candle cup with flat horizontal bobeche. Inverted baluster shaft with incised rings. Shallow saucer has circular finger loop with flat oval pad on top.

Marks and Dimensions
"OSTRANDER" and "& NORRIS" each in arc-shaped outline, stamped on underside. Height: 4¾". Diameter: 5¹⁄₁₆".

Maker, Locality, and Date
Charles Ostrander & George Norris (dates unknown), New York City. 1848–50.

Comment
The finest 19th-century candles were made from spermaceti oil, an important product of the flourishing whaling industry. These candles burned brightly and cleanly and lasted a relatively long time. Inexpensive candles of tallow or vegetable oils were less efficient because they burned poorly and guttered badly, requiring that chamber sticks, like the one shown here, have a commodious saucer to collect drippings not caught by the bobeche.

Hints for Collectors
Candlesticks and chamber sticks almost always have wide flared lips, called bobeches, to catch dripping wax. Some were designed with a bobeche as part of the candle cup, while many others had a removable bobeche, which has often become lost. Collectors should always strive to acquire examples retaining their original bobeche. This type of chamber stick always had a finger loop attached to the edge, but in many examples the original loop has broken off and been replaced at a later date. Examine a loop to be sure its color, finish, and signs of wear are consistent with those of the rest of the chamber stick.

Late Federal candlesticks

Description
Circular candle cup with flared bobeche. Knopped shaft with center section shaped as inverted baluster. Circular, stepped, and molded base.

Marks and Dimensions
"T.B.M. CO" and "3" stamped incuse on underside. Height: 6⅜". Diameter: 3½".

Maker, Locality, and Date
Taunton Britannia Manufacturing Company (1830–34), Taunton, Massachusetts. 1830–34.

Comment
The Taunton Britannia Manufacturing Company made some of the finest American pewter candlesticks. The pair shown here has pleasing proportions, careful finish, and sturdy construction. While the firm operated under the name Taunton Britannia for only a short time, it began production in 1823 and, after many name changes, is still in existence today as Reed & Barton. Because of the company's frequent reorganizations and name changes, these candlesticks can be dated fairly accurately by their mark.

Hints for Collectors
Candlesticks in this design, made by many firms, may be marked or unmarked. If marked, the collector can date them to a narrow time span. If unmarked, they must be dated more cautiously. During the 19th century, designs were often pirated by one maker from another, and an unmarked pair of candlesticks, though very similar to marked examples by one company, may have been made by a competitor.

312 Late Federal/early Victorian candlesticks

Description
Cylindrical candle cup with flared bobeche. Multiknopped shaft with center section shaped as inverted baluster. Circular molded base.

Marks and Dimensions
"J. WEEKES" stamped incuse on underside of one candlestick. Height: 7⅜". Diameter: 4¼".

Maker, Locality, and Date
James Weekes (dates unknown), New York City. 1820–43.

Comment
These very attractive candlesticks are simply constructed, with the shaft and base cast separately and soldered together. The hollow shafts were slush-cast, saving material and reducing the weight. The undersides of 18th- and early 19th-century candlesticks were usually skimmed, but later 19th-century examples were not. As a result, their undersides are slightly rough and look as if they have been rubbed with a cloth while partially molten. This texture was created by the parting agent, used to coat the interior of the mold before the molten pewter was poured so that the candlestick could be extracted easily.

Hints for Collectors
Since all pewter candlesticks made in the same mold are identical, it is very difficult to tell whether a pair has always been together. Single 19th-century American pewter examples can be paired by the persistent collector, and a pair is usually worth more than 2 individual sticks. The fact that only one stick of this pair bears a maker's mark might mean that these candlesticks were not originally together.

13 Federal candlestick

Description
Cylindrical candle cup with curved flared bobeche. Tall, knopped, conical shaft. Circular, flared, molded base.

Marks and Dimensions
"T. B. M. CO/1" stamped incuse on underside. Height: 12¼". Diameter: 5⅜".

Maker, Locality, and Date
Taunton Britannia Manufacturing Company (1830–34), Taunton, Massachusetts. 1830–34.

Comment
Most 19th-century American pewter candlesticks are between 6" and 8" in height. This unusual example, measuring over a foot tall, is the largest known to have been made for domestic use at the time. Aside from the Taunton Britannia Manufacturing Company, only a very few American pewterers, notably Henry Hopper and Thomas Wildes, seem to have made candlesticks of this size. Both Hopper and Wildes worked in New York City in the first half of the 19th century.

Hints for Collectors
The height, substantial weight, and pleasing design of this candlestick make it one of the most desirable of its type. Examples bearing the mark of their maker are worth considerably more than their identical unmarked counterparts, even if the latter can be safely attributed to the same maker on the basis of the molds used. In general, unmarked objects tend to be worth about one-quarter to one-third the price of marked examples.

Early Victorian candlesticks

Description
Spool-shaped candle cup has removable bobeche with broad gadrooned rim. Tapered cylindrical shaft with narrow neck flanked by 2 gadrooned borders. Flared, molded circular base with 2 gadrooned borders.

Marks and Dimensions
"FLAGG/&/HOMAN" in oval and "10" cast in raised letters under base. Height: 11". Diameter: 4¾".

Maker, Locality, and Date
Asa Flagg & Henry Homan (1847–1941), Cincinnati. 1847–51.

Comment
These finely designed and well-made candlesticks represent a relatively small body of midwestern pewter. Settlement of the areas along the Mississippi River during the 19th century brought with it manufacturing activity. Many of these firms were short-lived; others changed owners and products, adapting to the changing needs of the market. As the demand for both pewter and candle lighting declined during the 19th century, Flagg & Homan changed its production to electroplated tableware, thus ensuring the company's survival into this century.

Hints for Collectors
The mark on these candlesticks is unusual because it is cast in relief. A number of firms produced identical designs, and this type of candlestick was also made on the East Coast, most notably by the Meriden Britannia Company. Many such pieces are unmarked, and it is often impossible to make a definite attribution. Because midwestern pewter is rarer than its East Coast counterpart, it is sometimes more expensive, with candlesticks such as these, recognizing the maker's mark is very important.

Federal oil lamp

Description
Upright octagonal font with raised top. 2 tapered flared brass wick tubes pierce removable disk threaded into upper end. Tall conical shaft. Molded, flared, circular base.

Marks and Dimensions
"T. B. M. CO/1" stamped incuse on underside. Height: 14⅝". Diameter: 5⅜".

Maker, Locality, and Date
Taunton Britannia Manufacturing Company (1830–34), Taunton, Massachusetts. 1830–34.

Comment
Because molds were expensive and difficult to make, innovative pewterers circumvented the need for a large variety of them by using some for more than one form. For instance, the base and shaft of this lamp were cast from the same mold used to make a candlestick. Although 18th-century pewterers are known to have used molds in this way, it was not until the 19th century that the practice became widespread. In spite of the similarity of such forms, they were sold separately rather than as sets.

Hints for Collectors
The impressive size and unusual shape of this lamp would make it especially attractive to both collectors of pewter and collectors of lighting devices. Most pewter lamps from this period have a cylindrical font; the only known examples with an octagonal font were, like the one shown here, made by the Taunton Britannia Manufacturing Company. Such lamps are thus relatively uncommon and costly, but well worth seeking.

Victorian oil lamp with magnifying lenses

Description
Vertical drum-shaped font with flat circular burner having 2 short brass and tin wick tubes. Shallow pocket on 2 flat sides of font holds removable convex glass lens in circular hooded frame. Short baluster shaft; molded, stepped, flared base.

Marks and Dimensions
"ROSWELL GLEASON" stamped incuse on underside; "PATENT" in rectangle stamped on top of each lens frame. Height: 8½". Width: 5". Diameter: 4¾".

Maker, Locality, and Date
Roswell Gleason (1799–1887), Dorchester, Massachusetts. 1840–60.

Comment
Among the many devices invented during the 19th century to increase the brightness of artificial illumination was the short-lived magnifying lens. One or 2 lenses were attached to an oil lamp in front of the flame, substantially improving light output; this practice was related to the medieval technique of placing a water-filled glass globe before a candle to magnify its flame. These lamps were sometimes referred to as "bull's-eye lamps."

Hints for Collectors
The lenses on these oil lamps are removable for cleaning and for refilling the font, and naturally some have become lost over the years. Such lamps have a narrow slotted pocket on one or both sides into which the lens tab is inserted, but occasionally even these pockets have been removed. Always examine the flat sides of the font for such evidence, since it may adversely affect value. Replacement of a missing lens with a new one is difficult and quite expensive; therefore, avoid incomplete examples, unless you do not intend to replace the lens.

Victorian double-bellied oil lamp

Description
Molded double-bellied font; wide circular opening at top has lip with 2 upright tabs threaded to accommodate horizontal brass thumbscrews; 1 thumbscrew missing. Interior of font fitted with 2 wick tubes, one inside the other, made of tinned sheet iron. Urn-shaped support encircled by ring of pierced square holes. Short cylindrical shaft; flared, slightly dished circular base.

Marks and Dimensions
"ENDICOTT/&/SUMNER" with scrolls flanking ampersand, in scallop-edged rectangle, stamped under base. Height: 9⅛". Diameter: 4⅝".

Maker, Locality, and Date
Edmund Endicott & William F. Sumner (dates unknown), New York City. 1846–51.

Comment
The 19th century was an age of much experimentation in lighting devices, and oil lamps from this era illustrate the constant efforts to produce more light. Most pewter oil lamps had simple burners with one to 6 wick tubes. This lamp, however, is most unusual because it has a cylindrical wick, unknown in any other pewter example. The cylindrical wick, commonly used in brass lamps of the period, was a radical departure from simple woven wicks; it allowed air to flow both inside and outside of the wick, thus providing more complete combustion and cleaner, brighter light.

Hints for Collectors
This lamp originally had a tapered glass chimney, held in place with the thumbscrew atop the font. Although the chances of finding an appropriate period replacement are slim, collectors should not pass up a lamp as unusual and important as this one unless it is unrestorable.

Late Federal oil lamp

Description
Cylindrical font with screw-in cap that holds 2 short, cylindrical burners made of tinned sheet iron. Multiknopped shaft with belted barrel-shaped section at center. Circular, stepped, molded base.

Marks and Dimensions
"A. PORTER" in serrated rectangle, stamped under base. Height: 8¼″. Diameter: 4⅜″.

Maker, Locality, and Date
Allen Porter (dates unknown), Westbrook, Maine. 1830–38.

Comment
Before the advent of kerosene in the 1860s, oil lamps were popular lighting devices. The type shown here has 2 short vertical tubes for woven-cloth wicks. It was designed to burn animal or vegetable oil and was made in a variety of sizes, from slightly over 2″ to 14″. Fonts and shafts also varied widely in design. Most 19th-century pewterers who made lamps also produced candlesticks from the same mold, substituting a candle cup for the oil font.

Hints for Collectors
Allen Porter and his brother Freeman were among the few pewterers who worked in Maine. But because Freeman was in business for a longer time, much more of his work has survived. Since Allen Porter's work is rarer, collectors are willing to pay more for it, even though the only significant difference in the work of the brothers is their marks.

Victorian 2-burner oil lamp

Description
Cylindrical font with molded top and bulbous lower section. 2 short horizontal arms at 90° to each other. Disk with knurled edge screwed into short upright cylinder at end of each arm; cylinders contain 2 short wick tubes of brass and tinned sheet iron. Knopped shaft and flared circular pedestal. Applied disk on top of font with "PATENT APPLIED FOR" stamped incuse.

Marks and Dimensions
"YALE & CURTIS N.Y." in D-shaped outline stamped on underside. Height: 8½″. Width: 5¼″. Diameter: 4¹⁵⁄₁₆″.

Maker, Locality, and Date
Henry Yale & Stephen Curtis (dates unknown), New York City. 1858–67.

Comment
Most 19th-century pewter lamps have only one central burner and are quite simple. Attempts to design lamps with greater light output usually meant changing the shape or location of the burners. Though most such efforts produced only slight improvements, the happy result for collectors is the great variety of 19th-century lamp forms available today.

Hints for Collectors
Pewter oil lamps can be found easily and for reasonable prices. Seek marked examples, although an unmarked lamp might be worth acquiring if it has several unusual features, such as a recorded patent date, an experimental burner, or, as on this lamp, an unusual font/burner relationship. Avoid lamps that have been drilled for wiring or sloppily repaired with lead solder; such repairs are often most evident around the mouth of the font or at the joint between the shaft and the base.

Description
Font cylindrical toward top and bulbous below; domed upper end has short neck into which is threaded removable disk pierced by 2 tapered flared wick tubes of brass and tinned sheet iron. Short inverted baluster shaft. Flared, dished, circular base stepped and molded.

Marks and Dimensions
"M. HYDE/40" stamped incuse on underside. Height: 8⅞". Diameter: 4⁷⁄₁₆".

Maker, Locality, and Date
Martin Hyde (dates unknown), New York City. 1850–60.

Comment
Two basic types of combustibles were used in lamps before kerosene became popular. The more traditional was oil, such as whale and vegetable oils, which burned slowly and steadily with fairly short wicks. The other type, a mixture of alcohol and turpentine, was known as burning fluid; this volatile fuel required lamps with long flaring wicks so that the flames would be kept away from each other and away from the fluid in the font. In spite of this precaution, many fluid lamps exploded in use, cutting short the popularity of burning fluid.

Hints for Collectors
Many 19th-century pewter oil or burning-fluid lamps are available today. When a maker's stamp is present, it is almost always located under the foot. Do not convert such lamps to electricity; this diminishes their visual interest and value.

Description
Inverted bell-shaped font with hemispherical dome having short neck. Neck threaded with removable disk pierced with 2 short cylindrical wick tubes of tinned sheet iron. Knopped shaft has C-shaped handle with spur at top. Dished circular base.

Marks and Dimensions
"BROOK FARM" in arc-shaped outline, stamped on underside. Height: 7¼". Diameter: 5¹⁄₁₆".

Maker, Locality, and Date
Brook Farm (c. 1841–47), West Roxbury, Massachusetts. 1844–47.

Comment
Brook Farm, an "Institute of Agriculture and Education," was a short-lived communal group established in the mid-19th century in West Roxbury, near Boston. Founded by transcendentalist George Ripley and his wife, Sophia, Brook Farm was an experiment in group living; each member owned a share of the community, and each was required to perform certain duties, mainly agricultural. The group attracted many luminaries: Nathaniel Hawthorne was a member, and distinguished visitors to the farm included Ralph Waldo Emerson, W. H. Channing, and Margaret Fuller, among others. The main building was destroyed by fire in 1844, and this calamity soon led to financial disaster for the community.

Hints for Collectors
Lamps of this type, while plentiful, have usually lost their burners. Also, some that originally had handles soldered to the shaft have lost them. Collectors should examine the shafts of these lamps for color differences or other surface irregularities that may indicate the loss of a handle.

Victorian oil lamp on gimbals

Description
Inverted pear-shaped font with short circular neck, into which is threaded a flat cap with 2 short cylindrical tubes of tinned sheet iron. Gimbaled font fitted with copper rivets to swing in narrow circular frame, which in turn swings in U-shaped frame. Circular molded pedestal with small hole in edge opposite loop handle. Tinned sheet iron under base.

Marks and Dimensions
"YALE & CURTIS N.Y." in D-shaped outline and "3" incuse, all stamped on top of base. Height: 5½". Diameter: 4¹⁵⁄₁₆".

Maker, Locality, and Date
Henry Yale & Stephen Curtis (dates unknown), New York City. 1858–67.

Comment
To prevent spillage from a lighting device containing liquid fuel, the font was usually enclosed. A less frequently used solution, seen in this example, was to place the font in gimbals so that it would remain upright regardless of the angle of the surface on which it was placed. This type of lamp seems to have been used most often at sea.

Hints for Collectors
This type of lamp is rare. Most have an enclosed base weighted with sand for stability. Sometimes the bottom has been cut to remove the sand, which does not necessarily diminish the value of the object. Serious collectors should seek as complete an example as possible, including not only an intact base but also burner tubes, which are frequently lost.

Household Objects

The once-pervasive use of pewter resulted in an extraordinary quantity and variety of domestic objects. Pewterers' inventories and advertisements show that far more was made than survives today. Such things as ice-cream molds, curtain rings, candle molds, still worms (the coil in which alcohol condenses when being made), cranes, syringe pipes, bedpans, chairpans, water plates, measures, barber's basins, and colanders are but a few of those that can be documented to American pewterers. Other basic but relatively rare objects include sundials, funnels, flasks, church tokens, spittoons, urinals, and baby bottles. Such an array creates a vivid picture of the extent to which pewter was used in early America.

Desk-top Articles
Many pewter implements were used in letter-writing. The inkwell was a simple cylindrical container, and usually had an insert of glass, ceramic, or sometimes iron to hold the ink. A more complicated variant of the inkwell, the standish, was fitted with compartments for nibs, quills, blotting sand, sealing wax, and sometimes even a candle to melt the sealing wax. Individual sanders were also made; these always had a concave top, so that the sand used to soak up the excess ink on a letter could be easily returned to the sander for reuse.

Bedpans and Related Household Objects
Prior to the advent of modern plumbing, pewter was widely used for bedpans, commodes, and urinals—essential and ubiquitous sanitary vessels for the home. Similarly, pewter was also employed for other once-common household articles, such as spittoons. The custom of spitting was eventually denounced in the late 19th century, when it was called a "vile habit practiced by intemperate and coarse fellows," and spittoons soon disappeared from American dining rooms and barrooms.

The Decline of Pewter
Pewter began to lose favor with Americans as early as the 1790s. Changes in household routine had made some pewter objects obsolete, while inexpensive silver plate became increasingly available. By the late 19th century, pewter had almost disappeared as a common household metal. It continued to be used only in a very limited context as a base for electroplated silver, but even there, eventually gave way to a sturdier, whiter metal known as German silver. The pewter objects once so commonplace are today almost unknown.

Modern artisans have rediscovered pewter. Working primarily by hand, they produce objects that can properly be thought of as works of art. Their work differs significantly from the products of earlier pewterers, not only in design but also in technique of manufacture.

Description
Domed top with small pierced holes and beaded border; tall pear-shaped body. Low, circular, flared and molded pedestal; underside with removable cylindrical stopper threaded to short projection.

Marks and Dimensions
Unmarked. Height: 5¹¹/₁₆″. Diameter: 2¾″.

Maker, Locality, and Date
Attributed to Thomas Danforth III (1756–1840), Rocky Hill (formerly Stepney), Connecticut, or Philadelphia. 1777–1818.

Comment
Salt and other condiments have always been important accompaniments to food, especially before the age of refrigeration. The caster, or shaker, came into being early in the 18th century, although no American pewter examples from before about the beginning of the 19th century are known. Whereas 20th-century shakers generally have removable caps, those shown here have a threaded metal stopper under the base.

Hints for Collectors
Although there are no known casters like these with genuine marks, this pair has been attributed to Thomas Danforth III, a prolific pewterer. Marks are of considerable importance, since their presence can increase the price of an object by 50 percent or much more. This provides ample impetus for forgers to apply spurious marks to unmarked objects; collectors are well advised to pay close attention to marks, comparing them to those on documented examples.

Late Federal/Victorian baby bottle

Description
Cylindrical cap with pierced nipple tip threaded to bulbous pear-shaped body with slender neck.

Marks and Dimensions
"BOARDMAN/& HART" in conforming outline, and "N-YORK" in rectangle, all stamped on underside. Height: 6½".
Diameter: 3¾".

Maker, Locality, and Date
Thomas D. Boardman & Lucius Hart (1828–53), Hartford or New York City. 1828–47.

Comment
Baby feeders simulating the female breast were made of many materials before the development of the rubber nipple. Wooden, silver, pewter, porcelain, earthenware, and even glass examples are known. All work on the same principle, having a small elongated knob through which the baby could suck the bottle's contents. Although efficient, bottles like this were rather unsanitary.

Hints for Collectors
Baby bottles are an uncommon but visually pleasing form. However, the removable screw cap can be easily lost. Rather than automatically rejecting a bottle lacking its cap, a collector may wish to purchase it if the price is lowered accordingly. Talented workers in pewter can make a replacement part, provided that an original can be located to serve as a model for an accurate copy. Although you can expect minor corrosion in a bottle like this, avoid a badly damaged example whose walls have developed holes.

Late Colonial/Federal flask

Description
Short circular neck with threaded cylindrical cap. Flattened circular body with molded ring on each side.

Marks and Dimensions
"I.C.H." in scallop-edged rectangle, and "LANCASTER" in rectangle, all stamped on underside. Height: 5½". Width: 4⅞". Depth: 2¼".

Maker, Locality, and Date
Johann Christoph Heyne (1715–81), Lancaster, Pennsylvania. 1756–80.

Comment
While a number of 18th-century pewterers' inventories record flasks, those by Heyne are the only early examples known today. Simple in form and bearing his mark on the underside, these flasks were probably intended for military use and never achieved widespread civilian popularity.

Hints for Collectors
Flasks were also made in Europe, and unmarked examples may be confused with Heyne's. Very little unmarked pewter by Heyne is known, indicating that he typically stamped his products, usually on the underside. Any unmarked object attributed to Heyne should be very carefully scrutinized, since his pewter is quite expensive. Authenticity can be readily determined by comparing the dimensions of an unmarked flask with those of a marked example; objects cast in the same mold will have identical measurements. Decorative details, however, such as incised rings or moldings, may vary because they were finished by hand.

Late Colonial funnel

Description
Deep conical body with molded lip, 2 incised encircling rings, and long tapered tube at narrow end.

Marks and Dimensions
"I•B" with fleur-de-lis above and below, all in beaded circle stamped under rim. Height: 7¹⁄₁₆″. Diameter: 5⁹⁄₁₆″.

Maker, Locality, and Date
John Bassett (c. 1696–1761), New York City. 1720–61.

Comment
The funnel is an ancient utensil that has remained virtually unchanged in form over the centuries. The only known 18th-century American pewterer's account book, that of Henry Will of New York, indicates that funnels were in considerable demand. Yet few have survived, and virtually all of them bear the marks of New York pewterers. With the decline in popularity of pewter about 1800, this form began to be made more often in tinned sheet iron, commonly called tin.

Hints for Collectors
Since pewter is a soft metal, markings on it can wear away fairly quickly. Thoroughly examine a seemingly unmarked object because its mark may be substantially worn and thus difficult to see. A marked object is, of course, always of greater historical interest and value than a comparable unmarked one. Funnels are straightforward, functional objects with minimal ornament, and are difficult to display. In spite of this, some collectors are willing to pay handsomely for a signed example that is in good condition.

Late Colonial/Federal urinal

Description
Flattened circular body with concentric incised rings on both
sides and around circumference. Straight-sided conical projection
attached obliquely to edge.

Marks and Dimensions
Unmarked. Height: 7⅜". Width: 5¾". Depth: 2½".

Maker, Locality, and Date
Unknown. England or United States. 1750–1830.

Comment
Pewter was a ubiquitous metal, serving in virtually every aspect
of early American life. While most surviving early pewter is
related to food and drink, the many other types of pewter objects
include picture frames, shoe buckles, buttons, mantel ornaments,
candlesticks, lamps, chamber pots, and urinals.

Hints for Collectors
Although very rare, urinals do not and probably never will
command the price of more common but prestigious forms such
as tankards. Although this example is made of good quality metal
and is well constructed and finished, the practical purpose of the
piece strongly colors collectors' reactions. Urinals were a
common domestic appurtenance in earlier centuries, but most
that survive are porcelain examples from Europe or the Orient.
No marked American pewter urinals have yet been discovered,
but several 18th- and 19th-century American pewterers are
known to have made them, meaning that a marked example may
one day turn up.

Federal bedpan

Description
Low circular body with convex side and large hole in top.
Hollow projection on side to which is threaded a removable
baluster handle at oblique angle. "W L + S" engraved in block
letters on side.

Marks and Dimensions
"ww" with foliate device above and below, all in serrated circle,
stamped on outside bottom. Length: 17¼". Diameter: 11½".
Height: 4¼".

Maker, Locality, and Date
William Will (1742–98), Philadelphia. 1764–98.

Comment
Although very common before the advent of plumbing, bedpans
from the 18th and early 19th centuries are quite rare today.
While pewter objects used in the dining room were often
ornamented in much the same way as their stylish silver
counterparts, straightforward utilitarian objects like bedpans
were not embellished. The few bedpans known today have
removable handles, presumably to aid in cleaning after use.

Hints for Collectors
Will is perhaps the best known of all early American pewterers.
Much information has been published about his life and
pewtering activity, and his work commands a premium over that
of lesser-known craftsmen. In spite of the unappealing nature of
the form, a bedpan made by him should be expected to sell for a
high price. Even so, an unscrupulous person could place a
spurious William Will mark on an unmarked English example
and be reasonably assured of making money.

Victorian spittoon

Description
Circular body with curved flared side. Low flared and molded pedestal. Removable, shallow, conical insert with molded rim and hole at narrow end; ring-shaped handle on side.

Marks and Dimensions
"E.SMITH" in serrated rectangle, stamped on underside. Diameter: 5¾". Height: 3".

Maker, Locality, and Date
Eben Smith (1773–1848), Beverly, Massachusetts. 1835–48.

Comment
Although modern etiquette forbids spitting in public, the custom was generally accepted in previous centuries, as is evidenced by the existence of spittoons, or cuspidors. Because of their humble purpose and the eventual disapprobation of spitting, few spittoons remain today. Most examples are quite simple, with removable liners for cleaning.

Hints for Collectors
While spittoons provide an insight into life in earlier centuries, they are not in great demand by collectors. As a result they can be acquired more reasonably than other, more desirable forms like porringers and beakers. Pewter spittoons were always made with a removable liner for ease in cleaning, and with a small ring handle that was usually soldered to the side of the object. If the liner is missing or the handle broken off, collectors should expect that the price be less than that asked for a spittoon in good condition.

Late Colonial/Federal commode

Description
Circular bowl with straight flared side. Horizontal lip with molded edge. Encircling lines incised intermittently. Circular, low, and flared foot.

Marks and Dimensions
"F•B" with fleur-de-lis above and below, all in circle, stamped on underside. Diameter: 11⅞″. Height: 8⅛″.

Maker, Locality, and Date
Frederick Bassett (c. 1740–1800), New York City or Hartford. 1761–1800.

Comment
The wide flared lip of vessels like the one shown here was used to hang them inside specially fitted chairs or stools, the seats of which could be removed for access to the commode, or chamber pot. Although the use of commodes, also called chairpans or close-stool pans, was widespread, few American examples survive that can be dated to the 18th or 19th century. Virtually all bear the marks of makers from New York City, even though commodes are listed in pewterers' inventories from every major urban center. Earlier generations of collectors, in the interest of gentility, misnamed these objects flower pots.

Hints for Collectors
The cost of an object is usually directly proportionate to its rarity. However, commodes—like other unappealing functional forms—do not follow this formula. Their unsavory practical associations discourage collectors from seeking them out and displaying them prominently with their teapots and tankards. So although commodes are quite rare, many do not command the higher prices of more desirable forms.

Federal inkwell

Description
Circular body with curved tapered side and flared molded lip.
Flat inset top pierced with a large central hole surrounded by 3
smaller equidistant holes. Multiple incised rings around sides.

Marks and Dimensions
"ww" with foliate device above and below, all in serrated circle,
stamped on inside bottom. Diameter: 3⅛". Height: 1¹⁵⁄₁₆".

Maker, Locality, and Date
William Will (1742–98), Philadelphia. 1764–98.

Comment
This inkwell is among the simplest of its type. The large central
hole originally contained a glass insert in which ink was kept; the
smaller holes were meant to hold writing instruments. Some
similar inkwells had a small hinged cover that prevented the ink
from drying out. Many were made in England, but early
American examples are rare.

Hints for Collectors
The inkwell was a favorite form among early 20th-century
fakers. Forgeries were made by cutting out a maker's mark from
the bottom of a genuine but battered American teapot and
incorporating it into an unmarked English inkwell in place of its
original base. The soldered edge of the new part, duplicating that
of the original, is difficult to detect if the solder has been given a
counterfeit patina. This efficient and often effective ploy created
a valuable American rarity out of 2 common inexpensive objects.
Examine such inkwells closely; the underside should show
convincing signs of wear, and all solder joints should be neat and
carefully finished.

Late Federal sander

Description
Spool with curved side and beaded rims. Concave top pierced with numerous holes.

Marks and Dimensions
"W. POTTER" in rectangle stamped on underside. Diameter: $2\frac{5}{16}$". Height: $2\frac{7}{8}$".

Maker, Locality, and Date
W. Potter (dates unknown), New England. 1830–40.

Comment
Prior to the advent of modern writing instruments and paper, the process of writing involved varied implements. One of these was the sander, a container with a pierced dished top through which blotting sand was poured onto writing to absorb excess ink. Afterwards, the sand was carefully poured back into the sander's concave top for later use. Sanders were made of porcelain, silver, wood, brass, pewter, and a variety of other materials.

Hints for Collectors
Sanders and other pewter writing instruments are rare. There was apparently an extensive market for vintage examples during the early 20th century, since many fakes were made at that time. To spot forgeries, familiarize yourself with genuine examples. Fakes tend to be thick-walled, heavy, and colored the dull bluish-gray of lead. The maker's mark, if present, is usually grainy, and the lettering, unlike that prevalent during the 18th and early 19th centuries, often lacks serifs.

Federal boxes

Description
Left: Circular flat lid with concentric moldings; fitted over shallow container. Right: Circular stepped lid with wide flared lip and concentric incised rings; hinged to shallow curved body with incised rings; 2 interior compartments.

Marks and Dimensions
Left: "BABBITT, CROSSMAN & C⁰." in rectangle and "2" stamped incuse on underside. Diameter: 4″. Height: 1⅛″. Right: "A.G" in rectangle stamped on underside. Diameter: 4⁷/₁₆″. Height: 1⅞″.

Maker, Locality, and Date
Left: Babbitt, Crossman & Company (1827–29), Taunton, Massachusetts. 1827–29. Right: Ashbil Griswold (1784–1853), Meriden, Connecticut. 1807–35.

Comment
Small circular pewter boxes held a multitude of objects, from communion wafers to watch and clock gears. Although it is usually impossible to determine precisely what a particular box contained, the hinged example shown here is believed to have held shaving soap and a brush.

Hints for Collectors
These small boxes were intended for personal use, so they rarely have elaborate decoration. Because they were used with little concern for their longevity, not many have survived intact; hinges are often broken and lids lost. Modest and relatively inexpensive today, these boxes offer interesting insights into the extensive use of pewter in everyday life. The example with the flared side and hinged lid is more unusual than the simpler straight-sided box.

Modern nut dish

Description
Smooth, tapered, oval vessel with flared sides and upturned lip.

Marks and Dimensions
"Shirley Charron" engraved in script on underside. Length: 11½". Width: 3¹⁄₁₆". Height: 3⅜".

Maker, Locality, and Date
Shirley Charron (b. 1935), Ridgefield, Connecticut. 1972.

Comment
In the past, pewter was favored because it was easy to work and could be brightly polished to resemble more costly silver. However, pewter melts at relatively low temperatures and wears out quickly, making it less suitable for heavy use in the kitchen than more heat-resistant metals. This accounts partly for its gradual fall from popularity during the 19th century. Only in the past few decades has it slowly begun to regain acceptance as a material for utilitarian household objects.

Hints for Collectors
This deceptively simple dish was carefully wrought from a sheet of metal hammered over forms. The hammering process gives the metal an uneven textured surface that is nonetheless smooth and reflective. Collectors of modern objects made of pewter or other base metals should always be certain that the artisan has signed and dated the piece. While this may seem insignificant at the time of purchase, such documentation is very important, especially if the object is sold at a later date. A collector who owns an unsigned work by a living maker should feel free to ask the artisan to sign the piece for him.

Federal sundial

Description
Flat square plate with circular hole surrounded by narrow molded frame in each corner. On front, cast graduated chapter ring with Roman numerals in hourly segments from 5 A.M. to 7 P.M., enclosing a perpendicular triangular projection with small compass rose at base.

Marks and Dimensions
"CHANDLEE WINCHESTER" in cast raised letters on front. Width: 5⅛". Height: 2⅞".

Maker, Locality, and Date
Goldsmith Chandlee (1751–1821), Winchester, Virginia. 1800–21.

Comment
Sundials are simple devices, having a triangular vertical gnomon that casts a shadow on an encircling, graduated chapter ring listing the hours. They were an important means of telling time in past centuries. Numerous early brass examples are known, but pewter ones are uncommon. In order to increase their accuracy, sundials were calibrated to the particular latitude in which they were to be used. This example, though not so marked, was calibrated to the 39th parallel, near Winchester, Virginia, where it was made. When ornamented, American pewter usually had cast decoration, such as the raised compass rose and the circular motifs of this sundial.

Hints for Collectors
A sundial like this would be an interesting addition to any collection of American pewter. Since sundials are awkward to display, they are not popular with collectors, and thus their rarity does not translate into great cost. Many sundials have been severely damaged by being pried from their base. Avoid damaged or heavily corroded examples.

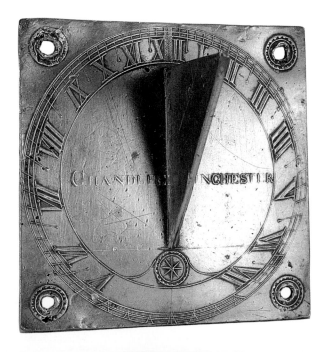

Federal communion tokens

Description
Left: Square with rounded corners. Front with "Wᵐ/MARSHAL/ 1775" in raised letters within sawtooth border. Reverse with "SCOT'S/CHURCH/PHILA." Right: Oval. Front with "ASSOCIATE/ CHURCH" in raised script letters. Reverse with "N YORK/1799."

Marks and Dimensions
Unmarked. Left width: ⅞". Right length: ⁷⁄₁₆"; width: ¹⁵⁄₁₆".

Maker, Locality, and Date
Left: Unknown. Philadelphia. c. 1775. Right: Unknown. New York City. c. 1799.

Comment
The custom of using communion tokens came to America with the Presbyterians; as early as the 17th century the tokens had taken hold in Episcopal churches as well, and their use persisted until the late 19th century. These tokens, presented to prospective members of the church upon passing a rigorous examination on the articles of belief, the Lord's Prayer, and the Ten Commandments, admitted new communicants to the communion table.

Hints for Collectors
The tokens shown here are made of pewter, but other materials, including paper, brass, copper, tinned sheet iron, and lead, were also used. Thousands exist in public collections, and other examples are available on the market at modest prices. These tokens were used infrequently, and consequently many remain in good condition. Buy only examples that have legible inscriptions and avoid those that are cracked, dented, or chipped.

Description
Box with one side curving upward to narrow edge. Topped by short neck to which is threaded stepped molded cap with hinged bail handle.

Marks and Dimensions
Crown over rose between 2 conjoined semicircular scrolls, upper one containing "HENRY WILL" and lower containing "NEW•YORK"; "HENRY•WILL/NEW YORK" with beaded line between, in rectangle; both marks stamped on back. Height: 10¾". Length: 12". Width: 5⅞".

Maker, Locality, and Date
Henry Will (c. 1734–c. 1802), New York City or Albany, New York. 1761–93.

Comment
In the days before central heating and insulated houses, the ways of keeping warm were limited. Since it was not always possible to stay close to an open fire, devices for carrying heat, such as bed warmers and braziers, were developed. These devices were usually made of iron or brass because of the intensity of the heat generated by embers and coals. With its low melting point, pewter could not be used to hold coals, but it could withstand the moderate heat generated by hot water. This foot warmer, with its screw-on cap, was filled with hot water. A person then could rest his feet on the sloping side to warm them.

Hints for Collectors
Although the foot warmer shown here is the only American example known, others will almost certainly come to light. When they do, their rarity will make them quite expensive. Astute collectors are more likely to recognize and avoid spurious examples if they are familiar with known and accepted pieces.

Colonial/Federal standish

Description
Shallow rectangular box with 2 lids hinged lengthwise along its
center. One side has 3 compartments containing a glass bottle
and a shallow pewter box with holes in top. 4 hemispherical feet.

Marks and Dimensions
4 pseudohallmarks ("HW"; seated female; leopard's head; and
rampant lion), each in rectangle with cut corners; crowned rose
within 2 opposed banners inscribed "HENRY WILL" and "NEW
YORK"; all stamped on each lid. Length: 7⅞". Width: 4¹¹⁄₁₆".
Height: 2¼".

Maker, Locality, and Date
Henry Will (c. 1734–c. 1802), New York City or Albany, New
York. 1761–93.

Comment
Before the 19th century, written communication required a large
number of accoutrements, including ink, pens, blotting sand, and
sealing wax. These articles were often kept in containers known
as inkstands or standishes, which were made of pewter, silver,
brass, or ceramic. Some standishes consisted of several small
separate vessels on a footed tray. Others were a simple box with
a hinged lid. Pewter examples sometimes consist only of a
cylindrical inkwell with a glass insert.

Hints for Collectors
During the 18th century, pewter standishes of this type were
made in England, and many were imported to America.
Documented American examples are scarce. If a standish is
offered as American, examine its marks carefully and check to
see that no part has been substituted; marked English lids are
sometimes replaced with fraudulent American ones.

Caring for Your Collection

Assembling a collection of silver, silver plate, or pewter requires time and dedication; the same kind of effort should be applied to maintaining and caring for your collection.

In general, collectors should acquire objects that are in fairly good condition; when repairs are called for, it is always best to seek the advice of a trained conservator who will have the knowledge and the equipment necessary to restore objects without damaging them or compromising their integrity.

Bear in mind that all polishes except dips contain abrasives of one sort or another that remove some metal along with the tarnish layer. Use mild polishes with tarnish inhibitors and apply them according to the directions on the container. Be careful to remove all polish, paying particular attention to recessed areas; residue is unsightly, and in some cases promotes corrosion. It is particularly important to remove all traces of liquid silver dips; they are very effective cleaners, but if not completely rinsed from the silver can be quite damaging.

Silver

Numerous industrial and household pollutants cause silver to tarnish; among the worst of these is sulfur, which is abundant in the air in industrial areas. Sulfur is also produced by oil-fired household furnaces and is even present in certain foods, such as eggs. While you cannot allay the production of these pollutants, you can take some steps to reduce their effects.

The simplest step is to store or display silver so that tarnishing agents cannot get at it. For storage, pacific cloth is excellent. It is soft, will not scratch the silver, and has a tarnish-inhibiting agent in it. Polyethylene also works very well, but it will not prevent silver from being scratched, so it should be used together with pacific cloth.

Collectors who prefer to display their silver can keep it in a case with glass doors. Camphor blocks or other tarnish-inhibiting materials may also be stored in the case to help the silver retain its luster. Some silver was originally patinated or textured as a part of its design. When you acquire silver that has been so treated, take care that patination or coloring is not lost by overzealous or improper polishing.

If you use your silver for eating or drinking, clean it immediately afterwards, especially if it was used in conjunction with eggs, salad dressing, salt, or any other highly corrosive foods. Salt, in particular, causes deep and unsightly pits. Some other common items are also very damaging to silver. One of the worst is rubber, which has a high sulfur content; keep rubber bands or other elastic of any type away from silver.

Lacquering is an effective way to inhibit tarnish, but requires the proper equipment and practice, and should be done by a specialist. Lacquering is suitable only for objects that are not to be handled extensively or used for eating and drinking.

The most ambitious restoration the general silver collector should consider undertaking is the removal of small dents with a rawhide or wooden mallet; any more difficult repair should be done by a reputable conservator. Silver objects should be restored in a way as close as possible to the way the original maker would have done it. It is also important that damage be promptly restored, before it becomes worse.

Silver Plate

The recommendations for the proper care of silver are even more important with silver-plated objects, which have only a very thin layer of the precious metal on their surfaces. Plated objects should be used as little as possible and polished infrequently. Lacquering, if properly done, is an excellent means of helping to preserve the thin coating of silver.

Some types of silver plate are very difficult to restore. Close-plated objects that have rusted under the silver coating present the greatest difficulty. Such damage is easily discerned because the silver surface, which should be absolutely smooth, has a bubbly appearance. At present, it is not technically feasible to restore badly rusted objects of this type, with the result that a rusted close-plated iron object will continue to corrode.

Electroplated objects can be readily re-electroplated without compromising their integrity. With fused-plated or French-plated objects, however, the matter is not quite so simple, since their original plating processes cannot be duplicated today. The decision to electroplate an object that was originally fused- or French-plated is subjective; most responsible collectors, however, choose not to.

A French- or fused-plated object with only minor silver loss can be locally silvered through a special electroplating process known as sponging, which is best left to trained conservators. The other serious problem with plated objects, especially those made of fused plate, are breaks that have been sloppily soldered with lead. Again, the correct restoration of this damage should be done only by a reputable conservator.

All of these restorations can be time-consuming and expensive. It is therefore best not to buy objects with severe damage or silver loss unless they are exceptionally rare or marked by a particularly desirable maker. Any antique French- or fused-plated object should reasonably be expected to have silver losses from handling, wear, and polishing. If no such losses are visible, the chances are good that the object has been electroplated.

Pewter

A pewter object that is not heavily corroded can be kept in good condition with periodic polishing. How often you polish your pewter depends on the environment: Cold and moisture will hasten oxidation, as will everyday household pollutants like airborne grease or emissions from a furnace. Do not expose your pewter to damaging agents any more than necessary. The less frequently a pewter object is polished, the better.

Lightly tarnished pewter should be cleaned with a mild commercial polish and a clean soft cloth. If moderately tarnished, 0000-grade steel wool can be used instead of a cloth, but never under any circumstances use anything more abrasive than that. Never polish pewter with a buffing wheel or other mechanical means; to do so creates a smeared effect on the surface, obliterates detail, and gives the metal an overly bright, mirrorlike surface that is universally disliked by collectors.

If pewter is black and covered with a heavy scale, stronger cleaning techniques, such as submersion of the object in lye or muriatic acid, are called for. However, inexperienced collectors should not attempt such cleaning because these liquids are toxic. Removing this type of scale should be done under careful advisement and by a well-trained conservator. The scale may be so thick that its removal will also remove the maker's mark or leave the object badly pitted and full of holes.

Generally, pewter collectors can sometimes remove dents or straighten distorted objects with a rawhide or wooden mallet. However, severely dented or distorted objects should be given to an experienced conservator.

Flatware Patterns

Many collectors focus their attention on just one area—silver and silver-plated flatware. And little wonder. With the arrival of the industrial age and the founding of large factories, the production of flatware flourished. Literally thousands of patterns were created, many of them in both sterling and electroplate. Although some patterns have passed from fashion, others are

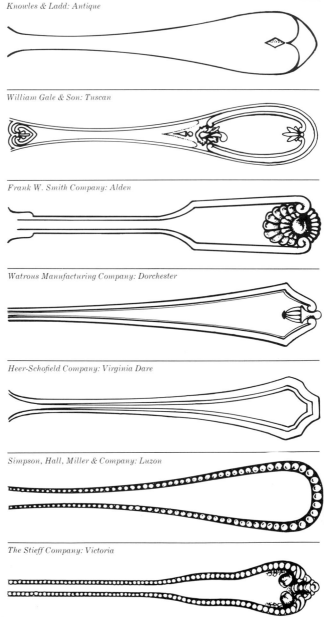

Knowles & Ladd: Antique

William Gale & Son: Tuscan

Frank W. Smith Company: Alden

Watrous Manufacturing Company: Dorchester

Heer-Schofield Company: Virginia Dare

Simpson, Hall, Miller & Company: Luzon

The Stieff Company: Victoria

still made today. A typical set of flatware might include not only the standard knives, forks, and spoons, but also a variety of miscellaneous serving pieces, including berry spoons, ladles, and meat forks.

The following illustrations indicate the incredible variety of patterns available to the collector today.

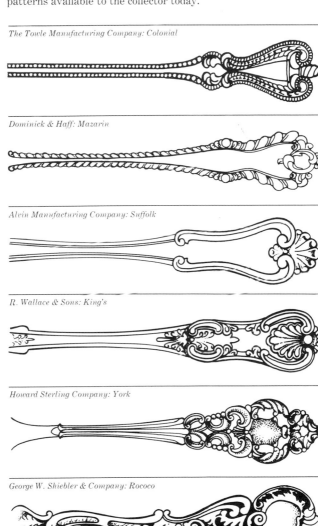

The Towle Manufacturing Company: Colonial

Dominick & Haff: Mazarin

Alvin Manufacturing Company: Suffolk

R. Wallace & Sons: King's

Howard Sterling Company: York

George W. Shiebler & Company: Rococo

Wood & Hughes: Humboldt

Flatware Patterns

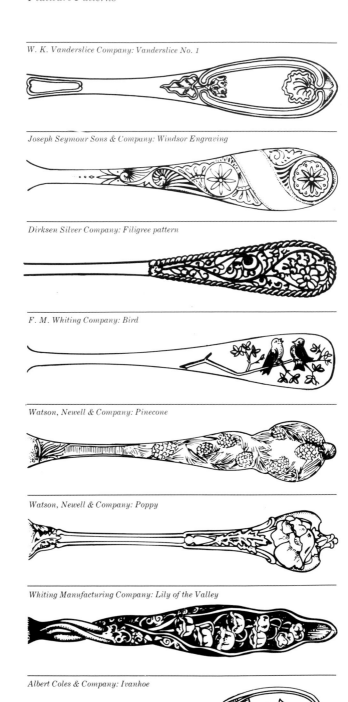

W. K. Vanderslice Company: Vanderslice No. 1

Joseph Seymour Sons & Company: Windsor Engraving

Dirksen Silver Company: Filigree pattern

F. M. Whiting Company: Bird

Watson, Newell & Company: Pinecone

Watson, Newell & Company: Poppy

Whiting Manufacturing Company: Lily of the Valley

Albert Coles & Company: Ivanhoe

Glossary

Acanthus   A spiny, broad-leaved, shrublike plant native to the Mediterranean region; used often in foliate ornament.

Anthemion   A stylized design, derived from the honeysuckle plant, of radiating, graduated petals. (*pl.* anthemia)

Applied   Made separately then added to the body of an object.

Arcaded   Ornamented with a series of arches on columns.

Attribution   A tentative assignment of an object to a maker based on circumstantial evidence.

Baluster   A short, pear-shaped shaft, usually with moldings at top and base.

Beaded   Decorated with a narrow band of adjacent beadlike balls.

Belted   Having a molding around the outermost circumference.

Bezel   In a box, the upper edge, over which the lid fits.

Bobeche   The flared cuplike part of a candlestick, used to catch melted wax; sometimes removable.

Boss   A raised area, typically circular or oval, on the surface of an object.

Bracket   An element, usually triangular and often decorative, added at a joint for strengthening.

Bright-cut   A type of engraving produced by short repetitive strokes of a cutting tool.

Britannia metal   A silver-white alloy of tin, antimony, and copper; sometimes also includes zinc or bismuth.

Cabriole leg   An S-shaped, usually tapered support.

Canted   Having corners cut at an angle.

Capital   The enlarged top of a column; often ornamental.

Cartouche   An area surrounded by ornament and reserved for engraving, usually of an owner's initials.

Chair-back   An upright rectangular appendage resembling the back of a chair in shape; often used as a thumbpiece on drinking vessels.

Chasing   Decoration created by hammering the surface of an object with small punches.

Claw-and-ball foot   A support in the shape of a bird's claw grasping a ball.

Close plating   A method of covering iron objects with a very thin foil of silver by using tin solder.

Collar   A narrow decorative flange applied around the rim or pedestal of a vessel.

Cove molding   A simple arc-shaped ornamental border.

Crenate   Having scrolled shaping, occasionally with engraved highlights, on the edge.

Crest   An ornamental device forming part of a coat of arms.

Cut-card work   Applied ornament, usually in the form of a border of flat stylized leaf tips.

Die stamping A fabrication technique in which a sheet of metal is stamped in a press; used to make ornament as well as objects.

Dished Having a concave surface.

Documentable Able to be assigned a maker, usually on the basis of strong circumstantial evidence, such as a bill of sale or verbal records.

Documented Proven to be the work of a particular maker, usually on the basis of a maker's mark.

Douter A small conical device used to extinguish a candle.

Egg-and-dart border A decorative molding consisting of stylized alternating ovals and pointed shapes.

Electroplating A method of coating an object with a thin film of silver by using electrolysis.

Engine turning Decoration usually consisting of wavy lines, cut into the surface of an object using a machine similar to a pantograph.

Engraving Decoration created by cutting grooves into the surface of an object with sharp pointed tools.

Escutcheon A protective shield, such as the shield surrounding a keyhole; often ornamental.

Ferrule A narrow element, usually made of wood or ivory, used in teapots and coffeepots to insulate metal handles.

Fillet A narrow molding encircling a vessel.

Finial The topmost portion of an object, often on the lid; usually decorative.

Flat chasing Decoration on flat surfaces created by small punches and a hammer.

Flatware Eating utensils; usually a spoon, fork, and knife and their variants.

Fluted Decorated with parallel vertical grooves.

Font In lighting devices, the portion of a lamp that holds the fuel.

Foot The supporting member or base of an object.

Foot rim A circular support attached to the base of an object; usually flared and molded.

Foot ring A circular support attached to the base of an object; usually straight, plain, and narrow.

French plating A method of using a heated iron to apply a very thin foil of silver to brass and copper objects.

Fused plating A method of covering a sheet of copper with thin sheets of silver through the use of heat and compression in a rolling mill.

Gadrooning Ornament consisting of narrow, parallel, vertical panels, usually tapering in width; the panels may be convex, concave, or alternatingly convex and concave.

Gallery A pierced ornamental border somewhat resembling a fence; used on the tops of vessels, especially in the late 18th century.

German silver An alloy containing approximately 50 percent copper, 40 percent zinc, and 10 percent nickel; first made in Germany during the early 19th century in imitation of the much older Chinese alloy known as paktong.

Gilt Decorated with a thin coat of gold.

Gimbal A frame, used to hold a lamp or other vessel, hinged in such a way that the vessel always remains upright; often used at sea.

Gothic script An elaborate style of lettering developed in medieval Europe and often used in engraving.

Greek key An angular line of ornament in the shape of alternating, interlocking Ls.

Guilloche Decoration consisting of 2 or more undulating, interlacing lines that form a series of conjoining circles.

Hallmarks Marks placed on English and European objects made of silver or gold. Hallmarks were required by law and indicate the maker, date, and place of manufacture; there is usually a fourth mark that certifies that the object meets a minimum standard of purity.

Hollowware Hollow-bodied vessels, usually associated with food or drink.

Hundredweight One-twentieth of a troy ounce, used in weighing gold, silver, and jewels; also called pennyweight.

Imbricated Having a repeating ornamental motif, each element of which overlaps the next.

Incuse Cut or stamped so that the pattern of letters or figures is below the surface of the object.

Japanned Having the surface painted with ornamental figures against a solid or mottled colored background, in imitation of Oriental lacquerware.

Knop A spherical or faceted ornamental knob on the shaft of a drinking vessel, candlestick, or other object.

Knurled Having low parallel ridges around the circumference to aid in grasping; similar to milling on the edge of a coin.

Lap jointing A method of attaching 2 objects end to end by overlapping them.

Linen mark A small, irregular, textured area made in the process of attaching a handle, found on the inside of some pewter porringer bowls and occasionally on other hollowware.

Mantling Ornament framing a coat of arms and usually consisting of leaves, flowers, scrolls, humans, animals, or mythological creatures.

Mat Having a surface textured by means of chasing or engraving.

Molded Having a shaped profile.

Nickel silver An alloy of about 50 percent copper, 40 percent zinc, and 10 percent nickel; silverlike in color, it is often used to make electroplated objects.

Ogee A molding with an S-shaped profile.

Paktong An alloy containing approximately 50 percent copper, 40 percent zinc, and 10 percent nickel; invented in China and brought to Europe during the 18th century.

Paneled Ornamented with a series of rectangular compartments.

Parcel-gilt Partially coated with a thin layer of gold.

Parting agent A powdery or liquid compound used to coat the inside of a mold so that castings can be easily removed.

Paw foot A support shaped like an animal's foot.

Pedestal A circular, square, or rectangular support between the body of an object and the base; usually flared and molded.

Pierced Having a series of foliate or geometric holes; piercing may be ornamental or just intended to allow a flow of air.

Pitch A black resinous substance made from distilled wood or coal; used to fill thin silver objects, it helped prevent them from becoming dented or distorted.

Plinth A square or rectangular support with architectural moldings.

Pseudohallmarks Marks on base metals, silver plate, and American silver in imitation of hallmarks; pseudohallmarks are not required by law and do not always have the same significance as true hallmarks.

Reeded Ornamented with a series of narrow, parallel, convex panels that resemble bundles of reeds.

Repoussé Ornamented with decorative elements that have been pushed up above the surface of the object.

Reserve A plain area in the center of a decorated panel; intended to be engraved with a name, initials, or coat of arms.

Ribbed Ornamented with a series of parallel or radiating lines.

Scroll An ornamental line resembling a loosely rolled piece of paper; a line that curves in on itself.

Sheet metal A broad, thin, flat piece of metal, formed either by hammering or by rolling in a mill.

Silver gilt Made of silver that has been completely covered with a very thin coating of gold.

Skim To place an object on a lathe and scrape its surface smooth.

Skirt A flared panel hanging below the main body of an object.

Slush casting A pewtering technique in which a mold is filled with molten metal; before the metal has thoroughly cooled, part of it is poured away, producing a hollow object.

Spinning A technique in which an object is shaped over a chuck on a lathe.

Spur A short, curved, pointed projection on a handle; used to aid in holding an object.

Stepped Having a series of graduated platforms, one on top of the other, that are used as a support for an object.

Strap handle A thin, solid handle on a drinking vessel that resembles a strip of leather.

Strapwork   Flat cutout shapes placed on an object; either structural or ornamental.

Strike   To stamp a mark on an object.

Swage   A wooden or metal form against which a piece of sheet metal is hammered in order to shape it.

Terminal   A decorative ending for an appendage; often seen on handles.

Touchmark   The name, initials, or symbol stamped on an object by its maker, usually for identification, but sometimes for ornament.

Troy measure   The measure used to weigh silver, gold, and jewels; one troy pound is equivalent to 12 ounces avoirdupois.

Turn   To place an object on a lathe and scrape it to shape it or to sharpen decorative detail.

Volute   A decorative spiral scroll.

Waterleaf   A broad flat leaf often used in ornament.

Weight value   The price assigned to the standard unit of weight (a troy ounce) of gold or silver.

Wrought   Hammered into shape on one or more anvils.

Illustrated Guide to American Makers and Marks

This table lists the American craftsmen and manufacturers whose work is featured in this book, along with their marks as they appear on the illustrated objects. The names are followed by birth and death dates, partnership dates, or operation dates, and by the primary location in which a maker worked. Makers of silver and silver plate are listed separately from pewterers.

Silver and Silver Plate

ALLAN ADLER

Allan Adler
b. 1916
Hollywood, CA

Joseph Anthony
1762–1814
Philadelphia

Thomas Arnold
1734–1828
Newport, RI

Joseph T. Bailey & Andrew B. Kitchen
1833–46
Philadelphia

BAILEY & CO.

Bailey & Company
1846–78
Philadelphia

NEW. ORLEANS

Horace E. Baldwin & Company
1842–53
New Orleans

BALDWIN & JONES

Jabez Baldwin & John B. Jones
c. 1813–19
Boston

W. BALL

William Ball
1763–1815
Baltimore

BALL, BLACK & CO.

Ball, Black & Company
1851–76
New York City

Jurian Blanck, Jr.
c. 1645–1714
New York City

Jacob Boelen
c. 1654–1729
New York City

Charles Oliver Bruff
1735–85
New York City

Cornelius van der Burch
c. 1653–99
New York City

Charles A. Burnett
1760–1849
Washington, DC

William Burt
1726–51
Boston

Daniel Carrel
dates unknown
Philadelphia and Charleston, SC

Simon Chaudron & Anthony Rasch
1809–12
Philadelphia

Chicago Silver Company
1923–45
Chicago

Hans Christensen
1924–83
Rochester, NY

21

Jonathan Clarke
1706–66
Providence and Newport, RI

 John Coburn
1724–1803
Boston

 Samuel Coleman
dates unknown
Trenton

 Albert Coles
d. 1886
New York City

 John Coney
1656–1722
Boston

 James Conning
c. 1813–72
Mobile, AL

 Elizabeth Copeland
dates unknown
Boston

 Thomas Dane
1726–c. 1795
Boston

 John David
1736–94
Philadelphia

 Junius Davis & Charles E. Galt
dates unknown
Philadelphia

DEMATTEO
STERLING
9

William G. Dematteo
1895–1981
Bergenfield, NJ

Derby Silver Company
1873–98
Derby, CT

H. Blanchard Dominick & Leroy B. Haff
1867–1928
Newark, NJ

Robert W. Ebendorf
b. 1938
New Paltz, NY

John Edwards
1671–1746
Boston

Samuel Edwards
1705–02
Boston

E.A.M
STERLING
78281

Elgin-American Manufacturing Company
1887–1950
Elgin, IL

William Faris
1728–1804
Annapolis, MD

Thomas Fletcher
1787–1866
Philadelphia

Thomas Fletcher & Sidney Gardiner
1808–27
Boston and Philadelphia

John W. Forbes
1781–1864
New York City

William Forbes
1799–c. 1864
New York City

William Garret Forbes
1751–1840
New York City

 STERLING **G. H. French & Company**
c. 1919–35
North Attleboro, MA

Daniel Christian Fueter
d. 1785
New York City

Moritz Furst
b. 1782
Philadelphia

William Gale & Nathaniel Hayden
1847–50
New York City

 William Gale & Joseph Moseley
1828–33
New York City

William Gale & John R. Willis
1859–62
New York City

 Baldwin Gardiner
dates unknown
New York City

GARNER & WINCHESTER **LEX.KY**

Eli C. Garner & Daniel F. Winchester
1842–62
Lexington, KY

P·G

Peter Getz
1764–1809
Lancaster, PA

W.Gilbert **New York**

William Gilbert
1746–1818
New York City

I·G

Joseph Goldthwaite
1706–80
Boston

Gorham Company
1831–present
Providence

STERLING

0 2 0 0
N

410
R·I·G
COIN

Martelé
950-1000 FINE

STERLING
GRAHAM

Anne K. Graham
b. 1942
Newark, DE

A.B.GRISWOLD&Cº N.O:H.

Arthur B. Griswold & Company
1865–1906
New Orleans

T·H

Thomas Hammersley
1727–81
New York City

M·H

Marguerite Hastier
dates unknown
New York City

J·HEATH

John Heath
dates unknown
New York City

LH

Lewis Heck
1755–1817
Lancaster, PA

A.H. **N.O.** 	**Adolphe Himmel** d. 1877 New Orleans
	William Hollingshead dates unknown Philadelphia
	Hiram Howard & Company 1878–1901 Providence
  	John Hull & Robert Sanderson c. 1650–83 Boston
	**Jacob Hurd** 1702–58 Boston
HUTTON 🦆	**Isaac Hutton** 1766–1855 Albany, NY
HYDE & GOODRICH	**Hyde & Goodrich** 1829–c. 1864 New Orleans
S.C. JETT	**Steven C. Jett** dates unknown St. Louis
W.B.JOHNSTON.	**William Blackstone Johnston** dates unknown Macon, GA
	George B. Jones, True M. Ball & **Nathaniel C. Poor** dates unknown Boston

William B. Kerr & Company
1855–1906
Newark, NJ
STERLING 766

Cornelius Kierstede
1675–1757
New York City

Jesse Kip
1660–1722
New York City

S.KIRK & SON **11.OZ** **Samuel Kirk & Son**
1815–1979
Baltimore

P.L.KRIDER
STANDARD
PHILADA

Peter L. Krider
dates unknown
Philadelphia

 BOSTON. COIN. **Vincent LaForme**
1823–93
Boston

⟨ L F ⟩ **La Secla, Fried & Company**
c. 1909–22
Newark, NJ

Jacob Leonard
dates unknown
Washington, DC

BR **Bartholomew Le Roux**
c. 1663–1713
New York City

K·L everett **Knight Leverett**
1703–53
Boston

H.LEWIS **Harvey Lewis**
d. 1835
Philadelphia

HARVEY.LEWIS

Edward Lownes
1792–1834
Philadelphia

Joseph Lownes
1754–1820
Philadelphia

Erik Magnussen
1884–1961
Providence

F.M.

Frederick Marquand
1799–1882
New York City

STERLING
ENTIRELY HAND
WROUGHT

Reino J. Martin

Reino J. Martin
b. 1923
Gloucester, MA

Seraphim Masi
active c. 1822–50
Washington, DC

Joseph Mayer & Brothers
1898–c. 1945
Seattle

STERLING
36

Meriden Britannia Company
1852–98
Meriden, CT

Meriden Silver Plate Company
1869–98
Meriden, CT

J.MOOD

John Mood
1792–1864
Charleston, SC

Nathaniel Morse
c. 1685–1748
Boston

Peter Müller-Munk
1904–67
New York City

PETER MÜLLER-MUNK
HANDWROUGHT
STERLING-SILVER
925
1000

James Murphree
d. 1782
Norfolk, VA

Myer Myers
1723–95
New York City

Nassau Lighter Company
c. 1915–22
New York City

John Owen
dates unknown
Philadelphia

Henry J. Pepper
c. 1790–1853
Wilmington, DE and Philadelphia

Alexander Petrie
d. 1768
Charleston, SC

John Potwine
1698–1792
Boston

Lewis Quandale
dates unknown
Philadelphia

Anthony Rasch
born c. 1778–1858
Philadelphia and New Orleans

MF'D & PLATED BY REED & BARTON 	**Reed & Barton** 1840–present Taunton, MA
	Paul Revere, Jr. 1735–1818 Boston
O.RICH. **BOSTON** ★ **fine** ★	**Obadiah Rich** 1809–88 Boston
S. Richard fecit	**Stephen Richard** dates unknown New York City
	Francis Richardson 1681–1729 Philadelphia
	Joseph Richardson, Jr. 1752–1831 Philadelphia
	Joseph Richardson, Jr. & Nathaniel Richardson 1777–90 Philadelphia
	Joseph Richardson, Sr. 1711–84 Philadelphia
	George Ridout dates unknown New York City
ROGERS, SMITH & Co. NEW HAVEN, CONN.	**Rogers, Smith & Company** 1857–98 New Haven, CT

PAT⁰ JUNE 13, 1868
PAT⁰ NOV. 3⁰ 1868

William Rouse
1639–1705
Boston

Pierre Casimir Rouyer
b. 1813
New Orleans

Robert Sanderson
1608–93
Boston

Carl Schon
dates unknown
Baltimore

Shreve, Crump & Low
1809–present
Boston

Simpson, Hall, Miller & Company
1866–98
Wallingford, CT

400

Thomas Skinner
1712–61
Marblehead, MA

Simeon Soumain
1685–1750
New York City

Robert Swan
c. 1748–1832
Philadelphia

Philip Syng, Jr.
1703–89
Philadelphia

Jacob Ten Eyck
1705–93
Albany, NY

Tiffany & Company
1853–present
New York City

Towle Silversmiths
1873–present
Newburyport, MA

Unger Brothers
1878–1914
Newark, NJ

Jacobus Vander Spiegel
1668–1708
New York City

Peter Van Dyck
1684–1751
New York City

John Vernon
1768–1815
New York City

Nathaniel Vernon & Company
1802–08
Charleston, SC

Robert Wallace & Sons
1871–1956
Wallingford, CT

Andrew E. Warner, Jr.
1813–96
Baltimore

Andrew E. Warner, Sr.
1786–1870
Baltimore

Joseph Warner
1742–1800
Wilmington, DE

Emmor T. Weaver
dates unknown
Philadelphia

Charles Whiting
1725–65
Norwich, CT

Wilcox Silver Plate Company
1867–98
Meriden, CT

WM. WILSON & SON

STERLING

5

William Wilson & Son
c. 1858–81
Philadelphia

Edward Winslow
1669–1753
Boston

Hugh Wishart
dates unknown
New York City

Henry Wood & Dixon G. Hughes
1845–99
New York City

W. Wood
dates unknown
Philadelphia

Thomas You
d. 1786
Charleston, SC

C.H. ZIMMERMAN

NEW ORLEANS

Charles H. Zimmerman
d. 1870
New Orleans

Pewter

Nathaniel Austin
c. 1741–1816
Charlestown, MA

Babbitt, Crossman & Company
1827–29
Taunton, MA

Frederick Bassett
c. 1740–1800
New York City and Hartford

John Bassett
c. 1696–1761
New York City

Joseph Belcher, Jr.
born c. 1751
Newport, RI and New London, CT

Joseph Belcher, Sr.
1729–78
Newport, RI and New London, CT

Thomas D. Boardman & Sherman Boardman
c. 1808–60
Hartford and New York City

Thomas D. Boardman & Lucius Hart
1828–53
Hartford and New York City

Timothy Boardman & Company
1822–25
New York City

Boardman & Company
1825–27
Hartford and New York City

Robert Bonynge
dates unknown
Boston

Parks Boyd
c. 1771–1819
Philadelphia

Cornelius Bradford
1729–86
New York City and Philadelphia

William Bradford, Jr.
1688–1759
New York City

Brook Farm
c. 1841–47
West Roxbury, MA

John Andrew Brunstrom
c. 1753–93
Philadelphia

CALDER **William Calder**
1792–1856
Providence

 Goldsmith Chandlee
1751–1821
Winchester, VA

 **Shirley Charron**
b. 1935
Ridgefield, CT

	George Coldwell died c. 1811 New York City
	Crossman, West & Leonard 1829–30 Taunton, MA
	Daniel Curtiss c. 1799–1872 Albany, NY
	Thomas Danforth III 1756–1840 Rocky Hill (formerly Stepney), CT and Philadelphia
	Peter Derr 1793–1868 Berks County, PA
	Fred Dodson b. 1921 Acworth, NH
	Edmund Dolbeare c. 1642–1711 Boston and Salem, MA
	William Ellsworth 1746–1816 New York City
	Edmund Endicott & William F. Sumner dates unknown New York City
	Asa Flagg & Henry Homan 1847–1941 Cincinnati
4800 **ROSWELL GLEASON** **10**	**Roswell Gleason** 1799–1887 Dorchester, MA
	Ashbil Griswold 1784–1853 Meriden, CT

Giles Griswold
1775–1840
Augusta, GA

Franklin D. Hall & Henry S. Boardman
c. 1843–60
Philadelphia

Samuel Hamlin, Sr.
1746–1801
Providence

Samuel S. Hersey
b. 1808
Belfast, ME

Johann Christoph Heyne
1715–81
Lancaster, PA

Martin Hyde
dates unknown
New York City

Samuel Kilburn
d. 1839
Baltimore

Elisha Kirk
d. 1790
York, PA

Richard Lee, Jr.
b. 1775
Springfield, VT

Richard Lee, Sr.
1747–1823
Springfield, VT

David Melville
1755–93
Newport, RI

Garry I. Mix
dates unknown
Wallingford and Yalesville, CT

Charles Ostrander & George Norris
dates unknown
New York City

 John Harrison Palethorp
dates unknown
Philadelphia

 Robert Palethorp, Jr.
1797–1822
Philadelphia

 Allen Porter
dates unknown
Westbrook, ME

 W. Potter
dates unknown
New England

 George Richardson
c. 1782–1848
Cranston, RI

SAGE & BEEBE. **Timothy Sage & Beebe (first name unknown)**
dates unknown
St. Louis

 Eben Smith
1773–1848
Beverly, MA

 Ebenezer Southmayd
1775–1831
Castleton, VT

T.B.M.CO
1 **Taunton Britannia Manufacturing Company**
1830–34
Taunton, MA

 Israel Trask
1786–1867
Beverly, MA

L.H. VAUGHAN
TAUNTON MASS.
PEWTER
Lester Vaughan
dates unknown
Taunton, MA

James Weekes
dates unknown
New York City

 Henry Will
c. 1734–c. 1802
New York City and Albany, NY

 John Will
c. 1696–1774
New York City

 Philip Will
1738–87
Philadelphia and New York City

 William Will
1742–98
Philadelphia

 Edward Willit, Sr., or Jr.
dates unknown
Virginia

 Henry Yale & Stephen Curtis
dates unknown
New York City

 Hiram Yale
1799–1831
Wallingford, CT

 **Peter Young**
1749–1813
New York City and Albany, NY

Price Guide

The current market price of antique silver, silver plate, and pewter is affected by such factors as scarcity of form, presence or absence of a maker's mark, physical condition of the item and the mark, and the importance of the maker to collectors.

The prices quoted here assume the item to be in very good condition, and where a mark is present, that the mark is clearly distinguishable.

Although auction prices, when taken over a substantial time period, and including a large sampling, may be an adequate guide to prices and trends, one must be aware that many forms come to auction very infrequently, and spirited competition may drive the price to an unrealistic level on that day. On the other hand, an item of importance that is not well advertised may sell for less than what would be considered normal.

The prices at which dealers offer specific items for sale is probably the best current guide to values. Although prices will vary somewhat from shop to shop, or area to area, competition in the overall marketplace will tend to keep prices generally confined to a much narrower range than would be experienced at auction sales only.

The educated buyer will always have a distinct advantage over those who have not studied the field. For example, some very rare and desirable forms lack a maker's mark. The collector who has become familiar with those forms may purchase a great prize at a fraction of its real value.

The broad guides to price presented here are a combination of dealer offering prices and auction prices; their range should encompass all but the widest variations. Some of the items included here are extremely well known and hence very expensive. A smaller number of objects are unique. It is more difficult to estimate their prices, because estimates are generally based on precedents or on prices paid for similar articles. In general, the actual sale price exceeds auction estimates if an item is both rare and great. The value of a great rarity may be substantially lowered if the item is battered or badly worn through years of disuse and lack of care, while an item in fine condition will sell at a premium.

Silver and Silver Plate

Plates, Trays, and Related Objects

Early American silver plates are rare and thus expensive, commanding $2000 to $4000 or more. Specialized Victorian plates are quite modestly priced, though those by a famous maker such as Tiffany may cost $200 to $400 each. Pairs and sets of plates are always more valuable. Trays range in price from $100 for a small modern one to $6000 to $20,000 for an early example that is large and elaborate. Victorian trays and platters are readily available for several hundred to several thousand dollars, depending on size and maker; smaller Victorian forms are often $100 or less.

1 **Federal plate** $5000–7000 (pair)
English plates, 9¾", of same date $700–900 (pair)
English plates, 10¾", of same date $1500–2000 (pair)
2 **Victorian plate** $300–350
3 **Victorian child's eating set** $1200–1500
4 **Late Colonial/Federal tray** $18,000–22,000
Similar English example c. 1750–75 $1200–1500
5 **Federal tray** $8000–12,000
Similar English examples $1200–1500
6 **Federal teapot stand** $1200–1500
English equivalents $150–250
7 **Modern bread tray** $100–150
8 **Victorian platter** $600–800
9 **Victorian tray** $2500–3000
10 **Modern compote** $600–800
11 **Early Colonial tazza** $12,000–15,000
Similar English examples $700–900
12 **Modern dish** $80–120
13 **Victorian/Modern sweetmeat dishes and spoons** $70–90 (single dish and spoon); $200–300 (pair)

Spoons, Knives, Forks, and Related Flatware

From $8 for a 20th-century electroplated spoon to $8000 or more for an early Colonial silver spoon by Hull and Sanderson—that is the tremendous range of prices collectors are willing to pay for American flatware. Pieces of Victorian and modern silver flatware generally cost from $15 to $100 each, and plated examples $5 to $25; fine Colonial and Federal silver flatware objects sell for hundreds if not thousands of dollars apiece. Elaborate Victorian ladles and serving pieces usually fetch $50 to $350, but earlier examples will cost $300 to $1500 or more, depending on the maker, craftsmanship, and rarity of form.

14 **Federal Onslow-pattern and octagonal-pattern ladles** $1200–1500 (left); $300–400 (right)
Similar English examples $500–600 (left); $200–300 (right)
15 **Victorian fused-plated ladle** $200–300
Similar English examples $60–80
16 **Federal and Colonial ladles** $1200–1500 (left); $400–600 (right)
Similar English examples $150–250 (left); $70–90 (right)
17 **Federal repoussé silver ladle** $800–1200
Similar English examples $200–300
18 **Victorian medallion-pattern pie server and fish knife** $80–120 (left); $120–150 (right)
19 **Victorian fish set** $300–400 (set)

20 **Federal fish knife** $200–300
   Standard English examples $100–150; imaginatively decorated
   English examples $200–300 or more
21 **Victorian crumber** $250–350
   English examples $80–120
22 **Modern Chantilly-pattern flatware** (left to right) $30–50;
   $15–25; $30–40; $15–25; $20–30; $40–60; $30–40; $60–80;
   $60–80; $50–70; $30–50
23 **Late Victorian flatware** (left to right) $40–60; $70–90;
   $30–40; $25–35; $15–20; $80–120; $30–40; $25–35
24 **Modern Richmond-pattern electroplated flatware** $8–12 (each
   piece)
25 **Late Colonial, Federal, and Victorian forks** (left to right)
   $80–120; $50–70; $40–60; $300–400
26 **Federal and Victorian knives** (left to right) $40–50; $70–80;
   $80–120; $200–250
27 **Child's Victorian Luxembourg-pattern spoon, fork, and
   knife** $120–150
   In original box $200–225
28 **Modern traveling knife, fork, and spoon** $150–250
29 **Victorian dessert spoon and early Colonial spoons** $25–35
   (left); $3000–5000 (center); $8000–12,000 (right)
   Dutch equivalent $400–800; English equivalent $600–800
30 **Victorian and modern souvenir spoons** $20–40 (each)
31 **Modern Art Nouveau berry spoon** $100–150
32 **Victorian parcel-gilt nut spoon** $125–175
33 **Victorian/modern oyster forks** $50–70 (left); $60–80 (right)
34 **Early Colonial sucket fork** $4000–6000
   English examples (also rare) $800–1200
35 **Early Colonial mote spoon** $2500–3500
   English equivalent $150–200
36 **Colonial/Federal marrow scoop and Federal tea-caddy
   spoon** $80–120 (left; unidentified maker); $600–800 (right)
   English examples $80–120 (left); $100–150 (right)

Table and Bar Accessories

Most of the objects in this section are small Victorian table
accessories ranging in price from $10 for a single butter plate to
$500 for an elaborate cruet frame. Numerous Federal items are
also featured; these are generally more costly. Most expensive
are the fine Colonial serving pieces and accessories, which
include a diminutive cream pail at $800–1200 and a singular
pierced dish ring by Myer Myers that would probably cost
$30,000 to $50,000 were it to come on the market.

37 **Federal spring-type sugar tongs and late Colonial/Federal
   sugar tongs** $100–150 (top); $600–900 (bottom)
   English examples $30–50 (top); $80–100 (bottom)
38 **Victorian grape shears** $300–400
39 **Victorian/modern gilt nut picks** $30–50 (each)
40 **Victorian skewer** $250–350
41 **Victorian and modern tea strainers** $150–200 (left); $80–120
   (right)
42 **Late Colonial punch strainer** $7000–9000 +
   English equivalent $800–1200; more ordinary English
   variants $200–300
43 **Victorian tea ball** $60–90
44 **Federal bottle label** $500–700
   Similar English examples $70–90

45 **Victorian silver-over-ivory corkscrews** $70–90 (each)
46 **Late Federal wine siphon** $500–700
47 **Late Colonial cream pail** $900–1200
    Similar English examples $300–500
48 **Victorian bottle coaster** $800–1200 (pair)
49 **Modern coasters** $50–70 (each)
50 **Victorian butter plate** $10–20
51 **Victorian knife rest** $60–90
52 **Modern sugar-cube holder or knife rest** $60–90
53 **Victorian table bell** $200–300
54 **Victorian bone holder** $300–500
    English equivalent $125–175
55 **Victorian electroplated napkin ring with vase** $100–150
56 **Victorian electroplated napkin ring** $15–25
57 **Colonial salt container** $15,000–25,000 +
    English examples $300–500
58 **Early Victorian salt dish** $300–400 (pair); $80–100 (single example)
59 **Victorian salt or pepper shakers** $50–70 (left); $70–90 (right)
60 **Early Colonial mustard pot** $20,000–30,000 +
    Dutch equivalent $1500–2500
61 **Late Colonial pepperbox** $2000–3000
    English equivalent $600–800
62 **Early Colonial caster** $30,000–40,000
    Similar English examples $1500–2000
63 **Victorian electroplated pickle caster** $80–120
64 **Victorian liquor frame** $1000–1500
65 **English George III fused-plated epergne** $800–1200
66 **Late Federal bottle frame** $2500–4500
67 **English George III fused-plated cruet frame** $200–300
68 **Victorian electroplated cruet frame** $300–500
69 **Victorian/modern toast rack and egg cup** $300–400
70 **Federal toast rack** $800–1200
    Similar English examples $250–350
71 **Early Victorian egg coddler** $1200–1500
72 **English Victorian electroplated coffee percolator** $300–500
73 **English George III fused-plated dish warmer** $80–120
74 **Colonial brazier** $8000–12,000
    English equivalent $800–1200
75 **Early Colonial skillet** $60,000–80,000 +
    English equivalent (would probably date somewhat earlier, from time of Charles II) $15,000–20,000
76 **Late Colonial saucepan** $3000–5000
    English equivalent $600–800
77 **Late Colonial dish ring** $30,000–50,000
    Similar Irish examples $1500–2000
78 **Late Colonial dish cross** $20,000–30,000
    English equivalent $600–900

Tureens, Vegetable Dishes, Sugar Bowls, and Related Objects
Most of the bowls and dishes in this section are large, elaborate covered serving pieces. The Victorian examples here begin at $300 for an unmarked electroplated meat cover to $7000 for a heavy and exuberant tureen by Tiffany. The Federal objects included are uniformly fine and thus costly—$2000 to $25,000; less expensive examples from this era are widely available today. At $4000 to $200,000, the prices of the Colonial bowls and dishes reflect their desirability.

79 **English Victorian electroplated meat cover** $300–400
80 **English George IV fused-plated vegetable dish** $300–400
   (single example); $700–900 (pair)
81 **Colonial/Federal silver-mounted coconut** $600–1200
   If attribution to Hammersley were proven, $4000–6000
   Similar Irish examples $300–500
82 **Victorian butter dish** $500–600
83 **Early Colonial sweetmeat box** $150,000–200,000 +
   Similar English examples $30,000–50,000
84 **Victorian electroplated vegetable dish** $250–350
85 **Victorian tureen** $5000–7000
   Example by same maker, but with less interesting
   decoration $2000–3000
86 **Victorian parcel-gilt tureen** $3500–4500
   New York version $1500–2000
87 **Federal tureen and tray** $5000–7000 (pair)
   Similar English examples from this date (generally without
   trays) $3000–4000 (pair)
88 **Federal tureen and tray** $20,000–25,000
   English examples with stand $7000–9000
89 **Federal tea caddy** $2500–3000
   Similar English examples $800–1000
90 **Colonial sugar bowl** $30,000–50,000
   Similar English examples $1500–2500
91 **Victorian butter dish** $800–1200
   Similar examples with New York maker's mark $500–600
92 **Late Colonial sugar bowl** $12,000–15,000
93 **Late Federal wine cooler** $10,000–15,000
94 **Victorian 2-handled cup** $300–400

Porringers, Bowls, Cake Baskets, and Related Objects
This group includes a monteith made by John Coney about 1700;
among the grandest and most valuable known items of early
American silver, it is worth perhaps half a million dollars or
more. Nonetheless, many of the objects included here are
reasonably priced. Numerous Victorian electroplated cake
baskets and bowls are available for under $200; silver examples
from this era will, of course, be more expensive. Federal silver
designs usually bring $500 to $3000, with exceptional pieces by
well-known makers commanding much more.

95 **Late Colonial bowl** $80,000–120,000
   Dutch brandy bowls (a smaller form from which this is
   derived) $1500–3000
96 **Late Colonial keyhole-handle porringer** $2000–3000
   Similar English examples $1000–1500
97 **Late Colonial sweetmeat dish** $5000–7000
   English or Irish examples $500–700
98 **Modern silver bowl** $400–600
99 **Colonial monteith** $500,000 +
   English examples $10,000–20,000
100 **Victorian electroplated punch bowl, tray, cups, and
    ladle** $1000–1500
101 **Modern bowl and ladle** $400–600
102 **Federal bowl** $4000–6000
    English equivalent $800–1200
103 **Federal compotes** $10,000–15,000 (pair)
    Similar English examples $3000–4000 (pair)

104 **Federal cake basket** $2500–3500
English equivalent $1200–1500
105 **Federal cake basket** $2000–3000
English equivalent $800–1200
106 **Modern bowl** $300–500
107 **Modern pierced bowl** $70–90
108 **Victorian olive dish** $300–400
109 **Victorian electroplated nut bowl** $100–200
110 **Colonial footed cup or bowl** $12,000–16,000
111 **Late Federal/early Victorian wirework cake or fruit basket** $2000–3000
112 **Victorian electroplated fruit basket** $100–200
113 **Victorian electroplated fruit bowl** $100–200
114 **Victorian electroplated fruit bowl** $100–200
115 **Victorian electroplated butter dish and knife** $80–120
116 **Federal bowl and French stand** $600–900
117 **Victorian electroplated cake basket** $100–200

Teapots, Coffeepots, Pitchers, and Related Objects
The most expensive objects in this section are the Colonial coffeepots and teapots, priced at $10,000 to $80,000 or more. One example, the late Colonial repoussé kettle-on-stand, is probably unique in American silver. Somewhat less costly are the Federal-era examples at $1500 to $30,000, although American coffeepots from before the mid-18th century are rare and accordingly expensive. Victorian coffeepots, teapots, pitchers, and ewers range widely in price from $500 to $3000 for silver pieces, and from $100 to $400 for plated examples. Streamlined teapots and coffeepots from the 1920s to 1960s often sell for $400 to $1200, but pieces by lesser-known or unknown makers usually cost much less.

118 **Late Colonial/Federal sauceboat** $2500–3500
Similar English examples $500–700
119 **Late Colonial sauceboat** $4000–6000
120 **Modern Martelé sauceboat and tray** $1200–1500
121 **Victorian pap boat** $300–500
Similar English examples (made until 1830–40) $150–200
122 **Late Colonial/Federal cream pot on pedestal** $5000–7000
Similar creamer by another American maker $600–900
English equivalent $150–250
123 **Modern Art Nouveau electroplated pitcher** $200–300
124 **Victorian pitcher** $2000–3000
English equivalent $800–1200
125 **Victorian ewer** $1200–1500
126 **Early Victorian ewer** $800–1200
127 **Victorian toby jug** $1400–1800
128 **Federal presentation pitcher** $30,000–50,000
Similar example by another New England maker $3000–4000
129 **Victorian pitcher** $700–900
130 **Colonial spout cup** $25,000–35,000
English equivalent $3000–5000
131 **Federal tankard** $2000–3000
Similar examples without spout $8000–12,000
English equivalent with added spout $700–900; without spout $1500–2000
132 **Late Colonial ewer** $30,000–50,000
English equivalent $3000–5000
133 **Late Colonial coffeepot** $20,000–30,000

134 **Federal rococo coffeepot** $12,000–15,000
   Similar English examples (usually slightly smaller than American ones) $1500–2500
135 **Victorian repoussé teapot** $1000–1500
136 **Late Colonial repoussé kettle-on-stand** $40,000–60,000 +
   English equivalent $2000–3000; if by Paul de Lamere $15,000–20,000
137 **English George III fused-plated hot-water urns** $1200–1500 (for both)
138 **Federal tea and coffee set** $7000–9000
   English equivalent $2500–3000
139 **Federal tea and coffee set** $20,000–30,000
140 **Colonial pear-shaped octagonal teapot** $80,000–120,000
   English equivalent $12,000–15,000
141 **Federal octagonal teapot** $1500–2500
   English equivalent $600–900
142 **Late Colonial pear-shaped teapot** $10,000–14,000
   English equivalent $800–1200
143 **Modern teapot** $400–600
144 **Modern coffeepot** $800–1200
145 **Modern double-spout coffeepot** $400–600
146 **Modern Art Deco coffee set** $1200–1500
147 **Late Colonial coffeepot** $50,000–60,000
   English equivalent $2500–3500
148 **Victorian electroplated ice-water pitcher** $100–200
149 **Victorian electroplated tilting ice-water pitcher** $200–400
150 **Victorian electroplated tilting ice-water set** $200–400

Mugs, Cups, Chalices, and Beakers
These vessels are priced for budgets of all sizes. Few collectors can afford the very early 2-handled covered cup by Blanck or the tall, lavishly engraved beaker by van der Burch, both extremely rare and priced in excess of $100,000. On the other hand, most collectors would not pass up a Victorian mug at $50 to $300 or even the larger Victorian pieces at $500 to $700. Most of the objects in this section fall between these extremes: For example, Federal mugs, goblets, and other drinking vessels are often priced at $500 to $3000.

151 **Victorian mug** $150–200
152 **Late Colonial cann** $2500–3500
   English equivalent $600–800
153 **English George III French-plated paktong cann** $100–400
154 **Early Victorian mug** $80–120
155 **Early Colonial mug** $3000–5000
   English equivalent $900–1200
156 **Victorian presentation mug** $125–175
157 **Victorian parcel-gilt mug** $250–300
158 **Federal pint tankard** $1500–2500
159 **Colonial quart mug** $6000–9000
160 **Late Colonial tankard** $40,000–60,000
   Comparable example by another Boston maker $6000–9000
161 **Late Colonial quart tankard** $40,000–60,000
   Equivalent flat-top English tankard $5000–8000
162 **Late Victorian silver-and-porcelain tankard** $300–400
163 **Victorian tankard of parcel-gilt silver, horn, and porcelain** $1500–2000
164 **Federal mug with lid** $800–1200

165 **Early Colonial 2-handled covered cup** $100,000–150,000 +
English equivalent $6000–8000
166 **Early Colonial caudle cup** $80,000–120,000
English equivalent $1500–2500
167 **Modern silver-and-porcelain broth cup, demitasse, and saucers** $5000–7000 (set of 12 cups or set of 12 demitasses)
168 **Victorian cup and saucer** $300–500
169 **Federal tumbler** $3000–5000
English equivalent $500–700
170 **Federal beaker** $700–900
English equivalent $300–400
171 **Late Colonial beaker** $20,000–30,000
172 **Victorian beaker or julep cup** $400–600
173 **Early Colonial beaker** $80,000–120,000
Dutch equivalent $5000–7000
174 **Victorian parcel-gilt goblet** $500–700
175 **Federal presentation cup** $1200–1500
English equivalent $300–400
176 **Victorian repoussé goblet** $300–400
177 **Victorian presentation goblet** $300–400
178 **Early Colonial chalice** $40,000–60,000
English equivalent $2000–3000
179 **Federal parcel-gilt goblet** $800–1200

Candlesticks, Lamps, and Related Objects

Devices for holding candles can be inexpensive: English plated candlesticks dating from 1750 to 1850 often cost $100 to $600. Yet American-made silver examples from the 18th century are very costly because they are so rare, and fine Federal candlesticks and candelabra can be nearly as expensive. Pairs are always in greatest demand. Early plated oil lamps made in England from 1790 to 1815 are plentiful at $500 to $3000. Later kerosene lamps are usually more affordable. The value of a lighting device of any kind is seriously diminished if the object is missing an element or has been damaged or altered.

180 **English George III fused-plated chamber sticks** $300–500 (pair)
$100–150 (single example)
181 **Colonial candlesticks** $100,000–150,000 (pair)
English equivalent $6000–8000 (pair)
Single example by Morse $20,000–30,000
182 **English Victorian electroplated candlesticks** $100–200 (pair);
$50–70 (single example)
183 **Federal candlesticks** $20,000–30,000 (pair); $3000–4000 (single example)
French equivalent $2000–2500 (pair)
184 **English George III fused-plated candlesticks** $400–600 pair;
$100–200 (single example)
185 **Victorian candlesticks** $1000–1500 (pair); $300–350 (single example)
186 **Colonial sconces and quillwork** $30,000–50,000
187 **Federal candelabrum** $12,000–15,000 (pair); $3000–4000 (single example)
188 **Victorian electroplated candelabrum** $500–700 (pair);
$200–300 (single example)
189 **English George III fused-plated Argand lamp** $2000–3000
190 **English George III fused-plated oil lamp** $800–1200

191 **English George III fused-plated Argand lamp** $800–1200
192 **English George III fused-plated oil lamps** $2000–3000
193 **Victorian electroplated kerosene lamp** $250–350

Boxes and Other Containers

These small containers are a relatively inexpensive collecting specialty. Victorian and 20th-century boxes and cases of amazing variety are readily available at $50 to $250. While Federal examples are usually far more costly, typical silver objects or plated examples may be found for $300 to $1000. Though small in size, Colonial boxes are large investments, sometimes selling for $4000 to $10,000 or even more.

194 **Late Colonial repoussé snuffbox** $4000–6000
   Scandinavian equivalent $400–500
195 **Colonial silver-and-tortoiseshell tobacco box** $5000–7000
   English equivalent $600–800
196 **Late Federal snuffbox** $2000–3000
197 **Federal fused-plated box** $400–600
198 **Federal skippets** $2000–3000 (each)
199 **Modern cosmetic case** $250–350
200 **Federal case and spectacles** $300–500
201 **Modern spectacles case** $80–120
202 **Federal etui** $700–900
203 **English and American Victorian calling-card cases** $200–300
   (each)
204 **Modern cigarette case and match safe** $100–150 (for both)
205 **Modern Art Nouveau cigar case** $250–350
206 **Victorian box** $100–150
207 **Federal vinaigrette** $800–1200
   Standard English examples $100–300; unusual examples are
   more expensive
208 **Modern enameled box** $1500–2000
209 **Victorian electroplated jewel casket** $150–200

Sewing and Desk Accessories and Other Personal Objects

The miscellaneous objects included here are, for the most part, modestly priced. Most types sell for less than $300, and many for less than $100. However, some of the earlier pieces or those that are particularly desirable will cost $1000 to $3000; and a rare Colonial baby's toy made of silver and coral may cost as much as $7000.

210 **Victorian pincushion holder** $80–120
211 **Federal knitting-needle holders** $40–80 (left); $80–120 (right)
212 **Victorian/modern letter clip** $60–80
213 **Victorian classical presentation medal** $200–300
214 **Late Colonial and Federal silver buttons** $100–200 (left);
   $200–300 (center and right)
215 **English George III shoe buckle** $250–350
216 **Colonial/Federal parcel-gilt Masonic medal** $2000–3000
217 **Victorian boatswain's pipe** $600–900
218 **Victorian Purim noisemaker** $600–800
219 **Colonial silver-and-coral baby's toy** $4000–6000
   Similar English examples $600–800
220 **Victorian chatelaine** $200–300
221 **European filigree posy holder** $70–90
222 **Modern vase** $300–400

223 **Late Victorian silver-mounted perfume bottle** $80–100
224 **Victorian parcel-gilt flask** $200–300
225 **Victorian/modern military hairbrush** $60–80
226 **Late Colonial dirk** $2000–3000
227 **Federal small sword and scabbard** $600–900 (for both);
   marked examples would bring a higher price
228 **English George III close-plated candle snuffer** $150–250
229 **Federal snuffer and tray** $2500–3500
   English equivalent $600–800
230 **Victorian curling iron and stand** $250–350
231 **English Victorian oil lamp** $250–350
232 **Modern cigarette lighter** $50–70
233 **Victorian silver-and-horn cigar lighter** $150–200
234 **Modern shell-and-silver ashtray** $100–150
235 **Victorian ashtray** $100–150
236 **Victorian electroplated card receiver and flower vase**
   $200–300
237 **Victorian electroplated card receiver** $60–90
238 **Late Federal/Victorian silver inkstand** $2000–3000
239 **English George IV fused-plated inkstand** $400–600

Pewter

Plates, Porringers, and Related Objects

The prices of the plates, dishes, basins, and porringers in this section range widely—from $12,000 for a scalloped-rim basin that may be one of a kind to $25–60 for a modern form such as a 1925 mayonnaise set. Typical circular plates and dishes from the Federal era are often available for well under $1000. Oval dishes as well as plates with unusual features, however, may cost $2500 to $8000. Many basins can be found selling for several hundred dollars, although covered examples or those by highly respected makers will fetch $2000 to $4000 or more. Common porringer forms, such as an unmarked crown-handle Federal example, may sell for as little as $250, whereas fine examples with an unusual handle will sell for upwards of $4000.

240 **English George III teapot stand** $250–350
241 **Colonial/Federal oval dish** $6000–8000
Similar English examples $400–600
242 **Early Colonial broad-brim dish** $6000–7500
Similar English examples $1000–1250
243 **Early Colonial multiple-reeded dish** $5000–6500
Similar English examples $500–750
244 **Late Colonial/Federal and Colonial smooth-brim plates** $3000–4000
Similar English examples $125–175 (right)
245 **Federal plates** $650–850 (left); $1750–2000 (right)
Similar English examples $125–175 (right)
246 **Federal deep dish** $2500–3000
Examples by Boardman or another fairly common maker $450–750
Unmarked examples $200–300
247 **Federal basin** $2800–3500
Similar English examples $200–250
248 **Federal lidded basin** $4000–4500
Similar examples (8–12″ in diameter), marked by Boardman, without lids $400–1500
Similar English examples (8–12″ in diameter), without lids, $175–500
249 **Late Colonial/early Federal basin** $10,000–12,000
250 **Modern mayonnaise set** $25–60
251 **Federal sugar bowl** $4500–5500
18th-century English examples $1000–1250
252 **Late Colonial/Federal salt dish** $600–800
Small late 18th- or early 19th-century English salts $75–150
253 **Federal footed basin** $650–850
Unfluted marked examples $450–650
Unfluted unmarked examples $250–350
254 **Federal crown-handle porringer** $700–900
Unmarked examples $250–350
255 **Federal geometric-handle porringer** $4000–5000
Unmarked examples $1000–1250
Similar English examples $500–700
256 **Federal flower-handle porringer** $1200–1500
Unmarked examples $300–400
257 **Federal porringer** $250–350
Similar examples without cast R mark $200–250
258 **Late Colonial/Federal porringer** $4500–5000
Unmarked examples $600–700
259 **Federal tab-handle porringer** $5000–7000
Similar examples with other makers' marks $2500–4000
Unmarked examples $600–800

Spoons and Ladles

Although spoons were the most commonly made form of pewter, they were not made to survive centuries of heavy use, and so are somewhat rare today. Still, pewter spoons constitute a relatively inexpensive collecting specialty. Unmarked examples from the mid-19th century may sell for as little as $10 to $20. Earlier spoons with uncommon shapes, decoration, or marks will command several hundred or even several thousand dollars. Ladles range in price from $100 for unmarked late examples to $2500 or more for rare 18th-century ones.

260 **Federal midrib-handle and fiddle-handle teaspoons** $300–400 (left); $250–350 (right)
Unmarked examples $25–40

261 **Victorian tablespoon and late Federal/Victorian teaspoon** $75–125 (left); $25–35 (right)
Unmarked examples $10–25 (left); $10–20 (right)

262 **Federal tablespoons** $2000–2500
Similar English examples $100–125

263 **Federal tablespoons** $600–800
Similar English examples with American-type decoration $125–250

264 **Early Federal slip-ended spoon and early Colonial trifid-handle spoon** $1200–1500 (left); $200–250 (right)
Similar marked English examples $200–300 (left)

265 **Federal midrib, wooden-handle, and fiddle-handle ladles** $2500–3000 (left); $600–800 (center); $300–450 (right)
Similar English examples $125–275 (left); $75–125 (right)
Unmarked examples $100–150 (right)

Teapots, Coffeepots, Pitchers, and Related Objects

While the fine 18th-century objects in this section are among the most expensive objects in American pewter, costing from $15,000 to $50,000 or even more, the great majority of teapots, coffeepots, and flagons sell for far less. In fact, many early Victorian examples are priced in the low- to mid-hundreds, and common Federal or English forms can be readily found in or below the $1000–2000 range.

266 **English Queen Anne lidless flagon** $25,000–35,000 +

267 **Federal flagon** $2500–3000
Examples without historical engraving $1500–2000

268 **Late Colonial/Federal flagon** $25,000–35,000 +

269 **Federal flagon** $2000–2500
2-quart marked example by Boardman $1800–2200
3-quart marked example by Boardman $2500–3000

270 **Federal lidless pitcher** $1000–1200
Similar examples by Rufus Dunham $300–500

271 **Federal lighthouse teapot** $1000–1200
Unmarked examples $400–600

272 **Late Federal/Victorian baluster-shaped teapot** $750–1000

273 **Federal bulbous teapot** $3000–4000
Unmarked examples $1200–1400

274 **Victorian teapot** $400–600 (marked examples by American makers)

275 **English George III coffeepot** $2000–2500

276 **Federal urn-shaped coffeepot** $50,000–75,000 +

277 **Federal flagon** $20,000–25,000

278 **Late Federal/Victorian coffee urn** $600–800

279 **Late Federal flagon on pedestal** $1200–1500
Similar English examples $200–500
280 **Late Colonial/Federal cream pot on pedestal** $4000–5000
Similar 18th-century English examples $1200–1800
281 **Late Colonial/Federal tripod cream pot** $7500–9000
Unmarked examples $3000–4000
Similar 18th-century English examples $1200–1800
282 **Late Federal/Victorian pitcher** $1200–1500
2-, 3-, and 4-quart marked examples $500–1200
283 **Late Federal/Victorian pitcher** $900–1200
Similar examples without covers $500–600
284 **Victorian octagonal tea set** $150–250 (each piece)
285 **Early Victorian teapot** $350–450
286 **Late Federal teapot** $350–450
287 **Late Colonial/Federal pear-shaped teapot** $20,000–25,000
Similar English examples $1250–1750
288 **Late Colonial/Federal teapot** $20,000–25,000
Similar English examples $1250–1750
289 **English George II teapot** $1200–1500
290 **Late Colonial/Federal egg-shaped teapot** $15,000–20,000
Similar English examples $800–1200
291 **European japanned kettle-on-stand** $750–900
Kettle alone $400–500
292 **Federal drum-shaped teapot** $15,000–20,000
Similar English examples $1250–1750

Mugs, Chalices, Beakers, and Related Objects
Many mugs and beakers differ only slightly in size, shape, and
detail, yet their prices vary greatly. Early objects in this
category stand out because of their unusual design, exceptional
workmanship, or the mark of a desirable maker; these are quite
costly, selling for $4000 to more than $15,000. More modest
forms, especially those that are comparatively late, unmarked, or
English, often sell for only one-fifth to one-tenth as much.
Examples with uncommon lids or handles or with cast or
engraved decoration are unusual and will fetch exceptional
prices.

293 **Late Colonial/Federal cann** $7500–9000
Similar 18th-century English examples $400–500
Similar 19th-century English examples $150–250
294 **Late Colonial tankard** $13,000–15,000
Similar English examples c. 1740–60 $1500–2000
Similar English examples c. 1790–1820 $850–1250
295 **Federal measure** $3500–4000
Examples with smaller capacities $800–3500
296 **Federal pint mug** $4000–4500
Similar English examples $400–600
297 **Late Federal 2-handled mug** $500–600
298 **Late Colonial/Federal strap-handle mug** $4000–4500
Similar unmarked examples $1500–2000
Similar unmarked pint-capacity examples $1250–1500
299 **Federal quart mug** $4000–4500
Similar English examples $500–750
300 **Federal infusion pot** $4000–4500
Similar English examples $400–600
301 **Late Colonial engraved tankard** $14,000–16,000
Similar unmarked examples $3000–4000

302 **Federal tankard** $15,000–17,000
Similar examples with "LOVE" mark $12,500–15,000
303 **Colonial and Federal beakers** $3250–3750 (left);
$700–900 (right)
Unmarked 18th-century examples $400–500 (left)
Unmarked examples $300–400 (right)
304 **Modern beakers** $40–100 (pair)
305 **Federal beakers** $4500–5500 (left); $400–500 (right)
Similar unmarked examples $75–125 (right)
306 **Victorian cup with handle** $450–500
Similar examples without handles $400–450
Unmarked examples without handles $75–125
307 **Federal 2-handled chalice** $275–350 (single example);
$550–750 (pair)
308 **Late Colonial and Federal chalices** $8000–10,000 (left);
$5000–7000 (right, single example); $12,000–15,000 (right, pair)

Candlesticks, Lamps, and Related Objects
19th-century pewter candlesticks, if marked by a maker,
generally range in price from $300 to $500; however, many late
unmarked candlesticks sell for $100 to $200. Marked pairs always
command a premium. The varied lamps in this section are priced
according to several criteria: the rarity of their form and design;
whether or not they are marked; and whether or not they are
complete and unaltered. Simple, unmarked Victorian fluid or oil
lamps are readily available for $200 to $300, while elaborate,
unusual examples by well-known makers cost $1000 or more.

309 **Federal or English George III candlesticks** $800–1000 (pair);
$350–450 (single example)
310 **Victorian chamber stick** $400–500 (single example);
$800–1000 (pair)
Unmarked single example $125–175
311 **Late Federal candlesticks** $350–450 (single example);
$800–1000 (pair)
Unmarked single example $150–225
312 **Late Federal/early Victorian candlesticks** $350–450 (single
example); $800–1000 (pair)
Unmarked single example $125–200
313 **Federal candlestick** $400–500 (single example); $1250–1500 (pair)
314 **Early Victorian candlesticks** $300–400 (single example);
$700–900 (pair)
Unmarked pair $300–400
315 **Federal oil lamp** $500–600 (single example); $1250–1500 (pair)
316 **Victorian oil lamp with magnifying lenses** $1000–1250 (single
example); $2000–2500 (pair)
Unmarked examples $450–650
Unmarked examples with 1 lens $400–500
317 **Victorian double-bellied oil lamp** $500–600
318 **Late Federal oil lamp** $400–500 (single example);
$1000–1200 (pair)
Unmarked single example $225–275
319 **Victorian 2-burner oil lamp** $750–1000
320 **Victorian fluid lamp** $350–450 (single example); $700–950 (pair)
Unmarked single example $200–275
321 **Victorian oil lamp** $500–600 (single example); $1000–1250 (pair)
Unmarked single example $250–350
322 **Victorian oil lamp on gimbals** $600–700
Unmarked examples $300–400

Household Objects

This section of miscellaneous pewter household objects includes many uncommon forms that are generally inexpensive. Because of their unsavory original functions, bedpans, commodes, urinals, and spittoons usually cost only $100 to $250; still, early examples by well-known makers will bring much more substantial prices. Other types of objects, such as funnels or sanders, are also often modestly priced. However, certain rare forms, such as foot warmers or standishes, can cost several thousand dollars, provided their American origin is documented; English examples are worth only a fraction as much.

323 **Federal casters** $250–350 (each)
324 **Late Federal/Victorian baby bottle** $2500–3500
    Similar English examples $600–800
325 **Late Colonial/Federal flask** $5000–7000
    Similar English examples $200–400
326 **Late Colonial funnel** $2500–3500
    Unmarked examples $500–750
    Similar English examples $125–250
327 **Late Colonial/Federal urinal** $150–200
328 **Federal bedpan** $2500–3000
    Similar examples marked by Boardman $400–700
    Similar English examples $150–250
329 **Victorian spittoon** $400–500
    Unmarked examples $125–200
330 **Late Colonial/Federal commode** $3000–3500
    Similar English examples $200–300
331 **Federal inkwell** $3000–4000
    Similar and later English examples $100–200
332 **Late Federal sander** $400–500
    Unmarked examples $125–175
333 **Federal boxes** $500–600 (left); $450–550 (right)
    Unmarked examples $150–200 (left); $175–225 (right)
334 **Modern nut dish** $25–75
335 **Federal sundial** $600–750
    Round unmarked examples $250–350
336 **Federal communion tokens** $125–150 (each)
    Similar English examples $25–75
337 **Colonial/Federal foot warmer** $4000–5000
338 **Colonial/Federal standish** $4000–5000
    Similar 18th-century English examples $275–400
    Similar 19th-century English examples $150–200

Picture Credits

Numbers in italics refer to pages.

Photographers

All photographs were taken by Rosmarie Hausherr with the exception of the following: *28, 54, 86, 91, 92, 93, 119, 124, 133, 146, 168, 176, 241, 278, 288, 319, 338.* Anne Krohn Graham photographed *28;* Helga Photo Studio photographed *93;* and Prather Warren photographed *54, 86, 91, 124, 168,* and *176.*

Collections

The following individuals and institutions kindly allowed us to reproduce objects from their collections:

Anglo-American Art Museum, Louisiana State University, Baton Rouge, Louisiana: *54* (Gift of Dr. and Mrs. C. C. Coles); *86* (Gift of Dr. and Mrs. A. Brooks Cronan, Jr.); *91, 124* (Gifts of the Friends of the Museum); *168* (Gift of Mrs. H. Payne Breazeale, Sr.); *176* (Gift of Dr. and Mrs. A. Brooks Cronan, Jr.).

John D. Barr: *314.*

Sewell C. Biggs: *56, 179, 226.*

The Brooklyn Museum, Brooklyn, New York: *241* (John W. Poole Collection); *278* (Gift of Arthur W. Clement); *288* (John W. Poole Collection); *319* (Gift of Mrs. Samuel Doughty); *338* (John W. Poole Collection).

Mr. and Mrs. Charles H. Carpenter, Jr.: *146;* photo courtesy Gorham.

Cooper-Hewitt Museum, Smithsonian Institution, New York City: *28* (Gift of Aaron Faber Gallery and Anne Krohn Graham); photo courtesy Anne Krohn Graham.

Martha S. Fennimore: *7, 22, 79, 188.*

James H. Halpin: *70, 127.*

International Silver Company, Meriden, Connecticut: *17* (top), *55, 63, 68, 100, 109, 112, 113, 115, 123, 148, 193, 209, 236.*

Museum of the City of New York, New York City: *3* (Gift of Miss Isabel Shults); *48* (Gift of Mrs. Bertha Shults Dougherty and Miss Isabel Shults); *64* (Gift of Newcomb Carlton); *69, 222* (Gifts of Miss Susan Dwight Bliss); *230* (Gift of Julian K. Roosevelt); *231* (Gift of Miss Susan Dwight Bliss).

Museum of Early Southern Decorative Arts, Winston-Salem, North Carolina: *92, 119, 133.*

Private Collections: *2, 8, 10, 12, 13, 17* (bottom), *18, 19, 21, 23, 24, 27, 31–33, 38, 39, 41, 43, 49–52, 58, 59, 66, 71, 82, 85, 93, 94, 98, 103, 107, 108, 111, 114, 117, 120, 125, 129, 132, 135, 137, 149, 151, 153, 154, 156, 157, 163, 167, 174, 177, 185, 199, 201, 203, 204, 212, 218, 221, 224, 232–235, 237, 334.*

Ian M. G. Quimby: *304.*

Charles V. Swain: *1, 9, 45, 53, 67, 72, 80, 84, 87, 104, 121, 141, 162, 164, 175, 182, 206, 210, 223, 225, 239, 240, 249, 251–253, 257, 261, 269, 273, 275, 279–281, 283, 289, 290, 294, 295, 311, 312, 318, 330.*

The Henry Francis du Pont Winterthur Museum, Winterthur, Delaware: *4–6, 11, 14–17, 17* (center), *19, 20, 25, 26, 29, 30, 34, 36, 37, 44, 46, 57, 65, 73, 74, 76, 83, 88, 89, 95, 96, 102, 105, 116, 118, 122, 126, 128, 130, 131, 134, 138, 139, 142, 147, 152, 155, 158–161, 165, 166, 169–172, 180, 181, 183, 184, 186, 187, 189–192, 196–198, 200, 202, 207, 211, 213–217, 219, 220, 227–229, 242–248, 254–256, 258–260, 262–268, 270–272, 274, 276, 277, 282, 284–287, 291–293, 296, 298, 299, 301–303, 305–310, 313, 315, 317, 320–329, 331–333, 335, 336.*

Yale University Art Gallery, New Haven, Connecticut: *35; 40, 42, 47, 60, 61, 62* (Mabel Brady Garvan Collection); *75* (Gift of Mr. and Mrs. Donald W. Henry, B.A. 1939); *77* (Mabel Brady Garvan Collection); *78* (Anonymous gift for the John Marshall Phillips Memorial Collection); *81* (The John Marshall Phillips Collection); *90, 97, 99* (Mabel Brady Garvan Collection); *101* (Gift of Mr. and Mrs. Davis W. Moore); *106* (Gift of William Core Duffy, Mus.B. 1952, Mus.M. 1954, and Mrs. Duffy); *110* (Anonymous gift to the John Marshall Phillips Collection); *136, 140* (Mabel Brady Garvan Collection); *143* (Gift of Mr. and Mrs. Samuel Schwartz); *144; 145; 150* (Millicent Todd Bingham Fund); *173, 178, 194, 195* (Mabel Brady Garvan Collection); *205* (American Arts Purchase Fund); *208* (Mrs. Paul Moore Fund); *238* (Mabel Brady Garvan Collection); *250* (Gift of Mr. and Mrs. W. Scott Braznell); *297, 300, 316, 337* (Mabel Brady Garvan Collection).

Bibliography

Silver
Avery, C. Louise
Early American Silver
New York: The Century Company, 1930.

Bacot, H. Parrott
Natchez-Made Silver of the Nineteenth Century
Baton Rouge, Louisiana: Louisiana State University, 1970.

Bacot, H. Parrott, and Carrie and Charles Mackie
Crescent City Silver
Baton Rouge, Louisiana: Anglo-American Art Museum, 1980.

Beckman, Elizabeth D.
Cincinnati Silversmiths, Jewelers, Watch and Clockmakers
Cincinnati: B.B. & Co., 1975.

Belden, Louise C.
Marks of American Silversmiths
Charlottesville, Virginia: University of Virginia Press, 1980.

Bohan, Peter, and Philip Hammerslough
Early Connecticut Silver, 1700–1840
Middletown, Connecticut: Wesleyan University Press, 1970.

Boultinghouse, Marquis
Silversmiths of Kentucky
Lexington, Kentucky: Privately printed, 1980.

Buhler, Kathryn C.
Colonial Silversmiths, Masters and Apprentices
Boston: The Museum of Fine Arts, 1956.
Paul Revere, Goldsmith
Boston: The Museum of Fine Arts, 1956.
American Silver, 1655–1825
Greenwich, Connecticut: The Museum of Fine Arts, 1972.

Buhler, Kathryn, and Graham Hood
American Silver
New Haven: Yale University Art Gallery, 1970.

Burton, Milby
South Carolina Silversmiths, 1690–1860
Charleston, South Carolina: The Charleston Museum, 1942.

Carpenter, Charles H., Jr.
Gorham Silver
New York: Dodd, Mead & Co., 1982.

Carpenter, Charles H., Jr. and Mary Grace
Tiffany Silver
New York: Dodd, Mead & Co., 1978.

Clayton, Michael
The Collectors' Dictionary of the Silver and Gold of Great Britain and North America
London: Country Life, 1971.

Cutten, George B.
Silversmiths of North Carolina, 1696–1850
Raleigh: North Carolina Department of Cultural Resources, 1973.
Silversmiths of Virginia, 1694–1850
Richmond, Virginia: The Dietz Press, 1952.
Silversmiths of Georgia, 1733–1850
Savannah, Georgia: The Pigeonhole Press, 1958.

Darling, Sharon S.
Chicago Metalsmiths
Chicago: Chicago Historical Society, 1977.

Fales, Martha G.
Early American Silver for the Cautious Collector
New York: E.P. Dutton & Co., 1973.
Joseph Richardson and Family, Philadelphia Silversmiths
Middletown, Connecticut: Historical Society of Pennsylvania, 1974.

Flynt, Henry N., and Martha G. Fales
The Heritage Foundation Collection of Silver
Old Deerfield, Massachusetts: The Heritage Foundation, 1968.

Gerstell, Vivian S.
Silversmiths of Lancaster, Pennsylvania, 1730–1850
Lancaster, Pennsylvania: Lancaster Historical Society, 1972.

Goldsborough, Jennifer F.
Silver in Maryland
Baltimore: The Maryland Historical Society, 1983.

Green, Robert A.
Marks of American Silversmiths
Harrison, New York: Robert Alan Green, 1977.

Hiatt, Lucy F. and Noble W.
The Silversmiths of Kentucky, 1785–1850
Louisville, Kentucky: The Standard Printing Company, 1954.

Hinds, Ruthanna
Delaware Silversmiths, 1700–1850
Wilmington, Delaware: Historical Society of Delaware, 1967.

Hood, Graham
American Silver
New York: Praeger Publishers, 1971.

Hughes, Graham
Modern Silver Throughout the World, 1880–1967
New York: Crown Publishers, 1967.

Jackson, Charles
English Goldsmiths and their Marks
Reprint of 1921 original edition. New York. Dover Publications, 1964.

Kauffman, Henry J.
The Colonial Silversmith
Camden, New Jersey: Thomas Nelson & Sons, Inc., 1969.

Knittle, Rhea M.
Early Ohio Silversmiths and Pewterers, 1787–1847
Cleveland: Privately printed, 1943.

Kovel, Ralph and Terry
A Directory of American Silver, Pewter, and Silver Plate
New York: Crown Publishers, 1961.

McClinton, Katharine M.
Collecting American 19th Century Silver
New York: Charles Scribner's Sons, 1968.

Metalsmith (quarterly magazine)
Clinton, Ohio: The Society of North American Goldsmiths, 1980–present.

New York State Silversmiths
Eggertsville, New York: The Darling Foundation, 1964.

Pleasants, J. Hall, and Howard Sill
Maryland Silversmiths, 1715–1830
Reprint of 1930 original edition. Harrison, New York: Robert Alan Green, 1972.

Rainwater, Dorothy T.
Encyclopedia of American Silver Manufacturers
New York: Crown Publishers, 1975.

Rainwater, Dorothy T., and Donna H. Felger
American Spoons, Souvenir & Historical
Camden, New Jersey: Thomas Nelson & Sons, Inc., 1969.

Reed, Helen Scott Townsend
Church Silver in Colonial Virginia
Richmond, Virginia: The Virginia Museum, 1970.

Rice, Norman S.
Albany Silver, 1652–1825
Albany, New York: Argus-Greenwood, Inc., 1964.

Rosenbaum, Jeanette W.
Myer Myers, Goldsmith
Philadelphia: The Jewish Publication Society of America, 1954.

Safford, Francis G.
Colonial Silver in the American Wing
New York: The Metropolitan Museum of Art, 1983.

Schwartz, Marvin D.
Collectors' Guide to Antique American Silver
New York: Doubleday, 1975.

Silver (Bi-monthly magazine; formerly titled *Silver-rama*)
Milwaukie, Oregon: The Silver Publishing Co., Inc., 1968–84.

Turner, Noel J.
American Silver Flatware, 1837–1910
New York: A.S. Barnes & Co., 1972.

Ward, Barbara and Gerald
Silver in American Life
New Haven: Yale University Art Gallery, 1979.

Warren, David B.
Southern Silver
Houston: The Museum of Fine Arts, 1968.

Williams, Carl M.
Silversmiths of New Jersey, 1700–1825
Philadelphia: George S. MacManus Co., 1949.

Silver Plate
Bradbury, Frederick
History of Old Sheffield Plate
Reprint of 1912 original edition. Sheffield, England: J.W. Northend, 1968.

Davis, Fredna H., and Kenneth K. Diebel
Silver Plated Flatware Patterns
Dallas: Bluebonnet Press, 1972.

Frost, T. W.
The Price Guide to Old Sheffield Plate
Clopton, Woodbridge, Suffolk, England: The Antique Collectors Club, 1971.

Hogan, Edmund P.
The Elegance of Old Silverplate
Meriden, Connecticut: International Silver Co., 1980.

Rainwater, Dorothy T. and H. Ivan
American Silverplate
Nashville: Thomas Nelson & Sons, Inc., 1968.

Snell, Doris
American Silverplated Flatware Patterns
Des Moines: Wallace-Homestead, 1980.

Torrey, Julia W.
Old Sheffield Plate
New York: Houghton Mifflin Co., 1918.

Veitch, Henry N.
Sheffield Plate
London: George Bell & Sons, 1908.

Wardle, Patricia
Victorian Silver and Silverplate
New York: Thomas Nelson & Sons, 1963.

Wenham, Edward
Old Sheffield Plate
London: George Bell & Sons, 1955.

Wyler, Seymour B.
The Book of Sheffield Plate
New York: Crown Publishers, 1949.

Wylle, Bertie
Sheffield Plate
London: George Newnes, Ltd., n.d.

Pewter
Bulletin of the Pewter Collectors' Club of America
Warwick, Rhode Island: 1934–present. (Semi-annual periodical)

Charron, Shirley
Modern Pewter: Design and Techniques
New York: Van Nostrand, 1973.

Cotterell, Howard H.
Old Pewter: Its Makers and Marks
Reprint. Rutland, Vermont: Charles G. Tuttle & Co., 1963.

Ebert, Katherine
Collecting American Pewter
New York: Charles Scribner's Sons, 1973.

Fulham, W. Ross
An Exhibition of Connecticut Pewter
New Haven: The New Haven Colony Historical Society, 1969.

Geffen, Jane, and Ida F. Taggert
Pewter in the Collections of The New Hampshire Historical Society
Concord, New Hampshire: New Hampshire Historical Society, 1968.

Hood, Graham
American Pewter: Garvan and Other Collections at Yale
New Haven: Yale University Art Gallery, 1965.

Hornsby, Peter R. G.
Pewter of the Western World
Exton, Pennsylvania: Schiffer Publishing Company, 1983.

Jacobs, Carl
Guide to American Pewter
New York: The McBride Co., 1957.

Kauffman, Henry J.
The American Pewterer
Camden, New Jersey: Thomas Nelson & Sons, Inc., 1970.

Kerfoot, J. B.
American Pewter
Reprint. New York: Bonanza Books, 1924.

Laughlin, Ledlie I.
Pewter in America: Its Makers and their Marks
Reprint. Vol. I and II. Barre, Massachusetts: Barre Publishers, 1969.
Vol. III. Barre, Massachusetts: Barre Publishers, 1971.

Montgomery, Charles F.
A History of American Pewter
New York: Praeger Publishers, 1973.

Myers, Louis G.
Some Notes on American Pewterers
New York: Country Life Press, 1926.

Peal, Christopher
More Pewter Marks
Norwich, England: Privately printed, 1976.
Addenda to More Pewter Marks
Norwich, England: Privately printed, 1977.

Thomas, John C.
Connecticut Pewter and Pewterers
Hartford: The Connecticut Historical Society, 1976.
American and British Pewter
New York: Main Street/Universe Books, 1976.

Silver and Silver Plate Index

Numbers refer to entries. This index has been divided into 2 parts; silver and silver plate are treated in the first part, and pewter in the second.

Pewter Index

Numbers refer to entries. This index has been divided into 2 parts; silver and silver plate are treated in the first part, and pewter in the second.

Staff

Prepared and produced by Chanticleer Press, Inc.
Publisher: Paul Steiner
Editor-in-Chief: Gudrun Buettner
Managing Editor: Susan Costello
Senior Editor: Mary Beth Brewer
Project Editor: Ann Whitman
Associate Editor: Marian Appellof
Art Director: Carol Nehring
Art Assistants: Ayn Svoboda, Karen Wollman
Production: Helga Lose, Amy Roche
Picture Library: Edward Douglas, Dana Pomfret
Drawings: Dolores R. Santoliquido, Mary Jane Spring
Visual Key Symbols: Paul Singer
Design: Massimo Vignelli

The Knopf Collectors' Guides to American Antiques

Also available in this unique full-color format:

Dolls
by Wendy Lavitt

Folk Art
Paintings, Sculpture & Country Objects
by Robert Bishop and Judith Reiter Weissman

Furniture 1
Chairs, Tables, Sofas & Beds
by Marvin D. Schwartz

Furniture 2
Chests, Cupboards, Desks & Other Pieces
by William C. Ketchum, Jr.

Glass 1
Tableware, Bowls & Vases
by Jane Shadel Spillman

Glass 2
Bottles, Lamps & Other Objects
by Jane Shadel Spillman

Pottery & Porcelain
by William C. Ketchum, Jr.

Quilts
With Coverlets, Rugs & Samplers
by Robert Bishop

Toys
by Blair Whitton